Aspen's Fund Raising Series for the 21st Century
Edited by James P. Gelatt, PhD, CFRE

Fund Raising
Basics

A Complete Guide

Aspen's Fund Raising Series for the 21st Century
Edited by James P. Gelatt, PhD, CFRE

Fund Raising Basics: A Complete Guide
Barbara Kushner Ciconte, CFRE, and Jeanne G. Jacob, CFRE

Planned Giving Essentials: A Step by Step Guide to Success
Richard D. Barrett and Molly E. Ware

Strategic Fund Development: Building Profitable Relationships That Last
Simone P. Joyaux, ACFRE

Capital Campaigns: Strategies That Work
Andrea Kihlstedt and Catherine P. Schwartz

Successful Special Events: Planning, Hosting, and Evaluating
Barbara R. Levy, ACFRE, and Barbara Marion, CFRE

Corporate and Foundation Fund Raising: A Complete Guide from the Inside
Eugene A. Scanlan, PhD, CFRE

Donor Focused Strategies for Annual Giving
Karla A. Williams, ACFRE

Aspen's Fund Raising Series for the 21st Century
Edited by James P. Gelatt, PhD, CFRE

Fund Raising Basics

A Complete Guide

Barbara Kushner Ciconte, CFRE
Associate Dean for Institutional Advancement
Washington College of Law, American University
Washington, DC

Jeanne Gerda Jacob, CFRE
Director of Development
American Society of Civil Engineers Foundation
Washington, DC

AN ASPEN PUBLICATION®
Aspen Publishers, Inc.
Gaithersburg, Maryland
1997

Library of Congress Cataloging-in-Publication Data
Ciconte, Barbara.
Fund raising basics: a complete guide / Barbara Kushner Ciconte, Jeanne G. Jacob.
p. cm. — (Aspen's fund raising series for the 21st century)
Includes bibliographical references and index.
ISBN 0-8342-0793-1 (pbk.)
1. Fund raising. I. Jacob, Jeanne G. II. Title. IIII. Series.
HG177.C53   1997
658.15'224—dc21   96-48719
CIP

Orders: (800) 638-8437
Customer Service: (800) 234-1660

About Aspen Publishers • For more than 35 years, Aspen has been a leading professional publisher in a variety of disciplines. Aspen's vast information resources are available in both print and electronic formats. We are committed to providing the highest quality information available in the most appropriate format for our customers. Visit Aspen's Internet site for more information resources, directories, articles, and a searchable version of Aspen's full catalog, including the most recent publications: **http://www.aspenpub.com**
Aspen Publishers, Inc. • The hallmark of quality in publishing
Member of the worldwide Wolters Kluwer group.

Editorial Resources: Brian MacDonald
Library of Congress Catalog Card Number: 96-48719
ISBN: 0-8342-0793-1

Printed in the United States of America

1 2 3 4 5

To my parents, Barbara and Lou Buschlinger, who throughout my life have been a constant source of love and support, and to my husband, Tony Ciconte, without whose humor, love, and understanding this book could not have been written.

Barbara Kushner Ciconte, CFRE

To my mother, Clara Cypreansen Jacob, who always told me I could do anything. Her indomitable Norwegian strength and spirit have instilled in me the desire to try all things and to do them all with the best of my ability. To my husband, Gerry Frank, without whose love, support, and expert editing skills I would not have been able to write this book.

Jeanne Gerda Jacob, CFRE

Table of Contents

Foreword

Fund raising is not an event; it is a process.

Edgar D. Powell
Accent On Philanthropy II

Fund raising. Development. Advancement. Resource Development. By whatever name, fund raising has been and continues to be an essential element of success for the nonprofit organization.

One of the characteristics that makes nonprofit organizations unique is our reliance on the demonstrable belief of others. For-profit organizations look to stockholders for essential capital. If the organization is successful, the investors will realize financial benefit. Their stock will increase in value, and they will enjoy the quarterly returns.

By contrast, nonprofit organizations seek an investment whose return is intangible. The financial buy-in is no less real, but the return on investment is very different indeed.

Most of us come to fund raising out of necessity. We are working for a nonprofit, either as staff or volunteer. We soon recognize that the organization's growth—if not its very survival—depends on our ability to convince others to part with some portion of their disposable income. In so doing, we are competing with: going out to dinner, buying new clothes, saving money for vacation, purchasing new software, saving for college . . . to say nothing of the myriad other organizations who are also seeking a donation. There are some one million charitable organizations in the United States, and literally thousands are established every month.

Which is why it is essential that we go about the challenge of raising funds in the very best ways possible. *Fund Raising Basics* will help chart the course. As its name implies, the book is about the knowledges and skills that are *basic* and requisite to an effective fund raising program. And as *A Complete Guide*, it is thorough; the reader will be introduced to the range of fund-raising approaches, from direct mail to major gifts, from special events to planned giving.

The nonprofit sector has undergone dramatic change in the last 30 years. And nowhere is that more true than in how we ask for funds. We have witnessed a shift from a concept of Charity to Investment. From "we need your support" to "we welcome your involvement." From a time when most of our funding was for general support, to a time when general support funds are among the most difficult to obtain. From the generalist to the specialist.

We have become more sophisticated in how we perceive what we do (Kotler & Fox, 1985), moving . . .

From	To
Panic reactions to negative deficits	Commitment by board & CEO to raise funds
Limited, short-term objectives	Strategic planning
Stopgap measures	Sound business management
Negotiating from weakness:	Negotiating from strength:
"Help," "Need," "Assist"	"Investment," "Goals," "Vision"
Car washes, bazaars, candy drives, Las Vegas nights	Proposals to foundations and corporations, endowments, wills & bequests

As fund raising has evolved, so too have the conditions in which funds are raised (Gelatt, 1992): (1) *The nature of the donor is changing.* As we enter the 21st century, the median age of the American population will be 36 years; it was about 28 years in 1970. The superannuated (the "old old") will be a burgeoning part of the population.

One in three persons will be from a minority background. Fund raising approaches that might have worked for a predominantly white, Protestant population in one part of the country may be singularly ineffective in another that is multicultural, multilingual, and multi-denominational.

One in two persons in the workforce will be women. Women with their own earning power also make their own decisions about which causes they will support.

(2) *The level of sophistication in fund raising continues to rise.* Fund raising may always be an art, but it is increasingly becoming a science. Successful fund raisers are becoming market-driven, asking "who wants, who needs" the services that the nonprofit organization provides, or might provide.

(3) *The scrutiny of fund raising is likely to increase.* Public scrutiny is being driven by two forces: concern about nonprofits in general and fund raising in specific (both influenced by unfortunate incidents such as that of William Aramony and The New Era Fund); and the public sector's need for ways to raise money without raising the traditional tax base.

At every level—federal, state, and local—the scrutiny is likely to increase. And much of it will focus on the raising and use of funds.

(4) *Increased competition for funds appears inevitable.* Some 100,000 new nonprofit organizations were created between 1975 and 1990. Virtually all of them seek funding. They will be joined by new entrants.

(5) *Overall, there should be a continued growth in philanthropy.* Even allowing for inflation, philanthropic contributions continue to rise.

(6) *Some things don't change:*

- People give to people, not places or things

- At base, fund raising is people who believe in what they are doing, who ask others to share in that belief

Fund Raising Basics: A Complete Guide was written by two of the best practitioners and teachers in the fund raising profession. Barbara Kushner Ciconte and Jeanne Jacob have both enjoyed outstanding careers as fund raisers. Their writing is crisp, sensible, and grounded in experience. As teachers of the art and science of fund raising, they not only know the subject, they know how to impart it to others.

I believe you will find this book to be a continual source of information to which you will return for advice. So will I.

James P. Gelatt, PhD, CFRE
Prentice Associates
Nonprofit Management Consulting
Adjunct Professor
Graduate School of Management and
Technology
University of Maryland
Editor, *Aspen's Fund Raising Series for the
21st Century*

References

Gelatt, J.P. 1992. *Managing nonprofit organizations in the 21st century.* Phoenix, AZ: Oryx Press.
Kotler, P. & Fox, K. 1985. *Strategic marketing for educational institutions.* Englewood Cliffs, NJ: Prentice-Hall.

Preface

During our eight years of teaching the Fundamentals of Fund Raising courses at The George Washington University's Center for Continuing Education in Washington, DC, we were continually asked what text we would be using to teach our classes. As there was no definitive text available, we used materials from many books and articles that our colleagues had written. Finally, when we were asked if we were interested in co-authoring a book on fund raising, we knew that we had the perfect subject *and* the answer to our problem of not having a fundamentals text available—we could write one! Thus began the journey that started with a need and an idea and finished two years later with a text entitled *Fund Raising Basics: A Complete Guide*.

With more than 35 years of fund-raising experience between us, writing this book became a collection of our own personal experiences in capital campaigns, special events, annual campaigns, planned giving, board development, and major gift solicitation. This text is intended not only for use in the classroom, but for all those interested in learning more about fund raising—those seeking to become development professionals, those raising money for or sitting on the boards of nonprofit organizations, or those who simply want to know how to raise money in a professional manner.

This book attempts to address all aspects of the development field to provide an overview for its readers. The extensive research done provides insight into many successful fund-raising programs, and the many opportunities available to those wishing for a career in development. In addition, ideas from other professional fund raisers are highlighted and shared with the reader.

The chapters are purposely kept short, as the text is intended as an overview. For those wishing to read more extensively on a subject, additional readings are suggested in the bibliography. Since a key trait of most development officers is a good sense of humor, we also chose to highlight the chapters with cartoons provided by Mark Litzler, Joseph Brown, and Carol Cable. Fund raising is not all work, it can be, should be, and most often is fun!

We welcome the readers to the professional world of fund raising and hope we have provided a book that can serve as a guide to successful fund raising.

Acknowledgments

We wish to acknowledge the organizations we have served and are currently serving as staff and volunteers for providing us with opportunities to grow and develop as fund raising professionals. Included among these are: for Barbara—the YWCA, NARAL, American University and the Washington College of Law, the Greater Washington, DC Area Chapter of the National Society of Fund Raising Executives (NSFRE), and for Jeanne—the American Society of Civil Engineers, *INN*dependent Management Group, the National Academy of Engineering, the American College of Nurse-Midwives, Youth for Understanding International Student Exchange, and NSFRE.

Also, recognition needs to be given to a number of special people whose leadership, guidance, mentoring, support, or friendship contributed to our own professional development in this field—for Barbara, those people are Rita Wasmuth, Bob Semple, Kevin Cornell, Paul Purta, and Sandie Fauriol; for Jeanne, those people include Tere Linehan, Gene Scanlan, Hugh Miller, Robert M. White, Ralph Landau, Stephen D. Bechtel, Jr., John F. Welch, Jr., Donald N. Frey, Curtis C. Deane, C.R. "Chuck" Pennoni, Carol Waite, Michael Walters, A.C. Burkhalter, Jr., Marcia Saumweber, Maynard Moore, and Barbara Waldorf. A special thank you, also, to our colleagues in the Washington, DC area and across the country who shared their fund raising experiences and insights with us.

Another important group to recognize is our students from The George Washington University Fund Raising Certificate program, many of whom are pursuing careers in development. Their eagerness to learn about fund raising and to become professional fund raisers inspired us to share with them our knowledge and enthusiasm for our work. We are proud of the work they are doing as development professionals for a variety of nonprofit organizations across the country.

We are indebted to others for their help in this project. Our thanks to Cathleen Williams at the National Society of Fund Raising Executives (NSFRE), to Mary Smith, Director, and Jan Alfieri, Coordinator, of NSFRE's Fund Raising Resource Center, who so willingly researched topics for us and were always cheerful in their assistance, to Toni Glover and Pamela Ciconte for their administrative support, Britt Moses, Assistant Director of Major Gifts at American University, and Suzy Tyahla, Assistant Director of Development at the Washington College of Law.

Thanks also to Mark Litzler who provided so many of the cartoons in this book. Litzler's cartoons have appeared in numerous publications including The Harvard Business Review, Barrons, The Wall Street Journal, The Chronicle of Higher Education, and The Chronicle of Philanthropy. He draws a weekly feature which appears in six American City Business Journal newspapers, and a monthly feature for The NonProfit Times. He is the development director for Kansas City's Truman Medical Center, and can be reached at 816-556-3159 or mlitzler@cctr.umkc.edu.

Of course, we wish to thank the team at Aspen Publishers—Jim Gelatt, Elizabeth Glaser, Loretta Stock, Kathleen McGuire, Ruth Bloom, Brian MacDonald, Bob Pursell, Kathy Argyropoulos, and Laureece Woodson for developing and including this book in their new *Fund Raising Series for the 21st Century*.

Also, our thanks to Susan Gaumont, Karen Gardner, Tom, Anna, and Robert Ciconte, Ellen Myerberg, Melanie and Sam Miller, Janet, Bill, and Amanda Baeder, Lee Brookshier Davis, Barbara Valentino, Kathleen, May-Belle, and Tom Chadbourne, Barbara Waldorf, Mary Fran and Matthew Freedman, Alice and Ted Cochran, Sheridan Gates, Helen and David Ross, Clara Jacob, Dorothy Davidson, Bernard Pagenstecher, Bobbie, Moe, and Mark Ruschman, Paul and Marguerite Bateman, and the many other friends who were patient with us, humored us, and constantly "checked in" to see how we were doing during the writing of this book. Their support, encouragement, patience, and understanding during the two years the book was in progress will never be forgotten.

Chapter 1
Philanthropy—An American Tradition

Chapter Outline

- Definition of Philanthropy
- History of Philanthropy in America
- A Tradition of Volunteerism
- The Relationship Between Volunteering and Charitable Contributions
- How Generous We Are as a Nation
- A Profile of a Donor
- Indicators That Affect Giving and Volunteering

Key Vocabulary

- Charitable Giving
- Demographics
- Development
- Donor
- Nonprofit Sector
- Nonprofit or Not-For-Profit Organization
- Philanthropy
- Volunteerism

> "We make a living by what we get, but we make a life by what we give."
>
> Winston Churchill

This quote by Winston Churchill captures the heart of the nonprofit sector and the strong sense of mission so prevalent among those who work within it. To successfully raise funds for a nonprofit organization, you must understand what philanthropy is and how it became an American tradition.

Definition of Philanthropy

The word "philanthropy" is Greek and means "love of mankind." According to the dictionary of the National Society of Fund Raising Executives, philanthropy is defined as (1) love of humankind, usually expressed by an effort to enhance the well-being of humanity through personal acts of practical kindness or by financial support of a cause or causes, such as a charity (for example, the American Red Cross), mutual aid or assistance (for example, service clubs and youth groups), quality of life (for example, arts, education, and the environment) and religion; and (2) any effort to relieve human misery or suffering, improve the quality of life, encourage aid or assistance, or foster the preservation of values through gifts, service, or other voluntary activity, any and all of which are external to government involvement or marketplace exchange. Philanthropy and volunteerism are uniquely American traditions, and their pervasive presence in our lives is often taken for granted.

History of Philanthropy in America

American philanthropy as we know it today began during colonial times. People focused on religion and higher education during the eighteenth century. Gradually, health, civic, and social causes, and the arts entered the picture as our young nation grew and prospered.

It is interesting to note that philanthropy in America before the American Revolution had its roots in necessity. It was the only means of building and sustaining the service institutions each community needed. Historian Henry Steele Commager has said

> Americans managed without energetic government for so long a time that they came to prefer voluntary public enterprise. If they wanted a college, they built one—and they kept on doing that into the 20th century; if they needed a hospital, they raised money for it; if they lacked books, they got together and collected them . . . because participation is the very essence of democracy, it is difficult to exaggerate the value of this aspect of American philanthropy. (Brakeley 1980, 1)

This statement rings true even today as more and more public support is sought to meet the rising tide of problems facing our society.

A Tradition of Volunteerism

The practice of philanthropy includes volunteer service in addition to gifts. Even in today's world with the many demands on our time by family, work, study, and leisure activities, people are undertaking volunteer work. Since 1988, Independent Sector, a coalition of charities and grant-makers, has conducted biennial national surveys of the giving and volunteering behavior of adults 18 years of age or older in the United States. Highlights of what it found in its 1994 survey, "Giving and Volunteering in the United States," include the following:

- About 48 percent of all adult Americans claimed they undertook some kind of volunteer work, donating an average of 4.2 hours a week.
- The combined efforts of these 89 million adults produced a staggering annual total of 19.5 billion volunteer hours, which is the equivalent of the efforts of 8.8 million full-time employees. The dollar value of this effort is about $182 billion yearly, a sum that surpasses the total amount of giving.
- Although millions of people work billions of hours doing volunteer activities, only one-fifth seek out the activity or assignment on their own.
- People offer many reasons for volunteering. Some are carrying on family traditions; others are asked by relatives, friends, members of their community, or people who represent a cause with which they

identify. Still others become involved because they believe their efforts will benefit friends or relatives.

The Relationship Between Volunteering and Charitable Contributions

Commager believed that "participation" was very much a part of the American philanthropic spirit. But how does one learn to "participate" or volunteer? A review of the current research shows that positive experiences as a youth can be one of the most important influences on generous giving and volunteering. Adults who belonged to a youth group, volunteered as a youth, did door-to-door canvassing to raise money, or participated in student government are the most likely to give and to volunteer. Parents who volunteered and served as role models for their families are also significant influences. Other major influences are active involvement in religious organizations and frequency of attendance at religious services.

Data from many recent studies and surveys clearly establish a relationship between giving and volunteering. Independent Sector's most recent survey revealed that 90 percent of individuals who volunteer for a nonprofit organization also make charitable contributions. Among those who do not volunteer, 59 percent contribute financially. We also learned that the average gift from households with volunteers was 55 percent higher than that from households without volunteers.

How Generous We Are as a Nation

Today, America's philanthropic spirit remains strong. Each year, the American Association of Fund Raising Counsel (AAFRC) Trust for Philanthropy publishes a report on U.S. philanthropy entitled *Giving USA*. The report compares current charitable giving with data collected since 1975. According to the latest issue of *Giving USA*, Americans gave an estimated $143.9 billion to charity in 1995, compared to $28.5 billion in 1975. This increase, nearly 11 percent more than in 1994, is the largest increase during the past decade and is based on many factors. These factors include a strong performance by the nation's economy as Americans saw their incomes increase by an average of 6.5 percent and the strong performance of the stock market with the Dow Jones industrial average breaking the 5,000 mark, which generated a burst of contributions of appreciated securities. Donors often give stock when its value has increased sharply because they can obtain bigger tax savings than they would if the stock were not as valuable. The editors of *Giving USA* speculate that some people who had not planned to give in 1995 might have changed their minds when the stock market began to boom. Contributors may have worried they would lose the tax benefits if their stocks' value decreased. A third factor influencing chari-

"CHARITABLE GIVING ISN'T THE ULTIMATE TEST OF ONE'S HUMANITY BUT IT GIVES US SOME NUMBERS TO PLAY WITH."

Source: © Mark Litzler.

table giving was the debate in Washington, DC about reducing tax rates, which may have motivated some donors to give while taxes were at current rates, giving them larger tax deductions. Because many different things affect giving, there always will be ebbs and flows in the patterns of charitable giving.

Exhibit 1–1 shows that individuals provided the vast majority of contributions, estimated at $116 billion, or 81 percent of all contributions. The remaining 19 percent was contributed by foundations ($10.4 billion), corporations ($7.4 billion), and individuals' bequests ($9.7 billion).

Regarding the types of organizations or institutions that receive contributions, not much has changed since the eighteenth century. Religious institutions remain the major recipients, followed by educational institutions. The breakdown of support for issues and causes is shown in Exhibit 1–2.

Religion

Churches and other religious groups received $63.5 billion in 1995, 5.4 percent more than in 1994. Religion forms the biggest category to which donors make gifts, accounting for 44.1 percent of all charitable dollars.

Education

Colleges and private schools netted $17.9 billion in 1995, which is an 8 percent increase from 1994. Contributions to private elementary and secondary schools are increasing.

Health

Giving to nonprofit hospitals, charities that "fight" diseases, and other institutions that are advocates for health

Exhibit 1–1 Sources of 1995 Contributions

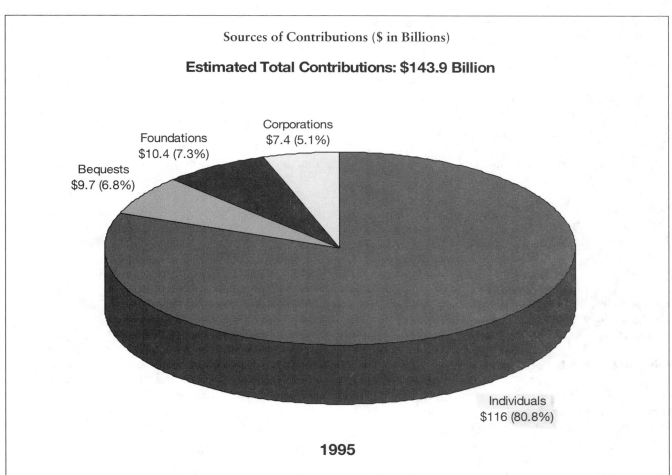

Sources of Contributions ($ in Billions)

Estimated Total Contributions: $143.9 Billion

Foundations $10.4 (7.3%)

Corporations $7.4 (5.1%)

Bequests $9.7 (6.8%)

Individuals $116 (80.8%)

1995

Source: Reprinted with permission from American Association of Fund Raising Counsel Trust for Philanthropy, Inc., *Giving USA, 1996 Edition,* © 1996, American Association of Fund Raising Counsel.

Exhibit 1–2 Uses of 1995 Contributions

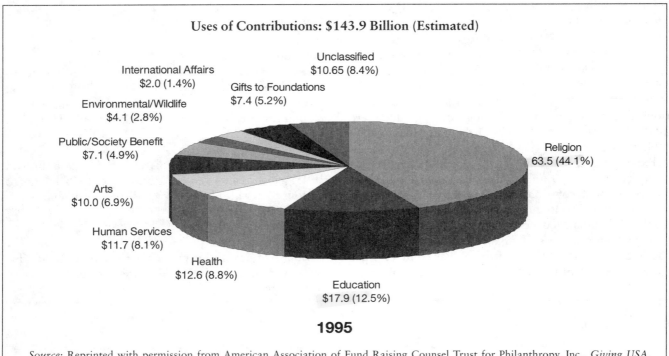

Uses of Contributions: $143.9 Billion (Estimated)

Unclassified
$10.65 (8.4%)

International Affairs
$2.0 (1.4%)

Gifts to Foundations
$7.4 (5.2%)

Environmental/Wildlife
$4.1 (2.8%)

Religion
63.5 (44.1%)

Public/Society Benefit
$7.1 (4.9%)

Arts
$10.0 (6.9%)

Human Services
$11.7 (8.1%)

Health
$12.6 (8.8%)

Education
$17.9 (12.5%)

1995

Source: Reprinted with permission from American Association of Fund Raising Counsel Trust for Philanthropy, Inc., *Giving USA,* *1996 Edition,* © 1996, American Association of Fund Raising Counsel.

causes increased by 9.2 percent, to $12.6 billion. This larger increase, up from 6.5 percent in 1994, was due to the fact that many large health charities are observing the results of dramatic changes made in their fund-raising programs several years ago. Giving to hospitals is also increasing.

Human Services
This was one of two categories to suffer from a decrease in donations, which was 0.2 percent—to $11.7 billion. However, it is much less than the 6.1 percent decline seen in 1994.

Arts, Culture, and Humanities
Giving to the arts rose 2.9 percent, for a total of $10 billion.

Public and Social Benefit
Charities categorized as "public benefit" organizations, ranging from Gifts in Kind International to civil rights organizations to consumer advocacy groups, received $7.1 billion, which is an increase of 17.4 percent over 1994. This group of charities experienced the largest increase in giving due in a large part to the amount contributed to organizations that accept donations of office equipment, computer software, and other goods. Gifts

in Kind International saw its contributions increase nearly 49 percent over 1994.

Environment and Wildlife
Contributions to environmental and wildlife-preservation organizations continue to increase. In 1995, $4 billion was donated, which was an increase of 12.5 percent. The report noted that policies favored by environmental groups were under attack in Congress in 1995 and that the groups reported on these legislative developments in their appeals.

International
After benefitting from the largest surge in giving in 1994, groups that provide international aid, such as famine and disaster relief, posted the poorest showing in 1995, which was $2 billion. The significant increase in 1994 was attributed to the prolonged press coverage of the civil war and massacres in Rwanda and the war in Bosnia. In the latest report, some groups cited donor fatigue and the loss of press interest in continuing international crises as causes of the decline.

A Profile of a Donor
Independent Sector and the AAFRC Trust for Philanthropy are only two of a growing number of organiza-

tions and individuals who are conducting research on donors and philanthropic trends. Information on changing demographics and future trends that will affect contributions to nonprofit organizations is critical. "The Heart of the Donor," a 1995 Direct Marketing Association Non-Profit Council study commissioned by the Russ Reid Company and conducted by Barna Research Group examines the beliefs and motivations of donors. The survey is based on a random sample of 1,164 donors nationwide. Key findings include the following:

- The average donor in the United States is a woman who is middle-aged, married, and college-educated. The median age is 43 years (average age of adults in the U.S. is 38 years). Median household income of donors is $39,100 (U.S. average is $31,200). Sixty-one percent of donors are female (51 percent of the U.S. adult population is female); 47 percent are college graduates (20 percent of the U.S. population are college graduates); 66 percent are married (54 percent of the U.S. adult population are married); and 89 percent are white (75 percent of the U.S. population are white).
- Eighty-two percent of donors who contribute to not-for-profit organizations also give to churches or other places of worship—48 percent on a weekly basis, 29 percent at least once a month, and 5 percent every other month.
- The most generous donors are those who have named not-for-profits as beneficiaries in their wills —on average, these people donate $558 per year, which is $385 more than the national median.
- People in their 30s, 40s, and 50s give at least twice as much as those who are younger and older.

Our changing demographics certainly will have a serious impact on the results of future studies concerning donor motivations. Minority populations such as Hispanics and Asians are increasing as the proportion of whites declines in every age group. The first wave of baby boomers has entered middle age. Senior citizens are living longer. These and other factors will not only affect giving but will also affect how organizations approach fund raising.

Indicators That Affect Giving and Volunteering

Even though the American people have a strong tradition of volunteering and charitable giving, many indicators can affect this tradition. First and foremost is the individual's economic well being and any perceptions he or she may have about having enough money in the future. The impact of changes in tax policy are important, too. Many people think that one of the prime reasons individuals make charitable gifts is because they can deduct them from their income taxes. Research shows that the issue of tax deductibility does not influence a donor's decision to make a gift but may influence the size of the gift.

> Our role as development professionals is to offer people opportunities to do great things, to challenge and inspire them, and to involve them in activities that make life better now and for future generations.

Major goals of recent national surveys and studies are to identify and monitor public opinion about charitable organizations. Because charitable organizations rely on public support through giving and volunteering, it is critical that public involvement and trust remain strong. It is no surprise to learn that past surveys reveal that positive attitudes toward charities are associated with higher rates of household giving and volunteering. However, in recent years, scandals involving the United Way and the New Era Foundation raise questions in the public's mind as to how charitable organizations are managed, and if they are honest and ethical in the use of their funds.

In response to a perceived shift in public opinion regarding charities, a group of leading organizations in the nonprofit sector developed a Donor Bill of Rights (Appendix 1–A). Although the document is written from the donor's perspective, it serves as an excellent guide for development staff to follow when working with their donors.

For both current and future development professionals, it is important to understand that our role is to offer people opportunities to do great things, to challenge and inspire them, and to involve them in activities that make life better now and for future generations. If we are successful, we will help to perpetuate the American tradition of philanthropy.

References

American Association of Fund Raising Counsel (AAFRC) Trust for Philanthropy, Inc. 1996. *Giving USA*. New York: American Association of Fund Raising Counsel.

Brakeley, G. 1980. *Tested Ways for Success*. New York: AMACOM.

Direct Marketing Association Non-Profit Council. 1995. *The Heart of the Donor.* New York: Direct Marketing Association Non-Profit Council.

Independent Sector. 1994. *Giving and Volunteering in the United States*. Washington, DC: Independent Sector.

National Society of Fund Raising Executives (NSFRE). 1996. *The NSFRE Fund-Raising Dictionary*. Edited by Barbara R. Levy and R.L. Cherry. New York: John Wiley & Sons, Inc.

Appendix 1–A
A Donor Bill of Rights

A Donor Bill of Rights

PHILANTHROPY is based on voluntary action for the common good. It is a tradition of giving and sharing that is primary to the quality of life. To assure that philanthropy merits the respect and trust of the general public, and that donors and prospective donors can have full confidence in the not-for-profit organizations and causes they are asked to support, we declare that all donors have these rights:

I.
To be informed of the organization's mission, of the way the organization intends to use donated resources, and of its capacity to use donations effectively for their intended purposes.

II.
To be informed of the identity of those serving on the organization's governing board, and to expect the board to exercise prudent judgment in its stewardship responsibilities.

III.
To have access to the organization's most recent financial statements.

IV.
To be assured their gifts will be used for the purposes for which they were given.

V.
To receive appropriate acknowledgment and recognition.

VI.
To be assured that information about their donations is handled with respect and with confidentiality to the extent provided by law.

VII.
To expect that all relationships with individuals representing organizations of interest to the donor will be professional in nature.

VIII.
To be informed whether those seeking donations are volunteers, employees of the organization or hired solicitors.

IX.
To have the opportunity for their names to be deleted from mailing lists that an organization may intend to share.

X.
To feel free to ask questions when making a donation and to receive prompt, truthful and forthright answers.

DEVELOPED BY

AMERICAN ASSOCIATION OF FUND RAISING COUNSEL (AAFRC)
ASSOCIATION FOR HEALTHCARE PHILANTHROPY (AHP)
COUNCIL FOR ADVANCEMENT AND SUPPORT OF EDUCATION (CASE)
NATIONAL SOCIETY OF FUND RAISING EXECUTIVES (NSFRE)

ENDORSED BY
(IN FORMATION)

INDEPENDENT SECTOR
NATIONAL CATHOLIC DEVELOPMENT CONFERENCE (NCDC)
NATIONAL COMMITTEE ON PLANNED GIVING (NCPG)
NATIONAL COUNCIL FOR RESOURCE DEVELOPMENT (NCRD)
UNITED WAY OF AMERICA

Design: Lipman Hearne/Chicago
11/93

Please help us distribute this widely.

Source: Reprinted with permission of the National Society of Fund Raising Executives (NSFRE), © 1993, Alexandria, VA.

Chapter 2
The Many Roles of Board, Staff, and Volunteers in Fund Raising

Chapter Outline

- Selection of Volunteers
- Knowing Who You Need on Your Board
- Adding Diversity to Your Board
- What to Look for When Recruiting Board Members
- Job Descriptions for Board Members
- Setting Clear Goals and Expectations for the Board
- Working with an Existing Board
- Techniques to Motivate Your Board into Action
- Board Training and Development
- Advisory Committees to Boards for Fund Raising
- Evaluating Board Members' Effectiveness
- How to Retire a Board Member
- Role of Staff in Fund Raising
- Communications Between Board and Staff
- Staff Expectations for Board Members
- Board Members' Expectations for Staff

Key Vocabulary

- Advisory Committee
- Diversity
- Prospect
- Internet
- The Three "G's"
- The Three "W's"
- Volunteer
- World Wide Web

Selection of Volunteers

Fund raising requires the use of volunteers at every level, from running the special event to chairing the board of the organization. Volunteers work with staff for the betterment of the organization whether programmatically or financially. Just as well-trained staff perform their jobs better than those who are untrained, volunteers who are trained will be more successful—and happier—than those left to their own devices. Therefore, it is as important to develop the professional volunteer as it is to provide enrichment to the best professional staff.

Before individuals even begin to volunteer their time for an institution, they should be provided with a job description as well as a packet of information about the organization. If they are being asked to work for or represent the organization to the public, they should be well-versed on the history, mission, goals, and objectives of the organization and the department or event for which they will be volunteering. If they are serving on the board, they must be able to guide the organization to the best of their abilities. By providing volunteers with appropriate information, they can be more competent and thus more successful in their chosen roles.

Selecting the right volunteer for an organization or project is just as important as selecting the right person to fill a staff position. Just as people select careers for different reasons, so too do they volunteer for different reasons. Susan Church (1988) states, "It is worth spending some time thinking about why people volunteer at all. Motives vary somewhat from person to person, but generally people volunteer for one or more of the following reasons:

> Just as well-trained staff perform their jobs better than those who are untrained, volunteers who are trained will be more successful—and happier—than those left to their own devices.

- They want to make a contribution to a cause in which they believe.
- They feel they need to fulfill business and/or social expectations.
- They are motivated by a desire for change.
- They want to have a sense of ownership and control that they can't find in a work situation.
- They want to learn new skills.
- They want to have fun and enjoy what they are about to do."

No longer is the average volunteer white, female, upper-middle class, married, and nonworking. Today, volunteers come from a variety of backgrounds: retirees (younger today than before because of downsizing of the military and corporations offering early retirement packages), minorities, youth, and even those actively employed. In the past, women were usually directed toward volunteering in hospitals or libraries, whereas men sat on the boards of prep schools, colleges, or universities. Women joined the Junior League, the PEO sisterhood, women's clubs, and other like organizations, whereas men often volunteered under the guise of membership clubs such as the Elks, Shriners, Rotary, Kiwanis, etc. Only when a community crisis or disaster brought them together, did men and women tend to volunteer jointly for a cause. Just as the stereotypical roles in the work place have mostly disappeared, so have the gender specific roles of volunteering. Service clubs are open to both sexes: men are volunteering for organizations once thought to be solely of interest to women, and women are asking for money to support the organizations for which they volunteer just like men have in the past.

Volunteerism is at the heart and soul of American culture. According to the *Chronicle of Philanthropy*, nearly half of all Americans (48 percent) volunteer! Some states even have offices and officials assigned to encourage volunteerism. The addresses of the state offices of volunteerism and names of their officials appear at the end of this chapter. This list was compiled by the Points of Light Foundation, a nonprofit organization in Washington, DC that encourages people to help charities.

> **Volunteerism is at the heart and soul of American culture.**

Volunteering is considered unique to the culture of the United States. Europeans are less likely to volunteer than Americans. In a survey of nine European countries conducted for the Volunteer Center U.K. in London, about 27 percent of Europeans said they had volunteered to help a charitable cause. European attitudes toward volunteering diverged sharply from one country to the next, stemming from differences in the ways that each country developed politically, socially, and culturally.

Currently, volunteerism in the United States is increasing among individuals in their 20s. This has been attributed to the increasing number of members of this generation who live at home, thus having more potential wealth (money not being spent on room and board) and time to volunteer (time not being spent on homemaking). Also, this group has been raised by parents who, for the most part, have been more socially conscious than generations before and have encouraged their children to become involved in causes.

Whatever the motivating factors—nationality, sex, race, religion, or interests—of the potential volunteers,

one thing they all have in common is the need to be recruited. The number of volunteer opportunities abound and successful programs are looking for volunteers in new places, with the Internet/World Wide Web being one such place.

Some say clever marketing devices or staff are the best recruiters of volunteers for an organization. The truth is that volunteers recruit other volunteers. Active, positive volunteers, excited about the work they are doing, will interest others in volunteering for the organization or cause much more quickly than ads placed in the newspaper, announcements on the radio, or other traditional techniques. Personal contact is the best way in which to recruit volunteers. Most people won't say no to someone they know and respect, no matter what the cause!

Vince Stehle (1993) lists several ways to recruit and manage volunteers. They are the following:

- Write job descriptions for volunteers.
- Provide flexible hours.
- Seek advice from experts.
- Get staff members, volunteers, and others to enlist friends, family members, and colleagues.
- Be cautious about using newspapers, magazines, television, and radio.
- Stress how the volunteer will benefit from working with a charity.
- Offer short-term opportunities.
- Eliminate barriers that make people reluctant to volunteer.
- Seek volunteers with specific skills.
- Tailor publicity to appeal to members of particular racial or ethnic groups.
- Make appeals upbeat.

Flexible time is especially important to volunteers today. Because many volunteers are employed full-time, they must be able to fit their volunteer efforts into already tight schedules. Thus, they seek shorter-term opportunities and may seek those that offer them the opportunity to learn new skills. To attract these volunteers, barriers must be eliminated that would make them reluctant to volunteer at an organization. Important and insightful information on recruiting, training, motivating, and retaining volunteers may be obtained from your state office of volunteerism. See Appendix 2–A for a listing of these offices.

If the goal is to find volunteers to assist in fund raising, then make sure that this is stated up-front. Also, provide the volunteers with a job description. Include with the job description a copy of the Bill of Rights for Volunteers (Exhibit 2–1). Susan Church (1988) also states that

> to increase volunteer leadership and participation in fund raising, development officers should do the following:

Exhibit 2–1 Bill of Rights for Volunteers

1. The right to be treated as a co-worker, not just as free help, not as a prima donna.
2. The right to a suitable assignment, with consideration for personal preference, temperament, life experience, education, and employment background.
3. The right to know as much about the organization as possible—its policies, its people, its programs.
4. The right to training for the job, thoughtfully planned and effectively presented training.
5. The right to continuing education on the job—as a follow-up to initial training—including information about new developments and training for greater responsibility.
6. The right to sound guidance and direction by someone who is experienced, well informed, patient, and thoughtful, and who has the time to invest in giving guidance.
7. The right to a place to work—an orderly, designated place, conducive to work and worthy of the job to be done.
8. The right to promotion and a variety of experiences—through advancement to assignments of more responsibility, through transfer from one activity to another, through special assignments.
9. The right to be heard—to have a part in planning, to feel free to make suggestions, to have respect shown for an honest opinion.
10. The right to recognition, in the form of promotion and awards, through day-by-day expressions of appreciation, and by being treated as a bona fide co-worker.

Source: Reprinted with permission from The Points of Light Foundation, *Making Volunteers Feel at Home,* © 1996. For more information, contact Jeff Brightbill at (202) 223-9186.

- Help provide a climate in which fund raising is a logical outgrowth of an exciting and productive organization's program;
- Ensure that volunteers are involved with other aspects of the organization—programs, policy development, etc.—along with fund raising;
- Recruit an ally (or allies) from the volunteer group to spearhead the revision of volunteer job descriptions and recruiting policies with special attention to specific expectations about fund raising;
- Ask volunteers to do what volunteers do best—don't waste the volunteer's limited time on work done more appropriately by staff;
- Give volunteers what they need to succeed (materials, training, practice, and recognition);
- Respect volunteer time—make requests specific and reasonable;
- Have a written fund raising plan, developed with volunteer participation. This plan should be specific as to what volunteers will do (and when) and what will be handled by staff; and
- Define success correctly. A volunteer who makes five calls that result in refusals is not a failure. He or she is a fund raiser.

> **Just as it is important to know how to recruit volunteers, it is equally important to know what to look for when recruiting volunteers for an organization's board.**

Knowing Who You Need on Your Board

Just as it is important to know how to recruit volunteers, it is equally important to know what to look for when recruiting volunteers for an organization's board. It is not always easy to identify new board members, and in smaller communities, many organizations are competing for the same people. Most board members are recruited for their wealth, but not all successful board members are wealthy. A successful board will comprise a diverse group of multi-background and multi-talented people who have a strong desire to serve and a keen interest in the organization. When selecting potential board members be sure to include the following in a review and analysis.

Sex

Is there a fairly equal representation of both women and men on the board? How will the rotation pattern of the term limits affect this representation? Has a list of qualified candidates of both sexes been composed?

Age

What is the average age of the current board members? Is there a balance among youth, middle age, and seniors? What is the age of those who will be leaving the board each year as their terms expire? Have candidates of similar ages to those who have left or of ages needed to balance the representation on your board been identified to fill these positions?

Race or Ethnic Origin

Has a conscious effort been made to balance the membership of the board to coincide with the race or ethnic origin of the membership or constituents? Have those of a different race or ethnic origin who have the skills and qualities needed by your board to meet its mission been sought? Have individuals of different races and ethnic origins been identified to fill positions of current board members whose terms next expire? Are there board members who represent African Americans; Native Americans; whites; Asians; Hispanics; Pacific Islanders; etc.?

Geographic Representation

Have members been selected from all parts of the United States or the world? Do the board members represent the geographic distribution of the organization's membership and/or constituents?

Expertise

Do the board members have the expertise that is needed to run the organization? Is there someone with a legal background? Is there a professional fund raiser? Does someone have a background in personnel management to assist you in personnel issues? Is there a public relations professional?

Access

Do the board members have access to people with wealth? Are they leaders in the community and able to open doors to other leaders and groups that can assist the organization?

Adding Diversity to Your Board

Robert Coles (1994) raises some serious questions regarding diversity. He states,

> Many board of directors and volunteer groups have made commendable efforts to integrate on the basis of sex and race. But here's a touchy point: Most organizations have done little to integrate on the basis of social class. You will find wealthy black trustees, successful women or the wives of well-to-do men, but you won't find many working-class people. Of course, let's be candid: working-class people don't offer much in terms of financial assets. But people of diverse backgrounds offer other points of view that are very important. We need a sort of affirmative action to involve all sorts of people on our boards and in the volunteer community.

What to Look for When Recruiting Board Members

Probably the most effective way to identify new board members is to ask those currently serving on a board to identify individuals they think would make good members. Give them an idea of the type of persons that are trying to be recruited for the upcoming openings. Provide them with age, sex, race, and geographic needs as well as the skills and access that are being sought. The number of potential board members identified by the current board probably will be surprising. Staff recommendations are another source of leads as are former clients of the organization.

Some boards have a nominating committee whose sole responsibility is to identify potential board members. They seek recommendations from community and civic leaders, from other professionals in the field, and from active board members of similar organizations; they even invite the organization's constituencies to send in nominations. Often a questionnaire similar to that in Exhibit 2–2 is used.

Job Descriptions for Board Members

All volunteers, whether chairperson of the board or envelope "stuffers," need to receive job descriptions. Just as a staff person would never be hired without a job description, a volunteer should never be brought on to do a task without a clearly defined written role. According to Janice E. Toohey (1986), volunteer job descriptions should be "designed directly from the planning forms. Include:

- Job title;
- Assignment's starting and ending dates;
- Qualifications;
- General responsibilities;
- Specific required tasks;
- Duties or meetings;
- Person or position supervising the volunteer;
- Number of hours per day/week/month needed; and,
- Site where work is to be done.

Job descriptions give volunteers ideas of definite work needed by the organization and provide the volunteer director with a guide for recruitment." For an example of a job description, refer to Exhibit 2–3.

Also, it is important to be able to evaluate a volunteer's work. By having a written job description, the volunteer's progress or lack of progress, successes, and failures can be discussed. In addition, by reviewing a job description in advance, a volunteer may decide that this is not the project that matches his or her skills or interests. It is better to know this in the beginning than after the project has begun and it becomes necessary to replace the volunteer and train someone new.

All volunteers should be interviewed to determine their interests, knowledge of the organization, skills, work habits, and attitudes. (Refer to Exhibit 2–4 for an example of a volunteer assessment form.)

> **All volunteers, whether chairperson of the board or envelope "stuffers," need to receive job descriptions.**

Exhibit 2–2 Board of Directors Member Questionnaire

NAME _____

HOME ADDRESS _____

_____

CITY/STATE/ZIP CODE _____

TELEPHONE _____ FAX _____

E-MAIL ADDRESS _____

EMPLOYER _____

TITLE _____

OFFICE ADDRESS _____

_____

CITY/STATE/ZIP _____

TELEPHONE _____ FAX _____

E-MAIL ADDRESS _____

PREVIOUS EMPLOYMENT DURING LAST TEN YEARS

POSITION	COMPANY	LOCATION

EDUCATION

SCHOOL/COLLEGE/UNIVERSITY/LOCATION/YEARS ATTENDED/DEGREES

_____

_____

_____

_____

HONORS/ACHIEVEMENTS

_____

_____

_____

continues

Exhibit 2–2 continued

SOCIAL AFFILIATIONS/CLUBS/MEMBERSHIPS

_____

_____

_____

_____

PROFESSIONAL ORGANIZATIONS

_____

_____

_____

BOARD MEMBERSHIPS

_____

_____

_____

_____

CHILDREN

NAME   AGE   SCHOOLS ATTENDING/GRADUATED FROM

_____

_____

_____

_____

PERSONAL INTERESTS/HOBBIES

_____

_____

_____

_____

_____

This may be done by the director of volunteers, if the organization has a position such as this, or by the staff person needing the volunteers. It is imperative that the volunteers and staff supervising them have a good working rapport. The staff must be able to lead and motivate the volunteers, and those volunteering their time must feel positive and enthusiastic about the organization and its staff to work effectively. Just as members of the professional staff need to feel proud of their position within the organization, so, too, do the volunteers. Just as members of the staff need to be stimulated to maintain their motivation, so, too, do the volunteers. Just as members

Exhibit 2–3 The Arizona Children's Home Foundation Board of Trustees

RESPONSIBILITIES

- Review and approve the mission for this board.
- Serve as advisors for the positioning of the Arizona Children's Home Association (ACHA) in each community.
- Work with the support of the Executive Director and the Chief Executive Officer to sustain fund-raising programs for ACHA services, including such activities as:
  Prospect Identification
  Prospect Review
  Prospect Cultivation
  Prospect Solicitation
- Support the advocacy efforts of the ACHA Board of Directors.
- Develop a strategy, with the support of the Executive Director and development staff, for implementing a $5 million campaign by the year 2000.
- Respond to community interests and needs as related to the welfare of children in Arizona and the possible involvement of the ACHA.

THE MISSION:

The mission of this board is to generate funding to enable the Arizona Children's Home Association to provide therapy and services that will foster healing and promote the emotional well-being of families and children in Arizona.

CRITERIA FOR NOMINATION:

- Individuals with visibility in the state and demonstrated commitment to children and families.
- Dedication to providing the optimum treatment programs for all children and families in need.
- Individuals with influence and ability to facilitate significant gifts.
- Individuals who represent cultural and ethnic diversity.

MEMBER RESPONSIBILITIES:

- Attendance at an orientation meeting or board retreat.
- Attendance at quarterly meetings.
- Commitment to serve on at least one committee.
- Willingness to serve as an advocate for the Arizona Children's Home Association.
- Involvement with the public relations program in your community.
- Commitment of an annual personal and/or corporate gift to the Foundation.
- Willingness to engage in friend raising and fund raising for ACHA.
- Participate in the annual Board evaluation.

TERMS OF SERVICE:

- Each member will be eligible to serve three consecutive three year terms. After three terms, a one year hiatus is required before re-election.

Courtesy of the Arizona Children's Home Foundation, 1995, Tucson, Arizona.

of the staff want to be promoted, so, too, do the volunteers. When establishing a volunteer program, approach the project as if new staff were being hired. Go through all of the steps—write the job description, place the ad, interview the applicants, "hire" the person, provide the proper introductions to the organization, train the individual to be equipped to handle the position, evaluate the performance, provide motivation, and recognize and reward success.

Keep in mind what Toohey said: "Always remember that volunteers are contributing their free time to your cause. They are under no contract obligation to continue; their commitment might be greater than that of some staff people."

Exhibit 2–4 NSFRE/DC Volunteer Assessment

The NSFRE/DC Chapter is one of the most active NSFRE chapters in the country and we want to make this a rewarding affiliation for you. We have lots to offer with our informative monthly luncheons, educational roundtables, current job hotline, inspiring Fund Raising Days in Washington, and the list goes on. What keeps us ahead is new talent and fresh ideas. Please tell us about your interests and abilities so we can match you with an appropriate opportunity within NSFRE/DC.

What expertise are you willing to share and which skills do you wish to develop?
  (Please check those that apply.)

	EXPERTISE	INTEREST
• Organizing	_____	_____
• Telephoning	_____	_____
• Writing	_____	_____
• Interviewing in person	_____	_____
• Design and Layout	_____	_____
• Meeting the public	_____	_____
• Advocacy	_____	_____
• Recruiting others	_____	_____
• Finance	_____	_____
• Facilitating	_____	_____
• Other _____	_____	_____

TIME

Many members are fully active volunteers by donating as little as three hours per month.
Please indicate your availability to support NSFRE/DC:

1–3   4–6   6+   hours/month

Please attach business card or complete the following:

Name: _____

Title: _____

Organization: _____

Address: _____

Telephone (W) _____ (FAX) _____ (H) _____

Courtesy of Carol Shaw, National Society of Fund Raising Executives, DC Chapter, Bethesda, Maryland.

Setting Clear Goals and Expectations for the Board

Most members of nonprofit boards have been asked to be on their boards for one of three reasons: (1) their ability to bring in wealth, (2) their wisdom, or (3) the ability to work hard for the cause. These are commonly referred to as the "three W's" in fund raising. In his book, *Fund Raising: A Guide to Raising Money From Private Sources*, Thomas E. Broce (1986) cites seven qualities that he looks for in good fund-raising trustees. They are the following:

- a natural relationship with or interest in the institution;
- affluence or influence;

- a willingness to contribute sacrificially;
- enough interest in the organization to be willing to ask difficult questions and ensure that members of the staff are doing their homework in all areas of management and administration;
- an ability and willingness to communicate enthusiastically to others;
- willingness to be well informed about the institution's history, current operations, and future goals; and
- a sense of urgency about the organization's mission.

"Good trustees are precious commodities," states Broce. "Do not waste active people's time with busy work and show and tell. Involve them in the life of the organization in meaningful ways, and they will respond enthusiastically."

A properly trained, organized, and structured committee of volunteers is crucial to a successful organization. Equally important is the selection of the appropriate chairperson. With proper training, the chair will be able to lead and motivate the board or committee to the betterment of the organization. An excellent list describing how crucial a well-trained chair is to the success of the committee, board, or organization is illustrated in Exhibit 2–5.

Working with an Existing Board

Most development officers inherit their board and other volunteers. They do not have the luxury of recruiting them. Unfortunately, this can also mean that the board comes with pre-set attitudes regarding fund raising. It may mean that they were recruited with the understanding that they were *not* to raise funds. If this appears to

be the situation, then the first step is to review the written job description for the board members. If this does not specify fund raising as part of the board members' roles, then the board must be convinced that

> Most development officers inherit their board and other volunteers. They do not have the luxury of recruiting them.

the criteria for membership and the job description both be changed. The development officer will need to rely upon help from the chairperson or other key volunteers to change the boards' attitudes.

If a board is in place and actively involved in fund raising, the job of raising dollars will be much easier for the development office staff. If members of the board accept fund raising as their responsibility, but just have not been doing it, and an active fund-raising committee is not in place, much more work will be required to build an active fund-raising effort among the board members.

The first step for the development office is to determine if the board members are accepting and acting upon their normal duties; making decisions on policies for the organization; ensuring the financial security of the organization; providing expertise and leadership in areas needed; understanding the mission and goals of the organization and representing them to the public; guiding the senior management of the organization when requested; remaining knowledgeable of the duties of the various staff and departments to evaluate the effectiveness of the organization; etc. If the board is "on top" of the basics, then the development officer can begin to determine which of the board members would best lead or assist with the board's fund-raising responsibilities.

Exhibit 2–5

A Board Chairperson does the following:

- Leads in setting committee goals and objectives, defining the work programs and monitoring its progress;
- Understands the decision-making process and knows how to lead the committee through it;
- Plans committee meetings, prepares the agenda, and arranges meeting time and location for maximum group convenience and effectiveness;
- Prepares and distributes the necessary materials and information for the committee to begin its work, and delegates responsibilities and tasks to appropriate committee members;

- Conducts the meeting firmly, but flexibly;
- Draws all committee members into the discussions;
- Keeps the discussion on track;
- Avoids imposing his or her opinions;
- Is sensitive to the needs and positions of other committee members;
- Sees that complete, accurate minutes are taken promptly at each meeting;
- Sees that costs are held within budget; and,
- Communicates often in appropriate detail with the rest of the organization.

Source: Reprinted with permission from Mark London, Effective Use of Volunteers: Who, Why, When And How, *Fund Raising Management*, August 1985.

Usually, one or two board members will emerge as the natural leader(s) for this role. If not, then one member must be identified who can assume leadership by being a liaison between the existing board and the fund-raising committee of the board about to be established.

The fund-raising committee of the board should do the following: solicit major gifts from individual members and from the leadership in the corporate and foundation world; train incoming board members to be solicitors by taking them along on fund-raising calls; set the standard for giving by making their personal gifts first—and generously; write solicitation letters or lend their signatures to those written by staff; chair memorial or capital campaigns, special events, or planned giving efforts; and lead other members of the board in fund-raising efforts.

Techniques to Motivate Your Board into Action

To motivate volunteers, staff must first empower them. Provide them with the training they need to succeed, the tools required to do their job, and the staff support necessary to complete the job successfully. Give credit to the volunteers for every success. Accept blame for every failure.

Staff members must provide the leadership and structure necessary for the volunteer effort to move forward. Develop job descriptions for the volunteers so their performances may be evaluated. Provide the volunteers with information that will help them with their assignments. Give them copies of the case statement, all fund-raising literature, and strategic plans of the organization. Share with them what they need to know and whatever else that could make their roles more substantial and fun. Volunteers want to be needed and want to perform tasks that make a difference.

Because most volunteers aren't comfortable asking for money, it is important for staff to train them in fund-raising techniques. Use other board members to assist in the process. Send a new volunteer on a fund-raising solicitation with a board member experienced in fund raising. Explain the reasons behind the campaign and take the volunteer on a site visit to see the work of the organization. Provide leadership and training. Review the volunteers' job description with them and provide time for feedback on their performance. Ask them for feedback. Keep an open channel of communication.

Don't attempt to manipulate volunteers to advance your own agenda. Never put a volunteer in the middle of an organization's turf war. Also, don't treat volunteers as a means to an end. They need to feel that what they are doing will make a difference; otherwise, they will lose interest.

Most important, give recognition for a job well done. This can be the number one method of motivation—peer recognition! When a board member has done an exemplary job in soliciting a prospect, share this with the other members of the fund-raising committee or board. Provide a regular format for recognizing efforts of the volunteers. Write a thank you letter; place an article in the organization's newsletter; recognize the volunteer at a special event. In some way, say thank you for a job well done.

Board Training and Development

After identifying board members' interests and determining their qualifications, appoint them to the appropriate committees. Provide them with the appropriate job description and then train, train, and train again. Never assume that a volunteer will know what to do because he or she has done it before. This organization's fund-raising needs may be completely different from those of the organization for which the board member had previously volunteered. Thoroughly explain the mission, goals and objectives, programs, and financial needs of the organization. Explain the time commitment necessary to perform the job at the level expected.

Remind board members up-front that part of their job description is to set an exemplary pace for those who will be asked to donate. Board members must be willing to give a "stretch" gift to a specific campaign and they must be willing to give annually to the organization. The organization's commitment to fund raising must start at the board level. Again, this message can be instilled through yearly training. Don't hesitate to bring in outside resources to train board members. It is important that they develop along with the organization. Just as staff members of the organization are encouraged to continually develop in their chosen field, so should the

"HEEEERE WE GO. BOARD RETREAT STRENGTH PAIN RELIEVER."

Source: © Mark Litzler.

board member be offered development opportunities. Select a motivational speaker on a topic of interest to the board; bring in an expert on planned giving to show the board that it doesn't need to be complex and that they can present the concept to prospective donors. Show the board members new ways and techniques to do their jobs well. The well-trained and motivated volunteer will be the successful volunteer.

Advisory Committees to Boards for Fund Raising

Board members are expected to raise money for their organizations as well as to set policy. The most effective way for a board to raise money is through a development or fund-raising committee. Those who have the strongest skills and interest in fund-raising work with the organization's development staff to direct and focus the fund-raising efforts for the other board members and committees. The members of this group should have previous fund-raising experience or strong ties with the corporate community. The development staff provides professional expertise to the committee and helps the committee establish goals. A job description should be provided to every member of the committee (as well as to all board members) so they know what is expected of them in their role as a fund raiser.

If the committee is large, strong, and sophisticated enough in fund raising, you may wish to establish subcommittees in specialized fund-raising areas. For example, if a member of your committee has a background in banking or law and is familiar with wills, estates, and trusts, you may wish to focus his or her energies on planned giving. If another one or two have strong ties to the corporate world, their energies may be best directed to raising money solely from corporations. The most important point to remember is that board and committee members must know what their roles are and these roles should not only be clearly defined, but they should be provided to members in a written job description.

If the board does not have members with the necessary experience to fund raise effectively, board members may wish to develop fund-raising committees whose memberships include other individuals than those currently on the board. This is one way of expanding the volunteer base of the board to assist with fund raising without increasing the overall membership of the board. Usually, the members of the advisory board or committee are from the corporate or private foundation community and are brought on specifically to help the organization increase its financial coffers. Commonly called corporate advisory boards (CABs) or corporate advisory programs (CAPs), these committees' goals are primarily of a fund-raising nature, but also include improving the communications network between the organization and the general public. Just as other members of the board are given job descriptions, so should members of the fund-raising advisory committee.

An excellent example of a job description for a development committee can be found in Exhibit 2–6.

As mentioned before, most individuals are selected to become members of nonprofit boards because they can bring wealth, work, and wisdom to the board. You will also hear the phrase "the three G's" used when referring

---

Exhibit 2–6 Job Description for a Development Committee

The purpose of a development committee is to lead the board in efforts to attract money and services that are necessary to carry out the mission of the organization.

The duties of the board development committee are to

- *Define the short-term and long-term funding needs of this organization with the help of the full board and administrator.* Funding appeals will be ineffective if we can't tell prospective donors exactly why our nonprofit needs funds.
- *Train the full board.* Little training is required to hold a modest fund-raising event—but most nonprofits need far more money than small events raise. The committee must become knowledgeable about planned giving, corporate solicitation, lobbying government bodies, grant-writing, and marketing.
- *Involve all board members in fund raising.* Each board member has the responsibility to do all he or she can to raise money for your nonprofit. The development committee must organize fund-raising activities to take into consideration each board member's unique talents.

- *Review progress on fund-raising goals—and inspire the full board.* The committee must not only report on the status of fund-raising efforts, it must be coach and cheerleader to the entire fund-raising team.
- *Make personal financial donations—and encourage your fellow board members to do likewise.* The best way to convince members of your community to give is to lead by example. Donations by the committee and other board members demonstrate that we believe enough in our nonprofit's mission to put our money where our mouths are.
- *Identify, cultivate, and enlist community leaders to serve on the funding development committee.* There may be a reservoir of untapped fund-raising talent in our community. The committee is responsible for finding it and putting it to good use.

Source: Reprinted from D. Struck and S. Campbell, *Board Fund Raising Manual*, p. 13, © 1992, Aspen Publishers, Inc.

> Most individuals are selected to become members of nonprofit boards because they can bring wealth, work, and wisdom to the board.

to nonprofit boards. The three Gs are Give, Get, or Get off! Board members are expected to give of their own personal wealth, get money from others for the organization, or get off the board. Nonprofit boards cannot afford to have someone who doesn't raise money. In addition to having a job description, it is a sound idea to have all board members sign commitment forms for both the amount of money they will personally give *and* what they will solicit from others. Exhibit 2–7 provides a sample format for this form.

Evaluating Board Members' Effectiveness

Volunteers need feedback. They need to know if what they are doing is correct or incorrect. They need both praise and guidance. Most organizations that develop and use an evaluation form with their volunteers find that their volunteers think that the effort is worthwhile. Some organizations averse to "performance reviews" for volunteers call their evaluations a "progress review." Others just don't like the term evaluation, and instead call it "feedback." Whatever it is termed, evaluations are important because they not only help the volunteer, but also the organization's staff. The evaluation is an opportunity for the volunteer to assess his or her own role with the organization and for the organization to assess its ability to select, guide, train, and motivate volunteers. Evaluation is a two-way street—the volunteer often sees things that need improvement that staff members don't and can help staff members redefine volunteer job descriptions that may not be manageable.

How can evaluations help remove "dead weight" from boards—the volunteer who doesn't follow through on his or her commitments or who exhibits passive-aggressive behavior? Establishing structure is the most effective way to resolve this type of problem. If there aren't board term limits, set them. If job descriptions don't exist, write them. If performance evaluations are not being done, initiate them. If every board member is evaluated according to his or her job description and a discussion is held regarding the progress made or not made, it opens the way for a healthy discussion of how to correct the lack of progress, reassign the person to a different responsibility, or discuss, based on facts, not emotions, the idea of that person leaving the board or not being asked to serve for a second term.

How to Retire a Board Member

At some point in every development officer's career, he or she will have to confront a board member who is no longer an active leader, who no longer produces for the organization—effectively, efficiently, or at all. Many times, this lack of action is not noticed at first, but appears gradually as the board member is "carried along" by the other members of the board. Sometimes this "awareness" will surface quickly, usually when an issue is brought before the board with which the member does not agree or cannot endorse for whatever reasons. Then it could just be the changing times—the board member cannot or will not change direction with the organization. The question is, "What should you do when this happens to you?"

Most organizations will have defined term limits with a set percentage of members retiring each year from their positions. Usually, terms are set for three years, with one third of the board rotating off each year. Some organizations have rules that allow board members to be re-elected for two consecutive terms and then they must "sit out" before being elected again. Other institutions will not allow board members to serve more than two terms. Some unfortunate organizations have no term limits and thus can find themselves with individuals who have been members of the board for ten, twenty, or thirty years. Why is this bad?

No organization can afford to have "dead weight" on its board. How to ask board members who have fulfilled their usefulness, as well as their time, to leave is as important as selecting members for the board. One method is to evaluate board members on a regular basis. Paid employees are usually first evaluated after their probationary period (three to six months) and then yearly after that, on or near the anniversary of their employment. Similarly, volunteers should be given a probationary period followed by an evaluation, and then evaluated yearly after that.

Role of Staff in Fund Raising

The director of development or chief development officer has the role of leading the fund-raising efforts. He or she is responsible for carrying out the work authorized by the board and making the day-to-day decisions of the office. The director is the liaison or bridge between the staff and the board, and consults the board for direction and guidance. The director should be knowledgeable of all types of fund raising including annual campaigns, capital campaigns, major gift solicitation, proposal writing, special events, direct mail, planned giving, etc. In addition, the director manages the functional responsibilities of the development office. He or she must be capable of leading the staff through the various phases of the fund-raising operation—planning and marketing; public relations; volunteer management and training; donor identification and solicitation; gift processing, reporting, and management; donor renewal, upgrading, recognition; etc. The director is expected to lead and

Exhibit 2–7

GIVE AND GET COMMITMENT FORM

Board member's name _____

My personal "giving" goal:

I personally pledge $_____to this organization to support our fund-raising objective.

   I would prefer to make: (Please check)
   ( ) One yearly payment
   ( ) Quarterly payments of $_____
   ( ) Monthly payments of $_____
   ( ) Weekly payments of $_____

(Rule of thumb: Each board member should give what he or she can. Some board members will be able to give more than others. But no matter what the amount you can give, it is important to set a giving example!)

My goal for "getting" donations:

As a board member I will personally get (raise) $_____ from outside sources.

I will solicit $_____for our special fund-raising event.

I will assist in building our donor list by submitting a total of _____ potential new donors.

I agree to participate in other fund-raising activities as needed. I accept this commitment as an understanding of my responsibilities as a board member.

_____
Board member signature

When you have the form signed, pass the information on to your administrator. He or she can then total up all the amounts for the entire board. Once you receive the totals, take a minute and fill out the blanks below. Then sit back and consider what a difference this money will make for your nonprofit!

If each board member meets his/her goals, the total raised will be:

1) Total amount donated by board members $_____

2) Total amount raised by board members $_____

_____

Total amount raised by board "giving" and "getting" $_____

Source: Reprinted from D. Struck and S. Campbell, *Board Fund Raising Manual*, p. 12, © 1992, Aspen Publishers, Inc.

---

motivate the staff to complete the tasks required to meet the department's goals.

As all department heads have budgetary responsibilities, so too does the development director. He or she must ensure that the work of the office is completed in a timely, efficient, cost-effective, and ethical manner. The director sets the tone for the office and motivates the staff as well as the volunteers. He or she is also responsible for keeping the executive director or president of the organiza-

tion and board informed of the activities of the department. There should be no "surprises" to report. Depending upon the size of the institution, there may be others to assist the director with office work.

Communications Between Board and Staff

It is important that open communications exist between the board and staff. As mentioned previously, a develop-

> A development director should not even consider a position in which he or she is not given direct access to the board of the organization at any time.

ment director should not even consider a position in which he or she is not given direct access to the board of the organization at any time. Use this access wisely. Know the difference between relevant and irrelevant information. Call upon the board members when there is a specific task for them to perform. Always follow through on what has been committed and within the time frame promised. Likewise, if asking a board member to perform a task, provide clear direction and give a time table for the results.

Ensuring that there are regularly scheduled meetings with board members is also important in keeping open communications between the board and development staff. The director of development should meet at least once a year with every member of the board. Be sure to have an agenda—review fund-raising goals with a new member; ask an experienced board fund raiser to attend a fund-raising conference with you; seek advice on a problem or opportunity; or introduce a board member to some facet of your operation that gives him or her new insight into the strength of your and your staff's work.

Most important of all, listen to what the board members have to say. They may provide the answer or an idea or insight to solve a problem for which the staff has been struggling for months to find the answer. They may have new ways of doing things that can work!

Staff Expectations for Board Members

Staff members can expect board members to do the following: be loyal and committed to the organization and its mission and purposes; attend all regularly scheduled board meetings; give generously of their own wealth and solicit funds from others to support the organization; enthusiastically support and represent the organization to the public; act as a liaison with the organization's many publics; maintain confidentiality; and actively participate in fund-raising activities including special events, gift evaluations, resource prospecting, developing a case statement for the organization, and soliciting prospective donors.

It is the staff's responsibility to make sure that the board is provided with adequate training to accomplish the previously mentioned tasks. If the board is not performing up to the expectations of the staff, then the staff must first look at itself to see if board members have been provided with the tools that they need to be successful.

Board Members' Expectations for Staff

Just as the staff has expectations of its board, so does the board have expectations of the staff. The board can expect the staff to know the nonprofit world and be able to guide the organization to reach its fund-raising goals successfully by use of strategic planning, which should direct the organization through many mazes and obstacles. The board will expect the staff to do the following: be professionals; design the overall fund-raising plan; develop all materials needed in the fund-raising effort; provide adequate orientation and training for the board and other volunteers; assist the board in making solicitation calls; provide the necessary materials to board members to solicit a prospect; establish the criteria necessary to accept and evaluate gifts to the organization; provide follow-up to all contacts made by board members; develop an acknowledgment procedure; and generally support the activities of the board. Board members and other volunteers can succeed only if they are provided with the proper training, motivation, and support by the staff.

Successful fund raising requires a team effort from both staff members and volunteers—requiring full energy on both sides. Just as in sports, fund raising requires a well thought out and well executed plan. This is developed by the staff in cooperation with the board, as its members will also want to have ownership. The meetings organized by the staff for the board should be planned well in advance, fit the schedules of most members, be organized so that time is not wasted, and include items to be discussed on which the board will take action or make decisions. Respect the time of the volunteer. Use it wisely. Don't ask too much of one group of volunteers and neglect others. Watch for overuse or "burnout." Volunteers who are kept informed, whose time is used judiciously, and who are respected for the talent they bring to the board will more often remain active and loyal to the organization than those whose time has been abused and interests have been ignored.

References

Broce, Thomas E. 1986. *Fund Raising: The Guide to Raising Money from Private Sources,* Second Edition. Norman, OK: University of Oklahoma Press.

Church, Susan. 1988. "The Volunteer's Role" in *Getting Started: A Guide to Fund Raising Fundamentals.* Chicago: National Society of Fund Raising Executives, Chicago Chapter.

Coles, Robert. 1994. "Doing Well by Doing Good: Why We Volunteer." *Advancing Philanthropy* (Spring).

Stehle, Vincent. 1993. "Finding New Ways to Recruit and Keep Today's Volunteers." *Chronicle of Philanthropy* (29 June).

Toohey, Janice E. 1986. "Care and Feeding—Some Practical and Innovative Ideas on How to Manage a Successful Volunteer Program." *NSFRE Journal* (Fall).

Appendix 2–A
State Offices of Volunteerism

Alabama
Governor's Office on National Community Service
11 South Union Street, Room 219
Montgomery, AL 36130–2751
Telephone: (334) 242–7110

Arkansas
Arkansas Division of Volunteerism
P.O. Box 1437, Slot 1300
Little Rock, AR 72203
Telephone: (501) 682–7540

Delaware
State Office on Volunteerism
P.O. Box 637
Dover, DE 19903–0637
Telephone: (302) 739–4456

Florida
Florida Commission on Community Services
Gulf Breeze Parkway
Gulf Breeze Office Park, Suite 331
Gulf Breeze, FL 32561
Telephone: (904) 934–4000

Georgia
Georgia Association for Volunteer Administration, Inc.
100 Peachtree Street
Atlanta, GA 30309
Telephone: (404) 679–5277

Hawaii
Hawaii Office of Volunteer Services and Special Projects
Office of the Governor
State Capitol
Honolulu, HI 96813
Telephone: (808) 586–7200

Illinois
Office of Volunteer Action
100 West Randolph, Suite 15–200
Chicago, IL 60601
Telephone: (312) 814–5225

Indiana
Governor's Voluntary Action Program
302 West Washington, Room E–220
Indianapolis, IN 46204
Telephone: (317) 232–2504

Iowa
Governor's Office for Volunteerism
State Capitol
Des Moines, IA 50319
Telephone: (515) 281–8304

Kansas
Kansas Office for Community Service
P.O. Box 889
Topeka, KS 66601
Telephone: (913) 575–8330

Source: Reprinted with permission from The Points of Light Foundation, *Volunteer—We Belong Together: The 1996 Volunteer Center Directory,* © 1996. For more information, contact Jeff Brightbill at (202) 223-9186.

Kentucky

Department for Social Services
Program Support Branch
275 East Main Street, Room 6–W
Frankfort, KY 40621–0001
Telephone: (502) 564–4357

Maine

Maine Commission for Community Service
State Planning
State House Station 38
Augusta, ME 04333–0038
Telephone: (207) 624–6011

Maryland

Governor's Office on Volunteerism
301 West Preston Street, Suite 608
Baltimore, MD 21201
Telephone: (410) 225–4496

Massachusetts

Task Force for a State Office on Volunteerism for
the Commonwealth of Massachusetts
9 Christopher Road
Randolph, MA 02368
Telephone: (617) 262–3935

Michigan

Michigan Community Service Commission
111 South Capitol Avenue
Olds Plaza, Fourth Floor
P.O. Box 30015
Lansing, MI 48909
Telephone: (517) 335–4295

Minnesota

Minnesota Office of Citizenship and Volunteer
Services
117 University Avenue
St. Paul, MN 55155–2200
Telephone: (612) 296–4731

Mississippi

Governor's Initiative on Voluntary Excellence
300 East Capitol Street
Jackson, MS 39201
Telephone: (601) 359–3175

Nebraska

Commission for National and Community Service
P.O. Box 98927
Lincoln, NE 68509–8927
Telephone: (402) 471–9107 or (800) 291–8911

New Hampshire

Governor's Office on Volunteerism
The State House Annex, Room 431
25 Capitol Street
Concord, NH 03301
Telephone: (603) 271–3771

New Jersey

New Jersey Governor's Office of Volunteerism
Department of Human Services
222 South Warren Street—CN 700
Trenton, NJ 08625
Telephone: (609) 984–3470

New Mexico

Commission for National and Community Services
Governor's Office
State Capitol
Santa Fe, NM 87503
Telephone: (505) 827–3000

New York

New York State Office for National and Community
Service
Division of Budget
State Capitol
Albany, NY 12224
Telephone: (518) 473–8882

North Carolina

Governor's Office of Citizen Affairs
121 West Jones Street
Raleigh, NC 27603–8001
Telephone: (919) 715–3470

North Dakota

Economic Development and Finance Department
1833 East Bismarck Expressway
Bismarck, ND 58504
Telephone: (701) 221–5330

Ohio

GIVE: Governor's Initiative on Volunteer Efforts
77 South High Street, 30th Floor
Columbus, OH 43266
Telephone: (614) 644–7644

Oklahoma

Oklahoma Office of Volunteerism
Office of the Secretary of State
1515 North Lincoln
Oklahoma City, OK 73105
Telephone: (405) 235–7272

Oregon

Department of Human Resources
Volunteer Program
500 Summer Street, N.E.—Fourth Floor
Salem, OR 97310–1019
Telephone: (503) 945–5759

Pennsylvania

PennServe: Governor's Office of Citizen Service
Department of Labor and Industry
1304 Labor and Industry Building
Harrisburg, PA 17120
Telephone: (717) 787–1971

South Carolina

Office of the Governor
1205 Pendleton Street
Columbia, SC 29201
Telephone: (803) 734–1677

South Dakota

Governor's Office for Volunteerism
500 East Capitol Avenue
Pierre, SD 57501–5070
Telephone: (605) 773–3661

Tennessee

Tennessee Commission for National and Community Service
302 John Sevier Building
500 Charlotte Avenue
Nashville, TN 37243
Telephone: (615) 532–9250

Texas

Texas Commission for National and Community Service
P.O. Box 13385
Austin, TX 78711–3385
Telephone: (512) 475–2289

Utah

State of Utah Commission on Volunteers
Office of the Lieutenant Governor
324 South State Street, Suite 240
Salt Lake City, UT 84114–7945
Telephone: (801) 538–8610

Vermont

Vermont Commission on National and Community Service
133 State Street
Montpelier, VT 05633–4801
Telephone: (802) 828–4982

Virginia

Virginia Office of Volunteerism
730 East Broad Street, Ninth Floor
Richmond, VA 23219
Telephone: (804) 692–1951

Washington

Center of Volunteerism and Citizen Services
906 Columbia Street, SW
Olympia, WA 98504–8300
Telephone: (360) 753–9684

West Virginia

West Virginia Department of Education
1900 Kanawha Boulevard
Building 6, Room 221
Charleston, WV 25305–0330
Telephone: (304) 558–2681

Canada

Voluntary Action Directorate
Department of Multiculturalism and Citizenship
Ottawa, Ontario, Canada K1A 1K5
Telephone: (819) 994–2255

Chapter 3
The Development Office

Chapter Outline

- The Need for a Development Office
- Major Functions of the Development Office and Staff and Resources Needed
- The Basic Requirements for Setting Up a Development Office
- The Development Office Budget
- Various Models for a Development Office
- Knowing When to Move from the One-Person Shop to a Larger Operation
- Expectations for the Development Office
- Suggested Publications for the Development Office Library

Key Vocabulary

- Back-Up
- Central Processing Unit (CPU)
- DOS
- Hardware
- Ink Jet Printer
- Laser Printer
- Megs
- Memory
- Modem
- Monitor
- Multitasking
- RAM
- ROM
- Slug
- Software
- Strategic Plan
- Surge Protector

The Need for a Development Office

The development operation within an organization manages all of the fund-raising activities of that organization. Not only do the staff members coordinate all of the development efforts of the various departments within the organization, but they also manage all of the office operations that support fund raising. The development office is an integral part of a nonprofit organization's operation. It is one of the main sources of revenue for an organization

> The development office should be considered a profit center for an organization and managed as such.

along with the membership, conventions and meetings, and publishing departments. The development office should be considered a profit center for an organization and managed as such.

Many nonprofit organizations claim they have no financial need for a development office. For example, organizations with many members may bring in enough money from their dues to support their organization's operations and, thus, think they have no need for fund raising. When particular departments within the organization wish to expand their operations, they usually take on the fund-raising responsibilities themselves—usually with little or no cooperation from other departments or direction from the senior management staff. This can work effectively and for a long time for many organizations until, suddenly, there is a need for coordination, usually brought upon by a crisis situation (for example, one department contacts a corporation or foundation that is being solicited concurrently by another department within the same organization). The potential donor will often ask, "Which one of your programs (or departments) do you want us to support?" Usually, it is at this time that a member of the senior management staff is called upon to decide which department should continue to solicit funding from that particular potential donor and which should step aside.

After this situation occurs several times, staff members affected by the situation will request that the organization find someone to coordinate these efforts so such conflicts will not happen again. Often, also at the same time, staff members will suggest that the organization hire a person to not only act as coordinator, but also as the initiator of gift solicitation. Staff members want someone hired to raise funds so they can attend to the job for which they were hired, and also expand the activities of their departments without diverting their energies from their day-to-day responsibilities and department operations. This is often how development offices are born.

Another reason that a development office is created may be that the institution has decided to embark upon a major fund-raising effort—a capital campaign for a new building, to underwrite programs, or to build an endowment. Thus, a development office may be started with no history of fund raising within the organization. Depending upon the reason for fund raising, having no history can be a major obstacle to overcome.

The size of the development operation will vary widely. Some organizations function for many years with a one-person development office. Others will grow quickly to three- or five-person operations. Yet others may employ from fifteen to more than twenty fund-raising staff. This chapter will focus mainly on the small to mid-size development operation. Larger operations, usually located within universities, have much more complex structures than this chapter will address.

The development functions should be an integral part of the organization's overall strategic plan. The fund-raising effort will depend upon the organization having a well thought-out mission statement and goals, and programs defined to support them. Development office staff members will then use these items to develop their fund-raising plans. These plans must be accepted and supported by the institution's board and senior management as part of the entire organization's efforts.

Development office staff members will perform various duties including the following: research and solicitation of gifts; processing of gifts received; maintenance of donor records; producing numerous reports for distribution among various audiences; writing proposals; gift acknowledgment letters and articles to promote the fund-raising efforts; planning special events to raise money, institutional awareness, or to enhance donor relations; training board members or other volunteers in fund-raising methods; planning and organizing major gifts and planned giving efforts; and providing support for their superiors when asked.

Major Functions of the Development Office and Staff and Resources Needed

Staff and resources for a development office will vary depending upon the functions of the office as well as the size of the organization. There are no set rules that dictate what number of staff or what size of office space will be needed to raise a set amount of money. Most organizations start small and grow only as money is raised. Following are brief summaries of the functions of a development operation and what staff requirements are necessary to perform those functions successfully.

Active Fund Raising

Most fund-raising departments are organized within annual fund, capital campaign, direct mail, special event, and estate planning activities. Trustee–led committees, along with other volunteers, perform many of these efforts. All activities are coordinated by the development office staff throughout the year to seek gift income for approved projects.

Donor Relations and Communications

Development staff members must maintain active contact on a continuing basis with all who support the organization. This includes internal departments as well as donors. Communications include information about board and staff activity, and reports on development progress. The development office should coordinate all communications with donors.

Services to the Organization's Other Departments and Staff

Personnel in the development office are available to the organization's administrative and departmental staff for professional assistance on projects appropriate for fund raising. Prospect research, proposal writing, prospect clearance, active solicitation, etc., are all duties development staff members can perform. Only the organization's projects with priority can command use of development office budget for fund raising. All other projects need to be funded by the department requesting assistance.

Gift Reports and Donor Record Files

All gifts are recorded in the development office. The type and number of gifts, and the complexity of the processing procedures depend upon the size of the institution, and the type and scope of the fund raising being undertaken. Gifts received can include cash, checks, securities (stocks and bonds), works of art, jewelry, real estate, planned gifts (charitable remainder trusts, bequests, etc.), and gifts-in-kind. The types of gifts that will be accepted by the organization must be decided in advance. A gifts procedure manual should be developed so the staff will know how to accept, record, acknowledge, and recognize gifts properly. All gifts will then be recorded, acknowledged, and recognized. Recording of gifts should be undertaken the minute they are received. Donors should be thanked for their gifts within 24–48 hours if possible. At the latest, each gift should be acknowledged within one week.

Reports listing gifts by source, purpose, and program must be produced on a regular basis (for example, unrestricted; restricted; annual fund; capital campaign; endowment; scholarship; research; education; etc.). These reports will remain confidential and be circulated only to those who need them. Pledges will be recorded and follow-up billing will be conducted. Permanent donor records will be maintained. They will include the gift history and all correspondence relating to gifts and pledges. Research information on donors and prospects will be collected. All these activities will be performed with sensitive personal data kept in confidence by development staff.

Credit should be given to donors for their gifts, whether appearing in a program, on a wall in a building, in newsletters, or in annual reports, or with donors publicly recognized at an event. It is the development office staff's role to develop the type of recognition that will be done and to ensure that it is carried out by either development office staff or the appropriate department within the organization.

The Basic Requirements for Setting Up a Development Office

Setting Up the Office
The development office serves not only as the fund-raising arm of the organization, but often as the public relations operation as well. Therefore, the appearance of the office is often as important as what it does. If other organization staff members, potential donors, or outside guests visit the office, they should

> The development office serves not only as the fund-raising arm of the organization, but often as the public relations operation as well.

be able to enter the space and view a highly effective, organized, and clean office with a staff that exudes professionalism, energy, organization, and effectiveness. Everything that is displayed within the office or produced by the office staff should display the highest level of quality. This office represents the organization and may be the first or only contact that a donor may have with the organization.

Equipment
When establishing a development office, it is often tempting to purchase all the equipment and supplies at one time. Before embarking upon this method, consider first what can be shared with or obtained from other departments within the organization. Also, it may be possible to obtain equipment on loan from affiliate agencies or from firms associated with the organization through its volunteers. Leasing (or leasing with an option to buy) is another option to consider before purchasing.

The following equipment is needed to set up a development office.

Computer
A development office will need to have at least one desktop computer that is compatible and linked with the organization's other computer equipment, networks, and software. Whether the operating environment is Windows-, DOS-, or Mac-based depends upon what is currently operational within the organization. If the organization is so new that no computer system has been selected, then an IBM PC compatible personal computer system is recommended, because many of the software packages used in fund raising and financial management are based on the DOS or Windows operating systems. Again, if the organization and development operation are so new that acquiring capital expenditures is not feasible, it is possible to lease computer equipment with the option to purchase once enough money has been raised. A number of organizations across the country work with nonprofits to help them acquire used computers. See Appendix 3–A at the end of this chapter for a list of such organizations. Larger development offices within a university system or large-membership organizations most likely will have a mainframe system. Usually, the reason to link with this system is to have access to the membership or alumni data which can then be downloaded into the development office computer system for manipulation.

The basic hardware needed to operate a development office includes the following:

- CPU

  The central processing unit (CPU) is the "heart" of the computer. When selecting a computer, refer to the requirements of the software that you will be using and make sure that the computer is capable of running all of the software at speeds necessary to perform the job. Get all of the power and memory that you need in the beginning. Don't "pinch pennies" at this stage. Make sure that the system is capable of being upgraded as technology changes nearly daily. Again, because of the rapidly changing technology, it may be wise to lease equipment instead of purchasing.

  Be aware that if there is more than one staff person, the office computers need to be able to "talk" with one another or be "networked."

- Monitor

  Select a monitor with a screen at least 15 inches diagonally or larger, especially if the office will be responsible for designing brochures and using graphics and drawing software packages.

- Keyboard

  There are many types of keyboards available today. Find one that is

- Modem
  comfortable to use and compatible with your equipment.
  A modem is necessary for telecommunications—e-mail, fax, web pages, etc.

- Printer
  A laser printer is necessary because the work that is produced by the development staff needs to be of superior quality. Do not even consider dot-matrix or daisy wheel printer systems. If you are looking at an ink-jet printer, consider one only for portability, as a back-up printer, or if you need to use it for color printing. Consider it as a second purchase after you have bought a top quality laser printer.

- Surge Protector
  This is a device that protects both hardware and software from being damaged by a surge in power through the electrical or phone wires. Some will even maintain a power supply for up to thirty minutes.

- Back-Up System
  It is vital that you have an external back-up system to maintain copies of your computer files. The files should be saved or backed-up on a daily or weekly basis. Services are available for a small monthly fee that will remotely back-up your system. Otherwise, you should purchase an external back-up system for your office.

- Service Contract
  One of the most important items to remember when purchasing equipment is the service contract. Make sure that it is as broad as possible and covers both parts and labor.

- Software
  Word processing software such as WordPerfect or Word is a necessity in the operation of a development office, as is a relational data base such as Paradox or d-BaseIII. There are several software programs available that have been designed specifically for fund raising. A sample listing of some of the companies that have designed software for this purpose can be found in Appendix 3–B at the end of the chapter.

Before selecting a computer software system to aid with fund raising, evaluate your needs and the services that each system provides. Consider the following when making your decision to purchase software: (1) DOS-based or Windows-based, (2) ease and flexibility of use, and (3) the support and training available to the customer and the cost of this support and training.

Chapter 4 of this book, "Using Technology in Fund Raising," provides more information regarding fund-raising data-base management systems.

Copier

One of the most important pieces of equipment required in the development operation is a high quality copier. The organization should have a high-speed copier that can run multiple copies, enlarge and reduce copy, collate and staple, and use various sizes of paper. If the cost of this type of copier is beyond the scope of the organization, then find the nearest copy center that has 24-hour service (or extended service hours including weekends), and make arrangements to open an account. Although reproductions of every-day correspondence can be made on small, slow, single-function copiers, there often will be a need to run multiple copies of proposal documentation and exhibits.

Postage Machine

A U.S. Postal Service survey reports that you could save up to 20 percent in postage costs using the right meter system. A postage meter will print the exact amount of postage needed. There are no trips to the post office because you are out of the exact denomination of stamps. Also, a meter prevents stamps from being available for personal use or theft.

In addition, accurate accounting of postage can be kept using a meter machine. Plus, staff members can use the meter to print postage right in the office, thus saving energy and trips to the post office for overnight delivery packages. By metering envelopes, time also is saved on mail delivery because metered envelopes don't have to be cancelled and postmarked at a postal station (the meter has taken care of these two steps).

The smallest to the largest organizations can develop their own identity by having a "slug" designed to carry a message promoting the organization which is printed to the left of the postage each time an envelope is put through the postage machine. This message can be changed to reflect different slogans, campaigns, anniversaries, centennials, etc. The small organization can look more official and efficient with the use of a postage meter.

A postage meter is also a time saver. Envelopes can be sealed and stamped in one step. There is no more "licking" of envelopes and stamps or "sticky" fingers when working on a mailing. When considering large mailings, it is definitely wiser to contract with a direct-mail house for these services. Most small offices will not have space available to organize such a mailing nor the staff to handle a project of this size.

File Cabinet

It is important to first consider the storage needs of the office—what is needed immediately and what will be needed in the near future and in the long range. In addition to establishing files, there undoubtedly will be a need for storing printed materials and office supplies. A storage cabinet may be required or a lateral file cabinet with drawers whose fronts lift up and slide back may be used for storage of paper, supplies, etc.

Every development office needs to have at least one filing cabinet with a lock. Any check that cannot be deposited in the bank on the day it arrives in the office needs to be kept in a locked and secure place. There also will be confidential documentation that requires a locked file.

Lateral file cabinets cost more but save space in an office, and the tops can be used for assembly of documents and to hold printers, postage machines, or other office equipment. Whatever type of file cabinet is selected, be sure to purchase one of good quality. Look for drawers that open smoothly and easily and that will not drag or tip if fully loaded. It is wiser to spend a little more and buy file cabinets that will last for many years under heavy use. Do not be afraid to purchase second-hand, used, or previously owned cabinets. Someone else may be upgrading and it could save much of your office's budget.

Calculator and Adding Machine

An adding machine or calculator with a tape is essential to balance the daily intake of money, run a tape of accounts, or accurately track the statistical breakdown of donations.

To make quick calculations, a small hand-held calculator can be easier to use than the adding machine. These are inexpensive and should be a "must" for a development office.

Telephones

There are many types of telephones and telephone systems available today as well as telephone companies to provide service to the fund-raising operation. It is important to understand what your immediate needs are and what your future needs will bring. If the organization is extremely small with only one office space, then a single phone line with a "call-waiting" feature may be sufficient. Most likely, if the organization has been in existence for awhile, it will have several departments with many offices, and the phones will be interconnected with many lines and options. If not, be careful in your planning and determine what your specific needs are today and what they may be in the future.

The development office should have a telephone number of its own, thus a separate line identified to use in publications; therefore, when phones are being answered,

the receptionist can respond to the call by identifying the foundation or development office as opposed to just stating the organization's name. Just be sure to price and compare various systems. Is it necessary to have a series of sequential telephone numbers that roll-over to the next when one is busy? Is an intercom system vital to the operation? Will a multi-line phone with teleconferencing capabilities make it easier to communicate with the fund-raising volunteers? Make sure that all options are considered and priced before installing phones and a phone system.

Telephone Answering Service

An answering machine or telephone answering service is required for times when the staff is speaking on one of the phone lines, or when the office is closed or unoccupied. An answering service can be provided either through the phone company or through private management companies. Whatever type of service is selected, make sure that the message recorded or read is clear, concise, grammatically correct, and professional. This is not the place to be "cute" or to "wish people a nice day." A sample message could read:

> "This is the ABC Foundation. We are currently unable to answer your call. Please leave your name, telephone number, date and time of call, and a brief message, and we will return your call as soon as possible. Thank you for calling the ABC Foundation."

Supplies

There are many office-supply companies available, many of which offer large discounts to their members and non-profit organizations.

Office Space

If the opportunity exists to select the offices for the development operations, consider that the space selected will need to be large enough for the following:

One-Person Office

The single office space will include a full-size desk with ample drawer space; one or more file cabinets with at least one with a lock; a computer with server, monitor, and keyboard; adequate work space—either a table or the top of lateral file cabinets; three chairs—one comfortable staff chair with good lumbar support and two guest chairs; printer; adequate lighting—both overhead and desk lamps; and other staples that are necessary to run an office.

Two- or Three-Person Office

Office space for two or three persons should include two or three rooms with desks, computers, and chairs for the

"THERE. I THINK I'VE UNJAMMED IT. YOUR PROPOSAL WAS CAUGHT ON A TECHNICALITY."

Source: © Mark Litzler

staff and guests. File cabinets and equipment usually will be kept in the outer office with the assistant and support staff. The director's office should be large enough to hold meetings or there should be access to other rooms within the organization in which to hold meetings—small or large conference rooms will do. Again, adequate lighting is a necessity.

Multi-Person Office

With more than three persons in an office, it is time to look for space with a reception area. This can be the space where one person is able to welcome guests, manage the phones, keep the files and the office equipment, as well as serve as administrative support for one or more persons. If possible, it is best to have a separate area away from the public's view for the office equipment and where activities such as collating, stuffing, copying, etc., are done. Also, the director should have a space away from the staff for confidential meetings, quiet space for planning, etc. Plus, it is imperative to have a place for volunteer help and meetings. This may be part of the development office space or space provided within the organization's complex.

Any development operation should be close to the president or executive director's office because he or she is frequently consulted or needed. Plus, placement of the office near conference, supply, and production rooms can provide access for meetings, storage, and work without having to pay for this extra space out of the development operation's budget.

Staff

Many development offices will consist only of one staff person, the director. This is usually if specific funds have been set aside for the director's salary for a single year. It is the expectation that the director will raise his or her own salary, plus the expenses of the office. Additional staff will be added only if the monies are raised in advance. Most institutions will not risk funding a two- to three-person office until adequate funds have been raised.

> Most institutions will not risk funding a two- to three-person office until adequate funds have been raised.

If enough money has been raised or budgeted for additional staff, the first person to be hired should be a highly qualified administrative support person. This person needs to be completely familiar with the software system used in the office as well as have an understanding of relational data bases. He or she must also have a good command of the English language, be a good speller, and an excellent grammarian. In addition, they must be discreet—they must be able to keep and maintain confidentiality. This person often will be the first person met by someone contacting the development office. Thus, good phone skills and impeccable personal grooming are essential.

In addition, this person also must be able to operate the printing and copying equipment, as well as understand filing systems. Look for a person who fits the personality of the office and organization.

When adding a third person to the office, the type of skills a person should have often depends upon the activities of the fund-raising operation. If there are many special events held, then someone to focus on events may be the next staff person to hire. If the office is operating a capital campaign, then a staff person to do research or to work with volunteer solicitors may be needed. Whatever the need, the third person is usually a junior professional brought on to support the activities of the director. The administrative work is usually performed by the administrative assistant with back-up support from the junior professional.

Office structures beyond the three-person staff will vary widely depending upon the activities of the development operations. There may be a large direct-mail operation requiring many staff persons, or a capital campaign may be large enough to command several—10 or more—staff persons. It is difficult to suggest any pattern of hiring after the third staff person has been hired. The position descriptions developed for hiring staff will reflect the direction that the development operation is taking.

The Development Office Budget

The size of the budget will vary, but the elements will remain the same for the small, medium, or large development operation. An example of a budget for a development office is illustrated in Exhibit 3–1.

Various Models for a Development Office

One-Person Office

The professional fund-raising executive must be a strong manager of people, time, and money. Individuals who manage a one-person office must be exceedingly well organized and capable of handling multiple tasks. This is a person who alone handles the following: volunteer training and development; office budgeting, financial planning, and fiscal management; direct mail production; proposal writing; donor solicitation, acknowledgments, and recognition; data entry and updating; purchasing and monitoring of supplies; research; all telephone calls and other communications; special events and receptions; etc.

The effective development officer must be able to manage all of the previously mentioned, plus recognize leadership ability in others. To effectively rate the development director, individual staff members, volunteer leadership and commitment, and the readiness of the organization, individuals may wish to review the checklist found in Exhibit 3–2.

Whatever the size of the development staff, the director must report to the most senior person in the organization—the CEO, the president, the executive director, the administrator, etc. The development director also must have access to the board of the organization. Be wary of the organization where the CEO wants all access to the board to come first through him or her. The development director must develop a relationship with the board to build a good fund-raising program. The board chair should alert the director of development of potential problems that the CEO may not want to admit. Anyone considering accepting the position of development director should always ask to meet with the board chair before accepting the position. Make sure that as director of development you

> Whatever the size of the development staff, the director must report to the most senior officer in the organization—the CEO.

will have the authority to make changes if and when needed.

Office with Both Professional and Administrative Staff

The office that has grown to include administrative staff will finally free the development executive of the clerical and administrative tasks that can be so time-consuming. Tasks that can be delegated to a secretary or administrative assistant include the following: ordering and monitoring supplies; opening and distribution of mail; reception and phone duties; gift processing, monitoring donor records, and pledge monitoring; research and files controls; computer data input, reports, and maintenance; and other secretarial and clerical duties. The executive's duties can then expand to include additional prospect solicitation, proposal writing, volunteer management and training, and strategic planning.

Integrated Within Other Departments in Organization

A more complex and highly structured development office will be found in large-membership, cultural organizations, or institutions of higher education. In a university setting, there will be several development operations in the various colleges or departments as well as a central office. Within this structure, there may be a vice-president of institutional advancement with directors of the following: the annual fund, the capital campaign, corporate fund raising, foundation relations, planned giving, research and records, public relations, alumni relations, and others. All of these report to the vice-president. In association fund raising, a similar structure may exist with the addition of directors of direct mail and membership reporting to the vice-president. Usually these offices will be connected through weekly meetings of their senior staff and electronically via interconnected computer systems. Communication is as vital to organizations of this size as it is to the smaller offices. Here there is more to coordinate, more diverse personalities to manage, and more money to raise.

Formal education is essential to the development of fund-raising staff of all levels. Training should occur both on the job and through continuing education. Classes in management, leadership, computer literacy, financial planning, tax laws, human relations, interpersonal skills, etc., should be included in the planning and budgeting process. Any professional staff member who may

> Formal education is essential to the development of fund-raising staff of all levels.

Exhibit 3–1 Development Office Budget

	Previous Fiscal Year	Current Fiscal Year	Estimated Next Fiscal Year
Development Salaries			
Director of Development	$ _____	$ _____	$ _____
Associate Director	$ _____	$ _____	$ _____
Assistant Director	$ _____	$ _____	$ _____
Research Assistant	$ _____	$ _____	$ _____
Special Events Coordinator	$ _____	$ _____	$ _____
Administrative Assistant	$ _____	$ _____	$ _____
Secretary	$ _____	$ _____	$ _____
Receptionist/Office Manager	$ _____	$ _____	$ _____
Temporary Employees	$ _____	$ _____	$ _____
Student Employees	$ _____	$ _____	$ _____
Sub-Total	$ _____	$ _____	$ _____
Fringe Benefits %	$ _____	$ _____	$ _____
Projected Pay Increases %	$ _____	$ _____	$ _____
Development Operations			
Office Rental	$ _____	$ _____	$ _____
Equipment Fees	$ _____	$ _____	$ _____
Purchases	$ _____	$ _____	$ _____
Rentals/Leases	$ _____	$ _____	$ _____
Maintenance	$ _____	$ _____	$ _____
Postage	$ _____	$ _____	$ _____
US Mail	$ _____	$ _____	$ _____
FED EX	$ _____	$ _____	$ _____
UPS	$ _____	$ _____	$ _____
Printing	$ _____	$ _____	$ _____
Telephone	$ _____	$ _____	$ _____
Local	$ _____	$ _____	$ _____
Long Distance	$ _____	$ _____	$ _____
Travel	$ _____	$ _____	$ _____
Local	$ _____	$ _____	$ _____
Out of Town	$ _____	$ _____	$ _____
Meals	$ _____	$ _____	$ _____
Tips/Gratuities	$ _____	$ _____	$ _____
Dues/Memberships	$ _____	$ _____	$ _____
Consulting Fees	$ _____	$ _____	$ _____
Supplies	$ _____	$ _____	$ _____
Entertainment	$ _____	$ _____	$ _____
Volunteer Committee Expenses	$ _____	$ _____	$ _____
Board Expenses	$ _____	$ _____	$ _____
List Rentals	$ _____	$ _____	$ _____
Mailing House Fees	$ _____	$ _____	$ _____
Books, Magazines, Periodicals	$ _____	$ _____	$ _____
Photography/Art/Design	$ _____	$ _____	$ _____
Awards/Plaques/Gifts	$ _____	$ _____	$ _____
Professional Development	$ _____	$ _____	$ _____
Insurance	$ _____	$ _____	$ _____
Sub-Total	$ _____	$ _____	$ _____
GRAND TOTAL	$ _____	$ _____	$ _____

Exhibit 3–2 The Effective Development Officer

For each item listed below, rate yourself and your organization's leadership as high (H), medium (M), or low (L) by circling the appropriate response.

Institutional Setting

1. Commitment to your organization's cause by the officers of the trustees/board	H	M	L
2. Leadership in promoting your organization's success by the officers of the trustees/board	H	M	L
3. Interest and commitment expressed in tangible involvement by a large majority of members of your trustees/board	H	M	L
4. Commitment expressed in terms of effort and results by the chief executive officer	H	M	L
5. Agreement of trustees/board and staff on the goals of the development program and methods for achievement	H	M	L
6. Accessibility of trustees, administrators, and development officer to one another	H	M	L
7. Supportive environment (budget, space, equipment, and personnel)	H	M	L
8. Community recognition of the worthiness of your cause	H	M	L

Personal Qualities

1. Ability to work with volunteers from a variety of backgrounds and interpersonal styles	H	M	L
2. Analytical/problem solving skills	H	M	L
3. Creativity	H	M	L
4. Using time and resources effectively	H	M	L
5. Ability to communicate effectively, orally and in writing	H	M	L
6. Willing and positive attitude	H	M	L
7. Listening skills	H	M	L
8. Seeking feedback	H	M	L
9. Balancing leadership and followership	H	M	L
10. Mentoring new professionals	H	M	L
11. Contributing regularly to my organization	H	M	L
12. Participation in at least one outside volunteer activity	H	M	L
13. Initiative as a self-starter	H	M	L
14. Ability to work with other staff as a member of the team	H	M	L

Relationships

1. Key volunteers and the Development Committee	H	M	L
2. Other volunteers and volunteer groups, especially fund-raising volunteers	H	M	L
3. The Chief Executive Officer	H	M	L
4. Co-workers and subordinates	H	M	L
5. Personnel from similar or cooperating organizations	H	M	L
6. Community leaders and wealthy individuals	H	M	L

Education and Training

1. Formal education (post graduate, B.A./B.S.)	H	M	L
2. Continuing education and specialized courses (e.g., NSFRE, etc.)	H	M	L
3. Internship or work experience under an experienced fund-raising professional	H	M	L
4. Participation in professional associations	H	M	L
5. Reading of pertinent literature	H	M	L
6. Exchanges/contacts with recognized development leaders	H	M	L

Expertise

1. Annual giving	H	M	L
2. Capital campaigns	H	M	L
3. Grantsmanship (foundations; corporations)	H	M	L

continues

Exhibit 3–2 continued

4. Commemorative giving		H	M	L
5. Special events		H	M	L
6. Direct mail		H	M	L
7. Phonathons (telemarketing)		H	M	L
8. Office technology, especially EDP uses		H	M	L
9. Developing public relations/marketing materials		H	M	L
10. Persuasive writing skills		H	M	L
11. Prospecting		H	M	L
12. Cultivation techniques		H	M	L
13. Recognition techniques for donors and volunteers		H	M	L
14. Budget development and monitoring		H	M	L
15. Volunteer recruitment and development		H	M	L
16. Supervisory skills		H	M	L
17. Case statement development		H	M	L
18. Public relations skills		H	M	L
19. Office administration		H	M	L
20. Utilization of professional fund-raising counsel		H	M	L
21. Setting goals and objectives		H	M	L
22. Setting priorities		H	M	L
23. Managing time		H	M	L
24. Taking remedial action; re-setting goals and priorities		H	M	L

This checklist draws extensively from items developed by Peter C. Barnard, Director of Development, Maine Medical Center, Portland, Maine, for a presentation entitled "The Profile of a Model Development Officer" for the Massachusetts Chapter, National Society of Fund-Raising Executives at the Harvard Club, Boston, Massachusetts.

Source: Reprinted with permission from the National Society of Fund Raising Executives, NSFRE Survey Course, Faculty Manual, 1994 version, Module VII: Development Office Operations, pp. I–13—I–16. Handout 2, Pages 1–4 © 1994 NSFRE, Alexandria, VA.

not have a baccalaureate degree should be encouraged to obtain one. Those having undergraduate degrees should be encouraged to obtain certification (CFRE, ACFRE, CAE), a master's degree, or doctorate.

A sample of the various activities of fund-raising offices with three persons and thirteen persons is shown in Exhibit 3–3.

The size of the development operation is not the most important aspect in determining the operation's success. A small, well-managed operation can raise as much money as a larger mismanaged development office. In a small or large operation, get to know the board immediately. Board members must have confidence in the talent and personality of the development staff. If they don't, it will be difficult to succeed. Also, be sure to know the organization's mission and programs. It is impossible to present the cause effectively to a potential donor if your homework hasn't been done or if your volunteers have not been trained to solicit donors.

If the organization is large, meet with the heads of all departments. Also, visit similar organizations within the community to see how their development operations are run. Pattern your operations after those that are successful. Carefully review your organization board, fund-raising history, and donor profile. How do they fit into the community? Are the community leaders on your board? Are they and others giving fully of their means? Have all giving opportunities been explored or has the organization been using only one or two methods? Why do the current donors support the organization? What is the profile of the average donor? Having a clear understanding of why people support the organization will help in the development of plans to expand this support.

The development director also should become actively part of the nonprofit professional world. By joining the National Society of Fund Raising Executives (NSFRE, general fund raising), the Council for Advancement and Support of Education (CASE, education), or the Association for Healthcare Philanthropy (AHP, hospital field), you will find colleagues that share the same successes and plights. These contacts may help you in your current position and can certainly open doors for you when seeking other positions in the development field. By sharing with and learning from your colleagues, you can better understand what makes a good development operation. Exhibit 3–4 lists the duties of a development officer and Exhibit 3–5 lists questions to consider for a successful development program.

Exhibit 3–3 Activities in the Fund-Raising Office

OFFICE STAFF ASSIGNMENTS

General Duties	Three-Person Office	Thirteen-Person Office
Leadership and direction	Fund Raiser	Fund Raiser
Fund raising	Fund Raiser	Three Fund Raisers
Office supervision, budget and personnel management	Secretary	Office Manager
Secretarial tasks	Secretary	Three Secretaries
Gift processing, donor records, pledge billing	Gift Records Clerk	Gift Records Clerk
Thank you letters, cards on all gifts	Gift Records Clerk	Gift Records Clerk
Research and files control	Gift Records Clerk	Gift Records Clerk
Computer records, in-put control, reports, etc.	Gift Records Clerk	Gift Records Clerk
Mail/phone/visitors	Secretary	Receptionist
Supplies, equipment	Secretary	Office Manager
Mail list preparation, coordinator, maintenance, control	Secretary	Data Entry Person
Mail assembly and distribution	Secretary	Data Entry Person
Personnel training and skill development	Secretary	Office Manager
Dedication, reception, benefit events	Everyone	Nearly Everyone
Plaques, awards, etc.	Fund-Raiser	One Fund-Raiser and Office Manager
Coordination of board and other outside support groups	Fund-Raiser	One Fund-Raiser and Office Manager

Source: Reprinted with permission from the National Society of Fund Raising Executives, NSFRE Survey Course, Faculty Manual, 1994 version, Module VII: Development Office Operations, pp. VII–16, Handout 5 © 1994 NSFRE, Alexandria, VA.

Exhibit 3–4 The Duties of a Development Officer

1. Serve the administration and board through fund-raising assignments.
2. Develop a plan that includes specific schedules and goals for obtaining funds from each public.
3. Promote loyalty, interest, and support between your institution and its publics.
4. Enlist, train, and raise effectiveness of volunteers making calls for donations.
5. Cultivate donors and prospects, and ask for donations.
6. Understand why donors give.
7. Be a partner with the Dean/President/Executive Director.
8. Be able to communicate.
9. Live up to a schedule.
10. Accept responsibility.

Knowing When to Move from the One-Person Shop to a Larger Operation

When the development officer has raised enough money to support more than one person and the tasks at hand require more than one full-time staff person, then it is time to hire a second person in the development office. If the program has been running successfully with two people, then it is time to consider the next step. This could be hiring a person to concentrate fully on grantsmanship—the researching and writing of proposals to support the many activities and programs of the organization. This is a time-consuming, full-time job that requires someone with excellent writing, research, and communication skills. If this proves successful after a year or two, then additional staff can be added when more money is raised to support them. This also may be the time that the board decides to embark upon a

1. Is your institution well regarded and highly respected in the community?
2. Is your mission considered important and necessary?
3. Is there wholehearted agreement among your administration and board concerning the importance of a development program?
4. Are your staff and board determined and committed to the success of the program?
5. Are they interested enough to provide both budget and time for your program?
6. Is top-level leadership available and interested in fund raising?
7. Can a sufficient corps of enthusiastic and dedicated volunteers be enlisted and trained to work on fund campaigns?
8. Is your development office staffed with competent and experienced fund-raising professionals who can direct your program?
9. Is your Chief Development Officer at the senior administration level in your organization?
10. Does your development staff have short-term and long-range goals?

Source: Reprinted with permission from W. Frank Elston, CFRE, FNAHD, "Prescription for a Successful Development Program," University of Texas Health Science Center, San Antonio, TX.

major fund-raising effort that will require additional personnel. These new staff members may be hired as consultants or permanently. If the decision is made to hire permanent staff, make sure that this decision fits with the long-range goals and budget of the department.

The final step in the expansion of a development operation is the beginning of a planned giving program. First, make sure that all other fund-raising programs are running well, then introduce planned giving into the picture. This move can start small just by including information on how to remember the organization in a donor's will in newsletters and other regular mailings. Seminars can be held for the board and major donors to introduce them to the many options of planned giving. At this point, a planned giving consultant could be brought on for advice, for direction, to run the seminars, and to write the articles.

> The final step in the expansion of a development operation is the beginning of a planned giving program.

Expectations for the Development Office

The expectations for the development office are set based upon the past performance of the operation. They also should be based upon successful completion of the development plan. The development office should complete a strategic development plan in concert with the strategic plan for the entire institution. Achievable goals and objectives should be set based on this plan, and the development staff should be held accountable for meeting only the goals and objectives listed in the master plan. It is easy to have high expectations of a development operation, yet if proper planning is not done, the fund-raising operation may fall short of its goals and expectations.

Proper planning makes it possible for the development staff to reach its goals. Improper planning can create a situation in which the staff may never be able to recover. Expectations may be set too high and be totally unrealistic. Establish a plan with a detailed timetable that is approved and accepted by the board or senior management. Define the role of the staff and the volunteers who will execute the plan, and clearly state what support is needed from the board or other institutional departments to make the plan succeed. With clearly written goals and objectives that are accepted by all, then and only then can the departmental staff be held accountable.

Suggested Publications for the Development Office Library

A development office is not complete without a library of professional resource materials. In addition to a dictionary, thesaurus, and a manual of style, all development offices should have fund-raising resources available. These could include the following:

The Chronicle of Philanthropy, Washington, DC.
Fund Raising Management, Hoke Communications, Inc., Garden City, NY.
Nonprofit Times, Cedar Knolls, NJ.
The Special Events Report, International Events Group, Chicago.
Advancing Philanthropy, National Society of Fund Raising Executives, Alexandria, VA.
Successful Fund Raising, Stevenson Consultants, Sioux City, IA.
The Foundation Directory, published by the Foundation Center.

The Corporate Fund Raising Directory, published by Public Service Materials.

The Leadership Library—Corporate Yellow Book, Federal Yellow Book, Leadership Directories, Inc.

Aspen's Fund-Raising Series for the 21st Century, Aspen Publishers, Inc.

Additional resources can be found in the Bibliography.

Appendix 3–A
Organizations That Help Provide Used Computers to Charities

Boston Computer Society
Computer and Peripheral Recycling Program
101 First Avenue, Suite 2
Waltham, MA 02154
(617)290-5700
Fax: (617)290-5744
E-mail: msa@bcs.org
Contact: Marlene Archer

Activities: Accepts computers that have hard drives, along with printers, monitors, and other such equipment. Provides volunteers to help with computer-related questions. Non-profit groups interested in receiving equipment or volunteer help must pay membership fees ranging from $100 to $300, based on the size of their budgets. Has started an electronic discussion group specifically for people running computer-donation programs. To subscribe, send an e-mail message to majordomo@bcs.org. In the body of the letter, type "subscribe comp-recycle-1."

Computer Bank Charity
15062-B 15th Avenue, N.E.
Seattle, WA 98155
(206)365-4657

Activities: Accepts and repairs donated computers and related equipment. Works primarily in the Seattle area, but will consider applications from elsewhere in Washington State when transportation can be arranged. Redistributes computers to individuals or non-profit groups at no charge; highest priority is given to people with disabilities.

Computer Reclamation, Inc.
912 Thayer Avenue, Suite 210
Silver Spring, MD 20910
(301)495-0280

Activities: Accepts donated computers and equipment. Gives most computers to non-profit groups in the Wash-

ington, DC area, but other organizations can apply for computers if they arrange for transportation. Requests a donation of $25 per computer from the recipient charity.

East-West Education Development Foundation
23 Dry Dock Avenue
Boston, MA 02210
(617)261-6699
E-mail: ewedf@lx.netcom.com
Contact: Stephen Farrell or Wayne King

Activities: Distributes refurbished computers and equipment to non-profit organizations and schools in the United States and other countries. Recipients are selected by the donors of the equipment, not by the East-West staff.

Free Bytes
One Buckhead Plaza
Atlanta, GA 30305
Mailing Address:
Post Office Box 550371
Atlanta, GA 30355-0371
(404)364-2136
Contact: Charlie Shufeldt

Activities: Provides computers to schools and non-profit groups, primarily in the Atlanta area. In most cases, organizations must pay $30 per machine.

Gifts In Kind International
Recycled Technology Program
333 North Fairfax Street
Alexandria, VA 22314
(703)836-2121
FAX (703)549-1481
e-mail: giftsinkind.org/productdonations
Contact: To donate, Doyle Delph; to receive, Lenore Belk

Activities: Accepts 386-level or higher computers and equipment for distribution to schools and non-profit

Source: Reprinted with permission from J. Moore, "Fixing Up Computers for Charity," *The Chronicle of Philanthropy,* May 18, 1995, p. 8.

groups that have paid a membership fee. Charges about $20–$30 per computer. Plans to work with 100 non-profit job-training programs across the country to temporarily store the computers, evaluate and repair them, and distribute them to charities and schools. Groups interested in applying to become a center should send a stamped, self-addressed envelope and request the Recycle/ Reuse Center application form.

Marin Computer Resource Center
757 Lincoln Avenue, Suite 19
San Rafael, CA 94901
(415)454-4227
Fax: (415)456-9492
Contact: Clay Thompson

Activities: Accepts any donation of computers and related equipment. Passes on machines in good condition to non-profit groups, schools, libraries, and low-income families; religious groups are not eligible. Recycles parts from very old models or those that cannot be repaired. Gives computers mainly to local groups, but organizations in other areas may apply as long as they arrange for transportation.

National Cristina Foundation
591 West Putnam Avenue
Greenwich, CT 06830
(203)622-6000
Contact: Yvette Marrin

Activities: Helps link companies and individuals interested in donating computers and equipment with non-profit groups and schools in the United States and abroad that serve people with disabilities. Does not handle distribution of the computers, but expects donors to send equipment directly to the intended beneficiary.

Non-Profit Computing, Inc.
40 Wall Street, Suite 2124
New York, NY 10005-1301
(212)759-23368
E-mail: npc@igc.org
Contact: John L. German

Activities: Accepts donated computers and equipment and redistributes them to non-profit groups, schools and government agencies, primarily in New York City. Provides training and computer repair. Makes donations to groups in other parts of the United States and in other countries when transportation can be arranged.

Non-Profit Services
1605 63rd Street
Emeryville, CA 94608
(510)658-4760
Contact: James Chao

Activities: Accepts working computer equipment and distributes it to member non-profit organizations in the San Francisco bay area. Organizations must pay a $30 annual membership fee.

Northwest Micro
6250 S.W. Arctic Drive
Beaverton, OR 97005
(503)626-2555

Activities: Reconditions computers and equipment traded in by customers. Gives equipment to local non-profit groups.

Appendix 3–B
Companies That Provide Fund-Raising Software

The Raiser's Edge
Blackbaud MicroSystems, Inc.
4401 Belle Oaks Drive
Charleston, SC 29405-8530
(800)443-9441
e-mail: sales@blackbaud.com
Web site: http://www.blackbaud.com

Fund-Master
Master Software Corporation
5975 Castle Creek Parkway North Drive #300
Indianapolis, IN 46250
(800)950-2999
e-mail: fundmast@iquest.net

DONOR II
Systems Support Services
8848-B Red Oak Boulevard
Charlotte, NC 28217-5518
(800)548-6708
e-mail: donor2@msn.com

Paradigm
JSI FundRaising
JSI FundRaising Systems, Inc.
44 Farnsworth Street
Boston, MA 02210-1211
(800)521-0132

Results/Plus
Metafile Information Systems, Inc.
4131 NW 41st Street
Rochester, MN 55901
(800)638-2445

For a complete guide to nonprofit fund-raising software, see the annual directory in the October issue of *Fund-Raising Management* magazine.

Chapter 4
Using Technology in Fund Raising

Chapter Outline

- The Future of Fund Raising
- The Need for a Technology Plan
- Assessing Your Needs
- A Comprehensive Fund-Raising Data Management System
- Evaluating Fund-Raising Software
- Using a Service Bureau
- Working with a Technology Consultant
- Information at Your Fingertips
- Fund Raising on the Internet

Key Vocabulary

- Computer Virus
- Database
- Electronic Funds Transfer
- Electronic Mail
- LAN
- Service Bureau
- Technology Consultant

The Future of Fund Raising

In these times of fierce competition for charitable contributions, nonprofit organizations must maximize their fund-raising potential. Fund raising needs to be more efficient and more productive. By doing so, a nonprofit organization can implement programs that serve the public good and meet the needs of its donors. Everything you read or hear today reinforces the belief that donors are increasingly more concerned that their contributions are used effectively. Because of the competition in the nonprofit sector, an organization must value its donors to retain their continued support. You will learn later in this book that it is much less expensive to renew a donor than to acquire a new one. In the current environment, donor information, the technology on which it depends, and its proper use will be the determining factors for an organization's success in fund raising.

> In these times of fierce competition for charitable contributions, nonprofit organizations must maximize their fund-raising potential.

When looking at an organization, one may find that many situations may exist that prevent the organization from using technology effectively. These may include the following:

- A donor database may not be current, may have many errors, or may be difficult to extract.
- Generating necessary reports may be difficult.
- It may take too long to get counts, segments, and data from the system and only one or two people may even know how to do it.
- Computer systems may be inadequate, overloaded, and/or used inefficiently.
- Donor database information may not integrate with accounting, fund-raising, membership, and other types of data.
- Organizations that have computer systems that use old hardware/software technology may view changes to these systems as too complex, too disruptive, and too expensive.

These examples illustrate some of the reasons a nonprofit organization may not be satisfied with the current use of its computers. Most lack sources of useful advice and support, fail to do adequate planning, are unable to afford the systems they really need, and lack the knowledge to apply computing power to their complex needs.

Today, there are many resources available to organizations. Nonprofit support groups are forming across the country to provide technical assistance, training, and exposure to a variety of software and hardware products. The Center for Strategic Communications in New York informs and educates nonprofit managers about how to take advantage of the evolving communication environment. CompuMentor, located in San Francisco, was formed in 1986 by a network of computer experts who wished to help nonprofit organizations join the computer age. For many organizations, the move to technology is hindered not only by a lack of expertise but by finances. Today, a growing number of foundations such as the W. Alton Jones Foundation make technology grants to organizations; companies such as IBM donate used computer equipment; and software companies such as Microsoft offer some software products free to organizations. Appendix 3–A lists some organizations in the United States that help provide used computers to charities. Another resource is consultants who specialize in computer-technology needs for nonprofit organizations that are not specific vendors of any particular software or hardware application.

The Need for a Technology Plan

Using technology such as computers, software, and modems requires an investment not only measured in dollars, but measured in staff resources as well. Many organizations budget only for the purchase of such equipment and not for the necessary training and support services that staff persons will need to be able to use the technology efficiently. Whether the purchase is small like a PC to do word processing or major like the purchase of a fund-raising software package, an organization wants to be sure it gets a solid return on its investment. This is achieved by making the correct choices and putting these new tools to their most effective use.

An organization can ensure getting the best return on its investment by developing a technology plan that establishes organizational goals and objectives. Not having a plan can lead to the purchase of hardware and software products that are not compatible or cannot easily exchange information. This could cause an organization to lose critical information or files for which there is no back-up.

Assessing Your Needs

The best way to determine your technology requirements is to do a needs assessment. This is a written analysis of your organization's current data management system and what the organization will need from a future system. To be able to plan effectively, an organization needs to look beyond the current day-to-day operation. Questions that need to be addressed include the following:

- Where is the organization now and where does it want to be in three to five years?
- What challenges will be encountered when implementing the strategic plan?
- What information will be needed to run the organization more effectively?

- What information is needed to better serve the organization's members or clients?
- How can effective communication and information-sharing both within the organization and with resources outside the organization advance the mission?

To begin, involve all appropriate staff in reviewing the current word-processing and data management systems. Staff persons should prepare lists of their particular department's needs and recommendations to use in discussions with other departments as the needs assessment process continues. A final needs assessment document should include the conclusions and recommendations resulting from this series of meetings. Exhibit 4–1 lists ways a needs assessment helps an organization.

After conducting a needs assessment, an organization must prioritize its technology goals. Determine the most critical areas for improvement. For some organizations, the need for hardware and software standards becomes critical. What type of machine? How much memory? Is it time to install a local area network (LAN) that would connect all staff, thereby enhancing communications and information sharing? Software standards are equally important. Are all staff using the same word processing and spreadsheet software? Is there a procedure for training new staff on software? Has the software been upgraded and should the organization change?

Security, virus protection, and data backup procedures protect an organization's investment. The importance of creating back-up copies of critical information cannot be overemphasized, and procedures should be practiced to ensure that it is accomplished. A data backup policy should include who is responsible for creating the back-ups, what information will be backed up, when the

---

Exhibit 4–1 Five Ways a Needs Assessment Helps an Organization

1. It defines in advance the organization's basic data-management requirements.
2. It creates a consensus of what is needed and expected from the new system among key groups of staff who use the information, who use the system, and who will help with maintenance and computer problems.
3. It justifies the need for a new system.
4. It establishes a timetable for the purchase of a new system.
5. It serves as a guide to help vendors know an organization's needs before their first meeting, and also weeds out those systems that do not fulfill an organization's requirements.

backups will be made, where the backup files will be stored, and how long backups will be kept.

If you have confidential information on your computer, and most development offices do, protect it by permitting only certain staff persons to have access by installing password protection. When looking at a particular software package, examine the security features it offers. Also, take steps to protect against computer viruses (a destructive software program designed to damage a computer system by destroying the information on the hard disk). You can install virus protection software on the machines. These programs are relatively inexpensive and can prevent serious damage to the computers.

As mentioned earlier, technology is an investment for an organization. It is not a one-time cost. Costs for technology should be planned for on a continuing basis. Staff training is essential to ensure that these new tools are used effectively. It is not enough to budget the purchase without budgeting training for staff. There are a number of for-profit and nonprofit organizations that offer training on different kinds of software fairly inexpensively. In addition to training, technical support and trouble-shooting assistance will be required. Does the software vendor offer technical support? Is there a fee for such support? Does the organization have an in-house technology expert? Can technology consultants provide the support needed?

Keep in mind that technology is constantly changing. An organization will need to periodically upgrade its software and hardware. One also must consider that an organization and its needs will change. For these reasons, an organization will need to continuously review and modify its technology plan.

A Comprehensive Fund-Raising Data Management System

Keep in mind what a computer can and cannot do. Computers track, sort, compile, and calculate. These functions are essential for a fund-raising program because they enable the computer to do the following:

- Store and retrieve biographical and gift information
- Track prospects
- Produce lists and mailing labels
- Prepare financial reports
- Create acknowledgment letters, receipts, and pledge reminders
- Create personalized appeal letters
- Track and record solicitations

The database and computer system should display information or data known as fields in an easy-to-read format. Exhibits 4–2 and 4–3 illustrate sample database screens in a Windows environment.

There will be different computer needs depending on the types of fund-raising programs being conducted by an organization. When determining technology needs, it is important to include any new fund-raising programs that will be initiated within the next three to five years. Exhibit 4–4 lists major components of a development program. Exhibit 4–5 helps an organization chart the types of current fund-raising activities going on and which activities will be added in the future.

The strengths and weaknesses of the current system are now identified. The next step will be to prioritize which programs have the greatest need for new or upgraded technology. Exhibit 4–4 can be used again to rank these programs from 1 through 10 with 1 being the highest priority for enhanced technology.

Evaluating Fund-Raising Software

There are a number of factors to consider when evaluating fund-raising software packages. First-time buyers are most often influenced by price, the level of ease to implement, and equipment needed. However, experience shows that a second-time buyer chooses to purchase a particular software package for very different reasons.

> Experience shows that a second-time software buyer chooses a particular software package for very different reasons than a first-time buyer.

Their selection is based on the level of technical support available, the reputation of the vendor, and the training provided. Important considerations, besides possible budget constraints, should be the quality of the product, training and installation, and ongoing technical support. Costs associated with software purchases alone can range from several hundred dollars to tens of thousands of dollars. Appendix 4-B lists where to find information about software packages.

After gathering information on various software packages, contact vendors to get basic information on their product and to request written information. You will need to provide the vendor some information about your current system and needs. Be prepared to tell the vendor how many records are on your current system, what your future needs will be, type of hardware currently in use, how many current users there are, and any serious limitation the current system has.

Questions to ask the vendor include the following:

1. How long has the company been in existence? How many clients currently use the software? When was the last upgrade?
2. What is the cost of fund-raising software? Are there other modules to add?

Exhibit 4–2 Biographical Data Screen

Gifts	Gift Entry	Pledges	Hon/Mem	Scholarships	Spare	Spare	Reports

Donor Info	**Add Donor**	Actions	Corp/Fdns	Appeals/Funds	Mailings	Quick Scan	Report Mgr

Basic Information	Secondary	Gift & Other Information	Add an Action Item

Biographical   DonorCatID: _____   Assigned To: _____ ⬍

Referred by: _____

Last Name: _____   Spouse: _____

First Name: _____   NickName: _____

Middle: _____

Salutation1: _____   Suffix: _____   **Secondary Address**

Salutation2: _____   Address: _____

Prof. Title: _____

Address: _____   City: _____

State: __ ⬍   Zip: ___ ___

City: _____   Phone (w/h): _____   _____

State: __ ⬍   Zip: ___ ___   Fax/Pager: _____   _____

Phone: _____   Alt. Phone: _____   Alt. EMail: _____

Fax: _____   Pager: _____   Notes: _____

EMail: _____

Source: Courtesy of Ciconte & Associates, Inc., 1996, Chevy Chase, Maryland.

3. Which word processors are recommended?
4. What hardware is required? What other equipment such as printers are needed?
5. What are the storage requirements?
6. What is the import capability for file conversion? Will the vendor do the conversion? What is the cost?
7. Can data be exported electronically to a mailing house or telemarketing vendor?
8. Where will training take place? What are the on-site costs? What are the vendor's headquarter costs?
9. What technical support is available? Is there an 800 number to call? What is the charge?
10. Can I talk to current users in the local area?

These companies will send a sample diskette along with a brochure. Be sure to ask if sample screens and reports are included in the materials because it is often simpler to review these than the diskette. Review this information as it relates to the needs you determined using the analysis worksheet in Exhibit 4–4. Come up with a list of no more than three and request that these companies present a demonstration of their software at your organization.

Each vendor will furnish a list of clients who are currently using their product. Call those clients whose fundraising programs would be most similar to those of your organization. There is no better way to learn if a product and vendor are all that they are purported to be than speaking to those individuals who use that product and vendor. Ask specific questions such as the following:

- How long ago did you install the system?
- What kind of hardware, operating system, and word processing do you use?
- Does your organization have an information systems department or computer support person?
- How did you convert your old files? What was the cost?

Exhibit 4–3 Giving History Screen

Giving History

Classification: Individual

Organization:

Last Name: Allen

First Name:

Total Gifts:

$5,500.00

Return to Previous Form

Preview Report

Print Report

Main Menu

Edit Contribution Data

	Date	Amount	Reason	CR#	Acc	Thk	Notes
▶	12/15/95	$100.00	Dues96			1	
	12/15/95	$300.00	Wickersham96			1	
	12/31/93	$5,100.00					
*		$0.00					

Record: 1 of 3

Source: Courtesy of Ciconte & Associates, Inc., 1996, Chevy Chase, Maryland.

Exhibit 4–4 Fund-Raising Program Needs Analysis

This list includes major components of a development program. Use C=Current, F=Future, or N/A=Not Applicable to determine needs.

1. annual giving _____
2. corporate/foundation _____
3. capital campaign _____
4. endowment campaign _____
5. donor research _____
6. honor/memorial/tributes _____
7. managing major donor cultivation _____
8. planned giving _____
9. special events _____
10. volunteer coordination _____
11. alumni/alumnae tracking _____
12. membership _____
13. other

_____ _____

_____ _____

Source: Copyright Systems Support Services/Donor II, Charlotte, North Carolina, 1995. Reprinted by permission.

- Do you find the system instruction manual helpful?
- How was the training conducted? On-site? At vendor? How many staff persons were trained? Would you make any changes in how the training was conducted?
- How responsive is the vendor when you call the 800 technical support number?
- How long does it take a staff person to enter 50 names and gifts?
- How long does it take to generate mailing labels?
- How many staff persons currently use the system? Are they comfortable with it?
- How do you back-up files? How often is it done and how long does it take?
- Would you select this same system again? What would you do differently?
- Do you have any suggestions for my organization in this process?

If a current user is in your area, visit the organization and see the system in use. Some fund-raising packages like Raiser's Edge have local support groups which can be most helpful.

Exhibit 4–5 Rating Your Current System

Rate your current fund-raising data management system on whether you are able to accomplish the following tasks and with what level of ease (1=easy; 2=somewhat easy; 3=somewhat difficult; 4=difficult; 5=cannot do).

Annual Giving

–Segmentation is available by:
constituencies
past giving history ____
amount of gift ____
recency of gift ____
renewing donors and members ____
current donors ____
LYBUNT (last year but unfortunately not this year) ____
SYBUNT (some year but unfortunately not this year) ____
first time donors ____
prospects ____
size of gift ____
giving to special funds, campaigns or appeals ____
–Allows for inclusion of information mentioned previously to individualize appeal and acknowledgment letters ____
–Mail merges acknowledgment letters for appropriate level of gift ____
–Tracks donor recognition and gift clubs ____
–Upgrades donors by specific dollar amounts or range ____
–For phonathon/telemarketing, the system can:
customize scripts ____
print forms ____
include last gift ____
include solicitor ____
include the targeted gift amount to be solicited and outcome ____
verify address ____
send reminders ____
–Ability to report on any and all of the previous ____

Corporation and Foundation Tracking

–Ability to track multiple contacts at a corporation or foundation ____
–Ability to track matching gifts with both "hard" and "soft" credit ____
–Ability to track board members, employees, and officers of a foundation or corporation ____
–Ability to track grant requests and proposal status ____
–Linkage between corporation or foundation records and individual records ____

Capital/Endowment Campaigns

–Ability to assign and track volunteer solicitations ____

–Ability to evaluate and rate donors and prospects ____
–Ability to track moves or action steps ____
–Ability to track prospect status during the campaign ____
–Ability to track and report on campaign structure and divisions at any level ____
–Ability to service pledges ____

Prospect Research

–The following biographical information is available to track:
first, middle, last name ____
maiden name ____
family linkages ____
company name for institutions and foundations ____
contact and position with the company ____
salutations ____
titles ____
source (alumni, parent, friend, patient) ____
group source (corporation, individual, foundation) ____
occupation ____
sex ____
activity code (such as donor or prospect) ____
special codes ____
membership levels and dates ____
social security number ____
nickname ____
date of birth ____
marital status ____
spouse information ____
children's names and information ____
affiliations (political, religious, clubs) ____
giving level or net worth ____
employer name ____
multiple addresses ____
position or title at work ____
profession (specialty) ____
employer information for spouse ____
hobbies, interests, avocations ____
organizations and clubs ____
colleges or universities attended ____
major and minor areas of study at college ____
degree(s) earned from college or university ____
graduation date from college or university ____
–Ability to import electronic screening information ____
–Allows for unlimited notes and comments ____

Management of Major Donor Cultivation

–Ability to evaluate and rate major donors and prospects ____

continues

Exhibit 4–5 continued

- Ability to track the next moves related to major donor cultivation ____
- Possesses tickler system by date and subject matter ____
- Allows for unlimited notes and comments ____
- Allows for assignment of staff, volunteer, primary, and secondary contacts ____
- Ability to track all correspondence history ____

Honor/Memorial/Tributes

- Ability to track:
  memorial and honor gifts ____
  bereaved family members ____
  relationship of bereaved family members to deceased ____
- Allows for personalized follow-up letter based on relationship of donor or bereaved family to deceased or honoree ____
- Ability to select which bereaved family members need to be acknowledged ____
- Ability to restrict memorial or honor gift to a specific fund ____
- Ability to split gifts to multiple memorials ____
- Ability to print memorial lists for newsletters and reports ____

Planned Giving

- Ability to evaluate and rate planned giving prospects ____
- Ability to track biographical and personal data and information ____
- Ability to track seminars attended and information requested from planned-giving mailings ____
- Allows for follow-up tracking and tickler system ____
- Allows for unlimited notes and comments ____

Special Events

- Provides for invitation and event list tracking ____
- Ability to track invitation and event responses ____

- Provides event specifics (seating, registration fees, foursomes) ____
- Ability to link with other development software ____
- Provides reports for flexible event reporting ____

Volunteer Coordination

- Can track volunteers by:
  interest areas ____
  service areas ____
  times available ____
  awards and recognition ____
  limitations ____
  hours ____
  attendance ____
- Ability to report on any and all of the previous ____

Other

Alumni Tracking

- Ability to track class year ____
- Provides linkage with alumni spouses ____
- Ability to track and bill dues ____
- Ability to track alumni by chapter ____
- Ability to track and manage class reunions ____
- Ability to link to other development software ____
- Ability to report on any or all of the previous ____

Membership

- Ability to track effective and expiration dates ____
- Ability to track category and renewal level ____
- Ability to track gift memberships ____
- Ability to process membership renewals and cards ____
- Provides linkage to other development software ____
- Ability to report on any or all of the previous ____

Source: Copyright Systems Support Services/Donor II, Charlotte, North Carolina. Reprinted by permission.

By following these steps, an organization should be able to select the fund-raising software package that best suits its needs.

Using a Service Bureau

Another option to meet the computer technology needs of a nonprofit organization is to use a service bureau rather than develop a comprehensive fund-raising data management system in-house. A service bureau is a professional firm that handles all facets of an organization's database

management for a fee. Gary W. DuBowy, President of Data Perfection, Inc., which provides this type of service to nonprofit clients, recommends that organizations first evaluate their needs and capabilities. A checklist that DuBowy recommends reviewing when considering whether to use a service bureau or have an in-house system is illustrated in Exhibit 4–6.

A service bureau basically will handle all aspects of an organization's data management system. This includes handling all hardware and software problems, which can be a great help to those organizations that do not have

Exhibit 4-6 Service Bureau Versus In-House System

1. One-person shop versus multi-user
2. Number of employees and/or users
3. Retention rate of employees
4. Competency of available staff to administer program, troubleshoot, train, update, and output
5. Number of records
6. Level of sophistication of fund raising
7. Level of detail in selecting data to segment the file
8. Number of ways data output is needed
9. Where and how production of direct-mail appeals, reply devices, acknowledgments, renewals, telemarketing, and fulfillment are done
10. The use of diskettes or tapes to output data
11. List maintenance

Source: Courtesy of Gary W. DuBowy, Data Perfection, Inc., 1996, Vienna, Virginia.

in-house information systems staff. File maintenance, production output, and system back-ups will be conducted on a regular basis by the bureau. Because a service bureau has the technology and the expertise of computer programmers, it can respond to job requests more readily. It is important that a service bureau provide online service to the nonprofit organization so that data can be viewed, downloaded, and uploaded to the organization's office. New system needs can be determined quickly and new ideas can be incorporated in the fund-raising program by the service bureau.

As you can see, a service bureau may be the answer for many nonprofit organizations. However, it must be understood that an organization's database is then no longer directly in its own hands but primarily in the hands of an outside vendor. If an organization should choose to pursue using a service bureau, it is recommended that the organization follow similar steps when evaluating the work of service bureaus as we covered in the section on evaluating software companies and their packages.

When evaluating the costs associated with using a service bureau, the number of records an organization has is a key factor. Services are based on a per record cost, so organizations with large databases will incur a lower rate than smaller organizations. A typical service package, which consists of storage of records, online capability for the organization, data entry, acknowledgments, cheshire labels, tapes, and reports, according to DuBowy, can average $.60–$1.20 per record per year, depending on the volume of records.

To locate names of service bureaus, contact the Direct Marketing Association (DMA) or one of its regional chapters such as the Direct Marketing Association of Washington (DMAW) for a copy of the *Source Book*, which lists service bureau companies. Also check the trade publications such as *The Chronicle of Philanthropy*, *NonProfit Times*, and *Fund Raising Management*.

Working with a Technology Consultant

With the explosion of technology and information now available to the nonprofit sector, a new type of consultant has joined other fund-raising consultants who work in the areas of resource development, direct mail, telemarketing, events, planned giving, and capital campaigns. Like the other fund-raising consultants who train and assist organizations to do more effective fund-raising, the technology consultant's role is to help organizations choose more personalized solutions for their hardware and software needs that will also increase the effectiveness and efficiency of the fund-raising program.

There are a number of situations in which a technology consultant could be helpful, such as (1) an old system that needs upgrading or replacement; (2) new initiatives or significant changes are to be undertaken that will affect the system; (3) a change in fund-raising, accounting, or membership management software is needed; (4) new communications expertise (for example, networks, network enhancements, and the Internet) is needed; (5) current technical support or vendor is inadequate or nonresponsive; and (6) current staff persons are not proficient in technology areas.

Anthony T. Ciconte, President, Ciconte & Associates, a consulting firm that provides technology assistance to nonprofit organizations and associations, states that the characteristics of a good technology consultant are the following:

- They are concerned about finding the right products and services for your organization, *not* with fitting your requirements to certain products and services.
- They are eager to explain technical items in sufficient detail to give you a clear understanding so *do not* hesitate to ask questions.
- They are concerned about your expectations.
- They are willing and able to train your in-house staff in a professional and nonintimidating manner.
- They are sensitive to your budget constraints and are willing to offer options based on spending limits.
- They *do not* claim to, or act like, they know everything.

When looking for a technology consultant, an organization should look for someone who has experience with the needs of nonprofit organizations, broad experience in the technology arena, vendor independence, flexible pricing, guarantees and warranties, post-project support, and at least three references whom you can contact. Exhibit 4–7 provides questions to ask prospective technology consultants, and Exhibit 4–8 provides questions a technology consultant can answer for your organization.

Generally, nonprofit organizations see the results of the assistance of fund-raising consultants in their bottom line—more donors and dollars raised. In the technology area, the results are seen in greater staff productivity; better access to accurate, timely information and donor histories; increased ability to segment donors for solicitation purposes; and reduced time to produce reports that give the organization the information it needs. These results will also have a positive effect on the organization's bottom line.

Information at Your Fingertips

CD-ROMs

Today, the need for more information at our fingertips brings the mass information storage device, the Compact Disk-Read Only Memory (CD-ROM) into the nonprofit workplace. Like a compact disc of music, the computer CD contains digital information that can be read only—you cannot write new information on it. The storage capacity of the CD-ROM, however, is so impressive that the volume of information is immense. Among the products available on CD-ROM are extensive directories. For that reason, this form of technology is now used when doing prospect research as part of an organization's fund-raising program. Specific CD-ROMs for prospect research are covered in Chapter 8.

> The need for more information at our fingertips brings CD-ROM into the nonprofit workplace.

Exhibit 4–7 Questions to Ask Prospective Technology Consultants

1. Are you affiliated with any specific hardware or software vendors? If so, do you work on commission?
2. How much experience do you have in the area(s) related to our particular needs?
3. Are you users of the products you recommend?
4. How will you support our organization after your recommendations are implemented?
5. What effect will your recommendations have on the office hardware and software systems?
6. Will you provide a detailed cost accounting for all services?
7. Can you recommend other specialists if necessary?

Courtesy of Ciconte & Associates, Inc., 1996, Chevy Chase, Maryland.

Exhibit 4–8 Questions a Technology Consultant Can Answer for Your Organization

1. What equipment can or should be retained or upgraded?
2. What equipment should be replaced?
3. What software products make the most sense for our specific requirements?
4. How do we best convert from one system or software product to another?
5. How do we best customize products for a particular organization?
6. What equipment and software should we purchase, lease, or upgrade?
7. Where and from whom should we acquire equipment and software products?
8. What types of maintenance agreements make the most sense?

Courtesy of Ciconte & Associates, Inc., 1996, Chevy Chase, Maryland.

Special equipment is needed to use CD-ROMs. Many new PCs come with CD-ROM drives. Other CD-ROM drives come as a kit with the accessories you will need, which may include an interface cable, cable, an adapter card, special software to run the driver, and extensions. Drives are available in internal, external, or portable versions. The computer that is used for accessing CD-ROM data does not need to be dedicated solely to that function. However, software provided by the manufacturer may need to be installed on the computer's hard disk and may take up considerable space. If the CD-ROM is hooked up to a single computer, consider how much use the system will get. If the CD-ROM will be made available on a network, make sure that the product is licensed as a networked product.

Like on-line services, CD-ROM products require that you either display information on the screen or print it out, so printing and monitor capabilities are important. A small or low resolution screen or poor quality printer may limit the value of the CD-ROM information. You will also need to make a choice of operating systems—Windows, MS-DOS, and Macintosh. Windows and Macintosh environments are more suitable for multimedia applications. Another considerable advantage to CD-ROM versions of databases is the graphic capability. Diagrams, graphs, charts, tables, illustrations, and animation are available.

One drawback to CD-ROM databases, however, is that they are not updated as frequently as on-line services. Some may be updated monthly whereas others may be updated only once a year. Some CD-ROM products are available on a subscription basis and can be expensive. Organizations need to determine the value of such technology services to its fund-raising programs before making the investment.

The Information Superhighway—The Internet

The Information Superhighway, Internet, and World Wide Web no longer are foreign terms to development professionals. Instead, they have become part of our vocabulary when discussing gathering and disseminating information. Nonprofit organizations are using this technology to communicate their message to members and potential members; to research information on prospective donors including corporations, foundations, and individuals; and to network with other organizations through e-mail, listservs, and newsgroups. Numerous articles and books are available on this subject and several publications such as *The NonProfit Times* and *Chronicle of Philanthropy* now feature a column on technology in each issue. Our purpose is to give you an overview in this chapter of some of the ways nonprofit organizations and their staff members are using this exciting new technology.

To get on the Information Superhighway, you must first select a service provider. Information service providers are companies that run sophisticated, high-speed computers that serve as giant electronic bulletin board systems and databases. The best known are America Online and CompuServe, with the addition of Microsoft's new Microsoft Network (MSN). Each of these takes a slightly different approach to what it offers, and the way it offers its service. All are similar in that they charge an hourly fee for connect time, and may charge a premium above this fee for special service and/or premium areas on the particular service. For example, CompuServe charges a basic monthly membership fee for its basic services, such as electronic mail and stock quotes. If you want to access many of the proprietary databases that

"The on-line search didn't turn up any new prospects, but I did find out that two of our current board members are deceased."

Source: © Carole Cable.

information vendors keep on-line, there is a surcharge above and beyond the base rates. The other vendors mentioned have similar structures, but because of the intense competition, all of these change frequently.

One of the most popular pieces of Internet software is Netscape. If you arrange your Internet access through a vendor other than the information services mentioned previously, you will probably end up using it. But if you are using CompuServe or America On-Line, use their software because it is easier. These information services are gateways onto the Internet, too. The Internet is actually millions of separate areas that exist on millions of different computers. Some of these Internet sites are located on computers belonging to giant corporations, others reside on someone's home PC.

Accessing the Internet is generally accomplished with a piece of software called a Web Browser. Internet sites are "visited" by specifying a Universal Resource Locator (URL) to the Web Browser software. A URL is actually the electronic address of the site you are trying to access. It is generally in the form of http:// or ftp://, with a string of characters following the two backslashes.

All forms of remote access, whether to a service such as CompuServe or America Online, or to the Internet, involve having your computer "talk" to another computer. This electronic conversation is accomplished with a modem. Depending on the computer you will be using the modem with, you may need an internal unit, external unit, or PC Card modem. The internal unit is the least expensive but it will have to be installed in an expansion slot of the computer. An external modem is a bit more expensive but it hooks up easily to just about any computer's serial port. PC Cards are small modems that are used in portables. In purchasing a modem, speed is also an important factor. If you plan to transfer graphic images from a service or Web page, you will need a higher speed modem (28,800 bits per second) to avoid spending so much time waiting.

The World Wide Web

The World Wide Web on the Internet is currently getting the greatest media coverage. The ease of navigating the web and the use of graphics have made this a popular place for individuals to go "surfing" and for organizations to set up their Internet web sites. The strength of the World Wide Web is linking together scattered bits of information into groupings that can be easily navigated and updated. This makes the World Wide Web a good place to get an overview of an issue or topic. Many organizations, associations, and foundations are using the World Wide Web to disseminate information about their programs and services. Some are also experimenting with fund raising on the Internet.

An excellent example of a charity using its web site effectively is the American Red Cross, http://www.crossnet.org (see sample pages in Figure 4–1). Clicking

American Red Cross Helps Families of TWA Crash

 1996 Olympic Games

News on Hurricane Bertha Clean-up Operations

FEMA's 1996 Tropical Storm Watch Information Web Page.

Protect Your Pet in a Disaster

Seniors Helping Seniors Prepare for Disaster

How to beat the heat at the Olympics and anywhere it's just plain

American Red Cross

Hurricane Bertha: *Wish you could do something to help?* You can.

1-800-HELP-NOW

1-800-257-7575 (Español)

Help Can't Wait

[**Red Cross News**] [**Virtual Museum**] [**Career Opportunities**] [**Community Disaster Education**] [**Find Your Local Chapter**]

This web site has been reviewed and rated by:

Back to the top of this page. . .

This web site is best viewed using _____ or later.

Copyright 1996 - The American National Red Cross

Figure 4–1. Sample Web Pages. Courtesy of the American Red Cross. All Rights Reserved in all Countries.

on the icons or the underlined text takes the user to related pages. By clicking on the line "News on Hurricane Bertha Clean-up Operations," users move to a page with news on the Red Cross's efforts to provide aid to storm victims. Entering a zipcode takes users to a page with information on the Red Cross chapter that serves that area. Another page gives users information on how they can help the Red Cross. Clicking on "Donate Now" takes users to a web page that provides information on why and how to give money to the Red Cross.

 **American Red Cross**

 Help Can't Wait

Ways to Contribute When Help Can't Wait

One of the best ways to help us help disaster victims and those in need in your community is through a financial contribution to the American Red Cross. Your donation means we can help those in need--immediately. Here are three ways you can help right now:

Donate Online. Make a secure donation now by credit card to the American Red Cross Disaster Relief Fund.

> Secure credit card donations can be made via any browser supporting the *"https"* security protocol such as Netscape Navigator, Microsoft Explorer, AOL's new version 3, Spyglass, and others. If your browser doesn't support https, you will get an error message when trying to access the donate online page. *If you cannot access this page, we suggest using one of the donation options below.*

Donate by Phone. Make a credit card contribution or pledge by phone.

Donate by Mail. Send a check to support your local Red Cross chapter or the American Red Cross Disaster Relief Fund.

> The American Red Cross is not a government agency and all Red Cross disaster assistance is free thanks to the generosity of people like you. Ninety-two cents of every dollar donated to the American Red Cross is spent on programs and services that help people in need. What's more, the value of your donation is increased by the fact that the ratio of volunteer Red Cross workers to paid staff is almost 50 to one.

Copyright 1996 - The American National Red Cross

Electronic communication also helps groups get feedback from the people they serve, the general public, and their donors. However, it is extremely important that an organization be prepared to respond to these messages in a timely fashion. That means having procedures for staff and volunteers to follow when handling these responses. The Red Cross's national office has a form on its web site that makes it easy for people to send an electronic message. As soon as an electronic request for information is sent to the Red Cross, an automated reply is mailed back with general information about the organization. The message says "Our slogan is 'Help Can't Wait' so until we read your message, we want you to have information on some of the topics that you have asked about most frequently." Volunteers then follow-up with personal replies.

One key to using a web site effectively is to make sure it gets updated frequently. Organizations need to keep their site exciting and new to keep people coming back to their sites. Since it is fairly simple to add the coding required to convert basic electronic documents into a form compatible with World Wide Web software, information can be added quickly. That is especially important to a group like the Red Cross so that it can communicate about current efforts helping victims of disasters.

Another example of a nonprofit organization's web site is the Nature Conservancy. Using a multimedia presentation of color, sound, and video, "Species Spotlight" profiles a different endangered animal each week using more than 20 video and audio clips. The organization tries to get users to become donors or volunteers by including "Get Involved" or "Join" buttons on numerous parts of the site. (See sample page in Figure 4–2.)

According to Amy Rakowski, direct marketing specialist at the Nature Conservancy, the Nature Conservancy is now receiving 88,000 hits per week (visitors to the site). Of particular interest is the Guest Registry page pictured in Figure 4–2. On this page, individuals complete a survey giving the organization information about themselves, their interest in joining and/or getting involved, and the type of literature they would like to receive. Rakowski reports that the Nature Conservancy received more than 1,000 surveys within the first two months of being online, and has collected excellent demographic information on members and potential members. Responding to these inquiries is very important, so the Nature Conservancy's Member Service Center has at least one full-time staff person and several volunteers assigned to follow-up each guest registry survey submitted. A free screensaver is the special "thank you" premium for submitting the survey. People can join the organization as well as renew their membership using the web site; however, according to Rakowski, it is too early to report any significant increase in membership. Type "http://www.tnc.org" to visit this site. See Appendix 4–C for a sampling of other organizations' on-line addresses.

Electronic Mail, Listservs, and Newsgroups

Another mode of communication has been added to sending a letter, making a telephone call, or sending a facsimile (FAX) of the document. It is electronic mail, commonly called e-mail. We use e-mail to communicate with co-workers, colleagues around the globe, and our members or alumni throughout the world. The Internet or e-mail can even take the place of a face-to-face meeting at a fraction of the cost. It is an effective way to issue important legislative alerts, report organization news, ask for suggestions or ideas, and poll members on a variety of topics without leaving the office.

E-mail allows us to communicate with people we have never met. We can ask questions, get advice, or discuss topics with persons who are knowledgeable. The most popular way to do this is through listservs or newsgroups on the Internet. For development professionals, there are a number of listservs set up for individuals interested in a variety of fund-raising and nonprofit issues. To get on a listserv, all you have to do is subscribe and you will begin receiving messages. One difficulty co-author Barbara Kushner Ciconte had when she first subscribed to fundlist was keeping up with the volume of messages she received every day, sometimes up to 100 messages. Fortunately, it is easy to cancel a listserv subscription. Because of the large number of messages posted, many listservs have a digest feature, which combines all daily postings into one message instead of many separate messages. We would recommend that you subscribe to a listserv on a subject of interest, read all the postings for a week or two, and then either ask for the digest, or be prepared to read many messages. If the topics are not of interest during the two-week period, it is suggested you follow the instructions to unsubscribe. Exhibit 4–9 is a short list of useful listservs.

The Usenet newsgroups are established to promote communication among users with similar interests. Unlike the list servers, there is no subscription. E-mail messages are not sent to individual mailboxes but are posted in repositories. A user who wishes to see recent postings or information on a particular newsgroup can "go to" the newsgroup and review the postings. Postings can be sorted by topic, date, or author. The user can respond to the entire group or to the author of the original posting. Newsgroups are good to use for making announcements about an organization, publicizing upcoming events, or for polling opinions on a specific issue. One such newsgroup for nonprofit professionals is soc.org. nonprofit.

Fund Raising on the Internet

As more and more organizations develop web sites on the Internet, the question arises whether these sites can be used to raise money for the organization effectively and inexpensively. In general, many organizations are exploring the possibilities of using this technology for fund raising. Health charities, environmental organizations, the United Way, and international-relief groups have made some progress in this area. Computer networks have certainly opened up new and exciting ways to communicate with donors and the general public, but many believe it will be years before significant dollars will be raised using this medium because of the potential for fraud. Because a large investment of money or technical expertise is not needed to get on a computer network, many fear that it will be easy to conduct false fund-raising appeals electronically. Nonprofit organiza-

 # Join Today!

JOIN The Nature Conservancy now for just $25 and receive our sturdy Nature Conservancy tote bag. The canvas tote measuring 16" x 13" x 3" is the ecologically smart answer to plastic bags when shopping -- and it's your FREE gift with Conservancy membership!

PLUS...when you join The Nature Conservancy you will receive....

Our bimonthly Nature Conservancy magazine. In its 40 exquisite ad-free pages, you will find captivating articles on the Earth's environment and inhabitants, all illustrated in full color.

A personalized membership card, which shows that you are taking an active personal role in preserving our endangered species.

Invitations to exciting field trips and special events at Conservancy preserves.

Opportunities to participate in local chapter activities to preserve endangered species in your own area.

Newsletters from your state Conservancy program, keeping you up to date on crucial state environmental problems.

A 10% discount on most purchases at The Nature Company, the nationwide retailer of natural history products.

AND....the satisfaction that you are doing your part to help preserve the world for all its creatures.

Click here to join by calling our 800 number

Click here to join by mail

Click here to join online

WELCOME WHAT'S NEWS NATURE CHAT WHERE WE WORK GET INVOLVED
CONSERVATION SCIENCE HOME SEARCH COMMENT JOIN INDEX

Figure 4–2 Sample Web Pages. Courtesy of The Nature Conservancy.

continues

Welcome to The Nature Conservancy's Guest Book
Please sign in!

We want to learn more about the people visiting our web site, so we appreciate your taking the time to tell us about yourself. After you've submitted your survey, you'll receive a thank you with instructions on how to download your screensaver.

Name:

First Name   Middle Initial
Last Name

Address:
Street Address
Apartment #
City
State
Zip Code

Home Phone #:
E-mail address:

Preferred method of contact:
E-mail Mail Phone

What is your operating environment?
MAC DOS/Windows UNIX Other

At what speed (with what method) are you accessing this site?
9600 bps modem
14400 bps modem
28800 bps modem
ISDN
T1
T3
Other

How did you learn about The Nature Conservancy web site?
Surfing the Internet through a service provider

AOL CompuServe Other

continues

Search engine -- *Please specify:*

Nature Conservancy Magazine

Media -- *Please specify:*

TNC printed material

      brochure
      letter
      other

Other -- *Please specify:*

MEMBERSHIP STATUS
Please check one:
I am a current member of TNC
I am a past member of TNC
I am interested in becoming a member of TNC
I am interested in general information about TNC

Are you a member of other conservation organizations?
No
Yes. Please list:

THE NATURE CONSERVANCY WEB SITE
What information do you want from TNC's web site:
Please check all that apply:
How to get involved
TNC literature
TNC office locations and contacts
TNC conferences and programs
Other:

TELL US ABOUT YOURSELF:
Occupation:

Age:

Sex: Female Male

Marital Status:
Married
Single/Never married
Divorced/Not married

continues

Number of children under the age of 18 living at home.

Education:
High School
Some college
Undergraduate degree
Some graduate work
Post graduate degree

Income:
Under $20,000
$20,000 - $50,000
$50,000 - $100,000
$100,001 +

Thank you.

**Thank you for your interest in The Nature Conservancy
and for completing our guest registry.**

Return to the top of the page.

WELCOME   WHAT'S NEWS   NATURE CHAT   WHERE WE WORK   GET INVOLVED
CONSERVATION SCIENCE   HOME   SEARCH   COMMENT   JOIN   INDEX

Copyright © 1996, The Nature Conservancy.

---

tions will need to be alert to any reports of fraudulent fund raising on the net. Early concerns regarding putting credit card information on-line have been addressed.

Development professionals agree that electronic fund raising would be less expensive than the current methods of direct mail and telemarketing that are used to reach large numbers of donors and prospective donors. The cost of distributing information on-line is usually much less than the paper, printing, and postage costs of direct mail or the long distance charges incurred in telephone appeals. Some commercial electronic services have waived or reduced their fees to allow nonprofit organizations to display information. Although the upfront costs may be less for fund raising on the Internet, new additional costs will be associated with the continuation

of the on-line service and staff needed to update and respond to inquiries and contributions.

Organizations that want to use this new medium for fund raising are facing two other challenges: (1) whether their donors and others who might contribute are on the net and (2) how aggressive they should be in the solicitation. Organizations certainly do not want to alienate any computer network users, especially on the Internet. To deal with these challenges, organizations need to know who among their donors are on-line. Requesting e-mail addresses as part of personal data updates will reveal just how many donors have access to this medium. Using this same group of individuals as a focus group will provide other important information on how they would like to be solicited for a contribution.

Exhibit 4–9 Listservs and How To Subscribe

To subscribe to any of these listservs, send an e-mail message to the address listed under "to." The text of the message should contain the information listed under "message." All of the listservs here require the subscriber's first and last names, separated by a space, but some require more information and others less.

CFRNET-L is for those involved in corporate and foundation relations.
TO: listserv@gibbs.oit.unc.educ
MESSAGE: subscribe CFRNET-L firstname lastname

FUNDLIST is for fund-raising professionals, many from universities and colleges, who discuss topics of interest including annual campaigns, major gifts, capital campaigns, and planned giving.
TO: listproc@listproc.hcf.jhu.edu
MESSAGE: subscribe FUNDLIST firstname lastname

GIFT-PL, run by the National Commission on Planned Giving, is for development and planned giving officers, many at academic institutions.
TO: listserv@indycms.iupui.edu
MESSAGE: subscribe GIFT-PL firstname lastname

PRSPCT-L is for nonprofit researchers and educational development professionals.
TO: listserv@bucknell.edu
MESSAGE: subscribe PRSPCT-L firstname lastname

To locate other listservs dealing with nonprofit organizations see the web page at http://www.tile.net/listserv.

As with other methods of raising funds we will cover later in this book, there are several basic guidelines to follow when using electronic communication to solicit contributions. They include the following:

- Planning is essential. Have a plan to develop and keep the home page updated, to communicate the organization's network address to donors and the general public, and to assign staff to respond to ongoing inquiries.
- Be sure to ask for a contribution. Make it easy for those visiting the home page to make a contribution. Be clear in your design and directions.
- Use what works with other types of fund raising. Try to be as personal as possible in the appeal as you are establishing a relationship with a donor. Include specific examples of how people are helped by donor contributions. Offer a small token or premium for those who respond on-line.
- Keep costs down. Look for volunteers or interns to help design the web site. Collaborate with other

nonprofit organizations in using electronic services such as Relief Net, which provides service to fifteen domestic and international relief groups. The Institute for Global Communications, which runs EcoNet for environmental groups and the PeaceNet human-rights network, posts the name and a basic description of each of its members on the World Wide Web. Depending on the amount of information and graphics needed, the charge runs from $30 to $300 a quarter.

Making Gifts Electronically—Electronic Funds Transfer

Banks and financial institutions advertise that the easiest way to bank today is from home using a computer. It also may become one of the easiest ways to make a contribution to a nonprofit organization. Electronic funds transfer, commonly known as EFT, is relatively simple. After receiving written authorization from a donor, credit card or checking account information taken over the telephone or via pledge cards is input into the organization's database. The information is then relayed to a processing company that verifies if there is enough money in the donor's account to cover the pledge. If the amount is approved for authorization, it is electronically debited from the donor's account and placed in the nonprofit organization's account for what is known as deposit settlement. Deposit settlement involves direct deposit of funds to the nonprofit organization's account. This process occurs within 48 to 72 hours after the deposit settlement file is transmitted.

> Using a computer may become one of the easiest ways to make a contribution to a nonprofit organization.

Through the use of making contributions electronically, nonprofit organizations receive donations faster and donors are relieved of writing checks. Costs can vary greatly depending upon the technology used to transmit check information. If an organization wanted to set up an EFT system, the cost of installation would range between $1,500 and $2,000. There is a transaction fee of between $2 and $4 for check debiting, depending on volume and any added services.

EFT has been available for nonprofit organizations for many years. But now organizations like the American Cancer Society are making the move to EFT to attract more support from the baby boomers whose lifestyle may not give them the time to read appeals or write checks. Instead, the American Cancer Society found during a marketing study that when the option of using a credit card to make a pledge was offered, people made larger gifts because it was easier to give a certain sum each month using their credit card.

Appendix 4–A
Case Study: Technology

Epilepsy Foundation of Greater Chicago

For years, the development office of the Epilepsy Foundation of Greater Chicago was an afterthought when it came to advancing institutional goals. Two years ago, however, the organization initiated a strategic shift that placed more emphasis on development. Two new staffers joined the organization to manage development and marketing responsibilities.

The shift in priorities required changes in technology. Current software didn't allow users to track the links between donors, their gifts, and the campaigns they responded to. Support staff, program staff, development, and the president got together to think of alternatives. Document production across departments was analyzed to promote consistency. The data collection and referrals process was analyzed to see what efficiencies could be gained.

The development staff sat down in the middle of this process and outlined their requirements. They decided that no one on staff had the time or inclination to learn a generic database package. At the same time, they didn't know what type of system to buy because they weren't entirely sure who they would be soliciting and how.

Development officials decided that given all of the uncertainty, it would be best to purchase a product that was robust enough to meet anticipated needs but not so expensive that they'd be locked into it forever. In three years they would reevaluate the development effort from top to bottom and if the software (or anything else) wasn't meeting their needs, they would move to something else.

Raiser's Edge was evaluated and ultimately rejected because it was too complex for the agency. Next on the list was FundMaster Lite, a slightly scaled down version of Master Software's flagship FundMaster software. The product got good marks for price and ease of use, but the fit wasn't quite right.

Finally, the organization settled on Target/I from Target/I Management Systems. The feature that most impressed officials was the availability of an ad hoc report writer that would enable them to analyze data in a myriad of ways. The company's level of technical support was also a critical factor in their decision.

Linda Jacoby, a development official for the organization, says, "By making a plan, we could see where we wanted to be and were able to hit the ground running. But it's going to take time. I think that we're going to have to be careful not to lose sight of what the software can do."

West Towns Visiting Nurses Association

West Towns Visiting Nurses Association receives most of its income from contracts and fees; the contribution from development is a small portion of overall income, but it plays a major role in strengthening ties to the community.

In 1990 Development Director Sue Svec decided that it was time to move away from the hundreds of scraps of paper holding 3,000 donor records that constituted VNA's donor system. "I wanted to automate because the list had grown bigger than I could manage manually," she says. "At the time it didn't seem too bad, but it's almost comical to look back on it now."

As a one-person department Sue didn't want a complex package, but she also wanted the option to grow one later. "I didn't want to change software every other year," she says. "I wanted something that was easy to use but also had upgrade potential."

At the time Svec was searching for a suitable product, Master Software released FundMaster (FM) Lite. It was a good match, and—after looking at other products to confirm her decision—Svec purchased and installed FM

Courtesy of Tim Mills-Groninger, Associate Executive Director, Information Technology Resource Center, Chicago, Illinois.

Lite. If the need arose she could upgrade to the full FundMaster with ease.

Three years later Svec is still a happy FM Lite user. The product's links between activity and source codes give her the ability to identify donor interests easily. She uses age and gender information from the clinical files to update donor profiles. That, plus FM Lite's ability to analyze gift profiles, repeat donors, event interest, and locations, has helped Svec meet her goal of strengthening the ties between VNA and its donors.

"All our fundraising events are growing because we're increasing our donor base, and we're also able to increase the giving per donor because we can target them better," she says.

Appendix 4–B
Where to Find Information About Software Packages

1. Non-Profit Software Directory—published by Hoke Communications in the annual October issue of *Fund Raising Management Magazine* (48 vendors)
2. The National Software Buyer's Guide for NonProfit Organizations—published annually by *Contributions* (47 vendors)
3. Management and Leadership Resources for Non-Profits—compiled annually by the Applied Research and Development Institute and published in the *Chronicle of Philanthropy*
4. Software information published annually by the *Non-Profit Times*
5. Software exhibitors at national meetings of such organizations as the National Society of Fund Raising Executives (NSFRE), Association for Healthcare Philanthropy (AHP), and Council for the Support and Advancement of Education (CASE)
6. General advertisements in publications previously listed
7. Referrals from nonprofit organizations using different software packages
8. Internet listservs and other online sources

Appendix 4–C
Organizations in Cyberspace

Greenpeace
http://www.greenpeace.org

National Organization for Women
http://www.now.org

Christian Coalition
http://www.cc.org

National Rifle Association
http://www.nra.org

The Nature Conservancy
http://www.tnc.org

American Cancer Society
http://www.cancer.org

Make-A-Wish Foundation of America
http://www.wish.org

National Urban League
http://www.nul.org

Non-Profit Resources Center
http://www.theriver.org/orgs.html#nonpro

National Society of Fund Raising Executives
http://www.nsfre.org

Independent Sector
http://www.indepsec.org

Foundation Center
http://fdncenter.org

Council on Foundations
http://www.cof.org

American Society of Association Executives
http://www.asaenet.org

The Internet Disaster Information Network
http://www.disaster.org

Information Technology Resource Center
http://www.mcs.net/~nponet

International Service Agencies
http://www.charity.org

American Red Cross
http://www.crossnet.org

Chapter 5
Developing and Evaluating Your Fund-Raising Plan

Chapter Outline

- The Critical Need for Planning
- Determining Organization Goals
- The Development Audit
- Setting Realistic Goals for Your Fund-Raising Program
- Involving Board and Volunteers
- Preparing a Budget
- Stages of a Development Program
- Cost-Benefit Guidelines—Return on Investment
- The Evaluation Process

Key Vocabulary

- Analyzing
- Cost-Benefit Guidelines
- Cost Per Dollar
- Development Audit
- Evaluation
- Fund-Raising Goals
- Planning
- Return on Investment (ROI)

The Critical Need for Planning

The need for strategic planning within the nonprofit sector has never been greater. Competition for charitable contributions has caused current and prospective donors to want more information about how organizations are managed, how their programs are serving the public good, and how their investment in the organization is being used. Through the planning process, organizations assess where they are, where they want to go, and how and when they will get there.

The truth is, however, that few organizations conduct effective planning. Among the barriers that get in the way, foremost is the issue of time. How many times have you heard or said yourself, "I have too much to do now to take time to plan." However, you and your organiza-

tion need to adopt the philosophy that planning does not take time, it saves time. Planning is not an easy task. Trying to forecast the future can be a difficult process, but it is necessary and can pay great dividends to your organization.

Planning

- builds a spirit of ownership within the organization's leadership;
- provides a structure, a framework that will serve as a guide for day-to-day decisions;
- focuses attention in a certain direction, thereby enhancing chances for success; and
- sets goals and objectives that promote the organization's growth.

Determining Organization Goals

It is important for development staff to be involved in the organizational planning process for two reasons. First, organizational goals must fit within the mission of the organization, thereby forming the basis for the case for support for donors. (See Chapter 6 for more information on the case for support.) Second, development staff persons, because of the type of work they do, may possess a better understanding of how the external constituencies view the organization.

When determining organizational goals, the task is to define what the organization is today, what it wants to become or do that will enhance its program in the future, whether there is a need for this kind of organization and service today and into the future, and what programs or services should be provided to achieve new or continuing objectives. It is essential to the process to examine the external environment that impacts the organization. Consideration should be given to competition of nonprofit organizations, trends in giving, the current economy, the political climate, and state and federal regulations. The purpose of this review of external factors is to identify opportunities and threats that the organization might encounter in the next three to five years. Another important element to analyze is the organization's internal environment. Physical facilities, leadership, staffing capabilities, and current level of financial support are among the areas to examine. Look at current strengths and weaknesses that need to be factored into the equation for success.

The Development Audit

A very effective planning tool used by nonprofit organizations is the development audit. Exhibit 5–1 depicts The Resource Development Assessment developed by Robert F. Semple, CFRE, a development professional and fund-raising consultant. This instrument is designed to provide an organization with a quick, graphic profile of its potential to compete for charitable dollars. It is not meant to be a substitute for an in-depth analysis of an organization's capacity to raise funds. Administered by professional counsel and completed by an organization's staff members and volunteer leaders, it will suggest where strengths and weaknesses lie within the overall resource development process.

The ten key result areas include the following:

- Planning
- The Board
- Volunteers
- Resource Development Staff
- Financial Resources
- Donor Research
- Fund-Raising Aids
- Fund-Raising Techniques
- Public Relations

Setting Realistic Goals for Your Fund-Raising Program

Now that the organization has set its future course, fundraising goals can be established. Development objectives (Broce 1986, 18) must be established to meet institutional goals. Donors give gifts to meet objectives, not simply to give money away. However, many people like to support worthy causes or efforts when they are presented with a challenging idea or program that is consistent with their interests.

> People like to support worthy causes or efforts when they are presented with a challenging idea or program that is consistent with their interests.

There are many ways to establish fund-raising goals and, all too frequently, development staff persons are not part of that process, but rather assigned a dollar goal based on the organization's operating budget. The fol-

lowing is a common scenario for how an organization might establish its goals:

1. Look at only the previous year's fund-raising results.
2. Look at next year's operating budget including additional programs, new staff, etc.
3. Project a reasonable increase, usually 10 percent.
4. Establish a goal through some compromise between the operating budget and the 10 percent factor, usually never less than the previous year.

A better approach to setting realistic goals would be to gather and analyze data collected during a three- to five-year period. This means that the organization must keep accurate records and be able to generate a variety of analytical reports. Before computers became fundraising tools (see Chapter 4), donor records, giving histories, and the results of the different methods of solicitation were kept manually. Some small nonprofit or-ganizations may still do this today, but for the growing number who use computers, the ways to track and analyze data are numerous, depending on the type of fund-raising software used. The analysis will reveal which types of fund raising have increased, decreased, or remained stable during this multi-year period.

Source: © Carole Cable

Exhibit 5–1 The Resource Development Assessment (abbreviated version)

Introduction

This abbreviated version of our Resource Development Assessment questionnaire is designed to provide an organization with a quick, graphic profile of its potential to actively compete in the philanthropic marketplace. It is **not meant to be a substitute** for an in-depth analysis of an organization's capacity to raise money. Normally, an expanded version is administered by professional counsel to a study group composed of the CEO, development staff, select board members, and key volunteers. However, in its current format, it will *suggest* where strengths and deficiencies lie within your resource development program.

Ten key areas have been selected for this brief investigation. These are areas known to have considerable impact on the success or failure of fund-raising programs. Please wait for the introduction to each section before selecting your answer. There are no right or wrong answers, only your *judgment* as to conditions that currently exist within your organization.

Each of the numbered statements is to be rated either as *Below Standard*, *Standard*, or *Above Standard*. These conditions correspond to a numerical scale of 1, 2, or 3 respectively. After you have made your assessment, place the numerical value in the grid adjacent to each statement.

After completion of each section, add the sub-totals to derive a cumulative score. Then transfer the cumulative score from each key area to the Resource Development Assessment Profile (attached).

Instructions

Assign a numerical rating to each item: 3 = **Above Average**; 2 = **About Average (Standard)**; 1 = **Below Average**.

After completing each section, add the sub-totals to derive a cumulative score. Then transfer the cumulative score from each grid to the Resource Development Assessment Profile.

A word of caution: Because every development effort responds to a unique set of circumstances, e.g., popularity of cause, staff expertise, budget, etc., some of these questions may not apply to you. If so, for purposes of this exercise, substitute another question you believe to be relevant.

Fund-Raising Environment

	Below (1)	Std (2)	Above (3)
1. External: capacity to compete with other nonprofit organizations performing similar services within your service area			
2. External: corporate gift *potential* within your geographic locale			
3. Internal: the board and volunteer leadership support for the resource development program			
4. Internal: office space and equipment to conduct business (e.g., FAX, computers)			

Donor Research

	Below (1)	Std (2)	Above (3)
5. Availability of reference materials including on-line capacity to conduct donor prospect research			
6. Prospect gift evaluation procedure			
7. Ability to retrieve donor gift data			
8. Frequency of gift analysis reporting			

continues

Exhibit 5–1 continued

Fund-Raising Techniques

	Below (1)	Std (2)	Above (3)
9. Effectiveness of board and volunteers in conducting face-to-face solicitation			
10. Dollars raised by special events			
11. Phonathon			
12. Direct mail program			

Fund-Raising Aids

	Below (1)	Std (2)	Above (3)
13. A case statement for support is available (**do not have one = 1; in the works = 2; complete = 3**)			
14. Caliber of written proposals to solicit contributions			
15. Capability of software packages in preparing proposals, acknowledgments, and statistical reports			
16. Availability of training materials to assist volunteers participating in fund-raising program			

Leadership

	Below (1)	Std (2)	Above (3)
17. The access board members have to funding sources			
18. The board's understanding of the resource development process			
19. The board's participation in soliciting gifts			
20. The board's percentage of gift participation in reaching annual goal (**Below = less than 25% participate; Standard = 25 to 75%; Above = more than 75% participate**)			

Volunteers (non-board members)

	Below (1)	Std (2)	Above (3)
21. Availability of volunteers to help solicit gifts			
22. Effectiveness of the volunteer orientation and training program			
23. Volunteer's percentage of gift participation in reaching annual goal (**Below = less than 25% participate; Standard = 25 to 75%; Above = more than 75% participate**)			
24. The recognition program for volunteers contributing their services			

continues

Exhibit 5–1 continued

Staff

	Below (1)	Std (2)	Above (3)
25. Development staff experience at designing and conducting fund-raising programs			
26. Chief development officer reports directly to the organization's chief executive officer (**No = 1; Sometimes = 2; Yes = 3**)			
27. Chief development officer has access to the board regarding resource development matters (**Never = 1; Seldom = 2; Frequently = 3**)			
28. Extent of development officer's opportunity to enhance fund-raising skills through workshops, seminars, and conferences			

Public Relations

	Below (1)	Std (2)	Above (3)
29. The access your organization has to the communications media			
30. The procedures to release information to the local newspapers, periodicals, and electronic media			
31. Name recognition organization has in the community			
32. Your organization's image in the community (**Poor = 1; Good = 2; Excellent = 3**)			

Planning

	Below (1)	Std (2)	Above (3)
33. Frequency of reviewing fund-raising plan to determine its effectiveness			
34. Involvement of key leadership in planning (CEO, development staff, selected board members and key volunteers)			
35. The budget allocation to support the plan			
36. The effectiveness of your current fund-raising plan			

continues

Exhibit 5–1 continued

Resource Attraction

	Below (1)	Std (2)	Above (3)
37. The overall ability of your organization to attract gifts from individuals			
38. The overall ability of your organization to attract corporate gifts			
39. The overall ability of your organization to attract gifts-in-kind			
40. The overall ability of your organization to attract gifts from private foundations			

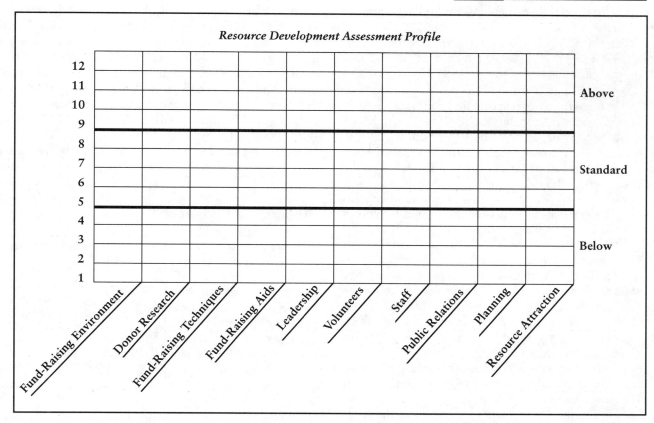

Source: Reprinted with permission from Robert F. Semple, Semple Bixel Associates, Inc., Nutley, NJ.

Look for the following when reviewing the data on the different types of fund-raising.

analyze

- Which generates the largest share?
- Which are the most reliable sources of income?
- Which are the least reliable sources of income?
- Which have the greatest potential for growth?

Once you have analyzed the results of your current fund-raising program, the next step in developing your fund-raising plan is to ask yourself the following questions:

plan or based on

- To which areas should you allocate more time?
- Which area(s) should you eliminate?
- Where would you involve more volunteers?
- Given a larger budget, in which areas would you invest more?

Keep in mind that different organizations will see varying results using the same methods of fund raising. For example, special events may be highly successful and appropriate for chapters of the American Heart Association, but may fail to raise significant funds for public radio stations. Annual campaigns can have differing levels of success from year to year based on committee leadership and composition. It is very important that volunteers remain motivated and enthusiastic about their tasks. A true-to-life example would be the following: Jane Smith, a board member, chaired the annual campaign committee last year, personally recruited twenty-five volunteers who in turn solicited ten prospects, each raising $25,000 for the organization. This year, Jim White, a well-known community leader, agreed to chair the committee, personally recruited ten volunteers who in turn solicited five prospects, each raising only $11,000.

An excellent tool to use when analyzing your fund-raising data and establishing your fund-raising goals is the form illustrated in Exhibit 5–2.

When using this or any other type of form that analyzes the fund-raising results, it is important to note any special circumstances that affected this year's results (Exhibit 5–3). Examples might include the receipt of a sizeable bequest or major gift that will not be repeated the following year. When developing the upcoming year's goals, the organization must plan how it will raise those funds through other means. For example, if a $10,000 gift was received, is there a new major gift prospect who will give at that level? Are there ten new prospective donors who will each contribute $1,000? Can you encourage twenty donors who gave $500 to increase their giving to $1,000 this year? Or will you look to other fund-raising techniques such as special events, foundation grants, or corporate support?

strategies vary

Involving Board and Volunteers

An organization's leaders and volunteers need to understand that fund-raising goals are targets, not fixed figures. Involving leaders and volunteers in the goal-setting process is an excellent way to educate them. Having them participate in an assessment of the institution's capacity to raise money, for example, using the Resource Development Assessment instrument, will give them a sense of ownership in the development effort. It also helps volunteer leaders better understand the role of the development office and what their role should be.

It is believed that each annual giving method requires three to four years to reach a level of maturity at which predictable levels of annual support can be projected. For an organization just beginning to build an annual giving program, it is important to maintain a positive environment for volunteers and staff. Successful programs build volunteers' confidence in their ability to perform and in the methods used. One positive outcome is that volunteers will continue to serve the next year, perhaps taking on a leadership role. This continuing involvement increases the potential for even greater levels of commitment from volunteers and donors.

Preparing a Budget

It is common for nonprofit organizations starting new development operations to choose to make a major investment in personnel alone. Believing that all the organization needs to raise funds is a development staff person is a critical error. The staff person is only one part of the investment. Funds to produce materials, do mailings, travel, set up record-keeping systems, hire secretarial support, and contribute toward other items are also required.

> Believing that all the organization needs to raise funds is a development staff person is a critical error.

Note that in the early stages of a development program, the costs of fund raising are a large percentage of funds raised. At best, it is a "break even" proposition. But, as a fund-raising program matures, the costs will be a smaller percentage of funds raised. Percentages will vary depending on the size of the organization.

To conduct an effective fund-raising plan, other items to consider including (in addition to personnel costs) are the following:

1. Design and printing
2. Postage and mail services

3. Supplies
4. Telephone
5. Photocopying
6. Travel
7. Food and entertaining
8. Professional services—photographer, entertainment for special events, consultants
9. Membership dues for professional organizations
10. Conferences and workshops
11. Computer needs—equipment, software
12. Public relations

Stages of a Development Program

As mentioned earlier in this chapter, planning is a developmental process. So, too, is an organization's development program. It is unwise for an organization to attempt to include every fund-raising method in the early years of its development program. It is best to begin expanding and enhancing those individual programs that have produced successful results for the organization. The development program illustrated in Exhibit 5–4 shows how a program advances through a number of

---

Exhibit 5–2 How to Plan Accurately for Next Year's Annual Fund

Do your board, CEO, and financial officer want you to accurately project fund-raising results for the coming year? If so, it *can* be done. And you can reach your goals.

There are two basic sets of figures that must be generated and compared to plan and project accurately. First, you need to determine what you are *likely* to accomplish—the amount of money that you are *likely* to raise next year based on past results. These figures will be logical extensions (increases or decreases), category by category, of what has happened during these past three years.

Pages two and three of this supplement will help you to measure three years' growth, category by category, and to use these growth figures to project what next year's figures are likely to be.

If where you are *likely* to be is where you *want* to be, then give yourself a gold star and pat on the back. Photocopy the completed pages two and three for your board, CEO, and financial officer and continue raising funds in the same manner as you have been. However, you may want to re-examine your institutional needs to determine what your fund raising goals *should* be.

On page four (columns O, P, Q) you will need to itemize specific objectives, fund raising category by category. These will add up to be your goal as it should be to meet all financial needs. Here's how to arrive at these objectives:

First, work with your CEO and department heads to determine what your fund-raising needs will be for next year. Discuss program growth, new equipment needs, new staff, and increases in numbers of people to be served. (Or, in some cases, reductions in these areas.)

Working with your financial officer, carefully estimate the costs of these changes. Add or subtract these costs from last year's department budget and allow for inflation.

Total all program or department budgets. Don't forget to add administrative costs. From the total, subtract assured income (fees for services, yields on investments, government contracts, continuing grants—all sources of income not related to next year's fund-raising efforts).

Now you have a net fund-raising goal. Estimate fund-raising costs by determining how much you are spending this year to raise your current income. Apply the same percent to your next year's goal. Add fund-raising costs to net fund-raising needs to determine your total development goal.

Using past experience as your guideline, break this total development goal down into fund-raising methods or categories on page four (lines 1–18, columns O, P, Q).

Finally, in columns R, S, and T, enter the differences between where you are likely to be (columns L, M, N) and where you want to be (O, P, Q).

continues

Exhibit 5–2 continued

	A	B	C	D	E	F
	TWO YEARS AGO			LAST YEAR		
	No. of Gifts	Total $ Raised	Average Gift	No. of Gifts	Total $ Raised	Average Gift
1. New Donor Acquisition Program	_____	$_____	$_____	_____	$_____	$_____
2. Reinstatement of Lapsed Donors	_____	_____	_____	_____	_____	_____
3. Renewal of First-Time Donors	_____	_____	_____	_____	_____	_____
4. Renewal of Ongoing Small Gift Donors	_____	_____	_____	_____	_____	_____
5. _____ (large gift club)	_____	_____	_____	_____	_____	_____
6. _____ (large gift club)	_____	_____	_____	_____	_____	_____
7. _____ (large gift club)	_____	_____	_____	_____	_____	_____
8. Board's Personal Call Program	_____	_____	_____	_____	_____	_____
9. Corporate Solicitation	_____	_____	_____	_____	_____	_____
10. Foundation Grants	_____	_____	_____	_____	_____	_____
11. Government Grants	_____	_____	_____	_____	_____	_____
12. Commemorative Giving Program	_____	_____	_____	_____	_____	_____
13. Yields on Planned Giving	_____	_____	_____	_____	_____	_____
14. Yields on Endowments	_____	_____	_____	_____	_____	_____
15. Telemarketing	_____	_____	_____	_____	_____	_____
16. _____ (special event)	_____	_____	_____	_____	_____	_____
17. _____ (special event)	_____	_____	_____	_____	_____	_____
18. Other Fund-Raising Income	_____	_____	_____	_____	_____	_____
19. TOTAL GIFTS	_____			_____		
20. TOTAL DOLLARS RAISED		$_____			$_____	
21. AVERAGE GIFT			$_____			$_____

Examine the fund-raising methods (1–18) and circle the number of each method used. For each method you use, fill in columns A, B, and C with accurate figures to show how well you did two years ago. Then, complete columns D, E, and F to reflect last year's results. To complete G, H, and I, take this year's results and project to year end.

continues

Exhibit 5–2 continued

G	H	I	J	K	L	M	N
THIS YEAR'S PROJECTIONS			Average Three-Year % Growth No. Gifts	Average Three-Year % Growth Total $	NEXT YEAR'S PROJECTIONS BASED ON THREE-YEAR TRENDS		
No. of Gifts	Total $ Raised	Average Gift			No. of Gifts	Total $ Raised	Average Gift
_____	$_____	$_____	____%	____%	_____	$_____	$_____
_____	_____	_____	____%	____%	_____	_____	_____
_____	_____	_____	____%	____%	_____	_____	_____
_____	_____	_____	____%	____%	_____	_____	_____
_____	_____	_____	____%	____%	_____	_____	_____
_____	_____	_____	____%	____%	_____	_____	_____
_____	_____	_____	____%	____%	_____	_____	_____
_____	_____	_____	____%	____%	_____	_____	_____
_____	_____	_____	____%	____%	_____	_____	_____
_____	_____	_____	____%	____%	_____	_____	_____
_____	_____	_____	____%	____%	_____	_____	_____
_____	_____	_____	____%	____%	_____	_____	_____
_____	_____	_____	____%	____%	_____	_____	_____
_____	_____	_____	____%	____%	_____	_____	_____
_____	_____	_____	____%	____%	_____	_____	_____
_____	_____	_____	____%	____%	_____	_____	_____
_____	_____	_____	____%	____%	_____	_____	_____
_____	_____	_____	____%	____%	_____	_____	_____
_____					_____		
	$_____					$_____	
		$_____					$_____

Take the increases (category by category) from year one to year two and add those to the increases from year two to year three. Divide by two to get an average. Divide the average increase by this year's results to determine average % growth (J and K). G + J = L; H + K = M. Do this for each of the methods you use in fund raising (1–18). Now, add L and M vertically. You have the *likely* number of gifts and *likely* dollars you'll raise if you continue development methods and procedures as you have in the past three years. Turn to page four.

continues

Exhibit 5–2 continued

	O	P	Q	R	S	T
	OBJECTIVES FOR NEXT YEAR			DIFFERENCES BETWEEN O, P, Q and L, M, N		
	No. of Gifts	Total $ Raised	Average Gift	No. of Gifts	Total $ Raised	Average Gift
1. New Donor Acquisition Program	_____	$_____	$_____	_____	$_____	$_____
2. Reinstatement of Lapsed Donors	_____	_____	_____	_____	_____	_____
3. Renewal of First-Time Donors	_____	_____	_____	_____	_____	_____
4. Renewal of Ongoing Small Gift Donors	_____	_____	_____	_____	_____	_____
5. _____ (large gift club)	_____	_____	_____	_____	_____	_____
6. _____ (large gift club)	_____	_____	_____	_____	_____	_____
7. _____ (large gift club)	_____	_____	_____	_____	_____	_____
8. Board's Personal Call Program	_____	_____	_____	_____	_____	_____
9. Corporate Solicitation	_____	_____	_____	_____	_____	_____
10. Foundation Grants	_____	_____	_____	_____	_____	_____
11. Government Grants	_____	_____	_____	_____	_____	_____
12. Commemorative Giving Program	_____	_____	_____	_____	_____	_____
13. Yields on Planned Giving	_____	_____	_____	_____	_____	_____
14. Yields on Endowments	_____	_____	_____	_____	_____	_____
15. Telemarketing	_____	_____	_____	_____	_____	_____
16. _____ (special event)	_____	_____	_____	_____	_____	_____
17. _____ (special event)	_____	_____	_____	_____	_____	_____
18. Other Fund-Raising Income	_____	_____	_____	_____	_____	_____
19. TOTAL GIFTS	_____			_____		
20. TOTAL DOLLARS RAISED		$_____			$_____	
21. AVERAGE GIFT			$_____			$_____

On page three, columns L, M, N tell you the numbers of gifts and dollars you are *likely* to raise if you continue using the same methods and procedures. Columns O, P, and Q, above, show what you should or want to raise. Line by line, subtract L, M, and N from O, P, and Q and enter the difference on the corresponding lines in columns R, S, and T. Method by method, procedure by procedure, what are you going to have to do *differently* to reach your objectives for next year? Develop a separate, detailed plan for each fund-raising method to be used.

Courtesy of David Barnes, Barnes Associates, Inc.

Exhibit 5–3 Year-To-Date Analysis

	YEAR A	%	YEAR B	%	YEAR C	THREE-YEAR AVERAGE
Direct Mail	$100,000	18.0	$118,000	23.0	$145,000	$121,000
Special Events	75,000	33.0	100,000	25.0	125,000	100,000
Major Gifts	175,000	14.2	200,000	12.5	225,000	200,000
Foundations	300,000	0.0	300,000	-25.0	225,000	275,000
Corporations	150,000	16.6	175,000	0.9	190,000	171,666
TOTAL	$800,000		$893,000		$910,000	$867,666
		+11.6		+0.2		

Note the following:

- Income has increased each year but at a declining rate of growth.
- Further research is needed as to why the foundations and corporations programs are not growing.
- How did volunteers, staff, and the external environment influence the direction and success of the program during this three-year period?

stages. Note that the length of time an organization's fund-raising program remains at a specific stage will vary depending on the organization. Exhibit 5–5 provides a simple action plan calendar.

SOP 88-2 vs SOP 97-1

Cost-Benefit Guidelines—Return on Investment

Recently, the issue of how much an organization spends raising funds is gaining attention. Questions about performance are on the rise from boards and managers, from donors and volunteers, from legislators and regulators, and from the media and the general public. The fund-raising profession currently does not have industry-wide guidelines and standards. This is due to the fact, as stated throughout this chapter, that nonprofit organizations do not conduct fund raising the same and that different types of fund raising programs perform differently for every organization.

> The issue of how much an organization spends raising funds is gaining attention.

According to Patricia F. Lewis, CFRE, President and CEO of the National Society of Fund Raising Executives (NSFRE), fund-raising executives always have been asked, "How much money have you raised?" But today, there are additional questions such as: "How much did it cost? Is that cost reasonable? How does our cost compare with others? What are the standards to measure performance? Can you estimate next year's results?" Answers are needed and so NSFRE has undertaken a study on the relationship between the budget invested in fund-raising activities and the results achieved. Exhibit 5–6 illustrates guidelines recently developed by NSFRE's task force for evaluation of fund-raising costs.

The two major organizations that monitor fund-raising activities of nonprofit organizations are The Council of Better Business Bureaus, Philanthropic Advisory Service (CBBB PAS) and the National Charities Information Bureau (NCIB). These two organizations report on whether charities meet standards that each has established for fund raising, governance, financial management, and public information. They do not approve or disapprove charities, but they urge potential donors to evaluate the importance of variations from these standards. To find out more about their standards, visit their web sites. For NCIB, type http://www.give.org, and for CBBB PAS, type http://www.bbb.org to access the sites.

James M. Greenfield, CFRE, FAHP, author of several books on fund raising, has done considerable research in this area. In his latest book, *Fund-Raising Cost Effectiveness: A Self Assessment Workbook*, he developed the Nine-Point Performance Index (see Exhibit 5–7) for organizations to use in evaluating their fund-raising programs and a listing of reasonable cost guidelines for solicitation activities (see Exhibit 5–8). Greenfield believes that there is more to performance management

Exhibit 5–4 Stages of a Fund-Raising Plan

Stage 1

1. Direct Mail
   – two to four appeals
2. Annual Giving Volunteer Committee
   – conducts personal solicitations
3. Special Gifts
   – mailing to board members
   – mailing to key volunteers and prospects
4. Special Events
   – general ticketed event
   – smaller events hosted by CEO or board chairperson
5. Foundations, Corporations, Government
   – conduct research on prospective funders
   – gather guidelines and other pertinent information
   – prepare letters of inquiries
   – develop proposals for key funders
   – institute a reporting procedure for funders

Stage 2

1. Direct Mail
   – renewal mailings to current donors
   – donor acquisition mailings
   – special mailings to lapsed donors
2. Introduce Mail/Phone program
3. Annual Giving Volunteer Committee
   – increase number of personal solicitations
4. Special Gifts
   – do special cultivation/informational mailings to current donors
   – introduce gift clubs
   – continue personalized mailings and increase number of personal solicitations
5. Special Events
   – expand successful general ticketed event to increase revenue by instituting a sponsor/patron structure
   – continue smaller events hosted by CEO, board chairperson, or major donor
6. Foundations, Corporations, Government
   – continue research on possible funders

   – set up meetings with current funders
   – target new group of prospects preparing letters of inquiries
   – prepare written proposals and continue reporting procedure
7. Planned Giving
   – introduce concept of wills and bequests in communications and newsletters
   – begin drafting gift policies for board approval
8. Memorial Giving
   – introduce concept in communications and newsletter

Stage 3

1. Direct Mail
   – renewal mailings to current donors
   – increase donor acquisition mailings
   – continue mailing special appeals to lapsed donors
2. Mail/Phone Program
   – continue program doing more donor segmentation
3. Annual Giving Committee
   – increase activity of committee
4. Special Gifts
   – continue cultivation/information mailings from CEO
   – expand number of gift clubs
   – identify prospects for special attention
   – continue personalized mailings and personal solicitations
5. Special Events
   – maintain current program with some enhancements
6. Foundations, Corporations, Government
   – maintain current program
7. Planned Giving
   – establish a bequest society
   – prepare special marketing materials on planned giving
   – do special mailings to selected prospects
8. Memorial Giving
   – continue to include information in communications/newsletter

than "bottom-line" analysis. To measure fund-raising performance, one must begin with individual program assessments.

The Evaluation Process

Nonprofit organizations need to view the evaluation of their development program as a continuous process. During the year, refinements and revisions often will be made as events and circumstances dictate. If you developed your fund-raising plan by analyzing past results and their cost-effectiveness, you already have begun.

The evaluation process does not conclude by viewing the bottom line only. There are a number of other factors that affect the success of your development program. As you proceed in your evaluation, here are some possible questions to pose:

- What was the performance level of the board, staff, and volunteers? Was new leadership revealed?
- Was the budget sufficient in all areas? Are there changes needed?
- Is your funding more or less diversified than before?
- Are computer technology support systems adequate?

Exhibit 5–5 Sample Action Plan Calendar

Months/Programs	Jan.	Feb.	Mar.	Apr.	May	June	July	Aug.	Sept.	Oct.	Nov.	Dec.
Direct Mail	Appeal Mailing				Appeal Mailing				Appeal Mailing			Appeal Mailing
Mail/Phone									Phone Program Donors and Lapsed Donors			
Annual Giving Committee						Recruit Committee			Personal Solicitations of Identified Prospects			End of Campaign
Special Gifts			Special Mailing						Invite to CEO/Board Chair Event		Special Mailing	
Special Events					Event					CEO/Board Chair Event		
Foundations Corporations Government	Research and Contact Potential Funders		Proposal Deadline			Proposal Deadline				Proposal Deadline		Report to Grantmakers
Planned Giving	Newsletter Mailing			Newsletter Mailing				Newsletter Mailing				

Exhibit 5–6 Guidelines Useful to Not-for-Profit Organizations for Evaluating the Appropriateness of Their Fund-Raising Costs

Fund-raising is a process which has many components, and there are investments which must be made in order to complete the process. Individual components of the fund-raising process should be evaluated as part of a total development program, and boards of directors of not-for-profit organizations should determine a reasonable rate of return on investment for their own organization based on prior results.

The following factors should be taken into consideration in evaluating the return on investment in fund raising:

- The age of the organization. A well-established organization will be likely to have a return on investment higher than a newly established not-for-profit.
- The age of the development department. A mature development department, professionally run, would be expected to produce a higher return on investment than a newly-formed department.
- Different methods used in the fund-raising process will produce different returns. For example:
  1. A donor acquisition mailing will have a much lower return on investment than a donor renewal mailing.
  2. A capital campaign will produce a much higher return on investment than an annual fund program.
  3. A newly established planned giving program may have zero return on investment for the first few years.
  4. The return on investment on a special event will be lower than that of a major gifts program.
- The size of an organization. The return on investment may be affected by the size of the organization.

- The profile of the constituency. The economic and geographic profile of the constituency solicited will have an effect on the return on investment.
- The location of the organization. An organization located in an affluent region of the country should expect a higher return on investment than one located in a less affluent area.
- The popularity of the cause. The cause and its level of acceptance by the community will affect the return on investment.
- The competition for funds. Within the community or constituency that the organization is appealing to for support, the competition by other organizations may lower the return on investment.

Responses to the following questions will indicate if proposals from outside vendors are in the best interests of the organization and its donors:

- What is the return on investment proposed by the vendor?
- What is the time commitment expected of staff?
- What is the time commitment expected of the board of directors and key volunteers?
- What is the amount of organizational funds needed?
- With what will the organization be left (skills, systems, enhanced volunteer involvement, expanded donor base, ongoing annual fund raising at a higher level, etc.) when the vendor has completed the project?

Courtesy of the National Society of Fund Raising Executives (NSFRE).

Exhibit 5–7 Nine-Point Performance Index

Basic Data

1. Participants	=	Number of donors responding with gifts
2. Income	=	Gross contributions
3. Expense	=	Fund-raising costs

Performance Measurements

4. Percent Participation	=	Divide participants by total solicitations made
5. Average Gift Size	=	Divide income received by participants
6. Net Income	=	Subtract expenses from income received
7. Average Cost per Gift	=	Divide expenses by participants
8. Cost of Fund-Raising	=	Divide expenses by income received; multiply by 100 for percentage
9. Return	=	Divide net income by expenses; multiply by 100 for percentage

Source: Reprinted by permission of John Wiley & Sons, Inc., from *Fund-Raising Cost Effectiveness: A Self-Assessment Workbook*, J.M. Greenfield, © 1996, New York, New York: John Wiley & Sons, Inc.

Exhibit 5–8 Reasonable Cost Guidelines for Solicitation Activities

Solicitation Activity	Reasonable Cost Guidelines
Direct mail (acquisition)	$1.25 to $1.50 per $1.00 raised
Direct mail (renewal)	$0.20 to $0.25 per $1.00 raised
Membership associations	$0.20 to $0.30 per $1.00 raised
Activities, benefits, and special events	$0.50 per $1.00 raised (gross revenue and direct costs only)*
Donor clubs and support group organizations	$0.20 to $0.30 per $1.00 raised
Volunteer-led personal solicitation	$0.10 to $0.20 per $1.00 raised
Corporations	$0.20 per $1.00 raised
Foundations	$0.20 per $1.00 raised
Special projects	$0.10 to $0.20 per $1.00 raised
Capital campaigns	$0.10 to $0.20 per $1.00 raised
Planned giving	$0.20 to $0.30 per $1.00 raised

*Benefit event cost allocations: To calculate bottom-line total costs and net proceeds from a benefit event, calculate and add the indirect and overhead support expenses to direct costs incurred and subtract from gross revenue.

Source: Reprinted by permission of John Wiley & Sons, Inc., from *Fund-Raising Cost Effectiveness: A Self-Assessment Workbook*, J.M. Greenfield, © 1996, New York, New York: John Wiley & Sons, Inc.

- Are gift-processing, acknowledgment, and tracking systems running efficiently?
- How well did your prospect research effort function?
- How well did your printed materials for fund raising and public relations perform?

In many ways, the evaluation process is yet a continuing audit of an organization's capability to raise funds successfully and effectively. Once completed, this evaluation becomes the basis for the next year's planning process.

References

Broce, T. 1986. *The guide to raising money from private sources.* Second edition. Norman, OK: University of Oklahoma Press.

Greenfield, J. 1996. *Fund-raising cost effectiveness: A self assessment workbook.* New York: John Wiley & Sons, Inc.

Chapter 6
Building Relationships for Your Organization Through Annual Giving

Chapter Outline

- The Role of Annual Giving
- Defining the Case for Support
- Solicitation Methods Used in Annual Giving
- Recruiting Volunteer Leaders
- Working with the Steering Committee
- Training and Managing Volunteers
- Using Gift Clubs to Motivate Increased Giving
- The Annual Campaign Calendar
- Effective Techniques to Increase Your Annual Campaign
- Evaluating the Campaign

Key Vocabulary

- Acknowledgment
- Annual Giving
- Brochure
- Case Statement
- Challenge Gift
- Constituency
- Donor
- Donor Pyramid
- Gift Clubs
- Matching Gift
- Personal Solicitation
- Reunion or Anniversary Giving
- Solicitor's Kit
- Steering Committee
- Unrestricted Funds

The Role of Annual Giving

An annual giving program uses the greatest variety of fund-raising techniques to introduce an organization's programs, services, and needs to the widest audience. Often considered the front lines or "trenches" of fund raising, annual giving seeks funds on an annual or recurring basis from the same constituency, or a broadening one, to be used for operating budget support. In the "pyramid of giving" illustrated in Figure 6–1, annual giving forms the base of the pyramid, because its purpose is to identify the largest number of donors and provide them with information about the organization. Annual giving is the first in a series of contacts with a donor that an organization hopes will develop into a long-term relationship leading to a major gift and/or estate or planned giving. Annual giving recruits new donors and brings back previous donors with the organization hoping that this will lead to increased gifts. It offers opportunities for donors to be involved as volunteers in special events and annual campaign committees. One very important purpose of annual giving programs is to identify potential leaders and prospective major donors. Throughout an annual giving program, you are friend-raising as well as fund-raising, thereby building relationships that are important for your organization's future. Exhibit 6–1 lists ingredients for a successful annual giving campaign.

Defining the Case for Support

Before you can develop a successful annual giving program, the priorities and needs of the organization must be identified. Additional funds are always needed so that organizations can expand their operations. However, keep in mind that the organization's mission statement sets the direction for specific programs and services that will benefit the public and meet the needs of the community being served. The case for support or "case statement" informs your donors and prospects who you are, what you are trying to do, and why. It presents the organization's objectives and needs as persuasively as possible so that a person will see the benefits of investing in that organization.

The case statement

- Gives the organization's history
- States its purpose and mission
- Outlines plans for programs and services to benefit society
- Shows how an organization differs from other similar organizations

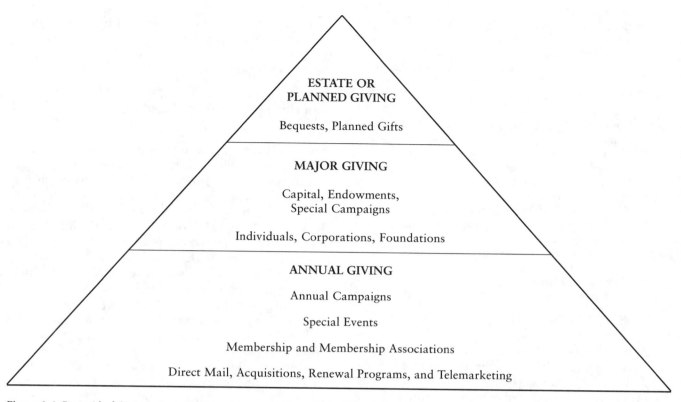

Figure 6–1 Pyramid of Giving. *Source:* Adapted by permission of John Wiley & Sons, Inc., from *Fund-Raising: Evaluating and Managing the Fund Development Process*, J.M. Greenfield, © 1991, New York, New York: John Wiley & Sons, Inc.

Exhibit 6–1 Ingredients for a Successful Annual Giving Campaign

1. A well-defined purpose
2. Extensive planning
3. An efficient organization
4. A realistic timetable
5. Meaningful benchmarks
6. Realistic assignments
7. Logical order

Source: Reprinted with permission from T. Broce, *Fund Raising, The Guide to Raising Money from Private Sources* pp. 86–87, © 1986, University of Oklahoma Press.

Given the tremendous competition for donors that exists in the nonprofit sector today, you must have a strong case for support. People will not give to organizations only because organizations say they need funds. People view their gifts as investments that help organizations and causes accomplish their objectives. Consider the following when developing your case for support:

- Relate the need to the community served.
- Demonstrate that the need is real and create a sense of urgency.

- Convince the donor that the need is worth supporting.
- Show that the organization itself cannot meet the need.
- Explain how the funds will be used.

Because the purpose of annual giving is to raise unrestricted funds for operating costs, it is sometimes more difficult to develop such a specific case for support. However, by focusing on the organization's mission and describing its programs or services, the case for funds may be made for general operational support, not restricted to a specific program or service. Exhibit 6–2 lists tips in preparing the case statement.

Because an organization appeals to several different constituencies—current donors, prospects, individuals receiving services, community members—you may need more than one case statement. A good test to use is to ask two key questions about each group: "What does this constituency know about my organization?" and "How much does this constituency care about my organization?" How your donors and prospects relate to these questions will com-

> Because an organization appeals to several different constituencies, you may need more than one case statement.

Exhibit 6–2 Tips in Preparing the Case Statement

1. Involve key staff, board members, donors, and volunteers.
2. Have only one writer.
3. The case statement does not need to be long.
4. Use simple, brief language that people can understand.
5. Be convincing and optimistic.
6. Present a positive image.
7. Base it on organization's strengths, not needs.
8. Project the future, not the past.
9. Tell the story with pictures and charts.
10. Make the case from the prospect's point of interest; be donor-oriented.
11. Demonstrate the capacity to solve problems that are important to donors.
12. Show that the organization's needs and wants are a good investment.

municate to you whether to have one case statement or several versions, and how to focus the case for each. The time invested in writing the case statement is extremely important. A well-developed case for support will serve as the basis for all development-related materials—annual giving brochures, appeal letters, training materials for volunteer solicitors, and public relations materials.

Harold J. "Si" Seymour was a pioneer fund-raising executive and consultant whose book, *Designs for Fund-Raising,* is often referred to as the "bible" of fund-raising. Seymour said, "People give to worthwhile programs rather than to needy institutions. The case must catch the eye, warm the heart, and stir the mind" (1988).

Solicitation Methods Used in Annual Giving

There are three basic ways to ask people for money: by mail, by telephone, or the most successful way—in person. Creatively combining these three methods makes for a successful annual giving program. The following are most commonly used in annual giving programs:

- Personal solicitation
- Gift clubs
- Telephone campaigns, telethons, telemarketing
- Direct mail

This chapter focuses primarily on using volunteers to do personal solicitations for an annual giving campaign. Information is included on how using gift club membership can be an effective way for volunteers to solicit increased gifts and new gifts. Chapter 9 also covers per-

sonal solicitation and how it is used to successfully secure major gifts for a nonprofit organization. More information on direct mail and telephone campaigns is found in Chapter 7.

Recruiting Volunteer Leaders

Volunteers are vital to a nonprofit organization. They govern and establish policies as members of the board of directors, help an organization offer its services as program volunteers, and most important, they enable the organization to achieve its goals as volunteer solicitors. To keep an active core of volunteers, an organization must maintain volunteers' confidence, use their time and talents effectively, and thank them regularly for the many contributions they make to the organization. (See Chapter 2 for more in-depth information.)

The first step in recruiting volunteer leaders is to plan the basic campaign structure. There are a number of ways you might structure a campaign. The simplest is to have an annual giving chairperson and committee. Search diligently for the best person possible for this position. The following are some qualifications to consider when looking:

- A generous donor to the organization
- A person capable of making a large gift and soliciting other large gifts
- A person with a strong commitment to your institution and its mission
- A person who has done significant volunteer work, who has done "hands-on" fund raising, and who likes challenges
- A person who is inspired by your organization and who can help recruit and inspire other key volunteers
- A successful business executive or community leader who is widely known and admired in the community

It is a good idea to go over the list of possible chairpersons with the CEO of your organization before contacting any of them. Because this individual serves as a spokesperson for your organization with donors and prospective donors it is important that the right person be selected. When offering a candidate the job, it is best that the CEO and/or chairperson of the board do it in person. They can answer any questions and discuss any reservations the person may have in accepting the position. This is not the time, though, to do any "arm-twisting" or minimize the duties involved. Serving as the annual giving chairperson takes effort, money, and commitment. You are not looking for a "letterhead" leader, but an active leader.

Working with the Steering Committee

Once the annual giving chairperson position is filled, you should immediately set up a meeting with him or her and set the plans for the campaign. The chairperson should be involved in planning each step of the drive. It is important that the chairperson have sufficient information about the organization's past fund-raising efforts so he or she can help set goals for the current campaign. Recruiting members for the steering committee is one of the first tasks. If you have developed a plan to solicit different groups within your organization and community such as board members, gift club donors, business executives, community leaders, and clients, it is important to have a volunteer chairperson from each group or constituency. As you think about possible candidates for these chairpersons, you are again looking for people who are available, willing to take part in the program, and have good contacts with potential donors and important groups. Once these chairpersons are recruited, they can begin recruiting other volunteers for their area of responsibility, thus increasing the number of volunteer solicitors. When determining how many volunteers are needed to complete the organizational structure, keep in mind that you should ask a volunteer to contact no more than five to six prospects. If you require more than this from your volunteer, the chances are that he or she will not complete their assignments.

The steering committee, chaired by the annual giving chairperson, sets the goals and policies, and assumes responsibility for the success of the campaign. The CEO of the organization must be an active member of the steering committee. The development officer is the staff liaison. In an annual campaign, the steering committee should be an action committee as well as a policy-making group. Setting goals and deadlines, approving strategies, and assigning major prospects make the committee feel involved and needed, thereby ensuring motivation and success for the program. Exhibit 6–3 provides the structure for a steering committee.

Training and Managing Volunteers

With your committee structure set, your next step is to train the volunteers. Do not simply assign tasks. Offer training so that you can inspire and build confidence in your volunteers to do a better job. Training sessions also will help you identify potential leaders for future campaigns.

In planning your training, consider the following:

- how much money you need to raise
- the complexity of your fund-raising plan
- the number of volunteers involved, and their knowledge and experience of your organization

Exhibit 6–3 Steering Committee Structure

Annual Giving Chairperson
Annual Giving Steering Committee Made Up of the
   Following Subcommittee Chairpersons:
     Board
     Gift Club #1 (Highest Giving Club)
     Gift Club #2 (Next Highest Giving Club)
     Business Community
     Clients
     Community
     Volunteers

- the volunteers' fund-raising experience
- amount of time committed by volunteers

Because many of today's volunteers are employed outside the home, you will need to design training sessions that use their time effectively. Depending on your group of volunteers, you may need to schedule a series of training sessions to be held on evenings and weekends. Do not present your sessions as lectures. Your volunteers will learn best by being active participants, so allow for open discussion and opportunities to practice the skills they need to be effective fund raisers.

Provide your volunteers the following opportunities during your training sessions:

- To meet, get to know one another, and begin forming a successful team
- To hear the executive director or chief executive officer and others discuss the "state of the institution"—its purposes, policies, and programs
- To understand completely the case statement—the goals, plans, and procedures—and to understand the strengths of the organization and its particular needs at this time
- To learn and understand the methods and techniques to be used in soliciting gifts
- To review the campaign's timetable, reporting dates, deadlines, and procedures
- To review the solicitation materials included in their kit (Exhibit 6–4)

The first objective of training is to provide volunteers with the necessary information and materials for them to be successful in their fund raising. While accomplishing this objective, you are showing your workers that you and your staff are behind them all the way, and are readily available for advice and help.

The development staff plays an important role in both managing and supporting the volunteers. The following are keys to managing volunteers effectively:

Exhibit 6–4 What To Include In A Volunteer Solicitor's Kit

General organizational brochures

Copies of the case statement

Lists of donors and prospects

Fact sheet of answers to questions most often asked

Information about making a gift and tax deductibility

Pledge cards and envelopes

1. Keep in regular contact with your volunteers.
2. Set up a schedule for progress reports.
3. Call meetings only when needed, so as not to waste their time.
4. If a volunteer can no longer fulfill his or her responsibility on the committee, accept the resignation graciously and look for a replacement.
5. If a volunteer is not "pulling their weight" on the committee, consult with the team captain and the annual giving chairperson about approaching the member. It is best if the volunteer leaders have a friendly but frank conversation with the member. He or she will either resign or agree to fulfill their commitment. The purpose of this meeting is to "clear the air."
6. Always make your volunteers feel they are an important part of the effort because they are.

You identified, recruited, trained, and provided tools and assistance to your annual giving campaign volunteers. Your volunteer program is now established. To ensure that this program continues to be a success, there is one basic key you must remember—to say thank you. Like all of us, volunteers need to be thanked for the job they do. Even if they are not successful, they still need words of appreciation and encouragement.

In Chapter 2, we covered a number of ways to provide recognition to volunteers. Depending on your organization, there are almost limitless ways to say thank you to your volunteers. At the very least, a word of thanks from you, as the development officer, and a letter from the executive director or board chairperson are appropriate. A certificate or memento from the organization also shows appreciation. Whatever you choose, volunteers will know your organization appreciated their efforts and will be more likely to serve on the annual giving committee again next year.

Using Gift Clubs to Motivate Increased Giving

One of the most successful ways for an organization to solicit larger annual gifts is to establish gift clubs. Gift clubs are created at those giving levels that produce the most funds in annual campaigns. The top category is usually gifts of $1,000 and above. The next range is gifts of $500 to $999. Experience shows that most individuals who can give $500 a year will instead contribute $1,000 to be a member of the most prestigious gift club, therefore fewer people donate $500. The next range is $250 to $499 with most of your donors contributing at the $250 level. The lowest category is $100 to $249 with the majority of members giving at the $100 level.

These gift levels or whatever other levels fit an organization's constituency form the basis for gift clubs. The name for each gift club should have special meaning for the organization. Using names of persons or places that played an important role in the history of the organization helps establish the importance of membership in these groups. For example at American University, gift clubs are named as follows:

- The President's Circle ($1,000 and above)
- The Hurst Society ($500–$999), named for the university's founder, John Fletcher Hurst
- The Mary Graydon Associates ($250–$499), named for the first dormitory and now student center
- The American Club ($100–$249)

When looking at the methods used in annual giving described earlier in this chapter, keep in mind that personal solicitation is reserved for the top gift clubs, whereas direct mail and telephone fund-raising approaches are used at all levels. (A further discussion of gift

> No volunteer solicitor should make a call until his or her own contribution is made.

clubs is found in Chapter 7.) Exhibit 6–3 illustrates that the two top gift clubs each have a chairperson who serves on the annual campaign steering committee. Keep in mind that it is best for volunteers to solicit individuals for gift club membership at the level they themselves can expect to contribute. No volunteer solicitor should make a call until his or her own contribution is made. The volunteer will then know what is expected of them and will be comfortable working with prospects in his or her giving range. He or she can tell prospects about the events they attend and communications they receive, which makes them feel more involved in the organization. Frequently using the names of the gift clubs in oral and written communications also shows the importance of these clubs to the organization.

The gift club structure increases the total of annual gifts and is also the best method to raise giving levels of donors. Each year donors should be encouraged to "move up" to the next gift club category. Experience shows that few people are offended by being asked for too much, and, by the same token, we have learned that few donors have suggested that the solicitor did not ask for enough.

The Annual Campaign Calendar

Because your annual campaign has a specific duration, it is important to set targets and deadlines for staff and volunteers. As illustrated in Exhibit 6–5, the annual campaign actually has three phases: planning, solicitation, and recognition. Depending on your organization's needs, this calendar could be used to develop a six-month, nine-month, or twelve-month annual campaign. To plan to do an annual campaign in less than six months means that insufficient time was allowed for the critical planning phase.

Effective Techniques to Increase Your Annual Campaign

Matching Gift Programs
Up until recently, this program benefited only educational institutions. Today, this program benefits a wide variety of nonprofit organizations including hospitals, arts organizations, cultural organizations, and social service agencies. A corporation with a matching gift program will match the contribution of its employees dollar for dollar up to a set figure. Some companies will match more than dollar for dollar and will match retired employees and employee spouse gifts. This is a terrific source of additional funds for all eligible organizations.

Challenge Gifts
A challenge gift can come from a foundation, government grant, or individual donor. It can be issued in several different ways—dollar for dollar, double the dollar, or whatever appeals to the challenger. With advice from the development staff, sometimes the challenge donor will match only new or increased gifts. Experience teaches us that the best time to issue a challenge is when your annual giving has reached a plateau or is declining.

Gift Clubs
As stated previously, establishing gift clubs is an excellent way to motivate increased giving. Common levels for such clubs are $100–249, $250–499, $500–999, and $1,000 or more. Using a variety of solicitation methods, donors should be encouraged each year to move up to the next gift club category.

Reunion or Anniversary Giving
Used primarily by educational institutions, a reunion celebration is an excellent device for soliciting new or

Exhibit 6–5 Annual Campaign Calendar

Phase One—Planning

- Recruit campaign chairperson and leaders.
- Prepare case statement, solicitation, and acknowledgment materials.
- Assemble steering committee.
- Set goals, make assignments, and evaluate prospects.
- Approve campaign schedule of tasks and events.
- Steering committee and staff recruit general volunteers.

Phase Two—Solicitation

- Solicit gifts from steering committee.
- Solicit gifts of $1,000 and more through personal solicitation and President's Circle special events.
- Solicit gifts of $500 to $999 through volunteer solicitation and Hurst Society events.
- Solicit lower giving categories using direct mail or telemarketing programs.
- Arrange public announcement of campaign—goal, gifts received to date—at an event and in organization's publications.
- Continue direct mail and telemarketing programs for all levels of gifts.

Phase Three—Recognition

- Acknowledge gifts and pledges promptly. Develop and implement a pledge reminder system.
- Announce successful completion of campaign—total dollars raised—in organization's publications.
- Hold special celebration dinner recognizing chairperson and steering committee members.
- Plan for honor roll listing of gift club members and donors in upcoming publications.

increased gifts. This model also can be used by organizations and institutions celebrating a special anniversary of their founding. Both reunions and special anniversaries call for different special events and are excellent public relations activities for the organizations. Structured as a mini-campaign, they follow the annual giving campaign model.

Evaluating The Campaign

As one annual campaign comes to a close, another begins. It is very important that staff and volunteers schedule a meeting to evaluate the past year's program and to make recommendations for the coming year. Those who should attend are the development staff, CEO of the organization, campaign chairperson and steering committee, and representatives of the board of directors. Every

"Shipwrecked or not, I never miss sending out my annual contributions."

Source: © Joseph A. Brown

aspect of the campaign is reviewed. To assist in evaluating the annual campaign, follow the checklist in Exhibit 6–6.

All sizes and types of nonprofit organizations engage in annual giving using some or all of the methods discussed here and in other related chapters in this book. These methods by and large have proven to be productive and profitable. The challenge for organizations and their development staff is to continually evaluate and refine these methods to increase their productivity and profitability. For additional information on annual giving, see *Donor Focused Strategies for Annual Giving*, by Karla Williams, another book in this series.

Exhibit 6–6 Checklist for Evaluating An Annual Campaign

BUDGET

1. Were expense projections accurate? Under? Over?
2. Were there any specific problem area(s)?
3. Were there any unexpected changes, situations, etc.?
4. Were there areas to cut for next year?

CAMPAIGN MATERIALS

1. Was the case statement well received?
2. Were the brochures effective?
3. Were supplemental materials—pledge cards, envelopes—easy to use?
4. Did volunteers find solicitation materials helpful? Did they suggest any changes?

CALENDAR

1. Was the schedule manageable?
2. Were any tasks omitted?
3. Did any areas need more time? Less time?

PUBLICITY

1. Was the campaign well publicized to internal publics? External publics?
2. What helped to get more publicity—campaign chairperson, event hosts, key volunteers?

3. What would you continue to do?
4. What would you change for next year's campaign?

CAMPAIGN LEADERSHIP, VOLUNTEERS, AND STAFF

1. Was the steering committee active in the campaign?
2. Were you able to recruit the number of volunteers needed?
3. Was the volunteer training effective? Well attended? Helpful?
4. Who should or should not be asked to serve again?
5. Was staff support available? Was it effective?

DIRECT MAIL/TELEMARKETING PROGRAMS

1. How did each direct mail letter do? Which were most effective?
2. Was the telephone follow-up effective?
3. What changes should be made for next year's campaign?

ANALYSIS OF GIFTS AND DONORS

1. How many new donors did you recruit? To which method did they respond?
2. How many donors were renewed?
3. How many increased gifts did you receive?
4. How many lapsed donors made a gift? To which method did they respond?

Reference

Seymour, H.J. 1988. Designs for fund-raising. Rockville, MD: The Taft Group.

Chapter 7

Using Direct Mail and Telemarketing to Build a Donor Base

Chapter Outline

- Using Direct Mail
- The Donor Acquisition Program—An Investment for the Future
- Testing and Analysis of Direct Mail Packages
- Types of Direct Mail Donors
- Donor Renewal Programs
- Upgrading Donors
- Reinstating Lapsed Donors
- Saying Thank You
- Trends in Direct Mail Fund Raising
- Using Telemarketing in Fund Raising
- Direct Mail and Telemarketing—A Winning Combination
- Working with a Telemarketing Company
- Working with Direct Mail and Telemarketing Consultants

Key Vocabulary

- Business Reply Envelope
- Closed-Face Envelope
- Constituency
- Donor Acquisition
- Lapsed Donor
- Mail/Phone Program
- Reinstated Donor
- Teaser Copy
- Telemarketing
- Wallet Flap
- Window Envelope

Using Direct Mail

There are entire books devoted to the subject of direct mail fund raising, some only on how to write the best direct mail appeal letters. A number of these books are listed in the bibliography. This chapter gives you an overview of important elements and tips to help you establish a direct mail fund-raising program.

Direct mail, an integral part of a fund-raising program, is a system by which we reach thousands of people. Direct mail can do more than just raise funds for an organization. It can also educate the public about an organization and its cause. Organizations of all sizes use direct mail to recruit new donors, renew current donors, and attract support from lapsed donors. Direct mail helps build an organization's donor base by

- Attracting new donors,
- Keeping donors informed of the organization's mission and programs,
- Nurturing a long-term relationship between the donor and organization, and
- Renewing donor support.

Keep in mind that direct mail is only one of several techniques used to raise funds. With the increasing costs of paper, printing, and postage, it remains an expensive way to raise funds. The appeal must be carefully thought out, and the budget must reflect the risk factor of any direct mail appeal—it may fail miserably, thereby incurring large expenses with no hope of recouping losses, it may barely break even, or it may be a wonderful success.

There are two factors that are of major concern when raising funds through direct mail. One is the intense competition for the philanthropic dollar today. The second is the ease in which the receiver can ignore the appeal by depositing it unopened in the wastebasket. In view of these two factors, it is important to avoid the following common errors if the letter is indeed opened (Gurin 1982, 122):

1. Inadequate Motivation. Create recipient motivation that leads from attention to interest and action. The lead of the letter should capture the reader's attention or he or she may never read beyond it.
2. Impersonal Approach. Make sure the signer has some type of connection with the recipient so that the letter can be a personal one.

3. Incomplete Planning. Second-rate planning usually guarantees second-rate results. Careful planning also can reduce the costs of the appeal and thus increase the net results.

When planning and writing a direct mail appeal, you will learn that many people have strong opinions about what they believe works best. Several popular misconceptions are (Gurin 1982, 122):

1. "An appeal letter should be no longer than one page." Statistics exist that prove that longer letters do better, meaning greater net results, than shorter letters. However, the rule to follow is that the letter should be long enough to make the case for support.
2. "This year's appeal has to be different than the one sent last year." Do not be afraid to repeat or re-phrase, though each year's letter should look different in some way than the previous ones.
3. "People don't read anything you send them." We know this is not true because of the success of direct mail fund-raising programs. However, with the volume of mail received today, people certainly cannot read everything, but they do read selectively—if you interest them. Exhibit 7–1 lists elements of a direct mail package.

Writing Effective Direct Mail

Basic pointers to follow when writing your direct mail appeal letter include the following:

1. Pretend you are writing to one person. Write from the prospective donor's viewpoint. What concerns the donor most? What do they feel strongly about? What do they want? Use current events to make your appeal timely. Make the donor feel that his or her past gift or new gift will make a difference.
2. Be clear about your basic proposition. Let them know on whose behalf you are addressing them. Tell them what you want them to do and why they will want to do that. State when you want them to do it and how they should go about making a contribution.
3. Have the letter look like a personal letter as much as possible. To do this, do not typeset the letter. Reproduce it from a computer-generated copy. Make sure the size of the font or print is easy to read. Include a date line. Indent paragraphs and vary their lengths. If possible, use a personal salutation. If you cannot, at least use "Dear Friend of the XYZ Organization." Know that a P.S. will be read so be sure you make good use of it.

To write an effective direct mail appeal, you need to plan your strategy. In the prewriting phase, decisions need to be made regarding the following:

Exhibit 7–1 Elements of a Direct Mail Package

1. Carrier envelope (window or closed, live stamp or postage metered)
2. Appeal letter (length determined by case for support)
3. Response card
4. Reply envelope (business reply envelope [BRE], no stamp, stamp)
5. Enclosure or brochure

- Who will sign the letter?
- What are the issues to stress?
- What focus will produce the best results?
- Who will be the audience?

With your strategy outlined you can now "put pen to paper." The tone used may vary from informal and friendly to serious depending on the appeal. You need to capture and hold the reader's attention. This means that the opening is the most important part of the letter. Begin with an attention grabber! Write with emotion and back it up with facts. People do not give because an organization needs money. They give because something in the letter aroused an emotion—concern, sadness, or anger. Write about the people the organization serves. Give the people names—use real people and stories if possible. Do not wait until the last page to mention money.

Develop a persuasive argument clearly, concisely, and vividly. Use simple words, not jargon. Use words that are active, concrete, and colorful. Sentence length gives rhythm to a letter. By varying sentence length, a rhythm is set that creates interest. The use of emphasis affects rhythm and interest. Call attention to pertinent phrases or paragraphs by using bullets, check marks, quotation marks, color, and photographs. Use underlining, but not too much. Almost as important as the opening is the closing—the request for action. Kay Lautman, CFRE, a well-known direct mail consultant and co-author with Henry Goldstein, CFRE, of *Dear Friend, Mastering the Art of Direct Mail Fund Raising*, says "Re-work the opening and closing paragraphs until they 'sing'" (1991).

But just how long should the appeal letter be? As mentioned earlier in this chapter, there is some debate on this matter. Keep in mind your audience. A four-page letter could be better if you are mailing to people

> **Make the appeal letter as long as is necessary to make a strong case for support.**

who may not know the organization, whereas a two-page letter may be sufficient for those who already know it. The rule, once again, is make the appeal letter as long as is necessary to make a strong case for support.

Designing the Direct Mail Piece

For a direct mail appeal to be effective, it must be opened! For that reason, the design of the direct mail package is important. This subject is also covered in greater detail in books on direct mail fund raising. The following is a checklist of items to be considered when designing a direct mail appeal.

1. Ink color
   –sets the mood
   –can be used in attention-getting devices
   –affects readability
2. Illustrations or photographs
3. The type and design of paper used
4. Envelope (important to get opened)
   –size
   –window or closed-face
   –plain, "teaser" copy, or photographs
5. Reply envelope
   –pre-printed address
   –postage paid—business reply envelope (BRE) or not
   –plain or wallet flap
6. The signer
7. Use of personalization
   –inside address and salutation
   –reference to past gift
   –reference time of last gift
   –reference programs and campaigns addressees responded to in the past
8. Enclosures
   –survey
   –request for names to add to mailing list

Once the appeal is written and designed, have more than one person proofread the appeal and review the package before it is either sent to the printer or reproduced for mailing. You will also need to decide how the appeal will be mailed. Options include first class (using a stamp, or preprinted indicia, or a metering machine) or nonprofit rate (preprinted indicia, metered, or a live nonprofit stamp). If you are using a BRE, you must first establish a business reply account at the post office, check to see if there are specific printing regulations, secure the permit required, and be sure to have funds in the account to pay for the return postage. Many organizations encourage donors to use their own stamps to save the organization mailing costs.

The Donor Acquisition Program— An Investment for the Future

There are three types of direct mail programs—renewal, upgrading, and acquisition. Renewal programs solicit previous donors to "renew" their support by continuing to contribute to the organization. This type of program serves as the foundation for an annual direct mail program. Upgrading programs are designed to not only renew donors but also to have the donor upgrade or increase their gift compared to last year's gift. However, no organization is assured that every past donor will give again or give a larger gift. That is why the need to regularly acquire new donors is so important to an organization's future. Acquisition programs are indeed developmental programs and are key to continuing to build a donor base.

Knowing how important acquisition programs are to an organization's future, one might ask why there is such difficulty in convincing the leaders of organizations to embark upon them. The primary reason is that acquiring new donors through direct mail can be the most expensive type of fund raising. Because these programs are developmental, an organization may not see any profit for up to three years. First-year acquisition programs will not raise any additional funds. The best scenario is a "break-even" one. During the second year, a small net profit may be seen. In year three, however, the organization will see increased net profits from the original pool of new donors acquired in the first year. More important than the income is the number of new donors you have added to your donor base. (See Appendix 7–A for a sample donor acquisition letter.)

Exhibit 7–2 provides an example of how a donor acquisition program works.

An organization invests in its future when it conducts an acquisition program. But before developing such programs, an organization should analyze its constituency because constituents are people, and people are prospects for support. The constituency can be identified as those who are currently involved with the organization, those who have been involved in the past, and those with the potential for some level of involvement in the future. These people hold a value for fund raising because they

---

Exhibit 7–2 An Example of How a Donor Acquisition Program Works

	Income	Cost
Year 1	$17,600	$17,600*
Year 2	10,788	1,280
Year 3	10,498	1,344
Year 4	10,716	1,408
Year 5	11,050	1,536
TOTAL	$60,652	$23,168
Minimum 5-year net	$37,484	

*Renting or purchasing mailing lists is a major expense during year 1.

can be identified as current and active donors, past donors who no longer give, or suspects and prospects who could contribute in the future.

But how does an organization get lists of people who may be interested in supporting it? Organizations can either rent donor lists from or exchange lists with other organizations whose donors may be likely prospects. For a fee, list management companies are available to assist nonprofit organizations in renting new lists and marketing their own lists for exchange. Renting lists is a major cost of an acquisition program. Arranging to exchange your list with another organization that has a list with an equal number of names is less costly. These costs are among the reasons why acquisition programs are so expensive. List management firms can be found in many of the fund-raising trade publications.

Although there are a number of risk factors associated with developing an acquisition program, we emphasize the importance of including such programs in the organization's overall fund-raising plan to continue building the donor base.

Testing and Analysis of Direct Mail Packages

An essential ingredient of a successful direct mail program is testing different packages. Possible elements to test include

- the message
- the envelope size and color
- the stationery size and color
- postage
- reply devices
- the length of letter
- the letter signer
- personalization
- additional brochure
- special enclosures

When testing, remember to test only one thing at a time, or test an entire package against a control package (one you have used successfully before). You will need to mail a large enough quantity to get a good sampling, but quantities will vary depending on the organization. Tests of direct mail packages are not appropriate for every organization. Experience doing tests of varying sample sizes will help organizations design future tests more efficiently.

A critical part of testing is the analysis of results. Make sure you code each test package so that the results can be interpreted accurately and easily. Mail the test and control packages at the same time in the same place. Keep to a minimum any outside factors that might af-

fect the test. Before changing the control package, you may want to test this same package with people from other lists. Review your results daily and weekly, charting the peak of returns and the drop off from the mailing. Consider the long-term results of the test by tracking continued donor giving during the next two years.

Analyzing the success of each type of direct mail appeal is very important for an organization's direct mail fund-raising program. Your fund-raising database management system can generate reports tracking these results (Exhibit 7–3).

Types of Direct Mail Donors

When you analyze your organization's donor base, you should be able to identify five types of donors.

1. First-Time Donor—Acquired through direct mail donor acquisition program.
2. First-Year Renewal Donor—Needs special treatment to create an ongoing relationship so that the gift will be repeated.
3. Ongoing Renewal Donor—Has given two or more years and should be asked to increase or upgrade his or her gift.
4. Special Gift Donor—Has been an ongoing renewal donor and, because of high level of confidence in organization, should be asked to do something special—bequest in will, planned gift, or a large one-time gift.
5. Lapsed Donor—Needs special attention because he or she has not given in one or more years. Donor needs to be convinced that past gifts were appreciated and important to the mission of the organization. Common terms used to describe lapsed do-

---

Exhibit 7–3 What To Track in Your Direct Mail Fund-Raising Program

1. Date sent
2. Number sent
3. Number returned
4. Average gift
5. Percentage return
6. Cumulative statistics (total received, response to date)
7. Comparison with previous year
8. Cost per mailing
9. Comparison of test results
10. Results versus expected return

nors are LYBUNT (last year but unfortunately not this year) and SYBUNT (some year but unfortunately not this year).

Donor Renewal Programs

An organization works hard to build its donor base. Renewing donor support is crucial to an organization's

> Renewing donor support is crucial to an organization's ongoing financial stability.

ongoing financial stability. A basic renewal system gives people more than one opportunity to renew their support. Through a planned series of mailings, donors are asked to renew their support as many as three times during the year. All mailings should be sent according to a timetable so that donors will have enough time to respond to one mailing before receiving the next. When developing your renewal appeal, follow what we covered earlier in this chapter pertaining to designing a direct mail appeal.

A suggested timetable for mailing renewals might look like the following:

First renewal mailing: January 11
Second renewal mailing: March 7
Third renewal mailing: May 3
Final renewal mailing: October 11

Even when using this formula, second and third renewal mailings may occasionally overlap with a donor's renewal check. Donors, like the rest of us, do not like to be reminded about a bill they have paid already. Therefore, it is very important that second and third renewal letters acknowledge that they might be crossing in the mail with a renewal check. The postscript is a good place to put this thought, "P.S. If you already have sent in your contribution, thank you—your gift and our letter have probably crossed in the mail."

The plan outlined in Exhibit 7–4 describes a strategy for first-time donors. Of the utmost importance is the ability to upgrade their giving in future years.

Upgrading Donors

In Chapter 6, you read about the donor pyramid—the simple graphic that illustrates a nonprofit organization's overall donor base. The bottom of the pyramid represents the bulk of an organization's members. Here is where we use direct mail. As you move up, the mid levels depict decreasing numbers of increasingly generous donors. At the peak are the organization's most generous supporters.

Exhibit 7–4 A Three-Year Plan for First-Time Donors

Year 1: Acquire first time gifts through general, restricted, and membership appeals. Develop strategies that will generate new gifts.

Year 2: Focus on retaining first-time donors. Develop strategies aimed at renewing the gifts at the same level. Do not be concerned with increasing gifts. The goal is to develop a "habit" of support. It is estimated that forty to sixty percent of first-time donors will renew.

Year 3: Begin to upgrade the donor. At this time, it is appropriate to try to upgrade the donor's level of giving. Develop strategies to increase support, including sending more than one appeal during the year, or asking for an unrestricted gift early in the year followed by a request for a specific program gift. Fifty to sixty percent of donors will make multiple gifts in a year.

The donor pyramid shows the tremendous potential represented by the pyramid's base. That potential can be realized only if the organization has a consistent strategy for moving its donors up through the levels of the pyramid. That strategy is known as the "ladder" that donors use to climb up the pyramid. This upgrade strategy includes the following (Blanton 1994):

- Educating donors about the mission and programs of the organization and the importance of ongoing donor support
- Acknowledging donor support
- Reminding donors of their level of support so that they identify with that level and move up and not down the pyramid
- Creating incentives and clear goals for upgrading support
- Showing donors that their gifts are effectively used to meet organizational goals. *STEWARDSHIP!!*

Steps in an Upgrade Program

The first step in an upgrade program is to review your donor file to identify a core group of donors. This group will be made up of donors who have consistently supported the organization because they care about its work. Look for amount of gift, recency of gift, and source of gift. By keeping track of the source of gift you will know to which appeal(s) the donor responded.

For example, a donor last contributed $25 to the year-end appeal, but also gave $30 in the spring for a new van to transport senior citizens and $20 in the summer to expand the homebound seniors meal program. Because last year's gifts totaled $75, this donor would be an excellent candidate for an upgrade program. If you are not able to store information about the source of gift, you would miss this individual when targeting prospects for similar campaigns.

A person's ability to give more can be identified by the following:

- the donor's maximum single gift in the previous 24 to 26 months
- the donor's cumulative annual gift for the previous year
- life-time total contributions of the donor
- size of the donor's average gift
- length of the donor's membership or support

Exhibit 7–5 provides a checklist to use to segment your donor file.

Different Types of Upgrade Programs

To motivate donors to give more than their customary $25 contribution or to respond to more than one appeal each year, you must create a structure for giving. Programs that encourage donors to upgrade their giving include the following:

Monthly Giving Programs

Establish a club for individuals who choose to make a monthly gift. You will find that many of your donors will consider giving $10 to $15 a month, which equals an annual gift of $120 to $180—a gift many of them would not consider giving at one time. By establishing such a club, you do not offend donors with the frequency of the mailings. Use the monthly mailings to this group wisely, reporting on ongoing programs and introducing new programs. Vary the signers, too.

Exhibit 7–5 A Checklist To Use To Segment Your Donor File

1. Membership or donor category
2. Recency of last gift
3. Amount of last gift
4. Amount of largest gift
5. Frequency of donations
6. Consecutive years of giving
7. Benefits or premiums received
8. Volunteer participation
9. Cumulative lifetime giving

Source: Reprinted with permission from Groman, J.E., Epsilon Non-Profit Letter, Vol. 7, No. 3, p. 2, © 1982, Epsilon Data Management, Inc.

Major Donor Clubs

This is a popular and successful way to encourage higher annual gifts. By using the file analysis to identify your file segments, you can set suggested club tiers that are within reach of each segment of upgradeable donors. Usually the minimum donation for the lowest gift club level is $100. Be careful when creating these gift clubs—do not offer excessive benefits or services because recent IRS regulations mandate that the value of goods or services received be deducted from the donor's charitable deduction. For the organization, it can also cut into the effective use of the contributions.

Cumulative Giving Programs

This type of program is more commonly used by institutions or organizations that have alumni. Specific levels are established to recognize lifetime giving. Once an alumnus reaches one level, the next level is waiting for him or her. Moving toward the next highest level is used in each appeal.

Matching Gift Programs

There are two types of matching gift programs. Many companies across the country offer corporate matching gift programs to encourage their employees to give. Companies will set formulas such as one-to-one or two-to-one in matching employee gifts. This is an excellent source of funds for many schools, universities, colleges, and a growing number of other types of nonprofit organizations. A second type of matching gift program is created by the nonprofit organization to motivate individuals to increase their gifts. When donors know that a matching gift fund will double the value of donations, the incentive to increase the size of the gifts is also doubled. Matching gift funds can be established through a foundation grant, major gift from an individual, or the organization itself.

Using Personalization in Your Appeal

Once you have identified your core group of donors, established a giving structure, and designed the appeal, it is time to decide how you will personalize your appeal (Groman 1982, 4). By making a gift, each donor already has formed a special relationship with your organization. By requesting an upgrade, you are attempting to strengthen that relationship. The more powerfully you can remind donors of their past involvement and what it has accomplished, the more likely it is that they will be committed to increasing their support.

We know that with computer technology we can use names, addresses, and personal salutations in our appeal letters. This is only the first step in personalization. Depending on what information you have in each donor record, you can include their length of continuous support, specific dates of donations, the appeals they responded to, and offices held in the organization. Always try to mention a donor's giving level with a suggestion to move to a new level or membership in a specific gift club. State how far a member is from a cumulative giving goal if you have a cumulative giving program.

Personalization also allows the organization to relate the appeal to a donor's needs and to their local community, and to explain how family and friends have been helped and will be helped in the future. Donors have a certain image of your organization and of how they fit into it. Fulfilling this image successfully is essential to their continued and increased support. Figure 7–1 lists how to move your donors up the giving ladder.

Reinstating Lapsed Donors

When setting fund-raising goals, you must also include objectives related to reinstating lapsed donors. A lapsed donor is defined as someone who has given to your organization in the past, but not during the last calendar or fiscal year, nor during the current calendar or fiscal year. Even if your goal is to raise as much money as you did last year, you will need to reinstate lapsed donors and/or acquire new donors.

> When setting fund-raising goals, you must also include objectives related to reinstating lapsed donors.

However, if your organization is like most, you will want to increase the number of gifts and dollar income over the past year. To do this you will need to both reinstate lapsed donors and acquire new donors, as well as upgrade the giving of those who renew.

Four major reasons why a donor lapses are

1. The donor feels unappreciated.
2. The donor is asked to give too much too soon.
3. The donor is asked to give too often.
4. The donor did not respond to particular appeal.

Keep in mind that of all those donors who have given to your organization for the past two or more years, consecutively, 10 percent to 20 percent will not give next year no matter how hard nor how often you try to renew their support in the coming year. However, to have fewer lapsed donors, you need to

- Nurture them.
- Listen to them.
- Act on their demands and complaints.
- Praise them for their past support.
- Let them know that you miss them.

Exhibit 7–6 lists how to reinstate lapsed donors.

Saying Thank You

The "care and feeding" of donors has three phases. They are the following:

- *information* • Inform—Educate donors about the organization, its needs, and how their support will make a difference.
- *involvement* • Involve—Encourage donors to act by making contributions or becoming volunteers for the organization.
- *investment* • Recognize—Thank donors in a timely manner and acknowledge their support publicly through the organization's publications.

Many organizations put much effort in the first two phases and then make the mistake of exerting less effort in the recognition phase. As you have read in the section

Test, Analyze, and Refine

Say "Thank You"

Use Personalization

Design A Well-Focused Appeal

Establish a Floor Value

Build A Giving Structure

Identify Core Group Donors

MOVE YOUR DONORS UP THE GIVING LADDER

Figure 7–1 *Source:* Reprinted with permission from Groman, J.E., Epsilon Non-Profit Letter, Vol. 7, No. 3, © 1982, Epsilon Data Management, Inc.

Exhibit 7–6 How To Reinstate Lapsed Donors

1. Do a mailing requesting address corrections using a newsletter or other special nonsoliciting mailing. A simple postcard can be an effective approach. Use the postcard to announce that the recipient will soon be receiving a special letter.
2. Continuously clean up your files by updating addresses, and purge those who cannot be located, are deceased, or have moved away (this is most appropriate for locally based organizations).
3. Treat the lapsed donors as a separate, special group. Send a series of personalized appeal letters stressing a different program each time and telling the donor how much good he or she has helped to accomplish with past gifts. (Note: After three mailings, 8 to 15 percent of lapsed donors should be reinstated.)
4. Once they renew, wait until the following year to solicit them again.
5. Once reinstated, do not ask them to upgrade their first renewal gift. Upgrading can begin after two consecutive years of giving.
6. Those who do not reinstate by mail should be contacted by telephone. (Note: With the correct approach, ten to fifteen percent should reinstate.)

Source: Reprinted with permission from D. Barnes, *National Fund Raiser*, Vol. 21, No. 2, December, © 1994, Barnes Associates.

Exhibit 7–7 Ways To Say "Thank You"

1. Personalized letter from CEO
2. Telephone call
3. Letters from others (president, volunteers, senior staff)
4. Personal visit (reserved for larger gifts)
5. Token-of-appreciation memento
6. Listing in honor roll of donors
7. Special events

first acknowledged by the preprinted card and then recognized by a personal call from the "top" person, which in turn is followed by a brief, personal letter from the same person making the call.

A thank you procedure is a must in any fund-raising program. People like to be thanked for their support, even though they may tell you differently. Remember that a timely and professionally executed thank you tells your donor that you know what you are doing, that you appreciate his or her willingness to support your organization, and that you look forward to a continuing relationship. Thank you efforts are cultivation efforts. You are establishing a link without asking for another contribution, but you are also getting your donor ready for a future upgrade request.

Trends in Direct Mail Fund Raising

To know what future trends may affect direct mail fund raising, one would turn to Mal Warwick, considered by many to be the "guru" of direct mail fund raising and who is the editor of *response!*, a monthly newsletter on direct mail and telephone fund raising. As we approach the twenty-first century, some trends Warwick (1992) foresees are

- There will be increased competition for charitable dollars.
- Baby boomer donors will be more sophisticated, demanding, and skeptical.
- Rising costs of postage and printing will increase costs of fund raising.
- There will be increased government regulation of direct mail fund raising.
- Donors will increasingly place a premium on known and trusted organizations.
- Donors will demand effective programs offered by nonprofit organizations of all sizes.
- Direct response technology will continue to proliferate and grow increasingly complex.
- The use of database marketing techniques will create more effective ways to use direct mail and telemarketing.

on reinstating lapsed donors, a donor who does not feel appreciated is much more likely not to renew his or her support. Therefore, it is extremely important for organizations to continue the same high level of effort throughout all phases of the care and feeding of its donors. Exhibit 7–7 lists ways to say "Thank you."

One would not use all these techniques for all your donors. Each organization sets minimum levels of gifts that warrant special attention from the CEO or board president. The important thing is to put an acknowledgment system in place so that thank you letters will be mailed within a short period—one rule of thumb is 24–48 hours. Preprinted cards and receipts are sufficient for gifts less than $100. In the $100 to $249 range, the preprinted card and receipt can be followed several weeks later by a personal letter from the president or chief executive officer thanking the donor on behalf of the organization and briefly mentioning how the donor's support makes a difference. For gifts of $250 to $499, the same procedure can be used with the addition of a personal telephone call from the chief development officer after the letter from the president or CEO, once again emphasizing how much the contribution meant to the organization. For some organizations, a gift of $500 or more signals a larger than usual contribution, which is

- Fast growing ethnic minorities will create challenges for fund raising.

Using Telemarketing in Fund Raising

Telemarketing is commonly used today to market a wide variety of services and products. It is also an effective way for nonprofit organizations to solicit contributions from donors and prospective donors because, unlike direct mail, it is more similar to a personal solicitation. Although we hear that many people do not like receiving these calls at home in the evening, telemarketing remains a very effective way to raise money for nonprofit organizations. Exhibit 7–8 lists why telemarketing is effective in fund raising.

Establishing a Telemarketing Program
Organizations need to evaluate what resources they have at hand when developing a telemarketing program. Does the organization have

- facility and equipment for phoning?
- core of volunteers who will call?
- staff who can train and monitor callers?
- technology that can generate the different types of materials needed for telemarketing?

If an organization can answer "Yes" to these questions, it has the ability to establish its own program using a volunteer caller program. Likewise, if an organization answered "No" to any of these questions, it should consider using one of a number of professional telemarketing companies working with nonprofit organizations, schools, and universities today. How to work with this type vendor is discussed later in this chapter. Exhibit 7–9 lists the steps involved in developing a telemarketing program.

What You Need to Get Started

Data and Materials
Before embarking on a telemarketing program, it is extremely important that your records are accurate. Your results will be affected if you are unable to reach a large number of your prospects. The data your callers need should include name, address, telephone number, previous giving, and special affiliations such as gift club membership, class year, parent, or special interests.

Location
The site for phoning must have multiple phone lines and enough space, and be convenient and safe for your callers. Few organizations beyond educational institutions have designated phone center space. Usually, callers are assigned to desks throughout the office. If the organization's office space is not suitable, contact educational institutions to see if they rent space to other organizations, or contact board members and donors whose offices would be more suitable. Regardless of whether the space you are using is your own or rented, remind callers to take their materials with them, keep the space clean, and leave a brief thank you note for the deskholder.

Follow-up Procedure
All pledges must be recorded clearly and accurately on the pledge confirmation form. See Exhibit 7–10 for an

Exhibit 7–8 Why Telemarketing Is Effective in Fund Raising

- It can be used to personally reach large numbers of donors and prospective donors.
- It helps donors better appreciate how their gifts are used, resulting in increased gifts to the organization.
- It increases donor involvement by giving them an opportunity to speak to an organization's representative.
- It gathers important donor information about reasons for giving as well as data for keeping records accurate and current.
- It allows better communication with donors in times of calm and crisis.
- It allows the organization to express its gratitude in person!
- It is an excellent way for volunteer callers to become more involved with the organization, see the organization's needs more clearly, and become better donors themselves.

Exhibit 7–9 Steps Involved in Developing a Telemarketing Program

- Identify prospects to call.
- Enlist callers.
- Find site.
- Produce pledge cards.
- Produce support materials such as scripts and fact sheets.
- Segment pledge cards based on giving history or special affiliations.
- Train callers.
- Call prospects and ask.
- Follow-up pledge immediately and through a regular reminder system.
- Give appropriate thanks.
- Report results.

Exhibit 7–10 Pledge Confirmation Form

Jane Smith, '81
555 Oak Drive
Milton, MD

Home (301)555-8963
Work (202)555-4972

GIVING HISTORY:

Date	Amount	Fund	Type
11/01/83	$25.00	Annual	Cash
11/05/90	$100.00	Annual	Pledge Pay
02/27/92	$100.00	Annual	Cash
01/08/93	$100.00	Annual	Pledge Pay
10/20/95	$500.00	Bldg	Pledge Pay

Total Given: $825.00
Largest Gift: $500.00
Latest Gift: $500.00

☐ Pledge $ _____   Matching Gift $ _____
☐ New Donor/Increased
☐ Will give (Unspecified)
☐ Undecided
☐ Refused/Reason_____
☐ Do Not Call
☐ Sent Gift Earlier
☐ Send Information

☐ Mastercard   ☐ Visa   ☐ Discover
_____ / _____ / _____ / _____

Exp. Date _____ / _____

CALL RECORD

Caller	Date/Time	Comments

NEW ADDRESS   ☐ HOME   ☐ BUSINESS

_____

Telephone _____

OFFICE USE ONLY

Entered on _____ By _____

Mailed on _____ By _____

Washington College of Law
The American University
4400 Massachusetts Avenue, NW
Washington, DC 20016–8084
(202)885–2609

Thank you for your pledge of $ _____ to the Annual Appeal made on _____.

Your participation and your support are greatly appreciated. _____
Caller

My employer will match my gift. The matching gift form ☐ is enclosed/ ☐ will be sent later.

Please send your check payable to the
Washington College of Law by April 30.
☐ Mastercard   ☐ Visa   ☐ Discover
_____ / _____ / _____ / _____
Exp. Date _____

Contributions are deductible for income tax purposes to the extent provided by law.

Source: Courtesy of American University, Washington College of Law.

example. The bottom part of the form is sent to the donor the following morning, and the top part of the form is used to record the pledge and any updated donor information on the system. Using a tally sheet each evening is a convenient way to double-check totals. For all large pledges and for any questionable pledges, have someone else re-call the donor immediately to thank him or her for the specific pledge amount. Check all pledges and responses six weeks later.

Establish a reminder system that will mail reminders at least every 30, 60, and 90 days to those pledgees who have not yet fulfilled their pledge. Some reminder systems are more frequent, using a four-, eight-, and twelve-week schedule. Either will significantly increase your fulfillment rate by 30 to 50 percent. Use the reminder to once again thank the donor and include a reply card and envelope.

Setting Goals

As with any fund-raising program, you must establish goals for your telemarketing program. In doing so, understand the need and urgency for funds, review past successes of the program, and note any special circumstances that will affect results such as a challenge grant, new organizational leader, or special opportunity. Look at each donor segment individually and build each segment's goal separately—current donors, lapsed donors, non-donors.

How many calls must you make? Some rules of thumb to consider are the following:

- Effective callers will dial 50 numbers during each two-hour session.
- Effective callers will reach 25 to 30 prospects each session.
- Staff members can manage 20 callers each session.

Establishing a Budget

Items to include in your budget are

- computer data conversion costs for forms and letters
- printing costs—forms, letterhead, envelopes, etc.
- telephone costs
- food and amenities for volunteers
- salaries for paid callers
- postage

Recording Results

Statistics are critical when evaluating the success of your telemarketing program. First, you must track the individual results of each of your callers. See Exhibit 7–11 for a checklist of items to include on the nightly tally sheet for individual callers to be totaled for the night's results.

Keep a record each year of the number of calling nights held and program totals from each category. That way you will be able to set realistic and attainable goals for the next year's program.

> Statistics are critical when evaluating the success of your telemarketing program.

Using Volunteer or Paid Callers

The length of time your telemarketing program will run is a major determining factor regarding whether you should use volunteer or paid callers. Programs that use volunteer callers are usually shorter in duration (average, two weeks) because it is more difficult to get long-term commitments from the callers. Those programs that run four to six weeks are best staffed by paid callers or contracted out to a telemarketing firm.

The Volunteer Caller Program

Your first task will be to find volunteers who agree to participate in the telemarketing program. If you know of volunteers who have done this before, be sure to ask them again. You may even need to hold a "recruitment phonathon" to get more callers. As was discussed in previous chapters, it is very important to give your volunteers the proper recognition and appreciation they deserve. Giving them the tools to be successful is also extremely important.

Once you have commitments from your volunteers, schedule training sessions that provide opportunities for them to practice making calls using the prepared script. A training session can be held either before the start of the telemarketing program or at the start of each night's calling. The training should include the following:

- the case for support
- the reason for the call
- specific procedures regarding how someone can make a gift

Exhibit 7–11 Statistics Checklist

1. Name of caller
2. Number of calls made
3. Number of pledges received
4. Number of dollars pledged
5. Number of unspecified pledges made
6. Number of refusals
7. Number of non-contacts (bad addresses and telephone numbers)
8. Average gift
9. Number of increased and decreased gifts
10. Number of new gift club members
11. Number of new gifts pledged

- ways to request a specific amount
- ways to overcome objections
- steps to increase last year's gift

Match up new callers with more experienced callers. Start new callers off with current donors whom you are calling to renew their support. Remember soliciting gifts is a difficult task even for the most experienced caller so you need to reinforce their experience by praising good performance immediately. Also, mix the cards so that no one gets all the non-donors; ring a bell for each pledge of $100 or more; create team rivalry; and offer special prizes. When the program is completed, be sure to send thank you letters including a report of the results to the volunteers. List their names in publications.

Like many volunteer programs, this type of program can be demanding on staff, because they will need to contact volunteers to confirm their attendance, conduct continuing volunteer training, and be a constant cheerleader and motivator to keep the enthusiasm of volunteers at the highest level.

Paid Callers

As with recruiting volunteers, you will need to interview and hire paid callers. Seek individuals who may have experience in telemarketing or who are eager to participate. Require a minimum of hours or nights per week. These callers will be paid to attend a training session, one that is more intense than the volunteer session. Evaluation and feedback are key to successful programs. Staff or hired calling supervisors need to monitor calls regularly. Callers should be critiqued with constructive comments to help them be more successful. Like the volunteers, reward good performance. Those callers who are performing poorly should be re-trained. However, those callers who consistently underperform should be terminated.

The Most Important Tool for Callers— The Script

The training session should focus on the best ways to use the prepared script. Instruct the callers that this is a tool, one that gives them the information they need to encourage prospective donors to contribute. It is always best that callers use as conversational a tone as possible when making a contact. Encourage callers to underline and asterisk those key areas of the script they need to remember when making a call. Exhibit 7–12 provides a basic script format, and Exhibit 7–13 provides a sample renewal and upgrading script.

Overcoming Objections

Even though callers have a prepared script with which to work, they will be more successful if they are good listeners. We hope each contact will be a two-way conversation so that the caller can gather important opinions and beliefs expressed by the donor that explains why he or she gives. The following are some common objections and how a caller could respond.

Objection: "I really can't do anything now."
Response: "I understand. But I'd like to suggest making a pledge now that you could fulfill before the end of our fiscal year on April 30."

Objection: "I'm busy and I can't talk to you now."
Response: "Oh, I understand. I'll call you back. Would later this evening, tomorrow, or next week at this time be more convenient?

Objection: "The only time I hear from you is when you want money."
Response: "We try to stay in touch with everyone throughout the year using newsletters and communications from the president but our annual appeal is too important to present only by mail. That's why we're calling to talk with you personally."

Objection: "I cannot afford anything because (some family or personal tragedy)."
Response: "I'm very sorry to hear that. We appreciate your past support and hope the next time you can join us in this program."

" ... SORRY. WE GAVE IN THE CAR."

Source: © Mark Litzler

Exhibit 7–12 Basic Script Format

Opening
Verify that this is a convenient time to speak.
Include an acknowledgment of thanks for past support.
Verify receipt of lead letter.

Case for Support
Highlight several things the organization is doing.
Emphasize how donor support makes a difference.

First Ask
Ask for largest target gift.
If not successful, move to "second ask."

Second Ask
Ask for next target gift level (less than "first ask").
If not successful, move to "third ask."

Third Ask
Target a small increase over last year's gift.

Closing
If solicitation is not successful, thank individual for their time.

If solicitation is successful, thank them, take down pertinent information, and verify current address.

Exhibit 7–13 Sample Renewal/Upgrading Script

Opening
Hello, is Mrs. Jones in? Hello, Mrs. Jones, my name is Jim Greene and I am calling on behalf of the American Heart Association—Montgomery County Chapter. I am calling to thank you for your past support and to tell you what your gift enabled us to do this past year.

Case for Support
(Caller should choose two different highlights to test which ones seem to be more compelling to the largest number of people.)
During the past year, Montgomery Heart

- Had dietitians and volunteers at twenty-three Montgomery County supermarkets for our fourth annual Food Festival. This year our theme was heart-healthy brown bag lunches
- Held our "Great Salt-Out Day" in area restaurants, corporate cafeterias, dining establishments, and school cafeterias, educating people about the alternatives to using salt
- Provided summer internships to ten gifted Montgomery County high school students at the National Institutes of Health through our student science program
- Helped to fund specific research such as the development of echocardiography being done by Dr. Daniel Savage at the National Center for Health Statistics

First Ask
As you know, there is still much more to be done. That's why I am calling to invite you to join our Second Century Club with a gift of $200. You may use a credit card to make your contribution directly, or make a pledge at this time. (PAUSE)

If yes—That's wonderful. Your gift will really help. Do you wish to use a credit card? Would you prefer I send you a pledge card and envelope? May I verify your address please? Thank you again. Goodbye.

Second Ask
Would you consider a gift of $150? (PAUSE)

If yes—That's wonderful. Your gift will really help. Do you wish to use a credit card? Would you prefer I send you a pledge card and envelope? May I verify your address please? Thank you again. Goodbye.

Third Ask
Then, would you consider a moderate increase over your $100 gift of last year? (pause)—$125 is terrific. May I verify your address, please? Thank you again. Goodbye.

Closing
If maybe—I'll put a pledge card and return envelope in the mail to you. May I verify your address, please? Thank you. Goodbye.

If no—We thank you for your past support for the Montgomery County Chapter, American Heart Association, and hope you will consider us once again in the future.

Objection: "I'm really angry about…"
Response: "I'm sorry you feel that way. How can I help you?

Objection: "I just sent something in."
Response: "Oh, that's terrific. On behalf of (institution's name), thank you very much for your gift."

In all cases, the caller should thank each person who had an objection for spending time speaking with him or her. Often, all a person wants is some extra attention. The telemarketing program presents an excellent opportunity to provide it to him or her.

Direct Mail and Telemarketing—A Winning Combination

In this chapter, we discussed the individual benefits of including direct mail and telemarketing in your fundraising program. Each program can produce successful results. However, combining these two techniques in a mail/phone program will significantly increase those results. This program involves a pre-call or lead letter followed by a telephone call several weeks later.

The Lead Letter

The lead letter is used to make a strong case for support. It should be signed by someone who is recognized as being affiliated with the organization, such as the executive director, board chair, president, well-known board member, or celebrity supporter. Begin with a phrase or sentence that makes an emotional connection with the reader. Then link that emotion to the appeal. Tell the reader that they will be called during the next few weeks, describe the urgency of the need, and ask for a favorable response to the call.

Making the Call

It is believed that a prospect will make his or her decision to give during the first 12 seconds. Therefore, the

> It is believed that the prospect will make his or her decision to give during the first 12 seconds.

caller should link the call to the lead letter already received by highlighting only one or two items. You will then follow a similar script as described earlier in this chapter. Describe the highest giving club and ask the prospect to join. If that level is too high, negotiate an increase over past gifts. Get a confirmed gift and payment date. Thank the donor.

Working with a Telemarketing Company

For those organizations who want to do telemarketing but do not have the space to create their own phone cen-

ters, the answer is to work with an outside telemarketing company. The telemarketing company will provide many services usually handled by the organization's staff. Even with this high level of support, a staff person needs to act as a coordinator and liaison to monitor the telemarketing program. Exhibit 7–14 provides a listing of services typically offered by the telemarketing company and the accompanying organization staff's role.

Working with Direct Mail and Telemarketing Consultants

Depending on the size of an organization and its budget, an organization may seek professional advice on its di-

Exhibit 7–14 Delineation of Staff and Vendor Roles

TASK	STAFF	TELEMARKETING COMPANY
Develop scope of program	X	X
Provide data on donors	X	
Analyze data and put it in useable form		X
Provide publications and materials about organization	X	
Draft pre-call letters		X
Approve pre-call letters	X	
Provide samples of letterhead and envelopes	X	
Print letterhead, envelopes, and forms		X
Produce, sign, and mail pre-call letters		X
Draft scripts for callers		X
Approve scripts	X	
Train callers		X
Monitor and critique callers	X	X
Prepare daily and weekly reports		X
Send out pledge confirmations		X
Send out reminders		X
Prepare final report of results		X

rect mail and telemarketing fund-raising programs. There are many people and companies who specialize in direct marketing and direct mail fund-raising such as those mentioned earlier in this chapter. Consulting firms offer a variety of services including planning, creative strategies, copywriting, database analysis and management, and telemarketing services. Fund-raising trade publications list these firms in each issue.

To find the best consultant for your organization, call other organizations to find out which companies they have used. Interview several firms to learn how each one provides its services to its clients. As with all contracts, have your legal representative review it before signing it.

References

Blanton, Carol. 1994. Building the upgrade ladder. *Grassroots Fundraising Journal* 13, no. 3: 9.

Groman, John. 1982. New techniques for upgrading donors. *Epsilon Non-Profit Letter* 7, no. 3.

Gurin, Maurice. 1982. *What volunteers should know for successful fund raising.* Lanham, Maryland: University Press of America.

Lautman, Kay, and H. Goldstein. 1991. *Dear Friend: Mastering the Art of Direct Mail Fund Raising.* Rockville, Maryland: The Taft Group.

Warwick, Mal. 1992. Fund raising on the road to the twenty-first century. Garden City, New York: *Fund Raising Management*, January: 28–29.

Appendix 7–A
Case Study: Direct Mail Acquisition

Ronald McDonald House of New York

This package was created by Lautman & Company, an award-winning direct mail fund-raising firm with offices in New York City and Washington, DC.

This prospect package for Ronald McDonald House of New York was used to successfully build their donor file from under 2,000 to 24,000. While most prospect mailings expect to just break even or lose money, this package continues to net a small profit whenever mailed.

It is a simple, two-color package (black and red and tints of red) which includes a four-page letter, a contribution card bearing the donor's name and address, and a postage-paid reply envelope. Two photo cards, designed to look like black and white snapshots with handwritten captions on the back of each, are also included in the package.

The letter is easy to read, friendly, and personal. The lead creates immediate interest, beginning with an excerpt of a letter from an anxious parent whose child has been diagnosed with cancer. The lead, placed before the salutation, states the problem and sets the stage for the solution.

After the salutation, the copy moves immediately into telling the reader what the parents and child would have faced if there was no Ronald McDonald House for them to come to in New York while the child received cancer treatments. It quickly establishes the need for funds and asks for a reasonably sized gift of $20, explaining that the amount equates to what Ronald McDonald House charges per night for the family (as opposed to $200 or more for a hotel). Thus, the $20 gift size is not arbitrary, but meaningful.

This letter uses a P.S., which is one of the most important elements of a direct mail package, almost as important as the lead. The P.S. attempts an upgraded gift by showing the full cost to Ronald McDonald House for one night, which is well over $20.

The letter is four pages long and every page contains interesting, case-building information. Facts are included, but it is a human-interest package and not an institutional package. In other words, it is more about the families served than it is about the institution providing the services. Artwork is child-like and appropriate to the organization.

Ronald McDonald House
The Children's Oncology Society of New York, Inc.
405 East 73rd Street
New York, NY 10021

To Ronald McDonald House, New York:

Our little girl Lisa, just four years old, was diagnosed with cancer a few days ago. We have been up night after night worrying about her, and how we will be able to pay for the treatment she needs to save her life.

We want her to have the best care possible, and her doctor says a special treatment at Memorial Sloan-Kettering Cancer Center in New York is working miracles. We want a miracle for Lisa. But we don't know how we can afford to stay in New York for so many weeks, yet we cannot send her there all by herself. We heard you could help people like us. I don't know how else we'll be able to do this for Lisa.

Will you have room for us next week?

Dear Friend,

Letters like this can break your heart, but we get them all the time. Sometimes, when we're full, we have to say "no". This time, fortunately, we had room for Lisa and her mother.

Before the New York Ronald McDonald House was here to turn to, parents like Lisa's would have been on their own. They would have had to stay in expensive hotels, or find a temporary apartment to rent. Some would be forced to sleep on hospital chairs or cots. And some would have to send their frightened children to New York to undergo painful treatments alone... long, lonely days and nights away from mommy and daddy.

It was out of this great need that our House was born. And the compassionate generosity that keeps it open is what makes us "The House That Love Built."

And as you'll see, love is exactly what greeted Lisa and her mother when they arrived here a few days after we received their letter.

Lisa's first chemotherapy appointment was early the next morning. She would need chemotherapy 10 times a month for a year. The treatments would consume hours a day, and leave Lisa too sick to travel back and forth to her home, but not sick enough to be hospitalized.

Lisa and her mother would stay at Ronald McDonald House several times during the next 12 months. And slowly, as their terrifying ordeal became a courageous routine, <u>this House became a home</u>.

Like all guest families, they shopped for their own groceries and cooked their own meals. In the afternoons, when she felt up to it, Lisa played in the backyard, or watched cartoons in the living room. There were birthday parties and bingo games, books to read and videos to watch.

Most of all, there was <u>the strong support of other families</u> at the house -- both children and grown-ups -- who understood exactly what Lisa and her mother were going through, because they were going through it, too.

"If we didn't have Ronald McDonald House," Lisa's mother later told me, "I don't know what we would have done."

Over 3,500 children like Lisa have passed through the doors of the New York House in the past 10 years. Some have won their fight with cancer, and some have lost. But all were able to struggle together, in an environment of comfort and support no hotel could possibly provide.

That is why I'm writing to you today... to ask you to join FRIENDS OF RONALD McDONALD HOUSE to help us continue providing a supportive "home away from home" for families fighting cancer.

Here, at Ronald McDonald House, we serve children from all over the world and throughout the United States who come to New York's 12 renowned cancer research hospitals. **<u>Over 75% of the children who stay with us are here for treatments not yet available anywhere else in the world</u>**; as a result, **<u>last year we cared for children from 36 states and from 45 countries around the world</u>**. What doctors learn from their treatments helps young cancer patients everywhere.

Our Ronald McDonald House is a project of the Children's Oncology Society of New York. In 1978, we opened on East 86th Street in Manhattan with enough room to help most of the families who brought their children to New York for cancer treatment.

This past year, we moved into a much larger House on East 73rd Street. With room for 84 families, it is **the largest Ronald McDonald House in the world**, as well it has to be. <u>You see, New York is the number one destination of children and families struggling to overcome cancer, and miraculous treatment advances are bringing more families here than ever</u>.

And families invaded by cancer have unique needs that can't be met by hotels, hospitals or other ordinary short-term accommodations.

* Fighting a life-threatening illness... they need understanding and support.

* Referred to specialized hospitals far from home... they need a sensitive place to be together.

* Incurring huge expenses and great disruption to their

everyday lives... they need an affordable place to stay.

   * Undergoing painful and time-consuming treatments... they need
     privacy and dignity.

   Our House provides all these things, in a setting as close to a
real home as possible. Staff is at a minimum. There are no "white
uniforms" allowed. Parents shop for their own groceries and prepare
their own meals which saves a fortune compared to eating in Manhattan
restaurants.

   <u>And the best part of all is, we charge only $20 a night</u> -- about
10% of an average New York hotel room (a fee we waive whenever a family
can't afford it).

   Our 84 rooms provide visiting families with affordability,
convenience, privacy and a supportive environment that enables them to
focus all their energies on the critical task of getting well.

   There is, quite simply, no other place like it anywhere in New
York. Ronald McDonald House is not a hotel, inn, hospice, convalescent
home, or dormitory. (In fact, when we applied for a New York City
permit, an entirely new category had to be created just for us.)

   We call it "The House That Love Built." The reason is that
nowhere is love more abundant, needed, or meaningful.

   Love is visible here every minute of every day. In a five-year-
old patient telling his new friend not to be afraid. In a teenage girl
helping out in the office while her mother and brother are at the
hospital. In a group of parents from different parts of the world
finding the words to overcome language barriers to give each other
support.

   There are dozens of reasons why the House is worthy of your gift
of $20, $40, $60 or more, and why it's the only real option for
families facing cancer. If you were in their shoes, you'd understand
why:

Cancer in children can be devastating.

   With nearly 8,000 new cases and 1,500 deaths a year, cancer is the
chief cause of death by disease in children ages 1 to 14. (Some of our
guests are just two months of age.) Treatments have a high success
rate, but are not widely available in local hospitals. As a result,
families must travel great distances to cities far from their homes,
jobs, schools, and friends.

Most children fighting cancer do not stay in hospitals.

   That's because pediatric oncology treatments, mostly chemotherapy,
are <u>outpatient</u> treatments. Children are treated in the morning, remain
under observation during the afternoon, and leave in the evening.
Hospitalization is usually not necessary, and as we all know,
prohibitively expensive.

Hotels are not a solution.

At $200 a night and up, New York hotels are expensive, especially for stays of weeks or months. More important, children undergoing chemotherapy and other treatments suffer serious side effects. One child describes it as "like having the flu ten times over." Hair loss, endless nausea, weakened immune systems, weight changes and the inevitable fear -- these are not conditions to suffer in an anonymous hotel room in an overwhelming city.

Togetherness speeds recovery.

A room at Ronald McDonald House helps children fight for recovery as hard as they possibly can. <u>It can also increase their chance of winning</u>, because research has shown that positive surroundings are an important part of the recovery process. Doctors advise keeping families together during therapy because it increases the cure rate, and eases the pain and suffering caused by the disease and its treatment. Our House makes that possible.

All of this makes Ronald McDonald House not only unique, but absolutely necessary.

Without our House, most parents of children with cancer would have nowhere else to turn. Your gift will enable us to be here for as many of them as possible... to keep our rooms available at the affordable rate of just $20 a night, even though it costs us $120 per family a night... and to waive part or all of this fee for families in severe financial need.

Where else could your gift of $20, $40 or $60 buy so much hope... support... gratitude... and love?

<u>As you've read this letter, a child somewhere in the world has been diagnosed with cancer. His parents are about to embark on a frightening journey to Memorial Sloan-Kettering or another New York hospital. Chances are they'll be referred to Ronald McDonald House.</u>

With your help, we'll be here for them. We'll give them a place to stay, a source of support and compassion, and a chance to direct all their energies to the one thing that matters most of all: getting well.

Please join FRIENDS OF RONALD McDONALD HOUSE today. And on behalf of the children and parents your gift will help, I thank you.

Sincerely,

Vivian Harris

Vivian Harris
President

P.S. Even though our $20-a-night fee covers just 17% of our costs of $120 a night to house each family, we're committed to helping as many families as possible. If you can join our FRIENDS program with a gift of $20 or more, we'll send you our quarterly newsletter through which you'll get to see how <u>much</u> your gift helps. If you are able to give the full $120 it costs us to support a family for a night we will be especially grateful.

A copy of our latest financial report is available from this office or from the NYS Department of State, Office of Charities, 162 Washington Avenue, Albany, NY 12231.

104   FUND RAISING BASICS: A COMPLETE GUIDE

Ronald McDonald House

Dear Vivian,

    Yes, I want to join FRIENDS OF RONALD McDONALD HOUSE to give an affordable, compassionate "home away from home" for children with cancer and their families. I contribute:

❑ $20✱   ❑ $40   ❑ $60   ❑ $100   ❑ $120✱✱ ❑ Other $_____

L2C

John Q. Sample
1234 Anywhere Street
Anytown US 12345-6789

|..||||..||..||....||....|||..||..|||..||....||..||..||..|

*A room at our House costs a family just $20 a night — but it costs us much more.

**If you can give the full $120 it costs us to support a family for one night, we'll be so grateful!

Please make your check payable to Ronald McDonald House and mail it in the enclosed envelope to
Ronald McDonald House, 405 East 73rd Street, New York, NY 10021. Your contribution is tax-deductible to the full extent of the law.

---

*Your stamp on this envelope
will be an additional contribution
to Ronald McDonald House!*

Printed on 100% recycled paper

|||| ||||

BUSINESS REPLY MAIL
FIRST CLASS   PERMIT NO. 04365   NEW YORK, NY

POSTAGE WILL BE PAID BY ADDRESSEE

The Ronald McDonald House

The Children's Oncology Society of New York, Inc.
405 East 73rd Street
New York, NY 10021

NO POSTAGE
NECESSARY
IF MAILED
IN THE
UNITED STATES

|..||||..||....||..||....||..||..|||..||..|||

Courtesy of Lautman & Company, Washington, DC.

Chapter 8
Prospect Research

Chapter Outline

- Why Research Is Important
- How to Identify Prospects
- The Prospect Profile
- Staffing and Organization of the Research Effort
- Sources of Information
- Using Volunteer Screening Committees
- Public Information
- Using The Internet
- The Role of the Development Officer
- Other Benefits of Prospect Research for an Organization
- Ethical Issues and Confidentiality

Key Vocabulary

- Briefing Report
- Electronic Screening
- On-line Databases
- Prospect
- Prospect Profile
- Prospect Research
- Screening and Rating Sessions
- Suspect

Why Research Is Important

Successful fund-raising professionals reveal that only 10 percent of their time is actually spent soliciting major gifts whereas the other 90 percent is spent researching prospects and developing strategies. For that reason, it is extremely important for an organization to allocate resources to establish a prospect research program. The importance of research and knowing something about current and prospective donors was covered earlier in the chapters on annual giving and direct mail. You will see throughout this book that research plays a critical role in every type of fund raising. Methods for researching corporations and foundations are covered in those specific chapters. This chapter focuses on prospect research that helps identify individuals who could make major gifts to an organization.

Prospect research plays a critical role in an organization's continued growth. Identifying individuals who may be interested in an organization leads to greater financial stability and security for that organization. It also offers an excellent opportunity to identify new leaders, supporters, and volunteers. Involving current volunteers in the research process allows them to assist the organization in a meaningful way, too.

Fund raising is a process that involves three simple steps: identification, cultivation, and solicitation. These steps should not be separated, but instead viewed as on a continuum. Prospect research itself is a process that uses one name to lead to another or one piece of information to lead to additional pieces of information. The purpose of prospect research, therefore, is to collect data in an organized manner on individuals and organizations who might become significant donors to a specific non-profit organization.

While conducting research, keep in mind some of the reasons why people contribute to organizations. First and foremost, people give to people, not to organizations. That is why it is important to search for connections or linkages between people. Second, people can give only what they have, not what an organization may think they have. So it is necessary to search for information that will reveal a capability to give. Finally, even if an individual knows someone in the organization and has the ability to give, people give only when they are interested and involved in a cause or organization. Therefore, it is critical to research whether an individual has displayed any interest in the particular issue, cause, or type of organization.

How to Identify Prospects

There are several ways for an organization to identify prospective donors. The best way is to first use the people and information resources already found within an organization. These resources include board members, staff, volunteers, individual donor files, and special event files. Using mailing lists of other nonprofit, trade, or professional organizations; civic and city directories; names referred by the board, staff, and donors; and commercial lists rented from national or regional organizations is also common.

In the first phase of the research process, an organization will compile a list of "suspects." Suspects are those individuals who with further research may become qualified prospective donors for the organization. The most effective method of identifying new prospects is to consider those individuals who are currently involved or were previously involved with the organization. Look for those groups who make up an organization's "family." Among them would be the following:

- board members (current and past members)
- current gift club members
- current donors
- volunteers
- alumni (graduates, former patients, clients served)
- staff leadership
- affiliated groups (professors, physicians, parents, artists, other related professionals)
- advisory council members
- special event attendees
- those known to believe in the organization's work

Use the "family" groups identified previously to start a list. Segment the list in such a way that those who are or have been most involved, such as current and former board members, are at the top. Another segment would be donors who have given over a period of years or who have recently made a significant gift. Many of the names on the list will be identified as "suspects." A "suspect" is defined as someone who may have minimal interest or involvement in the organization. It is only through careful evaluation that an organization will qualify a number of these suspects as prospects. Further evaluation will result in fewer prospects that merit in-depth research. Exhibit 8–1 provides a checklist of questions used when evaluating prospects.

The Prospect Profile

When establishing a research system, an organization must develop a prospect research profile that, in a well-organized format, lists pertinent information about an individual. Computer technology plays a critical role in organizing and tracking needed information so that it can be used effectively during the cultivation and solicita-

> **Research should be cumulative and ongoing.**

Exhibit 8–1 Checklist of Questions Used When Evaluating Prospects

1. Does this person have strong ties to the organization?
2. Is this person linked in some way to the organization through family or business?
3. Is this person a donor or volunteer?
4. How often has this person contributed to the organization?
5. What was the largest gift made to date?
6. To which program or service was the largest gift directed?
7. Does this person attend events sponsored by the organization?
8. If not a donor, what is the ability of the person to make a significant gift?
9. To what other organizations is this person a major contributor?
10. How interested is this person in the organization and in what specific area?

tion of a prospect. Research should be cumulative and ongoing. A prospect profile should be regularly reviewed and updated, and new information should be shared with volunteers and staff to whom the prospect is assigned. Exhibit 8–2 lists the types of information you should include in the prospect profile, and Exhibit 8–3 provides a sample prospect file.

Besides the profile, individual research system files should include the following:

- news clippings mentioning the prospect
- articles about prospect from internal and external publications
- copies of all correspondence to and from prospect
- memos highlighting telephone contacts
- written reports by development staff on visits with donor

When developing your list of suspects, you will discover individuals who will be good annual gift prospects at this time and not major gift prospects. The definition of an annual gift prospect versus a major gift prospect will differ according to the size and needs of an organization. A donor who contributes $5,000 or $10,000 at one time may be considered a major gift donor by a community-based organization, but is viewed as an annual gift donor by a university or hospital. It is important to remember that today's annual donors are good prospects for future major gifts. Keep them on a list to be further researched in the future. Do more in-depth research on those suspects that have the greatest potential now.

Exhibit 8–2 Prospect Profile

Basic Information:

- name, address, telephone
- occupation and work address
- date and place of birth
- marital status and family data
- giving history with organization
- cultivation contacts and organizational events attended

Internal Information:

- gift potential evaluated by peers and professional staff
- solicitation assignments and results

More Comprehensive Information To Include for Selected Prospects:

- income and assets including sources
- directorships (profit and nonprofit)
- social, political, community associations and activities
- club memberships
- special interests

Staffing and Organization of the Research Effort

Nonprofit organizations of all sizes need to conduct research so that staff and volunteer efforts can be focused more effectively. Keep in mind that the president, executive director, and/or board chairperson should devote a majority of their time to the cultivation and solicitation of major gift prospects identified through research. The issue of how to find time for research is very common in nonprofit organizations. Many believe that unless a staff person can spend a significant amount of time doing research, it is not worth getting started. However, as is often the case, an organization already may be doing research but does not realize it because there is no formal procedure for collecting and compiling data. Many times nonprofit staff will see their donors' names in the newspaper, trade publications, or regional magazines. They may cut them out and bring them to the office, but then where should they be filed? How often does a staff person read through a listing of donors and sponsors in a program book to see if they see familiar names? Without realizing it, the research process is underway!

The question of who is responsible for doing research can be more complicated depending on the size of the organization. Certain routine tasks can be assigned to staff, depending on the experience of staff persons, or to volunteers. Training is important to ensure that research

Exhibit 8–3 Sample Prospect File

CONFIDENTIAL
EMIL J. GAUMONT (BA '78)
416836946

POSITION AND FIRM
President
Signet Communications, Inc.
Five Lanai Boulevard
Palo Alto, CA 94301
(415) 332-1984

RESIDENCE
3672 Grinnell Avenue
Palo Alto, CA 94312
(415) 665-8913

EDUCATION
B.A. Kogod School of Business, American University, 1978

PERSONAL/FAMILY HISTORY
born July 2, 1954
married Kathy Gaumont (B.A. Education, American University, 1979)
children Adam Gaumont - 11 years old; Ryan Gaumont - 9 years old

PROFESSIONAL/FINANCIAL INFORMATION
President, Signet Communications, Inc.
  Business: Telecommunications - Internet
  Sales: $3 million in 1994 (Dun & Bradstreet)
  Employees: 35

NONPROFIT AFFILIATIONS
Chairman of the Board, San Francisco Chapter, American Cancer Society
Member of Young Presidents
Trustee, Palo Alto Lutheran Church

AMERICAN UNIVERSITY RELATION
Alumnus

AMERICAN UNIVERSITY GIVING
President's Circle Member ($1000)

AMERICAN UNIVERSITY INTERESTS
Speaker, Kogod Business Roundtable

NOTES:
Visited by Dean Jones, Kogod College, and Development Officer, John Sherman - 2/23/96
Expressed interest in getting more involved with AU; agreed to participate in Kogod Business Roundtable program in San Francisco

Prepared by: Diane Pace, 5/1/96

Courtesy of American University Development Office, Washington, D.C.

is conducted and compiled in a consistent fashion. However, in many nonprofit organizations, the fund raiser is the staff person responsible for conducting research. This is the case because the fund raiser is able to review and evaluate information on specific prospects much better than some administrative support staff or volunteers. The fund raiser further plays a critical role by contributing new and updated information to the profile based on meetings and telephone calls with the prospect or individuals who have information on that specific prospect. (See the section on The Role of the Development Officer later in this chapter.) Volunteers also are key to providing information on suspects, which also will be covered later in this chapter.

College and universities are an excellent resource for those organizations just beginning to organize a research program. Educational institutions often have the most sophisticated research efforts because of the number and size of the capital campaigns they conduct. This was certainly true for co-author Barbara Kushner Ciconte when she joined the staff of American University in the mid-1980s as the university was planning its $100 million centennial campaign. A separate research department was created with two full-time staff persons and one part-time staff person to research and identify major gift prospects for the centennial campaign. The research department also tracked progress on prospects assigned to fund raisers and volunteers.

Sources of Information

Sources of information that are appropriate for an organization's goals and budget need to be identified and selected. Some sources will be readily available within the organization. As mentioned earlier, these include records and files on current and past board members, current donors, lapsed donors, people who have attended special events, and participants in the organization's programs. Personal contact by telephone or meetings can offer valuable information, too. Member and alumni surveys are also useful tools in gathering specific information needed.

An organization needs to establish a budget for publications. A good place to start is to subscribe to various newspapers, magazines, and professional-type journals and publications. This is where you will get the most recent information on prospective donors. Another excellent resource is the Foundation Center, an independent national service organization that provides an authoritative source of information on foundation, corporate, and individual giving. Reference Collections operated by the Foundation Center are located in New York, San Francisco, Washington, DC, Cleveland, and Atlanta. (Addresses for these collections are listed in Appendix 8–A.) Cooperating collections located in libraries, community foundations, and other nonprofit agencies

across the country provide a core collection of Foundation Center publications and supplementary materials. Special directories and publications that are the most helpful may be purchased on an annual basis and added to an organization's research library. Telephone books from major U.S. cities and zip code directories from the U.S. Postal Service are good to have in the research library, too.

The Foundation Center also offers nonprofit organizations membership in its Associates Program, which is a comprehensive fund-raising information service. Staff members from the Associates Program have access to all of the significant fund-raising research publications, electronic databases, and other resources to help organizations seek information on corporate and foundation giving, individual donors, and grantmaking public charities. They are experienced researchers who can be viewed as an extension of the organization's staff. The annual membership fee, which is currently $495, includes a reference service that is accessed by calling a toll-free number for up to ten calls a month, access to the Foundation Center's grantmaker updates, complimentary publications upon joining the program, and customized computer searches priced on the basis of the number of grant and/or grantmaker records.

Computer technology plays an important role in prospect research with on-line services such as Knight-Ridder Information, formerly DIALOG, and LEXIS-NEXIS, that offer subscribers access to thousands of publications. The Internet is also a wonderful resource tool. A number of companies now provide services that research and identify potential prospects through a process of electronic screening. These topics are covered later in this chapter.

Appendix 8–B provides information on how to research government sources of funding.

Using Volunteer Screening Committees

The main purpose of the screening committee is to classify or "rate" prospects according to general giving capabilities. A second purpose is to involve volunteers in a meaningful way that heightens their own level of involvement with the organization. During the initial screening, the primary task is to evaluate an individual's resources or capability to give rather than his or her interest in the organization or ways to involve the individual in the organization.

Screening and rating sessions, as they are called, are usually held in a group. The session, conducted by an experienced staff person, should be businesslike and held in a comfortable environment. Refreshments should be served. When recruiting volunteers to participate, it is important to inform them that their anonymity will be respected. At the session, the group as a whole should decide the best way to proceed. Other issues related to screening and rating sessions are covered in Chapter 9. Exhibit 8–4 lists elements of a screening and rating session.

Exhibit 8–4 Elements of a Screening and Rating Session

During the session:
- Participants are provided with suspect lists including pertinent home and business addresses, giving history for donors, and volunteer and board involvement.
- A broad range of giving levels such as $5,000, $15,000, $25,000, $50,000, $100,000, and $250,000 is used to evaluate suspects.
- Each session lasts one to two hours with a follow-up meeting scheduled later.
- Participants evaluate only those suspects they know or of whom they have knowledge.
- Participants may add or delete suspects as desirable.
- Confidentiality of participants' work is respected.

Key to the success of the volunteer screening committee is matching each participant with a specially tailored suspect list to review. Certainly, an organization cannot compile lists of individuals whom each participant is assured to know. However, some ways of tailoring the list include segmenting them by the following:

- region, state, city, and community
- occupation or profession
- class year or academic major for alumni committees
- parents for independent school committees

Public Information

As mentioned earlier in the chapter, there are many sources of information that are available to the public either at public libraries or at the Foundation Center and its affiliated libraries. Helen Bergan, the former chief of the biography division of the District of Columbia Public Library, shares in her book, *Where the Money Is*, (1992) a comprehensive listing of the many resources that are available to help nonprofit organizations. A number of these resources also can be accessed using CD-ROMs, on-line databases, and commercial services, which are discussed later in this chapter.

Library resources can be divided into the following categories:

- Biographical, such as *Who's Who in America*, *Current Biography*, and *Dictionary of American Biography*
- Professional Directories, such as *Martindale-Hubbell Law Directory* and *Who's Who* directories by profession
- Newspapers and Periodical Indices, such as *Business Periodicals Index* and *Reader's Guide to Periodical Literature*

Computer On-line Databases

Professional librarians and information specialists used to be the only ones to do research using on-line databases. But now, the on-line industry has become a major resource for development offices across the country. All that is needed is a computer, modem, communications software, and a system password. Keep in mind that many of these databases are available to users only for a fee. Exhibit 8–5 lists computerized databases.

> The on-line industry has become a major resource for development offices across the country.

LEXIS NEXIS/Mead Data Central

Many prospect researchers use on-line databases to access information in magazines, newspapers, news wires, newsletters, and government and electronic publications. LEXIS NEXIS began as LEXIS, which was the first commercial full-text legal information service to help those individuals in the legal profession research the law more efficiently. NEXIS is primarily a full-text news and business information service. Because of the cost, it is best to think of NEXIS as an expensive news service that should be used only when other hard copy and on-line resources are exhausted. The typical cost for searching for a name and retrieving all the relevant information varies between $30 and $100.

Knight-Ridder Information

Formerly known as DIALOG, Knight-Ridder Information is one of the better known bibliographic retrieval services and has more than 400 databases. Many of the databases on Knight-Ridder are electronic versions of

Exhibit 8–5 Computerized Databases

Library Research Services
Knight-Ridder Information
CDP Technologies, Inc.

Full-Text Retrieval Services
Dow Jones News/Retrieval Services, Inc.
Mead Data Central
Data/Times

Government Sources Online
Federal Assistance Program Retrieval Service (FAPRS)

Source: Reprinted with permission from M.D. Scott, "Using Online Databases for Prospect Research," *Fund Raising Management*, October, 1995, p. 45, © 1995 Hoke Communications.

printed references, such as *The Foundation Directory, Dun and Bradstreet's Million Dollar Directory, Standard & Poor's Registers*, and *Marquis Who's Who* directories. The start-up fee is $295, which gives you everything you need to get started including credit for $100 worth of on-line connect time, to be used within the first 90 days. An annual service fee of $75 keeps your password active. It is possible to search for databases using key words, location of grantmaker and recipient, names of officers, amount of grant, assets, limitations, purposes, and activities.

To make searching easier, use DIALINDEX first to identify databases with information on your subject. If the search "Gerald Hattlet" appears in the National Newspaper Index and not in the Magazine Index, this crucial information can be retrieved through the use of DIALINDEX before accessing the more expensive individual subject files. This technique is very helpful because costs will vary depending on the database, beginning at $1.00 a minute. Exhibit 8–6 provides a sampling of Knight-Ridder files used for prospect research.

Compact Disclosure

This database, which is available on CD-ROM and through Knight-Ridder Information, allows an organization to have unlimited access to all SEC filings of publicly held companies. The *Disclosure SEC Database* gives

---

Exhibit 8–6 Sampling of Knight-Ridder Files Used for Prospect Research

Database	File Number
American Business Directory	15
Biography Master Index	287
Corporate Affiliations	513
DIALINDEX	411
DIALOG Company Name Finder	416
D & B Dun's Electronic Business Directory	515
Disclosure Database	100
Encyclopedia of Associations	114
Financial Times Full Text	26
Marquis Who's Who	556
Moody's Corporate News—US	555
National Newspaper Index	211
SEC Online	541, 542, 543, 544
Standard & Poor's Register— Biographical	526
Time Publications	746

Source: Reprinted with permission from M.D. Scott, "Using Online Databases for Prospect Research," *Fund Raising Management*, October, 1995, p. 45. © 1995 Hoke Communications.

---

both current and historical financial data including the names of (1) all corporate officers, (2) all directors, (3) all owners, (4) all individual owners with holdings greater than approximately 5% of outstanding shares, and (5) all institutional owners; it also gives the salaries of top executives. Also, company names may be searched using subsidiary and cross-reference (former) words in name commands. Company records may be located according to financial information such as earnings per share ratio, geographic location (city, state, and ZIP code), Standard Industry Classification Code (S.I.C.), number of employees, or by key terms in the president's letter or management discussion text found in annual reports to stockholders.

Information on CD-ROMs

Chapter 4 discussed how CD-ROMs are helpful to an organization's development efforts. Because of its ability to store huge quantities of information, many research resources can be found on CD-ROM. Telephone, address, and ZIP code directories can be found on CD-ROM. Corporate information such as that found in *Standard & Poor's Register of Corporations, Directors, and Executives* is also available. A new research tool available on CD-ROM is BoardLink by the Taft Group. This CD-ROM includes more than 130,000 names of board members of the largest 1,000 corporations, 5,000 nonprofit organizations, and 6,000 philanthropic foundations, which will help organizations determine if they have contacts with any of these individuals.

Commercial Services

In the past, to get information on-line, you had to subscribe to one of the major database vendors. Now, many of these databases are available from one of several commercial services such as CompuServe, America OnLine, and Microsoft Network. These services offer easier searching techniques, often at a cheaper rate. These commercial services not only offer useful information for research but also for networking with the advent of listservs and on-line forums. Exhibit 8–7 provides a sampling of CompuServe files useful for prospect research.

Using the Internet

In Chapter 4 we discussed some of the ways nonprofit organizations are using and planning to use the Internet. Perhaps one of the areas where the Internet is most useful is prospect research. Because there are too many web sites to list, the following are several web sites designed to provide information to prospect researchers regarding which Internet sites are most helpful.

PRSPCT-L—The Listserv for Prospect Research

This listserv provides a forum for discussion of prospect research issues. Areas of discussion include research re-

Books in Print	GO BOOKS
Business Database Plus	GO BUSDB
Disclosure II	GO DISCLOSURE
D & B Dun's Electronic Business Directory	GO DUNSEBD
Magazine Database Plus	GO MAGDB
Marquis Who's Who	GO BIOGRAPHY
Phone*File	GO PHONEFILE
S & P Online	GO S & P
TRW Business Profiles	GO TRWREPORT

Source: Reprinted with permission from M.D. Scott, "Using Online Databases for Prospect Research," *Fund Raising Management*, October, 1995, p. 46, © 1995 Hoke Communications.

"I'm very confident of the accuracy of the data generated by our new donor-profile software. It put us all in the 'least likely to make a major gift' category."

Source: © Carole Cable.

sources, techniques, ethical issues, job announcements, conference details, and management. Although information on specific donors is usually not requested or distributed, individuals will post questions about foundations, techniques for rating and tracking prospects, or upcoming conferences.

To subscribe to PRSPCT-L you must send a message to LISTSERV@BUCKNELL.EDU that says SUBSCRIBE PRSPCT-L Firstname Lastname.

To unsubscribe, send a message to the address that says UNSUBSCRIBE PRSPCT-L.

To receive messages in a digest format, send a message to the address that says SET PRSPCT-L MAIL DIGEST. To send messages, use the address PRSPCT@BUCK-NELL.EDU.

University Web Sites

David Lamb, a researcher at the University of Washington, has an excellent web site that lists Internet sites by topic and includes a brief review. To get there, type http://weber.u.washington.edu/~dlamb/research.html.

Northwestern University's web site includes a diagram of the research department and links to almost 40 related web sites. To get there, type http://pubweb.acns.nwu.edu/~cap440/.

The Internet Prospector

This monthly electronic newsletter gives tips on the best information on the Internet. People who subscribe to *prspct-l* discussion list automatically receive a copy of the newsletter at the start of each month. More information and a sampling of newsletter items are available at a World Wide Web site. To get there, type http://plains.uwyo.edu/~prospect.

Electronic Screening

After retrieving as much information as possible through the other techniques described in this chapter, you still may need additional information on identified prospects or need to identify additional prospects. There are a number of firms that provide these services. For a complete listing of firms, check publications such as the *Chronicle of Philanthropy*, *NonProfit Times*, or *Fund Raising Management*. The firms listed offer many services and products that can help you determine a prospect's ability to give and propensity to give, attitudes toward various causes, general interests, and in-depth biographical and financial information.

Basically, one of these firms will match an organization's donor file against a number of national databases. New information such as updated addresses and telephone numbers, estimated household income, history of philanthropy, and net worth will be added to the file. An organization can develop its own criteria for electronic analysis to meet its needs. Keep in mind that this information is helpful, but must be reviewed and acted on by experienced prospect researchers and fund raisers.

The following are some of the firms that provide these services.

- Bentz Whaley Flessner (612-921-0111) Prospect Select uses household-based demographic information and wealth indication data in its prospect analysis service.
- CDA/Investnet (800-933-4446) provides a collection of major donor information services that identify and quantify the giving potential of prospects based on stock holdings, real estate ownership, and philanthropic giving.

- Epsilon (800-221-3767) "PRIZM" is a geo-demographic market segmentation and targeting system that sorts the 36,000 U.S. ZIP codes into 40 "lifestyle clusters," each with distinct boundaries, values, consumer habits, and political beliefs.
- Grenzebach Glier and Associates (312-372-4040) "PROSPECT PROFILE" provides comprehensive electronic screening and prospect identification, and "Individual Prospect/Donor Research" in a range of in-depth profiles.
- Marts & Lundy (800-526-9005) Computer modeling is used in its "POTENTIAL PLUS" electronic screening product. The model assigns ratings based on top donor traits by combining household data with an organization's constituent data.
- SIGMA Econometrics (312-616-1099) "SigmaPROFILE" and "SigmaPRIME" identify donor characteristics unique to an organization and use data from publicly available sources in its modeling.

William J. Messina (1994), vice president for development and college relations, Spring Hill College, relates his experience using the Marts & Lundy POTENTIAL PLUS for Spring Hill College. Marts & Lundy uses commercial demographic reviews (CDRs), a computer-assisted program, wherein data are machine-matched against a historical database to analyze a mailing list. Each name is identified by a sophisticated statistical analysis to determine where a person lives, kind of car driven, magazine subscriptions, credit-card ownerships, etc. The analysis will code the constituency into lifestyle groupings based on U.S. census data (including income, education, and home value).

Spring Hill College sent a list of 10,000 names that were run through several computer screenings. The screenings look at a number of items such as past giving, whether they have an American Express Gold Card, where they live (Do they live in a "nice" neighborhood?), whether they subscribe to upscale magazines such as *Forbes*, and motor vehicle information (What make of car do they own?). After completing the computer screenings, the list of 10,000 was reduced to 3,000 of the best prospects. Next, the top 1,000 on the 3,000 list were run through another screening, Invest/Net Match, to obtain stock holdings and net worth.

The POTENTIAL PLUS program assigned a Potential Plus Rating (PPR) and a Lifestyle Category Code (LCC). Potential Plus divides the list into 33 rating segments (PPRs 1–33) based on an individual's potential (ability and willingness to be a significant contributor) if properly cultivated and solicited. The best prospects have a PPR rating of 1 to 8.

Lifestyle category codes (1–47) are neighborhood descriptions and are based on the average statistics for the area in which the address is located. The database for assigning these descriptions contains Census Bureau data

with the addition of more current market research data. The codes for each record gave Messina information such as "high income, high home values, well educated, professionally employed, married couples, larger families, high incidence of teenagers, homeowners, homes built in the 1960s" or "older, low mobility, fewer children, singles, apartments, urban areas," to name a few of the 47 lifestyle category codes.

According to Messina, a commercial demographic review program does not replace your volunteers. Volunteers are needed more than ever because you will have some names that are rated high because they live in the country club section. We all know people who live in a nice area but may not have much money. The volunteers can tell you this. The CDR was very helpful to Spring Hill College because its constituency is all over the United States. This program, along with Spring Hill's volunteers, helped the school re-identify its alumni and build cultivation programs for the best prospects.

If an organization does use electronic screening, it is extremely important that the organization have a plan for how to use the information it receives. For example, assign a manageable number of prospects that have received a high rating to development staff so that a personalized cultivation program can be designed for each prospect. Or, include the top rated prospects in a special direct mail/telemarketing program to increase an organization's annual giving. The critical thing is to do something with these data and not just have the report sit on a shelf!

> If an organization does use electronic screening, it is extremely important that the organization have a plan for how to use the information it receives.

The Role of the Development Officer

Prospect research is an interactive process. While prospect research staff members gather information from a variety of sources described in this chapter, volunteers, development staff, and CEOs need to share additional anecdotal information gathered through contacts with the prospects and/or individuals who may know the prospects. Even the most innocuous bit of information can sometimes be a lead. To ensure that such anecdotal information is not forgotten or lost, it is important to have a procedure for documenting visits and telephone calls. Using a form such as the Individual Prospect Briefing Report in Exhibit 8–8 is extremely important for the prospect research effort. Such reports should be a part of the individual's record on the organization's database. Also, Exhibit 8–9 provides a sample request for prospect research, and Exhibit 8–10 provides a reference checklist.

Exhibit 8–8 Individual Prospect Briefing Report

CONFIDENTIAL

STAFF: Ellen Taylor, Director of Development, American University Law School
VOLUNTEER: Paul England, '86

REPORT DATE:	5/8/96
PREPARED BY:	Ellen Taylor
PROSPECT NAME:	Mark Evans, '86
BUSINESS ADDRESS:	Smith, Powell & Evans
	320 S. Charles Street
	Suite 1500
	Baltimore, MD 21201
BUSINESS TELEPHONE:	301-665-1389
DATE OF MEETING:	May 7, 1996

MEETING RECAP:

Paul England (Class of 1986, Class Gift Chairman) and I visited with Mark in his office in downtown Baltimore. Paul and Mark were classmates and study group partners while in law school. They had kept in touch since graduation, getting together with their families and referring business to one another. Mark specializes in intellectual property law.

Since Mark and I had not met before, Mark spent a few minutes acquainting me with his background—where he was from, where he had gone to college, why he chose to attend AU's law school. Mark was originally from New York, had grown up on Long Island, and attended Hofstra University there. He decided to go to AU's law school because of its reputation, location in the nation's capital, and two college friends were planning to attend. I told Mark that I had, too, grown up on Long Island and that my brother-in-law had graduated from Hofstra in 1984. We talked about our shared experiences growing up on Long Island. Mark expressed goodwill towards the law school, stating that he had received an excellent education at the law school and remembered several professors he thought were excellent.

Paul explained to Mark that he was serving on the committee planning their class's tenth reunion. In particular, he was chairing the class gift committee. Mark had received information from the law school regarding the date of the reunion weekend—September 20–22, 1996—and asked what were the activities planned. Paul described the weekend's events which included a program on Law and the Internet for which continuing legal education credits would be awarded to attendees. Mark was glad to hear the law school was sponsoring such a program. He told us he planned to attend the reunion.

Paul and I thanked Mark for his previous support for the law school which was $500 a year. Paul asked Mark to consider increasing his gift this year to $1,000 in celebration of their tenth reunion. The goal set for the Class of 1986 gift is $25,000. Mark agreed to do so and also offered to solicit other classmates for the class gift.

He mentioned several other Class of 1986 members:

Aaron Fisch - in New York working for a Wall Street firm
Sheryl Deckert - in Los Angeles in the corporate counsel office for Toyota Corporation
Meredith Janson - in Chicago in the investment area, working at Bear & Stearns
Tom Moran - in Miami in international law practice
Ellen Pace - in Baltimore—not practicing law; has family wealth

Mark agreed to call each one and encourage them to come to reunion weekend and to participate in the class gift campaign. I told him I would provide him with current addresses and telephone numbers and information he could send them about making a contribution.

FOLLOW-UP:

1. Ellen will send Mark a note thanking him for meeting with Paul and herself. Include information and materials to be used for contacting classmates mentioned.
2. Add Mark Evans' name to reunion committee roster.
3. Paul to contact Mark in June to see how he is doing on his calls.

PERSONAL OBSERVATIONS:

Mark spent over an hour with us. He has warm feelings for the law school. Mark is someone to cultivate and involve with the law school. Speak with faculty he mentioned in the intellectual property area to see if there are opportunities to invite Mark to speak to students. Ask him to become an Office of Career Services mentor.

Courtesy of American University Office of Development, Washington, DC.

Exhibit 8–9 Request for Prospect Research

NOTE: Please check to see if a research file already exists on this prospect before filling out the form! Thanks!

TO: DATE:

FROM: _____   PROSPECT NAME AND ID: _____

Information Needed:

____ Address/Telephone Number Update Only

____ Biographical

____ Degree Confirmation

____ Financial/Assets

____ Giving History

____ Other

Known Information: (What do you already know about this prospect?)

_____

_____

_____

Interest: (What makes this prospect important?)

____ Past Giving

____ Employment

____ News Article

____ Family Wealth/Status

____ Third Party Contact

____ AU Event

____ Other _____

Comments:

_____

_____

_____

_____

Date Information is Needed: _____
(Please allow two to ten days from date of request)

Courtesy of American University Office of Development, Washington, DC.

Other Benefits of Prospect Research for an Organization

The focus of this chapter is to explain how prospect research helps the overall fund-raising program. However, in the process, there are a number of added benefits. They include the following:

- identifying potential leadership
- identifying potential organizational volunteers

Exhibit 8–10 Reference Checklist

NAME: _____

ID: _____

____ Research File   ____ Research Report - date _____

____ Briefing Report   ____ Database screens

____ Dun & Bradstreet's Million Dollar Directory   ____ D & B Reference Book of Corporate Management

____ Standard & Poor's Register   ____ S & P Corporations, Directors, and Executives

____ Who's Who _____ (List which volumes checked)

____ Social List   ____ Greenbook   ____ Washington '9X/Baltimore '9X

____ New York and TriState Area Directors   ____ Relational Directory (Chicago)

____ Lusk's Real Estate Assessment:

Assessed Value of Home:_____ Bought for: _____

Additional Properties?_____ (List on back, if necessary)

____ U.S. Guide to Foundations Name Index _____

(List which foundation book)

____ National Directory of Corporate Giving (Company Foundations)

Degree Confirmation and AU Participation:

Alumni: ____ Transcript   ____ Yearbook   ____ Commencement Book

Parents: ____ Student Enrolled _____   ____ Financial Aid _____

Student SS# _____

Is DIALOG search needed? _____

Courtesy of American University Office of Development, Washington, DC.

- identifying potential volunteers and corporate sponsors for special events
- focusing resources and efforts more effectively
- serving as a cultivation activity for current leaders and volunteers, which gives them confidence in the organization and in their own abilities to help raise funds

Ethical Issues and Confidentiality

The area of prospect research can raise a number of questions concerning ethical issues and confidentiality from an organization's board members and volunteers. As they review the information on identified prospects, they may ask if the organization has such a file on them and who has access to review it. It is important that the staff members answer truthfully, explaining that files containing information on individuals' involvement and giving to the organization are important for the organization and that the compilation of these files is part of a researcher or fund raiser's job. Whether or not the person was involved in the research process, explain to them that all information gathered is found in the public domain. At times an organization must convince a concerned individual that prospect research does not constitute an invasion of privacy.

To assure board members and volunteers that prospect research is being conducted professionally, an organization should establish prospect research policies and procedures. The policies and procedures should include the following:

- Security of paper and computer filing systems
  Are the file cabinets locked?
  Who has access to the files?
  Who can view a prospect's database screens?

> The areas of prospect research can raise a number of questions concerning ethical issues and confidentiality.

- Dating and marking materials "confidential"

  Do you have a stamp marked "confidential"?

  Do you date materials and mark them "confidential"?

  Do you print trip reports and other confidential material on dark colored paper so copies would be difficult to read?
- Setting up a distribution list for information

  Do you have a set distribution list?

  Do you ask individuals to check off whether they have read materials and send on to next person on list?
- The researcher being granted access to only certain institutional records

  Can the researcher have access to fund raiser files?

  Can the researcher contact volunteers directly concerning a prospect?
- Designating who does the research

  Are specific staff members assigned to do research?

  What role should support staff play?

  Should temporary help ever be used?

It is important to gather only relevant information about a prospect and not report negative characteristics or information learned through a meeting, telephone call, or from an individual who knows the prospect. To ensure that information is relevant and not negative, put your prospect research effort to this simple test. If a board member requested to see his or her file after a recent board meeting, would you feel comfortable having him or her read the file?

An important outcome of the burgeoning field of prospect research was the creation in 1987 of the Association of Professional Researchers for Advancement (APRA), an organization dedicated to serving the prospect research community. With a growing number of regional chapters, this organization holds an annual national conference as well as many regional conferences and meetings hosted by its chapters. APRA developed a code of ethics in 1992 to assist prospect researchers and all fund-raising professionals in dealing with ethical dilemmas arising in the course of their work. The code is based upon the belief that everyone has a fundamental right to privacy. (See Appendix 8–C.) For information about APRA, call 630-655-0177 or write to APRA, 414 Plaza Drive, Suite 209, Westmont, IL 60559; e-mail address apra@adminsys.com; or type http://weber.u.washington.edu/~dlamb/apra/APRA.html to access the APRA website.

Reference

Messina, William. 1994. Selecting the Best Prospects. *Fund Raising Management*, March: 34–35.

Appendix 8–A
Reference Collections Operated by The Foundation Center

The Foundation Center*
8th Floor
79 Fifth Avenue
New York, NY 10003
212-620-4230

The Foundation Center†
312 Sutter Street, Room 312
San Francisco, CA 94108
415-397-0902

The Foundation Center*
1001 Connecticut Avenue, NW
Washington, DC 20036
202-331-1400

The Foundation Center†
Kent H. Smith Library
1422 Euclid, Suite 1356
Cleveland, OH 44115
216-861-1933

To see if there is a cooperating collection in your area,
call 800-424-9836.

The Foundation Center†
Suite 150, Grand Lobby
Hurt Building, 50 Hurt Plaza
Atlanta, GA 30303
404-880-0094

Core collection consists of
The Foundation Directory 1 and 2, and Supplement
The Foundation 1000
Foundation Fundamentals
Foundation Giving
The Foundation Grants Index
The Foundation Grants Index Quarterly
Foundation Grants to Individuals
Guide to U.S. Foundations, Their Trustees, Officers
    and Donors
The Foundation Center's Guide to Proposal Writing
The Literature of the Nonprofit Sector
National Directory of Corporate Giving
National Directory of Grantmaking Public Charities
National Guide to Funding in…(Series)

*Has a complete set of U.S. foundation information returns (IRS Form 990-PF)
†Has IRS Form 990-PF returns for the southeastern, midwestern, and western states, respectively

Appendix 8–B
Researching Government Grants

Many nonprofit organizations rely on funding from the federal government to support their services and programs. Government grant support is very restrictive, requiring extensive reporting and management requirements. However, government grants can provide the largest dollar support for specific programs. Those nonprofit organizations that are successful in receiving government grants regularly keep in contact with federal agency staffs to monitor any changes or reductions in federal programs. They continuously educate public officials about the needs that those programs support while observing lobbying restrictions on nonprofit organizations.

Because of substantial cutbacks in government funding in recent years, many organizations that have received government funding now seek funds from private sources such as individuals, foundations, and corporations. However, depending on the type of nonprofit organization and the services it provides, government funding still may be available. Researching current government funding at the national, state, and local levels, therefore, is extremely important. Two primary sources of such information published by the federal government are listed in the following.

1. The Catalog of Federal Domestic Assistance (CFDA)

    This directory of thousands of federal programs, projects, services, and activities that provide assistance or benefits to the American public is a primary source of potential funds. It contains financial and nonfinancial assistance programs administered by departments and establishments of the federal government. Assistance includes, but is not limited to, grants, loans, loan guarantees, scholarships, mortgage loans, insurance, and other types of financial assistance, including cooperative agreements, property, technical assistance, counseling, statistical and other expert information, and service activities of regulatory agencies.

    To use the CFDA, look at the indexes. The Subject Index is the most commonly used index to look for government sources that would be interested in an organization's program or project. It is important to note the CFDA number that references each funding program. A floppy diskette version of the CFDA in ASCII text may be purchased from services administration by calling 202-708-5126.

2. Federal Assistance Program Retrieval System (FAPRS)

    This system uses a key-word search to match with federal grant programs; the user is provided with CFDA programs that are related to the desired grants areas.

3. The Federal Register

    Another primary source for federally allocated funds, the Federal Register, makes all government meetings, announcements of granting programs, regulations, and deadlines public. This information is available on-line via Government Printing Office access and is linked to the Foundation Center web page.

4. Commerce Business Daily

    This publication is also available on-line and announces the accepting of bids on government contracts, another source of funds for nonprofit organizations.

5. Agency Newsletters

    A number of federal agencies publish their own newsletters to inform the public about their programs and the availability of funds. Information how to apply or submit a proposal is available.

A number of commercial publications are available to assist government grantseekers with their pursuit of funds. The following are included among them.

1. *Federal Assistance Monitor*

    Twice a month, this 16- to 18-page publication produced by CD Publications (800-666-6380) provides a review of federal funds announcements, private grants, rule changes, and legislative actions affecting all community programs, including those in social services, the arts, education, and health. Each listing includes details on eligibility requirements, application deadlines, dollar amounts, and contact names and telephone numbers. The *Federal Assistance Monitor* provides updates on previously reported activities.

2. *Federal Support for Nonprofits 1996*

This annual publication by The Taft Group focuses only on those federal programs that give grants to nonprofit organizations, approximately 800 in all, and includes a listing of the actual grants awarded by each federal program. Each program description includes the following: program name; program's identification number, which allows reference to government publications; contact name, address, and telephone number; name of federal agency administering the program; description of the program; dollar range of past grants and average amount awarded; eligibility requirements for both applicants and beneficiaries; total giving by program for the most recent three years on record; application procedures and guidelines; types of recipients, with name, amount, and description; and types of assistance, from project and formula grants to direct payments on loans.

3. *Federal Grants and Contracts Weekly*

This weekly publication, produced by Capitol Publications, provides up-to-date federal announcements for support of projects in education, scientific and social research, community development, AIDS prevention, mental health, and other areas. This publication also includes a monthly supplement with information on sources of nongovernment private funds.

4. *Federal Money Retriever*

A Windows-based version of the *Catalog of Domestic Assistance* issued twice a year, this software contains information about $1 trillion worth of programs administered by 53 federal agencies. One-year licenses include updates. Limited, less expensive versions for users interested in a single subject such as housing, the arts, or the humanities are also available from Magic Valley Technologies Corporation (800-804-5270).

Appendix 8–C
APRA Mission Statement

The mission of the Association of Professional Researchers for Advancement is to foster professional development and promote standards that enhance the expertise and status of development research and information service professionals worldwide.

To fulfill its mission APRA will direct its energies to the following goals:

- To promote professional growth and advancement
- To advocate the highest standards of performance and ethical behavior
- To facilitate interaction among research, development and information professionals, and their representative organizations
- To advance the role of research in the development field
- To develop and maintain an administrative organizational plan that will support the organization

---

APRA Statement of Ethics

As representatives of the profession, Association of Professional Researchers for Advancement (APRA) members shall be respectful of all people and organizations. They shall support and further the individual's fundamental right to privacy. APRA members are committed to the ethical collection and use of information in the pursuit of legitimate institutional goals.

Code of Ethics

In their work, prospect researchers must balance the needs of their institutions/organizations to collect and record information with the prospects' right to privacy. This balance is not always easy to maintain. However, the following ethical principles apply:

I. **Fundamental Principles**
    A. **Relevance**
       Prospect researchers shall seek and record only information that is relevant to the fund raising effort of the institutions that employ them.

    B. **Honesty**
       Prospect researchers shall be truthful with regard to their identity, purpose and the identity of their institution during the course of their work.

    C. **Confidentiality**
       Confidential information pertaining to donor or prospective donors shall be scrupulously protected so that the relationship of trust between donor and donee and the integrity of the prospect research professional is upheld.

D. Accuracy

Prospect researchers shall record all data accurately. Such information must be verifiable or attributable to its source.

II. Procedures

A. Collection

1. The collection and use of information shall be done lawfully.
2. Information sought and recorded may include all public records.
3. Written request for public information shall be made on institutional stationery clearly identifying the sender.
4. Whenever possible, payments for public records shall be made through the institution.
5. When requesting information in person or by telephone, neither individual nor institutional identity shall be concealed.

B. Recording

1. Researchers shall state information in an objective and factual manner.
2. Documents pertaining to donors or prospective donors shall be irreversibly disposed of when no longer needed (e.g., by shredding).

C. Use

1. Non-public information is the property of the institution for which it was collected and shall not be given to persons other than those who are involved with the cultivation or solicitation effort or those who need that information in the performance of their duties for that institution.
2. Only public or published information may be shared with colleagues at other institutions as a professional courtesy.
3. Prospect information is the property of the institution of which it was gathered and shall not be taken to another institution.
4. Prospect information shall be stored securely to prevent access by unauthorized persons.
5. Research documents containing donor or prospective donor information that are to be used outside research offices shall be clearly marked "confidential."
6. Special protection shall be afforded all giving records pertaining to anonymous donors.

Recommendations

1. Prospect researchers shall urge their institution to develop written policies based upon the laws of their state defining what information shall be gathered and under what conditions it may be released and to whom.
2. Prospect researchers shall urge the development of written policies at their institutions defining who may authorize access to prospect files and under what conditions.
3. Prospect researchers shall urge their colleagues to abide by these principles of conduct.

Source: Reprinted with permission from the Association of Professional Researchers for Advancement, Westmont, IL, © 1996.

Chapter 9
The Use of Personal Solicitation in Major Gift Fund Raising

Chapter Outline

- The Importance of a Major Gifts Program
- Elements of a Major Gifts Program
- In-Depth Evaluation of Prospects
- How to Get Started
- Managing the Solicitation Process
- Why Major Donors Give
- Ways to Involve and Cultivate Relationships with Prospects
- The Successful Solicitation—Overcoming the Fear of Asking
- The Successful Solicitation Visit
- How to Say Thank You
- Ways to Recognize Major Donors
- Stewardship—The Practice That Ensures Future Major Gifts

Key Vocabulary

- Cultivation
- Development Audit
- Face-To-Face Solicitation
- Identification
- Research
- Stewardship

The Importance of a Major Gifts Program

For an organization to be successful in fund raising, a major gifts program is critically important. As recently as in the 1980s, experts believed that 80 percent of an organization's fund-raising support came from only 20 percent of its donors. However, results of more recent capital campaigns conducted by nonprofit organizations reveal that nearly 90 percent of the campaigns' total goals came from only 10 percent of the donors. Regardless of whether the amount is 20 percent or 10 percent, it is clear that major gifts play a significant role in an organization's success. These gifts are contributed by individuals, foundations, and corporations. In this

chapter, we will focus on major gifts from individuals. Chapters 10 and 11 cover corporate and foundation giving.

In the early years of its development program, an organization may not yet be ready to embark on a major gifts program. It is important to first establish a broad base of support using direct mail, telemarketing, and special events. These programs enable an organization to educate the public of its mission, program, and services while soliciting support. Enhanced visibility for the organization is an added benefit to the broader-based fund-raising activities. To evaluate whether an organization is ready to launch a comprehensive major gifts program, an organization should analyze its current situation including board and staff leadership, fund-raising and public relations efforts, and organizational planning and management. The development audit discussed in Chapter 5 is one way to evaluate readiness. Another method to analyze the ability to raise major gifts is to use the weighting form such as the one in Exhibit 9–1.

If an organization chooses (and it should at the correct time) to launch a major gifts effort, it is important to invest adequate time, resources, and personnel so that programs and strategies that invite major gifts will be in place. The following checklist highlights what should be in place.

Does the organization have the following?

- major donors on the board
- influential people from the community on advisory committees
- a system of gift clubs to upgrade donors
- a program to recognize donors (for example, listing of donors in publications)
- ways to cultivate donors (for example, newsletter, events, special communications)
- a compelling case for support
- a public relations plan
- a development committee focusing on major gifts
- a strategic plan

A Criteria	B Guidelines	C Score (1–3) ×	D Weight	E Total
Organization Age	1. 1–3 years 2. 3–10 years 3. 10+ years		1	
Annual Budget Size	1. Below $50,000 2. $50,000–$100,000 3. Above $100,000		1	
Percentage of Repeat Contribution	1. Under 40 percent 2. 40 percent–60 percent 3. 60 percent		2	
Program Appeal for Donors	1. Urgent 2. Urgent and cost effective 3. Urgent, cost effective, and "fashionable"		3	
Board Motivation for Fund Raising	1. None solicit 2. Some but less than once a month 3. More than once a month		3	
Amount of Publicity	1. None 2. Some but less than once a month 3. More than once a month		2	
Income Bracket of Best Donor Prospects	1. $50,000 or less 2. $50,000–$100,000 3. $100,000+		3	
$100+ Donors' Involvement in Your Programs	1. Under 20 percent 2. 20 percent–50 percent 3. Over 50 percent		1	
Donor Recognition	1. Thank you letters only 2. Special events for special gift donors 3. Special gift clubs		2	
Long-Range Plan	1. Verbal 2. Informal 3. Written		2	
			Grand Total	

Interpreting your score: 20–30 = you have poor chances of getting major gifts; 30–47 = you have fair chances; over 47 = excellent.

Courtesy of A.H. Edwards, Vice Chancellor for University Advancement, University of Arkansas, 1996.

- a budget describing programs and services that donors can understand
- materials that look professional

With a majority of these items in place, an organization is indeed ready to launch a major gifts program.

Elements of a Major Gifts Program

One cannot stress enough that fund raising is a process. It is a series of steps and actions that will hopefully lead to a contribution for an organization. This is certainly the case in raising major gifts. Therefore, the necessary steps include the following:

- Identification—First identify individuals capable of making a major gift to the organization.
- Research—Conduct research on an individual's family, background, interests, and financial situation to prioritize capability and inclination of giving.
- Cultivation—Once identified, develop strategies to involve those individuals in the organization so that they will choose to make a major gift.
- Solicitation—At the appropriate time, a specially selected individual or individuals will invite the donor to make a major investment in the organization.
- Stewardship—Acknowledge, thank, and recognize the donor's generosity. Good stewardship often results in additional future gifts.

The first two steps, identification and research, were covered in Chapter 8. In this chapter, we will focus primarily on the remaining steps—cultivation, solicitation, and stewardship.

In-Depth Evaluation of Prospects

In the previous chapter on prospect research, we discussed the methods to use when moving an individual from "suspect" status to "prospect." One of the methods covered involved screening and rating sessions using key volunteers and staff. The information shared at these sessions is used to evaluate an individual's capacity to give or current inclination to give to a specific organization. Prospect rating forms are useful tools in this process. These forms range from simple to complex depending on an organization. A common feature in all is the use of a weighting factor to distinguish which criteria are most important when determining ability to give. Exhibits 9–2 and 9–3 illustrate two different versions of prospect rating forms.

Researching and evaluating prospects can be a sensitive area, especially for the first-time volunteer commit-

tee member. Questions such as "Isn't this an invasion of privacy?" or comments that a volunteer is uncomfortable sharing information about people they know must be addressed. In

> Researching and evaluating prospects can be a sensitive area, especially for the first-time volunteer committee member.

Chapter 8, we discussed the need for organizations to adopt policies and procedures to ensure that issues of confidentiality and ethics were addressed. However, when faced with these types of questions and comments, an organization must be prepared to show how the rating of gifts plays an integral role in the fund-raising planning process. Gift rating helps by doing the following:

- Setting realistic goals for what can be raised—The process of gift rating will assess how many gifts at various levels can be anticipated and how that relates to the total of gifts needed to reach the goal. If the representation needed is not demonstrated, an organization will need to re-evaluate its goals.
- Using volunteers more effectively—By doing gift rating, volunteers can make a specific request based on research and information, which enables them to be more successful in their efforts.
- Establishing specific donor opportunities for giving—Knowing the range of gifts needed, an organization can establish different opportunities for support to meet the needs and interests of donors as well as those of the organization.
- Reducing the organization's cost of raising money—The more closely the staff and volunteers can come to the most appropriate level for the donor the more likely they will be successful in soliciting a gift, thereby enabling staff and volunteers to pursue other prospects according to the campaign timetable and not delaying the overall campaign.

How To Get Started

Given that an organization has now identified a pool of qualified major gift prospects, often it will seem overwhelming regarding how to begin. Chapter 14, which focuses on capital campaigns, describes how the campaign timetable dictates the schedule and program of major gift solicitations. Here we will discuss how a major gift solicitation program fits into an organization's annual development plan.

When getting started, select a manageable number of prospects (five to ten) for whom specific cultivation and solicitation strategies will be developed. Keep in mind that it could take from 18 to 24 months, up to even

Exhibit 9–2 Prospect Rating Form

> 1. Rate each prospect 1–5 in each category (5 is highest)
> 2. Multiply by "weight"
> 3. Add totals

Prospect _____

Date _____

Criteria	Score (1–5) ×	Weight	Total
Common Interest		2	
Financial Ability		3	
Commitment to Philanthropy		1	
Commitment to Our Organization		3	
Linkage With Our Organization		1	
Time Window		3	
Personality		1	
Past Solicitation Success		2	
Common Politics/Philosophy		1	

Grand Total
(Highest Score = 85)

Courtesy of A.H. Edwards, Vice Chancellor for University Advancement, University of Arkansas, 1996.

36 months, to successfully close a major gift depending on the prospective donor. Staff should designate specific time on their calendar to work with these prospects and the volunteer(s) involved in the strategy. These volunteers are specially selected because they know the prospect and the organization. They can include board members, the CEO, or other major donors. Each individual prospect should have a file that contains a copy of a research report and any other materials collected on that prospect. As the solicitation process proceeds, this file also should include briefing reports on telephone conversations and meetings. It is very important to record any and all contacts with the prospect and key volunteers. These contacts also can be referred to as "moves." This moves concept, which is designed to manage major gift solicitations, was developed and first used many years ago by David R. Dunlop at Cornell University.

As a solicitation strategy is developed, gift objectives will be identified for the organization and prospective donor. Designing ways to involve a prospect in an or-ganization—the cultivation process—needs to be a part of the solicitation plan. Later in this chapter, we will present some suggestions regarding the types of cultivation activities that are available to organizations. Keep track of the number of moves, the frequency, and by whom on a monthly basis. As solicitations are completed, new prospects from the pool can be added following the steps described previously.

Managing the Solicitation Process

Significant time and effort on the part of the development professional is spent "managing" the solicitation process. This includes keeping track of contacts and visits by the CEO, board chair, or volunteer, documenting these contacts, ensuring that the appropriate follow-up is completed, and planning the next step in the solicitation strategy. To keep up with this process, a type of tracking form or report is needed. Exhibits 9–4 and 9–5 illustrate two versions of such a form.

Exhibit 9–3 Capacity To Give Matrix

NAME OF PROSPECT—Mary Able

INDICATORS OF WEALTH	WEIGHT (col. 1)		VALUE (col. 2)		RATING (col. 3)
BUSINESS/PROFESSION	.25	×	3	=	75
EDUCATION	.10	×	1	=	10
RESIDENCE	.20	×	3	=	60
FAMILY	.15	×	1	=	15
VOLUNTARISM	.10	×	2	=	20
INTEREST	.20	×	3	=	60

1.00

240
TOTAL

DECISION FACTOR	ALPHA GIFT RANGE	ALPHA'S EQUIVALENT
270–300	A	$100,000
240–269	B	$ 75,000
200–239	C	$ 50,000
150–199	D	$ 25,000
100–149	E	$ 10,000
1–99	F	$ 5,000

INDICATORS OF WEALTH
BUSINESS—Position, ownership, evidence of advancement
EDUCATION—Private school, prep, and higher education of spouse and children
RESIDENCE—Neighborhood, street, style of house, cars, other properties
FAMILY—Parents, grandparents, in terms of evidence of affluence
VOLUNTARISM—Leadership in church, community, service clubs, etc.
INTERESTS—Hobbies, vacation sites, cultural, recreation
WEIGHTS—Determined by previous experience at generating gift income. The factors considered most important receive the highest numerical weight.
VALUES—Judgmental estimations scored on a numerical value scale: Low = 1, Medium = 2, High = 3
RATING—The product of multiplying the weight in col. 1 by the value in col. 2
DECISION FACTOR—The total of the rating column is then assigned to the appropriate numerical range under the heading "decision factor." There are six possible ranges (1–99 through 270–300) and each of these corresponds to an alphabetic code. The highest gift would be "A" where the total of col. 3, the decision factor, fell within the 270–300 range. Try it, it works.

Source: Reprinted by permission from Robert F. Semple, Semple Bixel Associates, Inc., Nutley, N.J.

Why Major Donors Give

> To be successful in securing major gifts, or gifts at any level, a nonprofit organization needs to know why people give.

To be successful in securing major gifts or gifts at any level, a nonprofit organization needs to know why people give and, especially, what motivates certain individuals to make major gifts to hospitals, universities and colleges, schools, social service agencies, arts organizations, or to any other nonprofit organization. An organization may want to collect its own data by surveying its donors regarding why they support that organization.

Several general studies conducted in the past help organizations understand the reasons why people give. Jerold Panas, a well-known fund-raising consultant, interviewed many major donors while writing his book,

Exhibit 9–4 A Simple Type of Tracking Form

<table>
<tr><td colspan="4" align="center">Sherman L. Lane
365 Mandel Road
Oceanside, New York 11755
516–221–0906 (H)</td></tr>
<tr><td>Date</td><td>Plan</td><td>Date</td><td>Action</td></tr>
<tr><td>1/15</td><td>Bob Gates to talk with Sherman Lane's sister about his interest in North Shore Hospital.</td><td>1/31</td><td>Eleanor Smith (Sherman's sister) told Bob that Sherman is in Florida now. She plans to see him in mid-February when she goes to Florida.</td></tr>
<tr><td>1/31</td><td>Bob Gates plans to speak to Dr. Hart, head of the cardiac unit, about his relationship with Sherman Lane.</td><td>2/3</td><td>Dr. Hart tells Bob he recently saw Sherman for a check-up and had a good conversation with him about the hospital. Knows Lane is appreciative of the care he got at North Shore.</td></tr>
<tr><td>2/5</td><td>Dr. Hart will set up a meeting with Lane and Gates in April when Lane returns from Florida. Meantime, call Eleanor Smith the end of February when she returns from Florida.</td><td></td><td></td></tr>
</table>

Exhibit 9–5 Solicitation Tracking Report

Prospect:
Irma Reckman
3765 Sycamore Place
Chandler, AZ 85224
602–839–2255

Key volunteer:
Jane Morgan, Board Chair

Secondaries:
Ellen Hayes, Executive Director, YWCA of Maricopa County
Marcia Stone—board member
Alicia Patterson—Y-Teen volunteer

Staff Manager:
Susan Gaumont

Gift Objective:
$10,000 for Y-Teen Leadership Program

Plan: Irma is a member of the YWCA Board of Directors; is very interested in youth and the Y-Teen program. Plan is to solicit $10,000 to fund the upcoming Y-Teen Leadership Conference.

Recent Events: 9/3—Jane Morgan and Alicia Patterson met with Irma to discuss future planning for the Y-Teen program. They briefed her on the preliminary plans for the leadership conference and the cost of the conference. Irma expressed interest in helping and asked to see a detailed budget. 9/17—Ellen Hayes and Alicia Patterson met with Irma to go over the budget and solicit ideas for community leaders to invite to participate in the conference. Irma made some suggestions about the budget.

Follow-up: Schedule a meeting the week of 10/4 for Jane Morgan and Ellen Hayes to solicit Irma for her gift.

Mega Gifts—Who Gives and Gets Them. He also surveyed development professionals to learn what they believed to be the reasons for giving major gifts. Exhibit 9–6 ranks 20 reasons for giving by major donors and gives a corresponding ranking of those same reasons by development officers. Please note this ranking is not absolute but reflects the opinions of those surveyed. Other donors and development officers may disagree with the exact order.

Several patterns emerge when reviewing these rankings. First and foremost, the organization itself is a prime motivator because the top seven reasons deal with an organization's mission, board and staff leadership, purpose, and fiscal management. Next, the level of an individual's involvement and interest in an organization is a major motivating factor as seen in reasons six through eleven. The bottom of the list includes reasons related to ways of making a gift including tax considerations, printed materials, and guilt.

It is interesting to note that major donors and development professionals did not agree in their ranking of board service and influence of solicitor, which were tied for number one for development professionals while ranked 6 and 9 respectively for the donors. One explanation for this might be that, because of personal experience, those development professionals surveyed had found those two reasons quite compelling. Another might be that although it appeared that board service and solicitor were important, this was combined with an individual's belief and respect for the organization.

It is important to have an understanding of why a major donor gives, but there is no substitute for getting to know a prospective donor's own motivation for giving.

Exhibit 9–6 Why Major Donors Give

Major Donors' Ranking	Development Professionals' Ranking
1. Belief in the mission	2
2. Community responsibility and pride	7
3. Fiscal stability	8
Regard for staff leadership	11
4. Respect for institution locally	6
5. Regard for volunteer leadership	6
6. Serves on board or official body	1
7. Respect for institution in a wider circle—region, state, nation	10
8. Adult history of involvement	5
9. Leverage or influence of solicitor	1
10. Great interest in specific project	3
11. Past involvement with personal benefit	14
12. Religious or spiritual affiliation of the institution	17
13. Recognition of gift	12
14. Uniqueness of project or institution	16
15. Challenge or encourage others	13
Actually involved in the campaign	4
16. Match gift made by others	18
17. Memorial opportunity	15
18. Tax considerations	9
19. Appeal or drama of campaign material requesting the gift	19
20. Guilt	20

Source: Reprinted with permission from *Mega Gifts—Who Gives Them, Who Gets Them*, Jerold Panas, Pluribus Press, Inc., 160 East Illinois Street, Chicago, IL, © 1984.

Ways To Involve and Cultivate Relationships with Prospects

The cultivation process is one of the most creative pieces in the development of the solicitation strategy. First, an organization should review its annual calendar to see what upcoming events, publications, and programs could be included in a general cultivation program. Next, new opportunities suited for a specific prospect need to be created. The list that follows highlights those types of events and publications that are excellent cultivation activities for groups of donors.

- invitations to special events
- open house events for donors to visit the organization's facility
- volunteer opportunities
- participation at seminars, conferences, and programs
- receptions and dinners
- invitations to serve on advisory councils, ad hoc committees, or task forces
- newsletters
- magazines and journals
- annual reports
- news clippings and press releases
- brochures

Many of these same events and publications also can be used when developing a specific prospect's solicitation strategy. Use a prospect's specific interests and skills to create other opportunities for involving him or her in the work of the organization. The following is a sampling of the kinds of cultivation activities you can create for a specific prospect:

Ask the prospect to

- Volunteer for an advisory council or special committee
- Offer advice
- Participate on a program panel
- Speak at a class, annual meeting, or special program
- Host an event in his or her home or office
- Join the board
- Attend a private dinner with the CEO
- Attend a testimonial dinner
- Accept a special award given by the organization
- Attend a special program or class not open to the public

The nonprofit organization can

- Provide special seating for the prospect at events
- Send the prospect special communications such as birthday cards, anniversaries, thank you letters, and congratulatory notes

- Feature the prospect in an article or interview in an organization publication such as a newsletter or magazine
- Recognize donors at organizational events

The Successful Solicitation—Overcoming the Fear of Asking

One of the biggest challenges for many development professionals is motivating board members and key volunteers to make personal visits to solicit major gifts. If you have ever served on a board or volunteered for an organization, you have heard people say they prefer calling people on the telephone or writing letters. They are willing to help raise funds but are not comfortable doing it face-to-face. There are a number of reasons why it is difficult to motivate even the most successful professionals on the board. They, like most people, suffer from the fear of being rejected, the fear of offending someone, the fear of appearing as a beggar, and most important, the fear of failure. Add to that a cultural "taboo" of discussing money with people other than family members, and you have an uncomfortable position for many people.

A proven method for motivating volunteers to make personal solicitations is through training. In Chapter 6, we covered how to train and manage annual campaign volunteers. Some of the elements of that training session can be included in training volunteers to solicit major gifts. In addition, training activities to help build the volunteers' confidence in both themselves and the organization will help bring a more positive attitude to the task at hand. If you are able to help a volunteer approach the task with greater comfort, you are well on your way to creating a successful solicitor for the organization. Make sure the volunteers know they will rarely, if ever, make a visit alone. Usually they will be part of a solicitation team consisting of the CEO or director of development, or another board member or volunteer. This also helps to make the situation more comfortable for everyone involved.

Volunteer solicitors should do the following:

- Believe in themselves.
- Believe in the project.
- Know the organization and specific project.
- Be knowledgeable about the prospect they are visiting.
- Tailor the presentation to the donor's needs and interests.
- Be good listeners.
- Be themselves.

Include ample opportunity to role play major gift solicitations in the training session(s). There is no substitute for having to "think on your feet." It is also important for individuals who will be making solicitation visits together to practice as a team for the flow of the meeting to go more smoothly.

The Successful Solicitation Visit

Ample time should be devoted to the earlier stages in a major gift solicitation—identification, research, and, especially, cultivation—to help ensure a positive result. Thus, the following scenario illustrates that the time is right to schedule a visit. An individual is identified as being a possible donor to an organization. Research was conducted by staff, and the individual was rated as a qualified prospect by staff and volunteers. During the past year, the prospect became involved with the organization by serving on the advisory committee, attending events, and meeting several times with the board chair and CEO. The following are basic steps in conducting a solicitation visit:

- greeting
- questioning
- listening
- presenting the proposal
- overcoming objections
- asking for the gift
- closing

Greeting

Start the meeting by taking a few minutes to catch up with one another. Ask about family members, business activities, mutual interests, acquaintances, etc. This is a continuation of establishing a strong relationship with the prospect. New information may be revealed during this time that could be important to the purpose of the visit. However, do not spend too much time conversing on a variety of issues because you want to be sure you have ample time to present your proposal, discuss any questions or objections, and solicit a positive response. Solicitation visits can last an hour or more depending on the prospect.

Questioning

Use a variety of open-ended questions to broaden the conversation and encourage discussion. It is important that the prospect think his or her advice is important to the organization. Some sample open-ended questions are the following:

- How do you feel about . . . ?
- What are the advantages and disadvantages of . . . ?
- Some people say . . . What do you think of that?
- If you were in our position, what would be your next step?
- Who else might be interested in this project?

Listening

We believe the most important skill necessary in soliciting major gifts is to be a good listener. Do not monopolize the conversation talking about the organization and the specific project. Respond to the prospect's comments and suggestions.

To be a better listener, you should

- Try to think like a prospect. During the time you have come to know this prospect, you'll begin to anticipate the kinds of questions he or she may ask. Keep the prospect's needs and motivations in mind.
- Limit your own and solicitation team member's talking. You cannot talk and listen at the same time. This is the advantage of making a solicitation visit with another person so that one can be an active listener at all times.
- Concentrate and focus on what is being said. Active listeners lean in toward the speaker, smile, maintain eye contact, take notes, if appropriate, and make comments such as "Yes," and "I see."
- Keep your own emotions under control, even though certain words, phrases, issues, personalities, and behaviors can trigger us emotionally. Do not stop listening while you think of a response.
- Often repeat and summarize what you heard. Be sure you have heard what they said. Verify by restating the information or asking for clarification.

"YOU MUST BE RATED CAPABLE OF MAKING A MAJOR GIFT. THE PRESIDENT OF YOUR COLLEGE IS HOLDING ON LINE TWO."

Source: © Mark Litzler

The Use of Personal Solicitation in Major Gift Fund Raising   131

Presenting the Proposal

You may have prepared a written proposal, but it is certainly not shared with the prospect during your meeting.

> By meeting with the prospect, you have the advantage of bringing your proposal to life in actions and words.

By meeting with the prospect, you have the advantage of bringing your proposal to life in actions and words. The solicitation team needs to present their case in a way that will excite the prospect. Ways to add excitement to your solicitation include the following:

- Use human interest stories.
- Tell a story.
- Use action words, drama, and humor when appropriate.
- State a problem and show how the donor can be part of the solution by helping the organization.
- Appeal to a prospect's senses and emotions.
- Quote other donors, clients, authorities, and experts on the merits of the program.

Overcoming Objections

There shouldn't be many serious objections to your proposal at the time of the meeting if the prospect has been properly cultivated. Again, listening skills are very important. During earlier contact with the prospect, the solicitation team would have learned if the prospect had serious concerns or questions about a possible project. They, then, should have addressed those concerns and helped the prospect feel more comfortable about the project if he or she seemed to have a real interest in that program. However, if the prospect comes up with some questions or objections at the time of the meeting, the solicitation team must be prepared to deal with them. Because there is no way to truly anticipate what objections a prospect may have, it is best to arm yourself with some techniques to overcome objections (Exhibit 9–7).

Asking for the Gift

The discussion leads to the moment of asking for the gift. It is extremely important that the solicitation team decide who will be the solicitor before walking in the door. You know the prospect is interested in the organization's programs, so take a positive approach in asking the prospect to make a gift. Let the prospect know the full cost of the project and ask if he or she can fund the entire amount, either as a current gift or through a pledge. As the solicitor, one might say, "David, Mary and I are delighted that you are interested in our arts in the classroom program for area elementary schools. We know that the cost of the program is $50,000. I can provide you with the budget. Will you consider funding this

Exhibit 9–7 Techniques To Overcome Prospect Objections

1. Be prepared to respond to comments such as "Prove that you will be able to do what you say you will do," and "Prove that your organization is the best one to advance this effort."
2. Prepare answers for objections heard from others in advance.
3. Bring up an objection before the prospect does, treat it as a minor point, and restate the benefits of the project.
4. Never argue with your prospect.
5. Do not inflate an objection by discussing it too much.
6. Never take an objection as a personal attack. Try to understand why the prospect is bringing up this particular objection.
7. Ignore excuses and weak objections.
8. Ask your prospect what he or she would do to solve the problem he or she brings up. Then suggest your organization as a means of doing that.
9. Turn an objection into a question—then answer it.
   "I understand how you feel . . ."
   "You have brought up an important question many people ask . . ."
   Get agreement on the question, then answer it with facts or a dramatic story.
10. Use the very effective technique of using words such as feel, felt, and found.
    "I understand how you feel . . ."
    "Others have felt the same way."
    "They found that . . ."

program with a gift of $50,000, either through a current gift or by pledging $10,000 a year over five years?"

Now, be quiet! Wait and listen for the prospect to respond. It is not easy to sit in silence because our first reaction will be to start talking. However, the prospect is the best judge of whether he or she can make a gift of the size you mentioned. By suggesting a multi-year pledge, you leave the door open to discussing other options of making such a gift rather than only an outright gift of $50,000.

The prospect may or may not choose to fund the full amount of your request. In spite of the research and relationship-building that has gone on, there may be a personal or business situation you are not aware of. Remember, do not take this personally. If the prospect responds with a lower figure, ask his or her advice about others who might be interested in helping fund this program.

The prospect may ask to have some time to think about the request or to discuss it with a spouse or family member. Tell them that this is fine but be sure to schedule a follow-up meeting while there. By setting a date and time to contact or meet, you will ensure a decision is made in a timely fashion.

Closing

If the solicitation is successful, offer your own thanks and gratitude immediately as well as those of the organization. Tell the donor that a staff person will contact him or her to confirm the pledge and payment schedule. Or, if the prospect has asked for time to consider the request, again, thank the prospect for his or her time and past support for the organization. Reconfirm the date and time to call or meet.

When summarizing the solicitation meeting, be aware of roadblocks that can sidetrack a successful solicitation visit.

- Not asking for the gift
- Not asking for a large enough gift
- Not listening—talking too much
- Talking about the organization and its approach rather than the client who benefits from the organization's services
- Making your presentation sound like a canned sales pitch
- Ignoring honest objections
- Forgetting to summarize before moving on to the "ask"
- Not having prearranged signals between solicitation members
- Asking for the gift too soon
- Not being flexible and not having alternatives to offer the prospect
- Speaking rather than remaining silent after asking for the gift

How to Say Thank You

Do not confuse saying thank you with recognition of a major gift, especially when a major donor asks for anonymity. Some major donors do not wish to receive public recognition, but that does not mean they do not want to know that their gift is appreciated by the organization and its leadership. It is a *must* to thank all donors; there needs to be a well-thought out plan for acknowledging major donors' generosity. By using the term plan, we do not mean to suggest delaying the sending of a thank you to develop such a plan. Instead, an organization should have an established process of who in the organization acknowledges major gifts. According to Panas (1984) a "rule of seven" is recommended, that is, thanking a person at least seven times before he or she is asked for a second gift. Seven times does sound a little excessive, but if planned properly over a period of time it can reap great rewards for the organization.

The following describes how simple it is to follow this rule.

A donor contributed $50,000 to endow a scholarship fund for a deserving law student. A letter from the president was sent, then a personal letter from the dean, then a handwritten note from the associate dean for institutional advancement, and then an official receipt from the Office of Institutional Advancement. Later in the year, the associate dean sends a letter to the donor informing him or her of this year's recipient and describing the recipient's background and interests. The recipient sends a thank you letter to the donor. The donor receives a personal invitation to the scholarship ceremony and reception and is asked if he or she would like to assist the dean in making the scholarship award presentation.

Other ways to say thank you can be of a more personal nature by taking into account the donor's interests and activities within and outside of the organization. Some examples include books, a video or photo album of a program's activities or project's construction, personalized gift baskets, or a limited edition drawing.

Ways To Recognize Major Donors

Organizations will want to publicly recognize the significant contributions made by their major donors. First, be sure that the individuals involved are comfortable with public attention by discussing with them the types of recognition an organization is planning. Publicizing major gifts in an organization's publications is an excellent way to not only thank the major donor but also to interest other potential donors to get involved with the organization. Magazines, newsletters, or annual reports can include an article about the donor and what his or her gift will enable the organization to accomplish. It is important to include some quotes regarding why he or she chose to make this gift. Use one or two photographs of the donor with his or her family or organizational leaders.

If an organization has conducted a capital campaign resulting in new facilities or programs, having a major donor's name associated with the facility or program is a wonderful way to recognize the donor. The names we see on university buildings, schools, or hospital centers, for example, are the result of major gifts to those organizations. Within those facilities, specific areas including rooms, theaters, or wings can bear the names of other major donors. This type of recognition is seen in lettering and plaques that indicate whose support made this facility possible. If the major gift endowed or created a new program, the donor's name could be associated with that program. Organizational letterhead and all references to that program in publications could bear the donor's name.

The following are two examples.

1. The naming of one of the courtrooms in the new law school building at American University—Brass lettering over the door reads, "Patrick R. Gardner (names have been changed) Moot Courtroom." Inside the courtroom is a brass plaque measuring 12" × 18", which reads, "This Courtroom is Made Possible Through the Generosity of Patrick R. Gardner, '66." A framed photograph of the donor and his daughter, Karen, '95, also hangs in the room.
2. The naming of an international student exchange program—The program is known as the Miriam Ward Fellows program and is referred by that name in all communications.

There are numerous opportunities and ways to publicly recognize major donors. Organizations also can create an opportunity that will have special meaning to the donor. Listed below are six other common ways to recognize major donors:

1. Arrange a testimonial dinner.
2. Designate the donor as a recipient of a distinguished service award.
3. Establish an award in the donor's name.
4. Conduct a special ceremony and event dedicating the facility or program that bears the donor's name.
5. Prepare a press release and circulate to print and electronic media in the cities of the organization and the donor.
6. Send an announcement to professional organizations of which the donor is a member for them to include in their publications.

Stewardship—The Practice That Ensures Future Major Gifts

The last phase in a major gift solicitation is stewardship. What is stewardship? It is the process whereby an organization continues to prove it is worthy of a donor's continuing support. It does this through the following:

- acknowledging the gift
- recognizing the donor
- honoring the donor's intent for the gift
- keeping the donor informed
- managing funds wisely
- using funds effectively to forward the organization's mission

The first two steps in the stewardship phase already have been described as standard operating procedures after successfully soliciting a major gift. It is extremely important that the organization honor the donor's intent for the gift. This responsibility usually falls to the development professional to monitor. An example of this type of monitoring occurs when dealing with scholarship awards. For example, each year, the development professional may serve on the scholarship committee for the law school. He or she reads the student applications and helps in selecting those candidates that match the scholarship criteria set up by the donor. Because the development professional is familiar with many of the donors and helped a number of them establish their funds, his or her role on the committee is to ensure that the donor's intent for the scholarship fund be honored. Regarding other types of programs that may be more general in purpose, the development professional should periodically check with the appropriate program staff person to get status reports on the program and the ways the gift is being used. For example, the development professional would check to see that the gift is being used for expenses directly related to the program if that was the intent of the donor.

Chapter 11 will discuss how important it is to follow a foundation's requirements regarding reporting how the grant is used. Because few individual major donors have this requirement, it becomes necessary for the organization to impose such standards on itself to keep major donors informed. This is often the weakest area in the stewardship phase for an organization. Unfortunately, development staff and volunteers are actively working with new major donor prospects and, therefore, may not have the time to steward past donors. This is a major mistake because those individuals who already have given an organization a major gift are the best prospects to make another significant contribution. Keeping donors informed about the organization and how their gift is being used is yet another way to show them that the organization appreciates their support. Do not worry that donors will feel the organization is in touch too often. It is best to err on the side of too much information than not at all.

Using the example described previously, it is easy to keep scholarship donors informed. Each year after the scholarship committee makes its selection, the development professional sends a letter to each donor informing them of who this year's recipient is and provides them with some information about the student's background and interests. An annual scholarship ceremony and reception held in January also provides the opportunity for donors to assist the dean in making the scholarship presentation and to meet the recipients. Good stewardship of the scholarship donors resulted in significant additions to established funds and the creation of new funds.

For the climate of an organization to be conducive to major gift fund raising, one must consider again the overall "health" of the organization in view of its leadership

> For the climate of an organization to be conducive to major gift fund raising, one must consider the overall "health" of the organization.

and management. Major donors must have confidence in the organization to manage their funds wisely and to use the funds effectively to forward the organization's mission. Therefore, it is critical to keep these donors informed of the organization's plans and status through special communications from the CEO and board chairperson. If serious organizational problems develop, be sure the major donors hear it first from the organization and not through the media. In being proactive with the donors, an organization can describe the problem and the solutions planned.

Reference

Panas, J. (1984). *Mega gifts—who gives them, who gets them.* Chicago, Illinois: Pluribus Press, Inc.

Chapter 10
Corporate Fund Raising

Chapter Outline

- The History of Corporate Philanthropy
- How and Why Corporations Give
- Corporate-Private Foundation Partnerships
- Research—Selecting the Right Corporation for Support
- Resources for Corporate Grant Information
- Writing the Corporate Proposal
- Submitting the Proposal
- Requests to International Corporations
- Waiting for the Decision
- Thanking the Corporate Donor
- Evaluating the Project
- Reporting to Corporations on Use of Funds
- Corporate Matching Gifts
- Cause-Related Marketing—Doing Well by Doing Good
- Corporate Sponsorships
- Non-Cash Assistance from Corporations
- Other Forms of Corporate Support
- Declining Corporate Support Because of Mergers and Acquisitions

Key Vocabulary

- Cause-Related Marketing
- Company-Sponsored Foundation
- Corporate Annual Report
- Corporate Brochure
- Corporate Foundation
- Corporate Giving Program
- Corporate Philanthropy
- Employee Matching Gift
- Federated Campaign
- Gifts-In-Kind
- Matching Gift
- Nine Ninety (990)
- Proposal
- Query Letter
- Rejection Letter
- Seconded Staff
- Seed Money
- Site Visit

The History of Corporate Philanthropy

Corporate philanthropy in North America began in the late 19th century when the railroads helped to build the YMCA hostels that housed railroad employees as they worked on the rapidly growing rail system in the West. Then, during World War I, the Red Cross began helping the civilians in war-torn Europe. After the United States entered the war in April of 1917, corporations were asked to help fund the international war relief efforts of the Red Cross, because the financial burden couldn't be carried by individuals or philanthropic organizations alone. The "Red Cross dividend" was created and enabled companies to request authorization from stockholders for a special dividend, or set amount of money, to be given to the Red Cross.

In 1921, the Internal Revenue Service (IRS) allowed businesses to make donations to charitable, medical, or educational institutions as long as these donations served the needs of their employees. This is termed "direct benefit" giving. Later in the 1920s, Community Chests and United Ways were organized based on the model of the war drives of the Red Cross. Then in the 1930s, Herbert Hoover moved quickly to marshal the resources of business and philanthropic organizations to deal with what he thought would be a short-term emergency, but which lasted nearly a decade—the Depression. But, there was no clear legal status given to corporate giving and corporations were advised by their attorneys that they should put their money into the communities where the workers lived. Again, the principle of "direct benefit" reigned.

It wasn't until 1936 that a lobbying effort by the Community Chests resulted in amendments to the IRS code that permitted corporations to contribute to charity, if a contribution did not exceed 5 percent of a corporation's net income. There was now a distinct difference between a charitable deduction and a business deduction, and businesses could claim one or the other, but not both for the same gift. Still, businesses were advised to "play it safe" and contribute only when it was clearly in their self-interest. During World War II, corporate charitable efforts were similar to those during the first world war. It wasn't until 1953 that the Supreme Court of New Jersey overturned the "direct benefit" rule. The new ruling stated that corporations had a larger social responsibility than that of just supporting programs that directly benefitted themselves. Unfortunately, guidelines still were not devised to assist corporations with their giving practices (Karl, 1982).

Also during the 1950s, corporations began to create foundations to separate the giving process from direct management of corporate staff. Foundations could set their own guidelines and either fund programs that directly benefitted the corporation or those that were of interest and were, perhaps, socially responsible, but had no direct benefit. In the 1960s and 1970s, corporate philanthropy took a sharp turn. No longer was it respectable to fund only those programs that would be of benefit to the corporation. "Self interest" and "direct benefit" took on negative connotations. There were the hungry to feed, the environment to save, and peace to bring to the world. Corporate philanthropy reached far beyond its own needs and communities. Corporations discovered the power of doing good and they realized that this power also could be profitable.

> Corporations discovered the power of doing good and they realized that this power also could be profitable.

When the Minnesota-based Dayton Hudson Corporation established a policy in 1945–1946 to give 5 percent in direct payments to charity, more than forty other Minneapolis and St. Paul corporations were motivated to follow suit. Kenneth Dayton, who was chair of the executive committee of the Dayton Hudson Corporation at that time, thought that "the purpose of business is to serve society," not to just serve business. *The Chronicle of Philanthropy* (Gray 1996) reported, "The company has donated more than $350 million to charities since the 5 percent tradition began. That has worked out to more than $19,000 a day. In 1995, the company gave 6.5 percent of its 1994 profits—or $28 million." Following the lead of the Twin Cities corporations, 5-percent clubs began to sprout in other cities. Of course, not every corporation agreed with this policy, and some realized that by giving 5 percent they would be giving more money to charity than the largest of the private foundations. Still, as the concept grew, philanthropic efforts of corporations expanded throughout the 1950s, 1960s, and 1970s. In the period between 1976 and 1981, corporate giving increased 16 percent.

Corporate philanthropy continued to grow until it peaked in the mid-1980s. The first half of the decade had been very profitable for corporations, and they responded enthusiastically to the Reagan administration's challenge to pick up the slack when government funding for nonprofit organizations was cut drastically. Also, in the 1980s, the American Express Corporation introduced "cause-related" marketing to the world of corporate philanthropy, and proved that a corporation could make money by directly aligning itself with a charitable cause. (For details, see the section of this chapter that addresses cause-related marketing.) Finally, there was a way to mix the two—direct corporate benefits and social responsibility.

In 1992, corporate giving to charities decreased for the first time in twenty years. Although it decreased only by 1.3 percent, this drop was indicative of the health of corporate America. Many companies were not doing well financially and were contributing less of their earnings to the nonprofit world. Six major corporations—Aetna Life and Casualty Company, Baxter International, PPG Industries, Texas Instruments, Textron, and Weyerhaeuser Company—gave nothing to their foundations that year. Donations from corporations totaled $5.9 billion, down from $6 billion the year before. This was the fifth consecutive year that donations had not kept up with inflation. Corporations were concerned with what causes their money was supporting and what they were getting in return for their contributions. Competition for this money was becoming more fierce as government funding and other sources were becoming more restricted. Corporate cash donations accounted for 86.6 percent of the $5.9 billion, whereas gifts of products accounted for 12.5 percent.

Many companies were forced to overhaul their contributions programs because of the recession. In 1994, thirty-five corporations reported in a survey to *The Chronicle of Philanthropy* (Dundjerski & Moore 1994) that "they had redefined their giving priorities during the past year; in most cases, they reduced the number of causes they support." Of the other companies responding, most had refined comprehensive changes they had adopted just two or three years previous.

The companies looked for new ways to direct their corporate giving to the programs that were more closely aligned with their own interests. The following are among the trends that emerged.

More International Giving—A growing number of corporations are starting or expanding contributions programs overseas.

A Surge in Matching Employee Gifts—Employees have been quick to take advantage of an increase in the number of companies that will match their gifts to charity. At Eli Lilly and Company, for example, the matching gift programs exploded from $200,000 when it began in 1980 to more than $5 million in 1996.

New Opportunities for Non-Cash Gifts—Recent mergers and layoffs by big corporations produced a surplus of office equipment at some companies. Many decided to donate what they could no longer use to charity. BankAmerica, for example, gave away $2 million worth of computers, desks, and other items after its merger with Security Pacific Corporation.

More Volunteer Programs for Employees—General Mills started a new program that offers seven or eight employees who are near retirement age time off from work to volunteer with nonprofit groups. James River provides information to high school students about jobs that do not require a college degree and helps train students for such positions. The company has recruited fifty other companies to help with the program.

Renewed Attention to Education—IBM announced that it would reduce its giving to higher education from half of all donations to about 5 to 10 percent, so it could give more to elementary and secondary schools. In 1993, IBM gave away $59.6 million in cash and $27.2 million in computers. Eaton Corporation, an electronics company, began helping first-year engineering students who are members of minority groups by providing each with a $2,500 scholarship, a summer internship at the company, and an employee mentor.

More Emphasis on Evaluation—Growing pressure to show successes of contributions programs has motivated General Electric, General Mills, Campbell Soup, and several other companies to start requiring charities to explain in their grant applications how a program will be evaluated. Companies like General Electric also have hired outside evaluators to determine the effectiveness of their giving programs—and make recommendations for change (Dundjerski & Moore 1994).

Another concern to appear in the mid-1990s is corporate chief executive officers' apparent lack of interest in philanthropy. Corporate foundation giving officers found that they had to justify their donations more frequently to ensure that they would receive the money needed for their budgets. This was found to be true even when the top corporate management had been supportive of the foundation's giving in the past.

Then, in the summer of 1994, ARCO fired the head of its foundation, a 13-year veteran who was highly respected in the field of philanthropy, at the same time it downsized the foundation by 40 percent. Others involved in corporate philanthropy heeded this as a "wake-up call" and sensed the urgency of aligning support for their foundations among the top management.

The focus of corporate philanthropy appears to have come full circle as corporations are again interested in how giving will affect their bottom line. Corporations are spending more time looking for ways to use their shrinking pool of money to improve their corporate image, elevate the morale of their employees, and expand their customers' loyalty. Still others seek to give their donations to programs that are more closely tied to their business interests.

Included in their strategies are the following:

- Forging closer links with the company's marketing, public-affairs, and government-relations departments.
- Focusing donations on themes or categories aligned with the company's business goals—and directed toward benefitting current or future customers.
- Ascertaining ways of measuring the impact of contributions on a company's balance sheet.
- Developing programs to make greater use of company employees as volunteers, including lending executives to charities.
- Promoting other non-cash forms of support, including donations of products, services, and employee expertise.
- Recycling money by lending it to charities at little or no interest, rather than giving it away (Greene 1995).

In 1995, 25 percent or more of companies' gifts were products. In 1996, corporations had a robust growth in profits (an 11.9 percent increase in profits for the largest 150 U.S. companies) and corporations said they would do more for charity. Yet, even with this leap in earnings, corporations were still trying to reduce the size of their giving staffs. Some companies even looked to outside companies to run all or parts of their philanthropic programs—a practice called "outsourcing." This practice had been used in corporate America for years, but this was the first time it affected corporate philanthropy.

The most dramatic example of outsourcing was when the Quaker Oats Foundation asked the Chicago Community Trust to administer all of its giving programs. Other companies that hire out their philanthropic programs have tried to keep the arrangements less visible than Quaker by having the contractors use the company's letterhead and forms and answer the phones with the company's name. Most companies are hesitant to try such outsourcing arrangements, for fear of mistakes that may tarnish their reputation and because of a possible lack of understanding by the public—their customers.

Even with downsizing, today's corporate philanthropy continues to comprise a bit of self-interest and a bit of social responsibility. Those searching for dollars from corporations can find most corporations' individual philanthropic policies described in detail in their published giving guidelines. Rest assured that at least for the remainder of the 1990s, companies will be pressured by their stockholders to not only produce a good bottom line, but to also show social responsibility.

> Even with downsizing, today's corporate philanthropy continues to comprise a bit of self-interest and a bit of social responsibility.

How and Why Corporations Give

Corporate philanthropy is versatile in its structure. Contributions to nonprofit organizations may be made in several ways, for example, cash gifts through a company foundation or directly given by the company, or through non-cash gifts, often called gifts-in-kind. Within a company, giving may be highly centralized or decentralized depending upon the corporation's philanthropic culture. Some corporations have large, full-time, staff operations spread throughout their divisions and subsidiaries to review proposals and coordinate giving, whereas others run a small, tight ship by having philanthropic decisions centralized within one office. Some corporations consider only cash gifts as part of their philanthropic effort, whereas others consider both cash and non-cash, gifts-in-kind to be part of their effort.

But, why do corporations give? And how much do they give? Will they continue to give as much in the future as they have in the recent past? Are there any trends in corporate giving? Do corporations give anything besides money? How can corporate support be obtained? This chapter will focus on these questions and the many others surrounding corporate philanthropy.

According to a study prepared for the Council on Foundations in May, 1982 by the renowned marketing survey company, Yankelovich, Skelly and White, Inc., corporate motivations for giving vary per company and its individual leadership. Reasons discussed and evaluated include the following:

1. The CEO dominates corporate giving decisions. Yet, CEOs agree that their boards of directors have a greater potential power, which is largely unrealized, to increase the company's giving in the future.
2. Corporate giving is an expression of enlightened self-interest. Generally it is not regarded as a form of corporate policy.
3. Many CEOs believe that corporate giving programs are underachieving their major corporate and social objectives.
4. Corporate giving is a poorly understood function in most companies and is relatively underdeveloped.

Further investigation into why corporations give away money brings forth many other reasons including: to build a positive public image, to increase revenues, to get tax deductions, to reward employees, and to improve the communities in which they operate. Some others give because it is the tradition of the corporation to support certain causes or events—national, regional, or local. Others give because they are perceived to exude good will and it puts them in good favor with their public. Others give because their CEO or board has aligned them with a certain cause. Yet others give because giving can create an environment of community responsibility, and this aura of good corporate citizenship actually may help them to attract new customers.

In many communities, this last reason may make a difference in how local customers perceive a corporation. Is it one that supports the community? Is it one that puts its contributions into the coffers of the organizations supported by those it employs? Does it have a matching gift program? Does it give time off to employees who wish to volunteer for a cause? Will it provide gifts-in-kind to the schools or other nonprofit organizations in the community?

Many national organizations care about the public's perception of them as much as their local or regional counterparts do. For example, because they supported local elementary schools, Apple Computer was an instant "hit" with educators around the country, and Levi Strauss and Company was giving nearly 3.5 percent to charities across the United States long before other corporations "got on the band wagon."

In 1995, corporations and corporate foundations gave an estimated $7.40 billion to nonprofit organizations. Of the total giving of $143.85 billion in 1995, corporations gave 5.1 percent, foundations gave 7.3 percent ($10.44 billion), bequests accounted for 6.8 percent ($9.77 billion), and individuals gave 80.8 percent ($116.23 billion). Corporate gifts increased by 10 percent from 1993. According to *The Chronicle of Philanthropy* (Murawski 1996), "Much of last year's increase was fueled by a big rise in donations from individuals, who gave 11.2 percent more than they did in 1994. But donations from companies and foundations also surged. The significant increase in giving reflected a strong performance by the nation's economy. Americans saw their incomes rise by an average 6.5 percent, the fastest rate of increase in five years. The strong performance of the stock market also spurred increased donations. The Dow Jones Industrial Average broke the 5,000 mark, generating a burst of contributions of appreciated securities."

This upsurge in 1995 was good news for charities. In 1994, corporate giving, if adjusted for inflation, showed an actual decline of 2.04 percent. This meant that for six consecutive years, corporate giving had not kept pace with inflation. Even though there were more dollars, they actually could do less good.

In the early 1990s, a corporate trend began of giving donations other than by directly giving cash. Many "gifts-in-kind" and other non-cash gifts were made. In the past, a request from IBM to underwrite a nonprofit organization's educational program could have meant a sizeable gift of cash. Today, they are giving computer equipment and training instead. Having thought of this idea later than Apple, IBM found that many of today's young adults had been taught as children on Apple computers

(Mac-based)—through Apple's early cultivation of elementary schools by giving computers to the classrooms. These children grew up to buy Apple computers and products. Now, IBM is providing the same equipment programs as Apple does to schools to ensure future customers.

In 1991, a national nonprofit organization approached IBM with a request of $100,000 to support its educational programs. Instead of receiving cash, the organization received $125,000 worth of computer equipment plus the expertise of the IBM staff to appropriately network the organization's computers so it could communicate internally and externally with its regional offices. The total gift was worth far more than the original amount requested, but still left the organization searching for money to support its educational programs.

Other corporations provide their products or even loan personnel to nonprofit organizations. Often, when an organization is embarking upon a capital campaign, the chair of the campaign will be the CEO of a major corporation. That chair will often "second," or loan, one or more of the company's staff members to work with the nonprofit organization to organize the campaign and provide assistance to the campaign's leadership team. Thus, the term "seconded" executive.

Also, corporations may provide nonprofit organizations with the use of their facilities free of charge. For the organization's board of trustees' annual meeting, the corporation may loan one of its conference rooms for the weekend. Some corporations even have provided loans to nonprofit organizations at below-market rates. These types of contributions are indispensable to the welfare of the nonprofit world and often are not included in the giving figures accredited to corporate America. According to *Giving USA* in their Annual Report on Philanthropy 1994, the corporation's median product and property donations (gifts-in-kind) increased by 74 percent between 1992 and 1993 whereas the median cash disbursements increased by only 52 percent.

Another interesting point observed by *Giving USA* was that corporate foundations actually gave more money to nonprofit organizations than they received from their parent company. To understand why and how, one has to understand that there are two types of corporate foundations. One type has been initially established by the parent corporation with a sizeable gift and then is in total self-control after that. The other receives cash each year from the corporation based on the earnings of the corporation that year.

Corporate-Private Foundation Partnerships

Something new has been happening in corporate solicitation fund raising. Ever since the Reagan administration began to cut deeply into the government support of the nonprofit world, the corporate community has been taking up more and more of the slack. The big surprise under the "Gingrich Era" was not that more government cuts were being made (that was expected), but that private foundations were busy courting corporations for support of their programs! Although still the exception, more and more partnerships and alliances are being formed between private foundations and corporations. For example, the Rockefeller Foundation and Bancomer in Mexico joined forces to sponsor a scholarship program. The Markle Foundation and an Oregon-based video games company collaborated to further a cause supported by the foundation—public interest applications of interactive media.

Perhaps one of the largest and most successful partnerships between a private foundation and a corporation is the one between the Robert Wood Johnson Foundation (RWJF), one of the largest foundations in health care, and HBO (Home Box Office), the cable programmer. Together, they work with the program "Comic Relief" to provide health care to the homeless via RWJF's twenty-two medical clinics set up across the country to help meet the medical needs of the homeless. Comic Relief raises the money through telethons carried on HBO. HBO pays the salaries and expenses of the Comic Relief staff, and all of the money raised goes to homeless people who are ill instead of paying administrative costs.

All of this potential—the up and down side—is detailed in an article by Smith (1995) in the *Corporate Philanthropy Report*. Smith sees some dangers in these partnerships. He states, "For non-profits that see the trend on the horizon, the danger isn't hard to detect. Their private foundation allies may decide to break with tradition by working directly with the business world. In other words, most of the nation's nonprofit organizations may be cut out of the loop." He also detects hesitation from the private foundations. "Indeed, true private foundation/corporate partnerships are still rare. The problem is that private foundation grantmakers—who rarely admit that their self-interests bias their funding decisions—are loathe to accommodate the self-interests of the very corporations they court."

Research—Selecting the Right Corporation for Support

Before writing any proposal, it is imperative that the grant seeker completely understand the reasons for seeking funds from the donor. What is the organization's mission? What are the organization's needs? What are the organization's programs? Why should a corporation support these needs or

> Before writing any proposal, it is imperative that the grant seeker completely understand the reasons for seeking funds from the donor.

programs? How will the money be spent? How is the organization spending its money now? A solicitor must be prepared to answer all of these questions and many, many more in simple, direct terms. If there are any problems with the organization—either programmatically or financially—a solicitor must be ready to respond to, or even initiate discussion on, these topics. There is nothing worse than being unprepared when being queried by a corporation.

In addition to knowing the organization inside and out, a grant seeker needs to know the corporation from which he or she will be soliciting funds. What are their guidelines? To whom have they made grants recently? What has been the size of their grants? Will the organization's mission and programs be of interest to the decision makers? It is important to know not only what the organization needs, but the corporation's interests and what it wants for itself. Does it have a specific image in the community, region, nation, or world that it wants to enhance? Does it have a public image problem that it wants to eliminate or erase? How can the organization be of benefit to the corporation?

Only when members of the development staff have completely exhausted asking and answering such questions, and have satisfactorily outlined responses to all of these, are they ready to begin to write a proposal to solicit funds from the organization. A successful proposal cannot be written if the author does not know the mission and needs of the organization or the interests and wants of the corporation. Many proposals are written with passion, but do not relay what the nonprofit organization wants. Others are so vague that they leave the potential grantor wondering what is being requested or what the organization is really all about. Ask someone outside of the organization to read the proposal. See if, to them, the proposal makes a "case" for giving. Often, those inside the organization know what they are trying to express, but they are unable to translate what they do and what they need into language that is understandable to someone outside of the organization.

Another technique used to prepare oneself for writing a strong proposal is to ask staff members of other organizations if you can read copies of "winning" proposals they have written. Many organizations are willing to share copies of their successful proposals, and even are willing to spend some time explaining why they think the proposals were successful. Of course, this sharing must then be reciprocal.

Other options also are available to those wishing to learn successful grant writing. One idea is to develop a committee of the organization's staff and board members to suggest ideas, assist in writing the proposal, or review the proposal at various stages in its preparation to ensure that it answers all of the questions mentioned earlier and represents the organization well. Often, grant writers think that the finely crafted proposal is what really sells the donor on the project. Most likely, it is a combination of factors and not just the proposal. No matter how erudite, if a proposal doesn't present the case clearly and succinctly to the potential donor and answer the right questions, then the project won't be funded.

In addition, successful corporate fund raising is always a matter of timing and relationship building. It may be several years before some organizations are funded because corporations are not aware of their existence. It is not uncommon for organizations to "court" potential donors for years before soliciting money from them. They are building relationships and establishing credibility. Then when they are ready to write a proposal, it will be received by people who are aware of the organization, its mission, and its needs. In addition, cultivation can lead to many other opportunities for the grant seeker. Corporate staff may attend special events held by the organization or may even provide "gifts-in-kind" to the organization long before making a grant to the organization. If one takes time now to know corporations and their world, it may pave the way for future, long-lasting relationships.

It is never too early to begin to compile files about corporations. Read the newspapers and business publications to clip articles regarding mergers and acquisitions; earnings and losses; hirings, promotions, and firings; and trends in the business or industry. Develop a profile on each corporation that could be a potential donor for your organization. Read through the corporations' annual reports and begin to develop profiles on each of the corporations. Find out what the corporation produces or sells, who their customers are, what their assets and liabilities are, and if the company is on a solid financial standing. Then determine who the officers or directors are of the corporation, who makes the decisions regarding charitable contributions—a committee or an individual—and who is the corporate giving officer—the contact person for proposals. Finally, review the corporation's giving history. What types of organizations are currently receiving grants? Do they support organizations in which their employees are involved? Do they provide "seconded" executives? Determine if there are any policies regarding supporting institutions such as yours. See Exhibit 10–1 for an excellent example of a profile form for researching corporate prospects.

Whatever steps are taken to prepare the proposal, never send a blind proposal—one that is mailed to a corporation with no cultivation beforehand. The adage "people give to people," proves true in corporate fund raising as well as in raising funds from individuals. Get to know the staff who handle the corporate contributions. In a small corporation in a small community, they may work in the public affairs office. In a larger community with a larger plant, or in a city that houses the corporate headquarters, there may be a separate foundation with staff to administer the charitable giving. To be successful, it is

Exhibit 10–1 Corporate Prospect Profile

COMPANY INFORMATION

COMPANY NAME: _____

ADDRESS:_____

_____

CITY: _____ STATE: _____ ZIP: _____

PHONE: _____ FAX: _____

BRANCH OPERATIONS: _____

_____

_____

PARENT COMPANY: _____

ADDRESS:_____

_____

SUBSIDIARIES: _____

PRODUCTS/SERVICES: _____

_____

_____

_____

CONTACT NAMES

CORPORATE CONTRIBUTIONS DIRECTOR

NAME: _____

TITLE: _____

ADDRESS: _____

CITY: _____ STATE: _____ ZIP: _____

PHONE: _____ FAX: _____

CORPORATE CONTRIBUTIONS COMMITTEE

NAMES: _____

_____

_____

_____

_____

_____

CHARITABLE GIVING

CORPORATE: _____

FOUNDATION: _____

MARKETING DEPARTMENT: _____

PUBLIC RELATIONS DEPARTMENT: _____

DISCRETIONARY FUNDS: _____

DETAILS: _____

_____

_____

_____

_____

continues

Exhibit 10–1 continued

TYPES OF CHARITABLE SUPPORT GIVEN

_____

_____

_____

_____

_____

CORPORATE LEADERSHIP

CHAIRMAN: _____

CEO: _____

COO: _____

HEAD OF MARKETING: _____

HEAD OF PUBLIC RELATIONS: _____

HEAD OF CORPORATE CONTRIBUTIONS: _____

FINANCIAL DATA

PROSPECT COMPANY

ASSETS: _____

REVENUE: _____

OPERATING INCOME: _____

MARKETING/ADVERTISING COSTS: _____

ANNUAL SALES: _____

PARENT COMPANY

ASSETS: _____

REVENUE: _____

OPERATING INCOME: _____

MARKETING/ADVERTISING COSTS: _____

ANNUAL SALES: _____

SUBSIDIARY

ASSETS: _____

REVENUE: _____

OPERATING INCOME: _____

MARKETING/ADVERTISING COSTS: _____

ANNUAL SALES: _____

SUBSIDIARY

ASSETS: _____

REVENUE: _____

OPERATING INCOME: _____

MARKETING/ADVERTISING COSTS: _____

ANNUAL SALES: _____

SUBSIDIARY

ASSETS: _____

REVENUE: _____

OPERATING INCOME: _____

MARKETING/ADVERTISING COSTS: _____

ANNUAL SALES: _____

continues

Exhibit 10–1 continued

SUBSIDIARY

ASSETS: _____
REVENUE: _____
OPERATING INCOME: _____
MARKETING/ADVERTISING COSTS: _____
ANNUAL SALES: _____

CORPORATE MARKETING PHILOSOPHY

MARKETING OBJECTIVES:
    LOCAL: _____
    REGIONAL: _____
    NATIONAL: _____
    INTERNATIONAL: _____

PRODUCT FOCUS:
    LOCAL: _____
    REGIONAL: _____
    NATIONAL: _____
    INTERNATIONAL: _____

PRODUCT ADVERTISING:
    LOCAL: _____
    REGIONAL: _____
    NATIONAL: _____
    INTERNATIONAL: _____

CONSUMER DEMOGRAPHICS:
    LOCAL: _____
    REGIONAL: _____
    NATIONAL: _____
    INTERNATIONAL: _____

SOURCES OF INFORMATION

SOURCE: YEAR:

_____
_____
_____
_____
_____
_____
_____

NAME OF RESEARCHER: _____

DATE: _____

Source: Courtesy of Gerry Frank, President, *INN*dependent Management Group, Alexandria, VA, 1994.

imperative to nurture the personal relationships. Don't be afraid to call corporate contacts to "run" ideas by them. Most people are flattered when others seek their advice.

It even may be possible to work with corporate staff to develop the proposal. If a good enough relationship has been developed, the corporate staff should be able to share what their interests are during the current funding cycle; what the "ceiling" is for the amount to be requested; if a program can be custom-made for the corporation; and what type of recognition would appeal to the corporation. It also is possible to learn if there is an opportunity to create employee programs or other tailor-made approaches. Don't forget to look for the possibility of developing promotional activities, taking advantage of cause-related marketing opportunities, or creating special market projects. Work with the corporation to clearly define in the proposal how the charity will handle the public relations and media efforts to create as much positive publicity for the corporation as possible. Before a corporation is even approached for a grant, it is also possible to learn, through these open discussions, what the corporation needs to obtain final approval on a project. Exhibit 10–2 presents a corporate visit report form.

Resources for Corporate Grant Information

Locating information on corporations requires research. There are more than 15,000 public corporations that file information with the Securities and Exchange Commission. Yet there are 9 million privately held companies that do not have the same reporting requirements as public companies. It is still possible to find information on these companies. The resources that follow will make the quest easier. See Chapter 8 for additional ideas.

Begin any search by using the traditional sources— *Million Dollar Directory, Ward's Business Directory of U.S. Private and Public Companies,* and the *Directory of Corporate Affiliations.* Most of these books are also available on CD-ROM format. There are also regional and local reference guides for use such as *Dun & Bradstreet Regional Business Directories, Sibbald Guides,* and *Manufacturers Directories.* Some of these resource books focus on specific industries (*Dun's Directory of Service Companies, Security Dealers of North America, Law Firms Yellow Book*), and some focus on international corporations (*World Business Directory, The World's Major Companies Directory, The European Directory of Medium Sized Companies,* the *Directory of European Business*). Many of these can be located in public or university libraries as well as the Foundation Centers located in several cities. It is unlikely that most development offices will be able to afford all of these resources. Of the many publications available, the ones most often included in development office libraries are the *Corporate Giving Directory, Corporate and Foundation Givers,* the *National Directory of Corporate Giving, Corporate Foundation Profiles,* and *The Corporate 500.*

Information on philanthropic programs for both public and private corporate giving programs can be found in publications such as the *Corporate Giving Directory, Corporate and Foundation Givers,* the *National Directory of Corporate Giving, Corporate Foundation Profiles, The Corporate 500, Matching Gift Details,* and the *Directory of International Corporate Giving.* Most of the information contained in these references also can be accessed on-line through DIALOG, DataTimes, LEXIS/NEXIS, and Dow Jones news retrieval. In most instances, it is much easier to search on-line than to use books, especially if you are cross-referencing material on various companies.

In addition to these reference materials, it is easy to access information by reading business journals and magazines. *Forbes, Fortune, Business Week,* and the *Wall Street Journal* all provide information on public and private companies. There are also other alternatives to consider. Reading the business sections of major city newspapers can provide invaluable information. Plus, local chambers of commerce may have business information available. All companies have to provide the Secretary of State with certain types of information. These files are available to the public. If the company is involved in any litigation, court records are available. These usually will include financial disclosures on the corporation and its executives. Plus, don't forget to just review the corporation's annual report. (See Appendix 10–A for a list that includes most of the resource materials available for research on corporations.)

Writing the Corporate Proposal

After completing all of the steps necessary for researching and cultivating a prospective corporate donor, it is time to develop the grant proposal. This process of putting together a good proposal can take several weeks to several months. After identifying a prospective donor and affirming the eligibility of the organization to receive a grant from the corporation, begin making a list of the ties or linkages that the organization and the corporation have regarding this project. When writing the proposal, weave these ties throughout. This is to confirm with the corporation that there are reasons for them to be interested in your organization and this particular project. Again, earlier cultivation should have established these ties or links. The proposal then builds upon this early work.

Keep the proposal short. Ten pages is long enough. If it can't be said in that amount of space, it probably isn't worth saying. All proposals need to have a cover letter that briefly summarizes the project. The cover letter should be signed by the most senior person in the organization, preferably the chair of the board, the president, or the executive director of the organization. The proposal itself should have a cover page with the name of the project; the name of the organization; its address, phone number, and contact person; date of submission; and the name of the corporation to which it is being presented. An executive summary should follow the cover page; it consists of one or two pages that provide a brief overview of the project, reasons why the corporation should fund the project, and the cost of the project to the corporation. Next comes the organization's back-

Exhibit 10–2 Corporate Visit Report Form

CORPORATE NAME: _____

ADDRESS: _____

_____

CITY: _____ STATE: _____ ZIP: _____

PHONE: _____ FAX: _____

E-MAIL: _____

NAME OF PERSON VISITED: _____

TITLE: _____

PHONE: _____ FAX: _____

E-MAIL: _____

ROLE IN CORPORATE CONTRIBUTIONS: _____

_____

_____

NAMES AND TITLES OF OTHERS ATTENDING MEETING: _____

_____

_____

_____

SUMMARY OF DISCUSSION: _____

_____

_____

_____

_____

_____

_____

_____

_____

_____

FOLLOW-UP REQUIRED: _____

_____

_____

_____

_____

_____

_____

PERSONS NEEDING TO BE NOTIFIED OF MEETING: _____

_____

_____

_____

_____

_____

_____

NAME AND TITLE: _____

DATE: _____

Source: Courtesy of Gerry Frank, President, *INN*dependent Management Group, Alexandria, VA, 1994.

ground information including its history, mission, programs, and the audience it serves. Again, this should be no more than one to two pages.

The "guts" of the proposal is included in the narrative, which is the part of the proposal that states the following: the case; the need; the objectives; the activities; the timetable; the reasons that the corporation should support the project; the names of those who will be responsible for the project; the amount of time they will spend on the project; the location of the project, if different from the organization's offices; the budget developed for the project; the plan for disseminating any materials developed during the project; how the project will be continued after the initial funding is exhausted; and plans for evaluating the success or failure of the project.

A paragraph or two should provide a conclusion to the proposal and direct the reader to the attachments at the end of the proposal. These attachments should include the following: the organization's tax-exempt charitable status under the IRS code; a copy of its IRS Form 990; an audited financial statement for the previous year; a copy of the current year's operating budget; a list of the names, titles, and affiliations of the board of directors; a list of the names and titles of senior staff; a list of current and relevant past contributors to the organization; an annual report; a development brochure; and any other material requested by the corporation or that appears to be necessary to make a successful case to the particular prospective donor.

Submitting the Proposal

Once the proposal is written, review the corporation's requirements to correctly submit the proposal. Carefully follow the directions given. Is the length of the proposal

"AS WE CONSIDER THE PROPOSALS, LET'S NOT FORGET WHO INCLUDED A GALLON OF ROCKY ROAD AS 'ATTACHMENT B'."

Source: © Mark Litzler

within the limits? Are all of the required attachments included? Have the appropriate people signed the document? How many copies of the proposal are required? Are the copies bound in the proper way? Is there a submission deadline? Is there a method of submission that the corporation prefers—mailed, hand-delivered, etc.? Don't forget to ask for a receipt from the company or courier selected to deliver the proposal. Keep the receipt to have a record of the proposal reaching the prospective donor.

Also, don't forget to have all of the in-house, organizational approvals completed well before the proposal delivery deadline. The finance department should review all budgets, and the publications department should use its resources to proofread the document for any typographical errors, redundancies, and inaccuracies. Make sure that enough time remains for "sign-off" by any necessary departments such as the president's office, the grant's office, or the department that will be running the project. Once all of these reviews have been completed, the proposal then can be submitted.

Remember that most corporate budgets are completed in the fall. Therefore, it is best to send a proposal to the corporation before September, especially if requesting large sums of support.

Requests to International Corporations

Requesting funds from international corporations is almost the same as soliciting funds from U.S.-based companies. Some cultures are different and require a different approach—most notably the Japanese. Patience is crucial when requesting support from Japanese companies. They tend to

> Requesting funds from international corporations is almost the same as soliciting funds from U.S.-based companies.

move slowly and cautiously, and consider every angle before making a decision. Also, Japanese companies usually will donate only from the profit side of their ledger and more often tend to fund high-tech research. They often consider their public image when supporting requests, and most often will fund projects from their public relations budgets.

Japanese companies must be nurtured just like any other company. An excellent example of "courting" Japanese companies is how the development staff at Youth for Understanding (YFU) International Student Exchange, which was headquartered in Ann Arbor, Michigan, in the 1960s and 1970s, and has been located in Washington, DC, since 1978, helped expand a student exchange program. YFU spent several years in the late 1970s and early 1980s discussing with the Toyota, Nissan, and Kikkoman corporations the many benefits of supporting the cost of sending students from the United

States to Japan as exchange students to live with Japanese families for the summer and, vice versa, the benefits of sending Japanese students to live in the United States for the school year with U.S. families and attend public schools. What finally transpired between the corporation and the organization were corporate-sponsored exchange programs between the United States and Japan. Toyota sponsored children of its employees in both the United States and Japan to participate in the YFU exchange program and paid all of the students' fees. Kikkoman, makers of soy sauce and other soy products, decided to sponsor student members of the Future Homemakers of America and the Future Homemakers of Japan to participate in YFU programs. Kikkoman's reason for this was simple—these students would be the future users of their products. Thousands of students participated in these corporate-sponsored programs over the years, and the program was so popular and successful that the corporations also made other capital gifts to the nonprofit organization. For example, one of YFU's three headquarters buildings was named the Nissan Building, after YFU received a large gift from the company, and Toyota also gave automobiles to the organization for its use. YFU was ahead of most other U.S.-based organizations in promoting cooperative efforts with Japanese corporations. They are proof that patience and "courting" pay off in soliciting funds from Japanese corporations.

Waiting for the Decision

After submitting the proposal, follow-up within ten to fifteen days to make sure that the corporation has received it and that it is complete and acceptable by their standards. Then, while waiting for the corporation's staff to meet and make their decision regarding your proposal, update them on any progress, new developments, or other grants received to support the proposal. Send copies of any positive publicity surrounding the project. Include a new annual report if a new one has been produced since submitting the proposal. It is important to use this time to the benefit of the organization. Don't let the corporation receive your proposal and then not hear from you. But, don't bombard them with useless information. Continue the cultivation process during this time just as you had done before. Remember that corporations give to successful organizations just as people do. Both want to be a part of a successful operation. Keep the company informed of any successes during this time.

Also remember that not all proposals can be funded. There is only so much money to give. It is disappointing and discouraging to receive a negative response, but it will happen, at some time, to everyone who submits proposals for funding. Often, it is because the problem hasn't been documented properly or the program's objectives do not match the interest of the corporation. Other reasons that proposals are not funded include the following: the project isn't cost efficient; the programs don't interest the company; the budget isn't within the range of funding available; the program is too ambitious in scope (or isn't ambitious enough); other organizations already have created the same programs within the community; the program cannot sustain itself and probably will fold after the funding is expended; the proposal writer didn't follow the corporation's guidelines; and the proposal was poorly written and included grammatical mistakes. Also, one sure way to have a proposal not be funded is to circumvent the staff who make the decisions and try to sell the project to a corporate board member, requesting that he or she tell the staff to fund the project (or, more subtlely, continually promote the project or organization to the staff). Be careful of using senior corporate contacts without cultivating the appropriate staff who manage the corporate giving program.

Thanking the Corporate Donor

A thank-you letter always should be written to the corporation, whether or not the organization receives funding from the proposal it submitted. If the corporation's response was negative, thank them for considering the proposal, and ask if they would be willing to meet with you either in person or over the phone to discuss the reasons why they didn't fund the proposal. Also, indicate that you would like to present other proposals for their consideration in the future and it would be helpful to know why they didn't find this one worthy of support. If the response was positive, make sure that the thank-you letter is sent promptly. A twenty-four- to forty-eight-hour turn-around is appropriate. In addition, include the ways they will be recognized for their support.

Corporate donors can be thanked additionally by providing recognition of their gift in the local media—both print and electronic. Their names may be added to a "wall of donors" or to a plaque hung in the organization's headquarters. A plaque or framed photo of the organization's project may be presented to the corporation to hang in a public place in their headquarters or at a local plant. The names of corporate donors can be included in the organization's annual report, and these donors can be invited to and honored at special lunches, dinners, or other events sponsored by the nonprofit organization. In addition, thanking a corporate donor may be as simple as asking for their advice, including their staff members when evaluating the project, asking them to serve on committees of the board or as board members, or sending them copies of letters of satisfied clients. Be creative, and remember, you can never say thank you enough times.

Evaluating the Project

Don't wait until the program has ended to evaluate the project undertaken. Begin by gathering data from the start of the project and continue throughout at assigned intervals. This will help you to remain on track with the project and can help you to magnify the value of the evaluation by providing data to your donors on an ongoing basis. If you find that you are not going to meet your objectives, an ongoing evaluation will give you an opportunity to take corrective action and to prepare your donors for a change of course or differing results than those for which you planned. Also, a timely evaluation may even lead to a better project. A donor even may be willing to pay for the evaluation, especially if it is included in the original budget.

The disadvantage of using staff members to conduct the evaluation is that they may postpone this work until the very end of the project, because they are too busy with the day-to-day details.

Reporting to Corporations on Use of Funds

Nonprofit organizations will be successful in fund raising only when they learn that successful solicitation does not end upon receipt of the gift from the donor, but instead, continues on as the nonprofit organization reports to the corporate donor on the use of the funds it received. "Corporate giving is a partnership between business and the community," states Burnell Roberts (1990). "Large corporations already are virtually saturated with proposals and funding commitments. Higher fund-raising goals in the future will require a broader donor base and more involvement by medium and small companies. Success in fund raising increasingly will go to those who close the loop on accountability and expand the loop on donor relations, and to those who treat the donor like the customer."

Spend time to invite the donors to a project site. Let them see their money at work. Show them the successful programs as well as those that weren't as successful. Keep them "in the loop" and they will be more likely to fund the organization again in the future.

Corporate Matching Gifts

More than 500 corporations offer a matching gift program to their employees. For every dollar given to charity, the corporation will match it either dollar for dollar, two dollars to one dollar, or, in more generous cases, three dollars to each dollar given. It is up to the donor to obtain a matching gift form from his or her company's personnel office. The donor must initiate the process. A listing of those corporations offering matching gift programs can be obtained by contacting the following:

Council for Advancement and Support of Education (CASE), National Clearinghouse for Corporate Matching Gift Information, Suite 400, 11 Dupont Circle, Washington, DC 20036–1261.

CASE even provides a leaflet that may be reproduced and used in a nonprofit organization's publications to promote this matching gift concept. See Appendix 10–B at the end of this chapter for an example of one museum's promotion of the matching gift concept.

Cause-Related Marketing—Doing Well by Doing Good

In the early 1980s, the American Express Company coined the term "cause-related" marketing when launching their fund-raising efforts to restore the Statue of Liberty. Each time someone used an American Express Card, American Express Travelers Cheques, or Travel Packages, or received a new AMEX card, a donation was made to the Statue of Liberty Fund. The corporation used extensive marketing and advertising to promote to the community the benefits of supporting the nonprofit organization that was providing the "facelift" for Lady Liberty. All the community would have to do was use one of the services of American Express. Since then, many more corporations have become involved in business partnerships with nonprofit agencies that can provide increased sales or revenues, raise recognition for both parties, and enhance the corporation's image.

This practice of cause-related marketing is synonymous to the old cliché of "doing well by doing good." Other examples of corporations partnering with charitable organizations that match up well with the businesses' products include Frookie's Cookies, makers of sugarless cookies, teaming with

> The practice of cause-related marketing is synonymous to the old cliché of "doing well by doing good."

the Diabetes Research Institute, and the makers of arthritis pain reliever medication joining forces with the American Arthritis Foundation. Other very visible partnerships that don't depend upon product identification include American Express and the "Share Our Strength" program, Coors Brewing Company and the "Literacy. Pass It On." message, and Sears and the Make-A-Wish Foundation. The corporation usually agrees to donate a percentage of the sales of a particular product to the nonprofit partner. It also may offer a fixed donation. The nonprofit organization in return lends its cause, prestige, constituency, and credibility to the corporation's product.

Funds to underwrite these partnerships come from the corporations' sales and marketing budgets, not from the corporations' foundations. Both the nonprofit organization and the corporation promote the partnership through advertising, point-of-purchase displays, direct mail, and other promotional opportunities. The corporation hopes that the customer will try a new product, thus increasing the corporation's profits. The nonprofit organization hopes for a new stream of revenue. And both hope that the increased publicity will bring a favorable public response for both the charity and the corporation.

In 1993, a survey of selected American consumers found that these consumers were likely to switch brands to buy a product that supports a cause when the price and quality are equal. In fact, 25 percent said that they were *very* likely to switch brands, whereas another 41 percent said they were *somewhat* likely to switch. It's obvious that cause-related marketing works because consumers are responding to the concept—consumers are motivated to change products while charities find new and reliable revenue sources. It is a classic win-win situation that produces higher sales, new revenues, greater recognition, and enhanced images.

Today, cause-related marketing is becoming the marketing tool of choice for companies in the 1990s. Cause-related marketing links fund raising to the use of corporations' products and services. Thus, the money to fund these efforts comes from the marketing budget of the company rather than from the company's foundation or community affairs department.

There is a difference between company sponsorships and cause-related marketing. A corporation that underwrites charitable activities such as public television programs, museum exhibitions, theater, opera, or special events will receive publicity, but not a direct financial return. Cause-related marketing, on the other hand, requires a formal contract between a corporation and a nonprofit for the express purpose of encouraging sales of the company's product while bringing publicity to the charitable organization. This contract establishes the amount of the gift to be given to the charity by determining the products sold or services rendered by the corporations to the public during a set period of time.

Cause-related marketing is also called joint venture marketing. To understand this concept, you have to understand the definition of marketing. Marketing is a process designed to bring about the voluntary exchange of values between an institution and its target markets through careful analysis, planning, and implementation of programs designed for the purpose of achieving organizational objectives. It is easy to see the parallels between marketing functions in a corporation and fund raising for a charity, and it is clear why corporations would want to form formal alliances with nonprofits.

People develop strong emotional attachments to certain charities or nonprofit organizations, especially if they have used the nonprofit's services at some time in their lives. For example, an elderly parent with a terminal illness may spend her last days in a hospice. The family may have strong positive feelings about the hospice's care of their loved one. Then, when these same people see that organization tied to a commercial venture such as a direct sale of a product, they often will increase their interest in that product and may ultimately purchase it. Their support is not so much for the product as it is for the nonprofit organization that helped them in a time of need.

Through a larger number of sales, the company's income increases. As a result, the company is able to share a portion of its incremental income with the nonprofit organization with which it has formed an alliance. The end result is that both the nonprofit organization and the profit-making corporation benefit from the partnership. And, the consumer has a sense of "doing good" by purchasing the product and thus helping the charity.

The National Easter Seal Society took the concept of cause-related marketing to a new dimension—that of "social responsibility marketing," which builds on the potential of cause-related partnerships. The corporations sponsoring Easter Seals extended their support beyond dollars by employing people with disabilities, becoming advocates for the disabled, and encouraging their employees to volunteer. Social responsibility marketing goes beyond cause-related marketing by adding a human dimension, one that will last much longer than any product promotion.

At the NSFRE annual meeting in Chicago in March of 1995, participants in the session, "Cause-Related Marketing: Boon or Bad Idea for Not-for-Profits?" thought that cause-related marketing would grow at the expense of corporate philanthropy. During the session, six recommendations were put forth for nonprofit organizations to consider before considering a cause-related marketing arrangement with a corporate sponsor. These six were the following:

- Consider your image.
- Carefully select your partner; tell the company how it will benefit.
- Develop a contract.
- Select the appropriate format.
- Maintain good communication.
- Apply ethical behavior standards.

Often, it is the corporation that seeks a nonprofit organization to sponsor or advance their corporate image. For example, when Oldsmobile, a division of General Motors, launched its "Aurora" philanthropic program designed to promote its new luxury sedan, Aurora, it underwrote six events in six major cities. The first event was a performance of *Sleeping Beauty* by the San Francisco Ballet. Not coincidentally, Aurora is the name of Sleeping Beauty!

Two other examples of partnerships between corporations and nonprofit organizations are Kinko's and

Sprint working together with the Make-A-Wish Foundation to provide free video conferencing for the children at the eighty-two Make-A-Wish chapters. The two corporations provide the children the opportunity to link with family or friends via one-hour site-to-site or multi-site transmissions at the 130 Kinko's branch offices. Nestlé Refrigerated Food Co., a division of Nestlé USA, Inc., is working with *Woman's Day* magazine in a campaign to raise awareness about wildlife preservation through an essay contest entitled "Kids Save the Animals." In return for promotion, Nestle will make a donation to the American Zoo and Aquarium Association.

In an article in the NSFRE Journal, Maurice Gurin, CFRE (1987), presents the disadvantages, if not the dangers, of cause-related marketing arrangements in the following six questions.

1. Does the corporate offer of financial support qualify as a tax-deductible contribution? If so, it obviously is an acceptable contribution to a voluntary organization.
2. Is it a "no-strings-attached" offer of outright financial support from a corporation's budget for public relations, advertising, or marketing? If so, it is an acceptable contribution.
3. Does the offer provide for a profit for the corporation? If it includes a built-in financial return to the corporation, the offer represents not a contribution but a share of the profits from a business transaction.
4. Could the offer of financial support weaken or debase a voluntary organization's case for public approval and philanthropic support, which is the organization's greatest resource for its continuing financial health?
5. Could the offer of financial support help to blur the public's understanding of the difference between philanthropy and business—a distinction that is essential if philanthropic support of our voluntary organization is to continue?
6. Could an outright offer of corporate support enhance the public regard for, and increase the sales of, a company marketing a product or service considered harmful to consumers?

Corporate Sponsorships

Holly Hall (1993) states that the IRS created a controversy in late 1991 when it declared that payments from corporations to organizers of college football bowl games were not charitable gifts but taxable unrelated business income (UBI) that the universities received in exchange for giving the corporations significant advertising exposure at the games. At the same time, many nonprofit organizations were relieved that putting corporate logos on the organization's materials handed out at special events (such as cups and t-shirts) would not be considered advertising and therefore would not be taxed. Nonprofit organizations look to build ties with corporations that provide for the company using the organizations' names in marketing. These arrangements can be lucrative to the nonprofit organization. Of course, there is the fear that corporations will try to take advantage of the nonprofits organizations' good names, but nonprofit organizations can benefit greatly from corporate sponsorships, especially if they are careful in constructing their deals. "Nonprofits should insist on a guaranteed minimum fee in exchange for the use of their logos," Hall continues. "What's more, nonprofits should insist that corporations specify in their advertising the exact portion of a product's purchase price that will go to the charity. They should stay away from arrangements in which the corporation advertises that the portion going to charity is limited to a certain amount, such as $300,000. Since consumers would have no way of knowing when the maximum of $300,000 had been reached, no one has any clue whether what they're paying is in fact going to benefit the cause."

The Olympic Games of 1996 were a prime example of the opportunities offered to the corporate world to financially sponsor a nonprofit organization's events. The Games held in Atlanta, Georgia, cost $1.6 billion to stage. Organizers of the Games planned early on to solicit corporate marketing dollars rather than rely upon traditional philanthropy or government grants. In addition to ticket sales, the sale of Olympic paraphernalia and commemorative coins, and fees paid by television stations to broadcast the games, corporate sponsorships were responsible for paying for the Games.

According to an article in *The Chronicle of Philanthropy* (11 January 1996), "The Olympic balance sheet is complex. More than $500 million comes from broadcast rights, bought by NBC and a handful of foreign television networks that will air the Games. Another $500 million comes from corporate sponsorships, which are fees paid by companies for rights to use the Olympic name and logo in advertising. Companies choose from three types of sponsorships:

- **Worldwide Sponsors**, which are limited to 10 companies. These are international corporations, such as Coca-Cola and Xerox, that have the right to promote their Olympic sponsorship in any of the 197 countries competing in the Games. Their contracts cover two Olympic seasons, both winter and summer Games.
- **Centennial Olympic Games Partners**, also limited to 10 companies. These are American companies, such as Home Depot, that don't have the international market of the Worldwide Sponsors and focus their Olympic promotion in the United States. They

can link themselves to two or more Olympic Games depending on their contract.

- **Centennial Olympic Games Sponsors**, which are unlimited in number. Twenty companies have signed up, but more are expected. These sponsors have a narrower market than the corporations in the top two categories. They pay lower fees for more-limited promotional rights. For example, Georgia Power only promotes its Olympic affiliation in the state, and the "Wheel of Fortune" and "Jeopardy" television game shows promote their affiliation only to their viewers.

Worldwide Sponsors and Centennial Olympic Games Partners pay up to $40 million each for sponsorship privileges. Centennial Olympic Games sponsors pay less, usually about $23 million each.

However, not all money from sponsorships and broadcast rights ends up in the coffers of the Atlanta Committee for the Olympic Games. A large chunk goes to the International Olympic Committee, which owns the rights to the Games, and the United States Olympic Committee, which provides technical assistance to American cities that run the Games and promotes sports in the United States. In the end, the Atlanta committee will receive 35 percent of the Worldwide Sponsorship money and 70 percent of the other two sponsorships. Its share of the broadcasting contracts is 60 percent.

Corporate sponsors pay for their promotional rights in cash, in-kind services, or a combination of the two. The IBM Corporation provided an elaborate computer system and personnel to the Atlanta Committee for the Olympic Games to become an Olympic Games Partner, while Home Depot paid $40 million cash for the same right."

Non-Cash Assistance from Corporations

More corporate giving officers and staff members of nonprofit organizations view non-cash assistance from corporations as a way for companies to expand their giving resources as their actual philanthropic budgets remain the same or even decline. Companies are interested in doing more with less because of corporate downsizing and the continual threat of economic recession. For years, small companies have offered "in-kind" contributions of products, supplies, facilities, services, equipment, seconded (loaned) personnel, below-market loans, and public relations assistance. Now, the larger, national and international companies are catching on to this idea and are beginning to understand how to fully integrate non-cash gifts with ongoing corporate grant-giving programs. In the beginning, most corporate CEOs considered philanthropy and social responsibility mostly in terms of cash donations. Non-cash gifts usually were not listed as part of the corporation's charitable contributions. Often these gifts were made by regional execu-

tives without notifying the corporate headquarters or by vice-presidents who took the cost of these gifts out of their budgets. These gifts were counted as the expense of "doing business." Today, this has changed, and corporations are including the cost of these non-cash, "corporate assistance" gifts as part of their total philanthropic dollars.

Corporate giving should not be considered suspect. It is possible to "do good" and still make a profit. Corporate giving that directly benefits the business does not necessarily alter its charitable nature. All aspects of business should be carried out while paying attention to social responsibility. It is possible to match the needs of the corpo-

> Corporate giving should not be considered suspect. It is possible to "do good" and still make a profit.

ration with the needs of the community. This just emphasizes the need for a well thought out giving program.

A nonprofit organization does not need to spend a lot of time or money persuading corporations to donate their products. There are organizations whose sole purpose is to help charities find such donations. See Appendix 10–C for a list of organizations that distribute donated goods.

The Chronicle of Philanthropy (Hall 1994) offers the advice of some corporate executives and charity officials for organizations that want to increase their contributions of products:

- Concentrate on small, local companies.
- Seek out companies that are rapidly growing or shrinking.
- Decide what products will be accepted.
- Plan for future needs.
- Get to know company buyers.
- Tell companies how their products can help.
- Pick up donated goods promptly.
- Set up an in-kind donations hotline.
- Consolidate requests.
- Challenge donors to match contributed items.

Additional information regarding the use of non-cash gifts to support nonprofit organizations can be found in *Corporate and Foundation Fund Raising: A Complete Guide from the Inside*, by Eugene A. Scanlan, PhD, CFRE, also in this series. A comprehensive publication, *Resource Raising: The Role of Non-Cash Assistance in Corporate Philanthropy*, offers information on all of the various types of non-cash gifts, brokerage services, and legal and tax aspects of non-cash assistance.

Other Forms of Corporate Support

Corporations may give products, lend executives, share expertise, offer internships, provide office space, or lend equipment in addition to giving cash gifts. In addition, many corporations assist nonprofit fund raising by participating in the local United Way campaign or other federated campaigns. In these campaigns, companies pledge a certain amount of money toward the campaign and then start collecting the money from their employees to meet the pledge. Each year a different employee is asked to chair the campaign for the corporation; goals are set; committees are established; presentations are made; solicitations are conducted; and money is collected. Even special events are held to raise the monies necessary to meet the goal pledged. Also, some companies even match the amount of money given by their employees. The collected money is then given to the United Way or another federated campaign as the corporate contribution to support the community's many charities.

Although there has been much criticism in recent years of the operations of the national leaders of the United Way of America, local United Way operations provide a long-standing alliance between the corporate world and the nonprofit world. In smaller communities, this tie remains firm and the two do much for the health and welfare of local residents.

Recently, corporations have cut back on seeking the involvement of their employees in these campaigns. Instead, some corporations are using electronic pledge cards and telephone solicitations in place of face-to-face solicitations with their employees. This has brought mixed reviews. According to an article in *The Chronicle of Philanthropy* (25 January 1996), "fund-raising federations that rely heavily on employee donations say that some of the technological devices used by companies are hurting contributions. As campaigns become more hands-off, it's more difficult for us to maintain that face-to-face relationship. It becomes a challenge to get our message out."

Some corporations and federated campaigns have used electronic campaigns for several years. Ameritech, Federal Express, the Gap, and General Motors use an automated telephone system to collect charity pledges, while IBM uses computer kiosks at seventy-five of its locations. Other companies have developed electronic pledge cards that allow employees to use e-mail to send in their pledges.

The greatest concern about these high tech approaches is that the human touch is lost. People give to people, not to machines. For a campaign to be successful, group meetings or a personal presentation most likely will be needed.

Declining Corporate Support Because of Mergers and Acquisitions

During two years in the 1980s, more than 4,300 companies changed ownership, and national corporate acquisitions increased 27 percent. Some companies merged voluntarily, whereas others were acquired involuntarily.

Small and mid-sized local companies were bought by large national and international corporations whose headquarters were elsewhere. These large, multinational corporations often did not take the time to learn where corporate gifts had been given in the past and even were accused of assigning too little grant money to outlying plant sites. This trend continues in the 1990s, and many business and philanthropic leaders are concerned about the decrease in corporate support in communities where such mergers have occurred. Often two companies have had strong corporate giving programs only to find that when they merge, giving doesn't double, it instead usually decreases to the level of one of the previous two. Plus, mergers often mean loss of jobs within the two corporate communities as duplicate departments are eliminated. The first to go is usually one of the corporate contributions departments.

Nonprofit organizations are usually the last to hear about mergers or takeovers. They are left in doubt about the continuation or renewal of their grants. It is especially difficult when a foreign corporation acquires a U.S. company, because philanthropy is not likely to be part of a foreign company's business. For example, when Grand Metropolitan PLC acquired Pillsbury Company in 1988, Minneapolis charities found that while Grand Met had an impressive giving record in Great Britain ($1 million per year), it paled compared to Pillsbury's philanthropic history ($8 million in the year before the merger). Even after a promise by Grand Met's senior U.S. corporate representative to match Pillsbury's previous giving, the corporation never equaled their support. Grand Met then proceeded to narrow its giving priorities to focus on families and children, thus leaving out many of the arts organizations who previously were supported by Pillsbury.

According to *The NonProfit Times* (1994), "Nonprofits complaining about downsizing at large corporations may want to consider a frequently overlooked alternative: small business. According to a recent study by the Indiana University Center on Philanthropy, small businesses (defined as firms employing 1 to 100 workers) in Indiana consistently give 3 percent or more of their net income to charity. The comparable figures on giving for medium-sized (101 to 500 employees) and large (500 or more employees) companies are 1 percent and 2.5 percent, respectively.

"Small business employees were also more generous than their big-firm counterparts, the study concludes. The average annual cash donation per employee was $264 for small companies versus $135 at medium-sized firms and $169 at large corporations. The message to community organizations is that they need to include small businesses in the mix. These contributions represent a relatively small percentage of the total amount of corporate giving, but that percentage is especially crucial to nonprofit organizations in small communities."

Even though the study found that larger corporations gave more frequently to the arts, educational, and cultural organizations and smaller businesses gave more often to international causes, all of those surveyed indicated that the greatest factor in determining where they gave was the organization that asked for their support. Again, even in corporate philanthropy, people give to what and whom they know—people give to people.

References

AAFRC Trust for Philanthropy. 1994. *Giving USA: The annual report on philanthropy.* New York: AAFRC Trust for Philanthropy.

Charities fear fallout of corporate mergers. 1996. *The Chronicle of Philanthropy 8*, no. 8 (8 February): 8–10.

Dundjerski, M., and J. Moore. 1994. A rebound ahead for corporate donations? *The Chronicle of Philanthropy 6*, no 22 (6 September):1–18.

Gray, S. 1996. Dayton Hudson Corporation's 5% philanthropic tradition turns 50. *The Chronicle of Philanthropy 8*, no. 19 (11 July): 17.

Greene, S.G. 1995. Companies seek to do well from giving. *The Chronicle of Philanthropy 7* (September 7): 13.

Gurin, M. 1987. Don't rush into cause-related marketing: Disadvantages and dangers. *NSFRE Journal* (Spring): 47–53.

Hall, H. 1993. Joint ventures with business: A sour deal? *The Chronicle of Philanthropy 5* (6 April): 21–22.

Hall, H. 1994. Getting good at getting the goods. *The Chronicle of Philanthropy 6* (12 July): 38–41.

High-tech fund raising: Boon or bane? 1996. *The Chronicle of Philanthropy 8*, no. 7 (25 January): 21.

Kane, B. 1982. Corporate Philanthropy: Historical Background. *Corporate Philanthropy*, Council on Foundations: 132–135.

Murawski, J. 1996. A banner year for giving. *The Chronicle of Philanthropy 8*, no. 16 (30 May): 1–34.

Olympic fund raising focuses on attracting large corporate sponsors. *The Chronicle of Philanthropy 8*, no. 6 (11 January): 9–12.

Roberts, B. 1990. Fund-raising for the 1990s: A changing partnership. *NSFRE Journal* (Winter): 14–16.

Small businesses pack charitable punch. 1994. *The NonProfit Times*, November: 8.

Smith, C. 1995. Can Private Foundations Woo Corporations: Corporate Philanthropy Report 10, no. 5: 1, 3–4.

Yankelovich, Skelly and White, Inc. 1982. Study prepared for the Council on Foundations.

Appendix 10–A
Resources for Researching Corporate Donors

Annual Reports—Individual annual reports of corporations of interest.

Moody's Investors Service, Inc., New York. Annual.
  Moody's Industrial Manual
  Moody's Bank and Finance Manual
  Moody's Transportation Manual
  Moody's Public Utility Manual
  Moody's Over the Counter (OTC) Manual

Gale Research (800-877-4253)
  Ward's Business Directory
  World Business Directory
  Ward's Private Company Profiles
  The World's Major Companies Directory
  The European Directory of Medium Sized Companies
  Directory of Major Companies in SE Asia
  Directory of European Business
  Companies International

The Foundation Center (800-424-9836)
  National Directory of Corporate Giving
  Corporate Foundation Profiles

National Register Publishing (800-521-8110)
  Directory of Corporate Affiliations

Datarex Corporation (415-896-1900)
  Corporate 500

John Sibbald Associates (312-693-0575)
  The Sibbald Guide Top 250

Standard & Poor's (800-221-5277)
  Security Dealers of North America
  Compmark Data Services (data on large corporations and their executives)

State Industrial Directories

City Directories—Boston: R. L. Polk and Co. (updated frequently; none for large cities).

Rand McNally International Bankers Directory—Chicago: Rand McNally and Co. Annual.

Polk's World Bank Directory, North American Edition—Nashville, TN: R. L. Polk And Co. Semi-annual.

Directory of American Savings and Loan Associations—Baltimore: T.K. Sanderson Organization. Annual.

Directory of Corporate Affiliations—New York: National Register Publishing Company. Annual.

Marketing Economics Key Plants—New York: Marketing Economic Institute (industrial plants with 100 or more employees).

Thomas Register of American Manufacturers—New York: Thomas Publishing Co. Annual.

The Taft Group (800-877-8238)
  Corporate Giving Directory
  Corporate and Foundation Givers
  Directory of International Corporate Giving

Dun & Bradstreet (800-526-0651) Annual
  Million Dollar Directory—Annual. (Businesses are worth over $1 million.)
  Regional Business Directories
  Dun's Directory of Service Companies
  Dun's Consultants Directory
  Middle Market Directory—Annual. (Businesses are from $½ million to $1 million net worth.)
  Market Identifiers (DMI)—(Information on all Dun & Bradstreet Company listings.)
  America's Corporate Families—Annual.

Monitor Leadership Directories (212-627-4140)
  Financial Yellow Book
  Law Firms Yellow Book

MLR Biomedical Information Services (215-790-7090)
  Medical and Healthcare Marketplace Guide

CASE (Council for Advancement and Support of Education) (800-554-8536)
   Matching Gift Details

The Standard Directory of Advertisers

Compumark Data Services

Bix Books, Inc. (800-486-1513)
   Book of Lists

Harris Publishing Company (800-888-5900)
   State Manufacturers Directories

Securities and Exchange Commission

DataTimes (405-751-6400)

DIALOG (800-334-2564)

Dow Jones News Retrieval (800-522-3567 ext. 52)

LEXIS/NEXIS (800-543-6862)

VENDOR LISTINGS

PROSPECT IDENTIFICATION:
   Marts and Lundy
   1280 Wall Street West
   Lyndhurst, NJ 07071

PROSPECT RESEARCH:
   American Prospect Research Association
   414 Plaza Drive
   Suite 209
   Westmont, IL 60559
   630-655-0177

ADDRESS VERIFICATION:
   PSA—Smart Names
   8800 Edgeworth Drive
   Capital Heights, MD 20743
   301-350-5600

   TRW—Information Services Division
   9861 Broken Land Parkway Drive
   Suite 401 South
   Columbia, MD 21046
   301-381-3200

   Wogan and Associates
   10046 South Western Avenue
   Chicago, IL 60655
   800-779-8309

   TransUnion
   7240 Parkway Drive
   Suite 400
   Hanover, MD 21076
   301-796-5544

TELEPHONE NUMBER RESEARCH:
   TeleMatch
   6820 Commercial Drive
   Springfield, VA 22159
   703-658-8300

Appendix 10–B
Matching Gift Programs

Check out your company's

Matching Gift Program

I f you work for one of the companies listed on the reverse, your generosity will be matched by an additional corporate gift. All you need is a Matching Gift Form from your company's Public Affairs Department. Complete the section designated for employees and mail the form to us. We'll take care of all the other details and paperwork. Your membership is vital to the future of the MUSEUM OF FINE ARTS, HOUSTON and we appreciate your continued support.

For more information:
call the Membership Office at 713/639-7550.

Corporate Matching Funds may not be used to increase your membership category or benefits.

MUSEUM OF FINE ARTS
HOUSTON

Matching Gift Companies

Air Products & Chemicals Inc.
Akzo Nobel Inc.
American Express Financial
American Express Foundation
Ameritech
Amoco Foundation, Inc.
AmGRIP
Apache Corporation
ARCO Chemical Company
ARCO Foundation
AT&T Foundation
Atochem North American
    Foundation
BankAmerica Foundation
Bankers Trust Foundation
Bank One, Texas, N.A.
Baroid Corporation
Black & Decker Corporation
The Blount Foundation, Inc.
Boeing Company
British Gas Explorations &
    Productions, Inc.
BP America Inc.
Caterpillar Foundation
Champion International
    Corporation
Charter Bank Houston
Chase Manhattan Bank
Chevron Corporation
Chubb & Son, Inc.
CIGNA Foundation
Citibank
CITICORP Foundation
Liz Claiborne Foundation
Coca-Cola Company
CogniSeis Development
Compaq Computer Foundation
Computer Associates International
Continental Group Foundation
Cooper Industries Foundation
Cray Research Foundation
Deluxe Corporation Foundation
Digital Equipment Corporation
Dixie Carriers, Inc.
Dresser Industries, Inc.
Dunn, Kacal, Adams, Pappas &
    Law
Eli Lilly & Company Foundation
Enmar, Inc.
Enron Foundation
Exxon Corporation
Federated Department Stores
Fireman's Fund Insurance
Georgia-Pacific
Glaxo, Inc.
GE Fund

John Hancock Mutual Life
Harcourt General Inc.
Hoechst Celanese Foundation
    Inc.
Houghton Mifflin Company
Houston Endowment Inc.
IBM Corporation
IMCERA Group, Inc.
Johnson & Higgins of Texas Inc.
Johnson & Johnson
JP Morgan
Kemper Securities Group, Inc.
Harris & Eliza Kempner Fund
Lyondell Petrochemical Company
May Stores Foundation, Inc.
Mayor, Brown & Platt
McFall & Sartwelle
McFall, Sherwood & Sheeny, P.C.
McGraw-Hill Foundation, Inc.
Merrill Lynch
The Mitsui USA Foundation
Mobil Foundation, Inc.
Monsanto Fund
MBank Houston
Nalco Chemical Company
The Neiman Marcus Group
The Northern Trust Company
Olin Corporation
Panhandle Eastern Corporation
Pitney Bowes
Pogo Producing Company
RJR Nabisco Foods
RJR Nabisco, Inc.
Santa Fe Pacific Foundation
Sara Lee Foundation
Sedgwick James, Inc.
Shearson Lehman Brothers Inc.
Harold Simmons Foundation
Sonat Foundation
Sun Life Assurance Company
    Canada
SBC Foundation
Tenneco Inc.
Texas Commerce Bank-Houston
Texas Instruments Foundation
Times Mirror
Transamerica Foundation
Travelers Companies Foundation
Union Pacific Corporation
Union Texas Petroleum
Vastar Resources, Inc.
Vista Chemical Company
Wells Design, Inc.
Westinghouse Electric Foundation
WMX Technologies

MUSEUM OF FINE ARTS
HOUSTON
1001 Bissonnet at Main • Houston, Texas 77005
713/639-7300 • TDD/TTY 639-7390 *(for the Hearing Impaired)*

Source: Produced courtesy of the Museum of Fine Arts, Houston.

Appendix 10–C
Resources for Nonprofit Groups Seeking Donated Products

PUBLICATIONS

Accounting for Gifts-In-Kind
Julia Lafferty and Ted Browning
Publisher: Ernst & Young
1225 Connecticut Avenue, NW
Washington, DC 20036
202-862-6000
Available from: Gifts In Kind International
700 North Fairfax Street
Suite 300
Alexandria, VA 22314
703-836-2121
4 pages
Published in 1992
Free

Computer Resource Guide: Computer Grants Directory, 4th Edition
Tracy A. Fetters and Debbie J. Zuver
Publisher: Public Management Institute
358 Brannan Street
San Francisco, CA 94107
415-896-1900
318 pages
Published in 1991
$160

Discover Total Resources: A Guide for Nonprofits
Publisher: Mellon Bank
Community Affairs Division
One Mellon Bank Center
Pittsburgh, PA 15258
412-234-8680
43 pages
Published in 1991
Free

NATIONAL GROUPS

Brother to Brother International
P.O. Box 27634
Tempe, AZ 85285-7634
602-345-9200

Gifts In Kind International
700 North Fairfax Street
Suite 300
Alexandria, VA 22314
703-836-2121

National Association for the Exchange of Industrial Resources
560 McClure Street
P.O. Box 8076
Galesburg, IL 61402-8076
309-343-0704

Second Harvest
116 South Michigan Avenue
Suite 4
Chicago, IL 60603
312-263-2303

REGIONAL GROUPS

Christian Appalachian Project
322 Crab Orchard Road
Lancaster, KY 40446
606-792-2897

Cornerstone Distribution Center
515 North Orange Blossom Trail
Orlando, FL 32805
407-649-4100

Helping Others Win
730 Northeast 55th Street
Portland, OR 97213
503-288-5110

Loading Dock
2525 Gywnn Falls Parkway
Baltimore, MD 21216
410-728-3265

Massachusetts Coalition for the Homeless
288 A Street
South Boston, MA 02210
617-737-3430

Materials for the Arts
New York Department of Cultural Affairs
410 West 16th Street
Fourth Floor
New York, NY 10011
212-255-5924

Metro Atlanta Furniture Bank
538 Permalume Place
Atlanta, GA 30318
404-355-8463

Provider's Resource Clearinghouse
3100 Blake Street
Denver, CO 80205
303-296-8580

San Francisco Clothing Bank
699 Eighth Street
Suite 6256
San Francisco, CA 94103
415-621-6100

Shelter Partnership
1010 South Flower Street
Suite 400
Los Angeles, CA 90015
213-747-1686

Surplus Exchange
1107 Hickory Street
Kansas City, MO 64101
816-472-0444

Volunteer Center
1215 Skiles Street
Dallas, TX 75204
214-826-6767

Source: "A Sampling of Resources for Non-Profit Groups Seeking Donated Products," *The Chronicle of Philanthropy*, July 12, 1994, p. 41.

Chapter 11
Raising Money from Foundations

Chapter Outline

- Definition of a Foundation
- Types of Foundations
- Planning an Effective Foundation Relations Program
- The Solicitation Process
- The Proposal Process
- The Proposal Is Accepted
- The Proposal Is Rejected
- Trends in Foundation Fund Raising

Key Vocabulary

- Community Foundation
- Corporate Foundation
- Endowment
- Family Foundation
- Foundation
- General Purpose Foundation
- Grant
- Operating Foundation
- Private Foundation
- Program Officer
- Proposal
- Public Charity
- Special Purpose Foundation

Definition of a Foundation

Another source of funds for nonprofit organizations and institutions are foundations. The Foundation Center, an independent national service organization that offers a wide variety of services and comprehensive collections of information on foundations and grants, defines a private foundation as "a nongovernmental, nonprofit organization having a principal fund of its own, managed by its own trustees and directors, and established to maintain or aid charitable, religious, or other activities serving the public good, primarily by making grants to other nonprofit organizations." Because most foundations have permanent endowments, they do not need to raise funds each year from the general public. They re-

flect the philosophy and beliefs of the individuals and corporations that establish them. Foundations are an excellent source of funds for new

> Foundations are an excellent source of funds for new approaches to tackling social problems.

approaches to tackling social problems and often will make multi-year commitments, up to three years, to address community needs.

According to the Foundation Center's *Foundation Giving* (1995), there are more than 37,000 private, community, and corporate foundations in the United States. The breakdown is as follows:

- 33,224 private independent foundations
- 1,956 private corporate foundations
- 374 community foundations

At least 75 percent of all foundations are small and unstaffed; they are run by volunteer boards, family members, or professionals such as bank trust officers and attorneys. Fewer than 10,000 foundations have assets worth more than $1 million or award more than $100,000 in grants, yet these foundations hold 96 percent of foundation assets and are responsible for 93 percent of all foundation grant dollars disbursed. Of these larger foundations, roughly one in four have paid staff. Seventy-five new foundations on average are formed each year; most of these are family foundations. Almost half of the largest foundations are found in the middle Atlantic and eastern north-central states.

Together, grantmaking foundations held more than $179 billion in endowment assets and awarded grants totaling more than $10 billion to charitable causes in 1995. However, this annual grant amount was only 7.3 percent of the $143.9 billion contributed to nonprofit organizations in the same year, according to *Giving USA 1996*. The breakdown of the $143.9 billion is illustrated in Exhibits 1–1 and 1–2.

Grants awarded by foundations are a small percentage of the total dollars contributed annually. For that reason, an organization should not devote too much of its staff time and effort to this area. The overall development program should include a variety of programs such as annual giving, planned giving, major gifts, corporate fund raising, and special events. Nonetheless, foundation fund raising remains an important source of funds for specific programs and initiatives.

Types of Foundations

There are several types of private foundations that distribute money to those who follow their application guidelines and are fortunate enough to be selected (Exhibit 11–1).

Planning an Effective Foundation Relations Program

An effective foundation relations program requires thoughtful planning for long-term development. Developing relationships with foundations that result in support will enhance all other fund-raising programs. The following are points to keep in mind.

- Foundations like to be pioneers; they look for innovation.
- People run foundations; they have specific interests and personalities.
- Foundations prefer to fund projects, not organizations.

- Giving criteria and areas of interest change from time to time.
- Foundation staff do not like to think that your financial stability depends almost solely on their funding.
- First approach foundations that have supported you in the past or are familiar with your organization.
- Do not circumvent foundation staff to sell your project to trustees.
- Be careful in using social linkages—it can backfire.

The Solicitation Process

First Step—Know Your Organization
It is extremely important for the staff involved in the solicitation of foundations to have an in-depth understanding of their organization. They should know what current programs and services their organization offers. Are there plans for new initiatives in the future? What are the current needs of the organization and what future needs will there be for the organization to fulfill its mission? One very important piece of information staff should know is the history of past contacts with foundations, including which foundations provided funding and which did not.

Depending on the organization, the development staff may or may not be directly involved in the overall planning for the organization. The advantage of having development staff involved in program planning is two-

---

Exhibit 11–1 Types of Foundations

Family Foundation—This is not a legal term but denotes those private foundations whose funds are derived from members of a single family. Generally, family members serve as officers or board members of the foundation and play an influential role in grantmaking decisions.

General-Purpose Foundation—An independent, private foundation that awards grants in many different fields of interest.

Operating Foundation—A private foundation that, rather than making grants, conducts research, promotes social welfare, and engages in programs determined by its governing body or establishment charter.

Private Foundation—As designated by federal law, a foundation whose support is from a single source (usually a person, family, or company) that makes grants to other not-for-profit organizations rather than operating its own programs. Its annual revenues are derived from earnings on investment assets rather than from donations. Private foundations are subject to more restrictive rules than public charities.

Public Charity—As designated by federal law, a foundation that, during its most recent four fiscal periods, has received one-third of its support from donations from individuals, trusts, corporations, government agencies, or other not-for-profit organizations—provided no single donor gives two percent or more of the total support for the period. Normally the charity must receive no more than one-third of its support from investment income. A public charity escapes the stringent rules that apply to a private foundation.

Special-Purpose Foundation—A public foundation that focuses its grantmaking activities on one or a few special areas of interest.

Corporate Foundation (covered in Chapter 10)—A private foundation, funded by a profit-making corporation, whose primary purpose is the distribution of grants according to established guidelines.

Community Foundation—A not-for-profit organization that receives funds and distributes them, or any income from them, for charitable purposes in a specific geographic area.

Source: From *The NSFRE Fund-Raising Dictionary*, (pp. 38, 41, 76, 123, 136, 142, 158) by John Wiley & Sons, Inc., New York. Copyright 1996 John Wiley & Sons, Inc. Reprinted by permission.

fold. First, staff can make a stronger case for support to potential funders when they have greater knowledge of the organization. Second, when staff members are aware of the current areas of interest within the foundation community, they can take part in helping shape future programs that will both fulfill the organization's mission and appeal to funders' interests. It is very important that an organization does not plan new programs only because they know foundations fund such initiatives, especially if a program does not fit within an organization's mission. Keep in mind that foundation program officers review proposals carefully to see if a new program or service furthers the mission of the organization. If it does not, it will not matter that the program falls within the foundation's giving interests, the proposal most likely will be rejected.

Researching Foundations

Finding foundations that may fund your organization can be an overwhelming task, especially for the one-person development office. It is best to narrow the focus of the research to only one or two organizational programs. Although there are a variety of approaches to identifying possible funding sources, there are three basic steps to follow.

1. Develop a broad list of prospects. Include foundations that have shown an interest in funding some aspect of your program. Look for foundations that fund organizations similar to yours or are interested in the same causes as your organization. Use subject, geographic area, or types of support approach.
2. Refine your list. Eliminate foundations unable to fund projects in either your subject or geographic area, or that do not provide the type of support needed.
3. Investigate thoroughly the foundations remaining. Gather information on staff persons, trustees, current financial status, application procedures, and most recent grantmaking activities. Call or write foundations on the final list and ask them to send you their latest annual report, guidelines, or other materials outlining their giving priorities. Information on a growing number of foundations can be found on the Internet. Visit The Foundation Center web site at http://fdncenter.org, which has links to many of these foundations. Or, visit a foundation's individual web site like the Charles Dana Foundation at http://www.dana.org/grant.html; the John D. and Catherine T. MacArthur Foundation at http://www.macfdn.org; the AT&T Foundation at http://www.att.com/foundation; or the Rockefeller Brothers Fund at http://www.igc.apc.org/rbf for specific information regarding their giving policies.

Sources for Researching Foundations

There are a number of sources available for researching foundations (Exhibit 11–2). Having a reference library in your own development office is a great help. To start your library, consider purchasing one of the published foundation directories (average price, $200). The *Chronicle of Philanthropy,* which is published twice a month, lists more recent foundation grants than the published directories. Materials such as annual reports, guidelines, and brochures that are available from individual foundations also belong in the reference library.

Technology is an added tool to use in the research process, with the introduction of software packages like Taft's Prospector's Choice and Orca's Foundation Directories on diskette and CD–ROM. More expensive than the published directories, these databases are more comprehensive and allow the user to manipulate the data to make the research process easier. The price range for this software is $400 to $1,000 depending on the specific package and number of users.

> Technology is an added tool to use in the research process.

For those organizations just beginning a foundation program or with no budget for building a reference library, the Foundation Center and its affiliated libraries across the country can help you in your research. (See listing of Foundation Center libraries in Appendix 8–A.) The Foundation Center also has copies of the IRS form 990, a form completed by private foundations containing their financial information. Check your local public library, too, because many now have the tools you will need for doing this type of research. If you live in a community that is home to a college or university, the school's libraries or development offices can be a rich source of current materials. Also, for those doing fund raising in the greater Washington, DC area, the office of the National Society of Fund Raising Executives (NSFRE) located in Alexandria, Virginia, has an excellent library open to members and nonmembers alike. Information also may be requested from the NSFRE Resource Center via phone (800-688-FIND) or mail.

Approaching Foundations

After completing the first phase of research, you should have a list of ten to twelve foundations to approach in the coming year. Make an initial approach by telephone to request additional information such as the foundation's annual report, guidelines, or other published materials. If, after reading the guidelines and other materials detailing the foundation's interests, additional information is still needed, a call to a program officer is in order. For example, an organization may have an educational program that looks like it fits nicely within the giving areas of a foundation. One could find out what specific level of education, that is, pre-school, elementary, secondary,

Exhibit 11–2 Available Reference Publications

The Foundation Center Publications
- *The Foundation Directory*—largest foundations
- *The Foundation Directory, Part II*—mid-sized foundations
- *Foundation Grants Index*—grants given by more than 1,000 of the largest independent, corporate, and community foundations
- *Foundation Grants Index Quarterly* (periodical)—updates on recent grants
- Grants guide series on various subjects
- Regional guides to grantmaking
- *Guide to U.S. Foundations, Their Trustees, Officers, and Donors*—information on more than 38,000 foundations
- *The Foundation 1000*—information on the 1,000 largest foundations
- *National Directory of Grant Making Public Charities*—information on 800 public charities that award grants
- *National Directory of Corporate Giving*—information on 2,600 grantmakers

- *Corporate Foundation Profiles*—235 of the largest corporate foundations

The Taft Group Publications
- *Corporate Giving Directory*—profiles 1,000 largest corporate foundations and corporate giving programs
- *Corporate Giving Watch* (periodical)
- *Foundation Giving Watch* (periodical)
- *Foundation Reporter*—top 1,000 private foundations
- *Directory of Corporate and Foundation Givers*—includes smaller, more regional grantmakers

Other Publications
- *Foundation News and Commentary*—Council on Foundations
- *The Chronicle of Philanthropy*
- *Corporate Philanthropy Report* (periodical)—Capitol Publications

or college, is of most interest. This call is an excellent opportunity to establish a relationship with a program officer by seeking his or her advice or help in preparing your proposal. However, it can also alienate a program officer to an organization if the staff person asks questions that are covered in the guidelines. One should be prepared to answer specific questions on the goals and costs of the program, and provide reasons why it is believed the foundation might be interested in your organization or program. A meeting can be requested while speaking to the program officer, if it seems appropriate. However, be aware that with the current volume of proposals received by foundations, it is becoming increasingly more difficult to arrange a face-to-face meeting for an organization with potential grantmakers.

A growing trend for approaching foundations is the "letter of inquiry." This letter, no longer than two pages, can be signed by the organization's chief executive, the chief development officer, a board member who heads the development committee, or someone from your organization with ties or connections to the foundation. It is used, based on the research completed, to introduce an organization and its programs to certain foundations. No specific request is made in the letter. (See Appendix 11–A for sample letter of inquiry.) A follow-up telephone call is then made to the foundation to verify its interest.

It is useful to develop a checklist or worksheet to help you keep track of the information you are collecting on selected foundations. This data also can be collected and tracked on an organization's computer database. An example of such a worksheet is the Foundation Prospect Profile in Exhibit 11–3.

Meeting with the Foundation

After sending a letter of inquiry to the foundations you placed on your priority list and confirming their interest by telephone, it is time to plan your face-to-face approach. The first decision to make is to decide whom you will take to the meeting. If you are not strongly versed in the organization's program initiatives or if the area is highly technical, make sure that you take a senior level staff member from your organization's program depart-

"MAN, THEY WEREN'T VERY ENCOURAGING."

Source: © Mark Litzler

Exhibit 11-3 Foundation Prospect Profile

Foundation's Name _____

Address: _____   Telephone Number: _____

President: _____   Contact Person: _____

1. Any previous grants awarded to the organization by the foundation?
2. Are there personal connections to the organization either by board members or CEO?
3. Is there a demonstrated commitment by the foundation to funding in the organization's field?
4. Does the foundation make grants in the organization's geographic area?
5. Is the organization's specific request for funding within the range of the foundation's grants?
6. Is there a foundation policy prohibiting grants for the type of support requested by the organization?
7. Does the foundation usually make grants to cover the full cost of a project/program or does the foundation prefer to be one of several grantmakers supporting a project/program?
8. Over what period of time does the foundation make awards? annual grants? multi-year grants?
9. What types of organizations does the foundation currently support? Who are recent grantees?
10. What are the deadlines for applying for a grant?

ment. If you are confident that you can answer detailed questions regarding the specific program for which you are seeking funding, then consider another source of support. If a member of your staff or board has a contact within the foundation, ask that person to accompany you. It is extremely important that the persons attending the meeting are well prepared. They must know what you expect from them that day, why you are seeking funds from this particular foundation, and what you are asking of the foundation. Meet with whomever is accompanying you to the meeting in advance and practice your solicitation. The meeting should be comfortable, but not casual, with a well-organized presentation that does not appear to be stilted or rehearsed. A team presentation can feel spontaneous, but in actuality be well orchestrated.

> A team presentation can feel spontaneous, but in actuality be well-orchestrated.

Is there an advantage of having a board member from your organization with you? Of course, if you select the right person. The last thing you want is someone who adds nothing to the meeting, who is present only because of his or her name recognition. The foundation officer can read that name on your letterhead. Instead, bring someone who can champion your specific cause, someone who is thoroughly involved with the issues and programs of your organization. This will mean carefully reviewing your board to select the proper individual for a specific foundation approach.

Working with a Program Officer

Foundation program officers come in all shapes and sizes with a variety of personalities. If you are fortunate, you will find a program officer who has not only read your letter of inquiry, but is interested in your project and wants to meet with you immediately. At the worst, you will find that you have either contacted the wrong person in the foundation or that the person is not interested in meeting with you at all and, no matter what their written guidelines say, he or she states that the foundation is not interested in funding your program. Somewhere in between is the reception that most development officers receive. It can be as nebulous as the program officer stating, "Follow the guidelines, submit your application, and you'll hear from us shortly," or as specific and encouraging as, "You fit within our guidelines and we would welcome a proposal from your organization."

If you find that interested, helpful program officer, don't be afraid to ask what you can do to make your proposal more promising. Read through the foundation's guidelines in detail, and ask what specifics they look for that may not have been written in the guidelines. Some program officers who are interested in funding a potential program or broadening their outreach to new organizations will work with you to develop a "winning document." Program officers have been known to call development officers and suggest that specific items be added or deleted from a proposal to make it stronger when being presented to the decision-making committee. It is truly good fortune to find the helpful and nurturing program officer.

A word of caution—don't take it personally if a foundation program officer does not return your calls or is not interested in your program even though on paper you appear to be an ideal "fit" for funding from his or her foundation. It may take several approaches, much nurturing, and several months or years before you are even granted a meeting. Don't give up. Program officers change; foundations expand to include new program initiatives; and you may have fine-tuned your proposal so that it is now just what the foundation wishes to fund. Keep the foundation on your mailing list for appropriate materials from your organization. Let them become used to hearing from you and learn the value of your organization to their community.

If you find that your organization falls into several of the foundation's giving categories, for example, both environmental and educational, make a decision as to which area your program is most likely to receive funding. Don't hesitate to ask the program officer for guidance. It may be that there is a much larger source of money for funding in one area than the other. Whatever you do, don't try to make your proposal fit both areas. Select one and make the strongest case possible for funding in the area you selected.

One of the greatest challenges a fund raiser encounters is finding the right foundation to fund a specific program. Sometimes you will find that you fall under the general giving guidelines of a foundation, but when you receive materials from the foundation you may realize that you do not fit exactly into their program efforts. At this point, you must determine how closely your program matches one or more of the foundation's program areas and what changes you can make so that your program will fit the specific guidelines without compromising the program's integrity. Minor adjustments are done frequently. Do not rewrite or redefine your program because you may put yourself in jeopardy of being turned down because the program does not fall within the guidelines of your organization's mission. Be creative; be cautious; but, foremost, be honest to yourself and to your organization.

Often you will complete your research only to find that the deadline for submitting proposals has passed. At this time, you can do one of two things. First you can proceed as planned, sending a letter of inquiry and then contact the foundation's program officer. Some foundations allow program officers to accept promising proposals after deadlines are past. Others are strict with their deadlines and allow no exceptions to the set deadline. If the former, proceed under the direction of the program officer and meet every extended deadline given to you. This is the time for you to "pull out all stops," because they have extended a courtesy to you. If the latter proves to be true and you are told that it is indeed too late for this round, then continue to nurture the program officer and submit everything in a timely manner to meet their next deadline. This is not the time to use influence to bypass the program officer to try to have the date extended by someone else. This will only antagonize the program officer and may preclude your proposal from being accepted at any time.

Another type of program officer you may encounter is the recalcitrant foundation program officer—the one who thinks that the foundation's money is his or hers and is not interested in helping you advance your proposal in any manner. This personality type exists in both large and small foundations. If you confront this trait in a program officer, don't try to fight it, just explicitly follow the foundation guidelines and treat the person with respect, but with an equal amount of distance. Then let the system work for you and respectfully ignore the program officer's recalcitrant behavior.

Most grants from foundations will be disbursed during a multi-year period. Often, programs require some fine tuning or even drastic change during the course of the funding years. If and when changes are necessary, immediately inform your program officer of the need to make changes, and make sure these changes will not adversely affect your funding. This also may include extending the deadline of the final product. Often, additional work will need to be done before the final report or product can be delivered. Dates can be extended for good reasons. Just keep your program officer informed. Program officers do not like to be surprised because they need to defend your program and funding to their board of directors. The cardinal rule is to keep your program officer apprised—of both your successes and failures. How you manage the grant is as important as having been awarded the grant.

The Proposal Process

It can take several months to put together a competitive grant proposal. Those months should be spent cultivating the potential funder and carefully planning, documenting, and internally reviewing the proposals. The following is a suggested time table for effective proposal development.

One to three months:
- assess organizational needs
- develop ideas for programs and projects that meet the organization's needs and could be funded by foundations
- prepare position or concept papers on new programs/ projects
- research potential foundation funders
- approach selected foundation for additional information
- submit a letter of inquiry
- develop goals and objectives for programs/projects and prepare specific plans for implementation

Three to six months:
- draft proposal, circulate for comment, finalize document, receive appropriate approvals

- submit the proposal by the application deadline
- schedule a face-to-face meeting, if possible
- await notice of acceptance or rejection from the foundation

Preparing the formal proposal is the last step in the process, not the first. Only when a foundation indicates an interest in the program or project based on your initial inquiry should you prepare a formal grant proposal. Follow carefully the instructions the foundation provides in its annual report or giving guidelines. Requirements may include limits on the number of pages, forms to be attached, necessary signatures, appendices allowed, and the number of copies to be submitted. See Exhibit 11–4 for important points to remember when preparing your proposal.

Recently, in an attempt to decrease the amount of paperwork that must be completed by grant seekers, some regional grantmaker groups have developed a common form. A complete listing of regional area grantmakers (RAGs) can be found on the Council of Foundations web site at http://www.cof.org/docs/rags.html. Appendix 11–B depicts the common application form for the

Delaware Valley Grantmakers, which was given the highest rating of twelve such forms in a recent issue of *The Grantsmanship Center Magazine*. This form was the first of its kind to be developed and serves as a model for the other regional associations of grantmakers. On the national level, the National Network of Grantmakers is developing its own common proposal form tailored for progressive funders.

The Proposal Format

There are several variations of the proper format for a written proposal. The following outline covers the key elements to be included. The sample proposal in Appendix 11–C is a variation from this outline but still does include these elements.

Cover Letter

The cover letter should be one to two pages long and provide a brief summary of the proposal and specific request. Always begin the letter with a reference to previous contacts such as telephone calls or meetings. Show how this request matches with the foundation's purposes and guidelines. Be sure the letter includes a contact name, telephone number, and is signed by the chief executive officer or board president.

Cover Page

The cover page includes the name of the program/project, the name of the organization, its address, telephone number, name and title of contact person, date of submission, and the name of the foundation to which the proposal is being submitted.

Proposal

The proposal itself should be five to ten pages long, if the foundation has no other set guidelines. Always follow the foundation's specific outline. However, if a foundation does not have an outline, use the one that follows.

Summary of the Need. Explain the problem to be addressed, and describe the need for the program/project locally, regionally, and nationally.

Background on Organization. Introduce the organization's mission, present its programs and services, geographic area, and constituencies served. State the sources of support for the organization.

Planned Programs, Activities, Projects, and Services. Describe in detail the purpose, goals, objectives, and action plan for the specific program for which you are requesting support. Explain how the activity relates to what other organizations are doing to solve the problem, but point out how it is different. Include information regarding the management of the program, the staffing, and how it will fit into the overall organization. A time table for implementation is also needed.

Exhibit 11–4 Points To Remember When Preparing Your Proposal

1. Be sure your organization is eligible to apply for a grant from the foundation.
2. Explain "who, what, why, when, where, how, and how much" concerning your organization and its program.
3. Present your case in a clear, concise, and logical manner.
4. Use headings and subheadings to assist the reader through the proposal.
5. Clearly link your program or project to the foundation's interests.
6. Set realistic goals and objectives for the program or project. Avoid too ambitious plans.
7. Establish a reasonable budget for the program or project.
8. Be certain the program or project has qualified leaders and staff.
9. Describe how the program or project is innovative.
10. Explain how your organization and others have worked to solve the problem addressed by the program or project.
11. If the funder supports only national or regional efforts, illustrate how the program or project can have an impact beyond your geographic area.
12. Be sure the funds you are requesting would be used to enhance a current program or create a new one, not to replace operating funds.
13. If applicable, provide evidence of collaboration with other organizations and outline sources of support.

Evaluation. Report on how the program will be evaluated. List how objectives will be evaluated, by whom, and when. The evaluation process will assess the program's progress toward its identified goals at specified and regular intervals.

Fund-Raising Plans. Explain how the program/service will be funded currently and in future years. List other foundations that are being approached but do not include the amount being requested.

Timeline. Describe the length of time the program/service will be in operation.

Specific Grant Request. State the purpose and amount of request including a timeline for a multi-year grant request. List any matching funds you have obtained from foundations or individuals.

Attachments. The following supporting documents could be added as appendices to the proposal.

1. Organization's Mission Statement
2. Proof of tax-exempt status under IRS Section 501(c)(3)
3. Financial Audit
4. Organization's Strategic Plan or Long Range Plan
5. Organization's Operating Budget
6. Specific Budget for Described Program/Service
7. List other foundation and corporate supporters; proof of matching funds or in-kind contributions
8. Listing of organization's current board of directors or trustees
9. Letters of agreement from other organizations collaborating in program/service
10. Letters of support from individuals who have been helped by the organization, program, or service
11. Job description of new positions; résumés of staff involved in program/service
12. Other collateral material such as annual report, brochures, etc.

Submitting the Proposal

If there is a submission deadline, it will be stated in the annual report and/or guidelines. Check to see if this is the date by which the foundation must receive the application or the date by which you should mail it. Foundations seldom extend their deadlines and usually will return late proposals; however, some will hold late submissions for review in the next cycle. Many foundations do not set deadlines. Instead, they may request that you submit a proposal a certain number of weeks before their next board meeting. Other foundations review applications as they are submitted.

Before a proposal leaves your organization, make sure you have obtained organizational approval, following internal procedures. You may need to have finance staff persons review the budget and the grants office or officer—if you have one—review the entire proposal. You also may need the approval of your organization's board of directors. Most importantly, be sure to have others proofread the entire proposal to make sure that the proposal does not contain any omissions, inaccuracies, or typographical errors.

Once you are sure the proposal is complete, submit the proposal by certified, return-receipt mail or express delivery so you will have proof that the foundation received it.

After the Proposal Is Submitted

After you submit your proposal, it is important to contact the foundation to make sure it has received it. This is also a good opportunity to once again request a meeting with the program officer, if earlier attempts to schedule a meeting failed. Ask the program officer if he or she has any questions about your submission or if there is any additional information he or she needs. Try to get some idea from the program officer regarding the timing and likelihood of funding.

If your organization receives funding from a foundation during the time another foundation is considering your proposal, call the program officer to let him or her know. Also inform the program officer of any other developments such as a change in senior staff or financial difficulties. If a problem arises for your organization, it is best to let the foundation know of the problem and of your organization's plan or solution.

> If a problem arises for your organization, it is best to let the foundation know of the problem and of your organization's plan or solution.

How Foundations Evaluate Proposals

Foundations consider the following when evaluating proposals.

- Importance of and need for the program or service
  1. from the foundation's point of view
  2. considering the needs of society
  3. regarding the value of your organization
- Effectiveness and soundness of the program's plan
- Feasibility of program
- Capability of organization to implement program
- Cost efficiency of program
- Duplication of services
- Continuation of a previous foundation commitment
- Interest of the foundation's trustees

The Proposal Is Accepted

When you learn that your proposal has been accepted and will be funded at the level requested, the first thing to do is to prepare a thank-you letter from the chief executive officer or president of the board to be sent to the foundation. If the program officer did not contact you regarding the acceptance, you should call and thank the program officer for his or her help.

It is important to know the reporting requirements of the foundation. Do they want a narrative-type report or fiscal reports? How often do they want to receive reports? What other information should you send to the foundation during the year—internal progress reports, newspaper articles? The organization is beginning a new relationship with a funder, so the objective is to maintain a good relationship with proper recognition and reporting. Keep in mind all activity is in preparation for the next approach to this foundation.

The Proposal Is Rejected

Foundations are not able to fund every proposal submitted to them. Therefore, it is not uncommon for an organization to learn that the proposal it submitted was rejected. As the development officer, you need to take advantage of this opportunity and call the program officer to find out why the proposal was rejected. Some reasons why proposals are rejected are listed in Exhibit 11–5. However, it is important for you to learn the specific reasons why your proposal was turned down. Here again, the program officer serves as an adviser and helper. Once you know why the proposal was turned

---

Exhibit 11–5 Why Proposals Are Rejected

- Format and Composition
  1. The proposal did not follow the foundation's guidelines.
  2. The proposal is poorly written and difficult to understand.
- Content
  1. The problem was not documented properly.
  2. The project objectives do not match the objectives of the foundation.
- The problem does not strike the reviewer as significant.
- The project budget is not within the range of available funding.
- The proposed project or program has not been coordinated with other individuals and organizations working in the same area.
- Prospective client groups have not been involved in planning and determining program goals.
- The foundation does not know the capabilities of the organization submitting the proposal.
- The program objectives are too ambitious in scope.
- There is insufficient evidence that the project can sustain itself beyond the life of the grant.
- The evaluation procedure is inadequate.

---

down, ask when you might submit another proposal, or ask about other foundations that might be interested in this program.

Trends in Foundation Fund Raising

Foundations are joining forces to leverage the power of their grantmaking, set joint agendas, and fund projects that are more national in scope. Because the costs of nonprofit organizations' programs are beyond the ability of a single small foundation to fund adequately, small foundations are developing regional associations like the Washington Regional Area Grantmakers and other topical groups. They share information about grantees and programs to disburse their collective grant dollars more effectively. Collaborative funding of such issues as AIDS and homelessness is common today.

Concerned with the potential for duplication of programs and services in the nonprofit sector, foundations expect grant seekers to establish cooperative networks and linkages with other related organizations to address many of society's most pressing problems. To achieve long-term and broad-scale impact, foundations prefer model programs, rather than one-shot projects. Directors and program officers like to make grants to programs that address significant problems and those that could reflect well on their foundations. Organizations need to develop programs that simultaneously serve two needy groups, thereby multiplying the effect of foundation funding. To increase a new organization's chances for funding, the organization should involve another trusted community organization in a joint proposal. Some foundations see themselves as catalysts in seeking solutions for today's problems. Increasingly, these foundations no longer accept proposals from organizations. Rather, they approach the individual organizations that are doing innovative programming in these areas to develop joint efforts.

Earlier in this chapter, a new kind of strategic relationship was mentioned, one developing between foundation staff and development officers. Foundations, in an effort to ensure that the grants they make are sound investments, are working with organizations to develop programs and services that help solve many of today's most pressing social problems.

Community foundations will play an increasingly important role in grantmaking. According to the Council on Foundations' survey of community foundations in the United States published in 1994, community foundations continue to grow. In the twenty years from 1973 to 1993, the assets of community foundations have increased from about $1 billion to nearly $10 billion. Although community foundations accounted for only 1 percent of all U.S. foundations in 1991, they awarded 5.9 percent of all grants, received 11.7 percent of all gifts, and held 4.9 percent of all assets that year. Findings from the survey confirm that because of the significant role living donors are playing in the growth of many community foundations, these foundations have added donor relations staff to help serve existing donors and to reach out to new donors.

For more information on seeking grants from foundations, see *Corporate and Foundation Fund Raising: A Complete Guide from the Inside*, by Eugene A. Scanlan, PhD, CFRE, another book in this series.

References

Association of American Fund Raising Counsel (AAFRC) Trust for Philanthropy. 1996. *Giving USA 1996*. New York: AAFRC Trust for Philanthropy.

Council on Foundations. 1994. Survey of Community Foundations. Washington, D.C.: Council on Foundations.

The Foundation Center. 1995. *Foundation Giving*. New York: The Foundation Center.

Appendix 11–A
Sample Letter of Inquiry

March 22, 1995

Charles R. Halpern
President
The Nathan Cummings Foundation
1926 Broadway, Suite 600
New York, NY 10023

Dear Mr. Halpern:

Thanks to your past support with a seed grant, Green Seal is a vibrant and growing organization and is in an exciting stage now. In the first couple of years, time was taken to establish, with a wide-spread review process, scientific criteria and standards in several product categories. We now have 237 products certified and standards published in 52 categories. And we continue to build momentum with many other products currently under review.

I write to inquire about presenting a proposal to The Nathan Cummings Foundation. With the current climate in the government of challenging the regulatory process, which may harm many of our environmental safeguards, and the strain of budgets forecasting the cutback of many programs, it is necessary to turn to the private sector to help protect our natural resources. Green Seal's current emphasis aims to organize institutions across the country and harness market forces toward purchasing environmentally preferable products, thus reducing environmental abuse at the source.

Recently, Green Seal initiated an Environmental Partners Program to assist institutional organizations such as businesses, universities, and local and state governments to provide leadership for organizations that care about the environmental impact of their purchases. In exchange for a commitment to buy products that cause less harm to the environment, Green Seal provides expert advice, assistance, and educational tools to develop and implement a "green" procurement policy.

Institutional consumers purchase over $100 billion in products and services each year. By altering their purchasing patterns, these institutions have the potential to greatly influence manufacturers to reduce their significant impact on the environment. For example, an institution purchasing 100 tons of recycled paper meeting Green Seal's standards would save 1,700 trees, 700,000 gallons of water, reduce air pollution by 6,000 pounds, and save over 200,000 kilowatt hours of energy. We currently have 93 Environmental Partners. By specifying environmentally preferable products on their purchase orders, these institutions can create quite a market force for protecting the environment.

In addition to our Environmental Partners, we are also working with two specific industry groups to develop a specialized buying guide geared to their particular needs. In the entertainment industry, we are working with 18 television and movie studios to analyze their special purchasing needs—such as particle-board for set designs—and developing policies to guide their purchases. We are also doing a similar study for the hotel industry.

With the support of The Nathan Cummings Foundation, we would also like to target the special purchasing needs for a transportation sector. We would specifically look to institutions who have a fleet of vehicles, like state governments, regional post offices, and car and truck rental agencies, to help them develop efficient maintenance and purchasing policies that would include such items as environmentally preferable lubricating oil and re-refined engine oil. A survey conducted by the National Conference of State Fleet Administrators found that over 1,200 alternative fuel vehicles are owned by 54 agencies and over 1,400 more are expected to be purchased in 1996.

The private sector needs to help reduce the environmental impact of products. Green Seal helps redirect consumer purchases toward environmentally preferable products to provide for a more sustainable society. Our Environmental Partners program's objective is to harness a market force through these institutions for environmentally preferable products, thus promoting more environmentally responsible manufacturing.

Green Seal seeks your support to help us enlarge our pool of Environmental Partners, target a transportation sector, and provide them with educational tools for adopting green procurement policies. Our budget for this project is $75,000. Enclosed is the budget for our Environmental Partners program, our organizational budget for this fiscal year, staff qualifications, and our Annual Report.

I plan to be in New York in the first and third week in April and would welcome the opportunity to meet with you to discuss this project.

Sincerely,

Carol B. Waite

Carol B. Waite
Vice President, Development

Enclosures

Courtesy of Carol B. Waite, CFRE, CEO, CBW Consulting, Former Vice President, Green Seal, 1995.

Appendix 11–B
Common Grant Application Form

Delaware Valley Grantmakers'
COMMON GRANT APPLICATION FORM

Date of application _____

Organization:_____

Contact person:_____Tel:_____

Grant Request:

$_____for General Support; Total Operating Budget_____
or
$_____for Project Support; Total Project Budget _____

Purpose of grant or Project name _____

Please answer all the questions in the order listed and title each section.
Please submit _____ copy(ies), without binders. Applicant may be
requested to provide additional materials. All agencies, even if
previously funded, need to include the following information:

A.   PROPOSAL SUMMARY (1/2 page)

B.   NARRATIVE (maximum of five pages)

    1.   Background. Briefly summarize the agency
        a.   History and mission;
        b.   Current programs, activities and
            accomplishments, with highlights of
            the past year.

    2.   Funding Request. Please include or describe
        a.   Current need;
        b.   Program objectives that address the
            current need;
        c.   Constituency served/involved;
        d.   Events and activities planned, with
            timetable for implementation;
        e.   Key staff/volunteers involved and their roles
            (Indicate any new staff/volunteers required);
        f.   Interaction with other organizations (if
            relevant).

-1-

3.   **Evaluation.** Please discuss
        a.   How you will define success (and, if applicable, how it will be measured);
        b.   How you will evaluate the effectiveness of your activities at the end of the funding period.

C.   ATTACHMENTS

1.   **Board of Directors.** Please include addresses and occupations and constituencies (ethnic, economic, consumer and/or neighborhood representatives).

2.   **Finances.**
        a.   Current agency annual operating budget (project budget if project funding is requested).
        b.   Funding sources for the organization:
          • 3 largest contributors in the last year, with amounts
          • Funding received or pending for this request
          • Anticipated future funding sources (if different from above)
          • Recent annual financial statement (audited if available).

3.   **Personnel.** Please attach resumes of top staff and relevant key staff/volunteers involved.

4.   **Other support material.**
        a.   A copy of the most recent IRS letter regarding your agency's tax exempt status;
        b.   Assurance that your organization is registered to solicit funds as required by the Pennsylvania Solicitation for Funds for Charitable Purposes Act, if applicable;
        c.   Annual report, if available;
        d.   Several examples of current relevant newspaper/magazine articles or reviews about organization's program, if available.

- 2 -

Delaware Valley Grantmakers'
COMMON REPORT FORM

All grantees must submit a grant report which is due_____
or _____one year from the date of the grant *or*_____ at the
time of the next application.

The report should be two to five pages in length. Please follow
the outline below as you write your report. A paragraph on each
topic should be sufficient.

* *

Grant number (if applicable)   _____

Date grant received_____

Organization _____

Contact Person_____Telephone number _____

Grant amount $_____for General Support

     or $_____for Project Support

Purpose of grant *or* Project name _____

1.   List and evaluate objectives you planned to accomplish
     at least in part with this grant. Briefly describe activities
     and people involved. Explain any obstacles you encountered
     and changes in plans. Note significant organizational
     changes that occurred during the year, e.g. staff changes,
     membership growth. Explain in what ways this year's
     experiences affected your objectives for the coming year.

2.   Describe your organization's major strengths and
     weaknesses relative to the following criteria. Did your
     organization's work:

     a. Benefit low-income and/or African-American,
         Asian-American, Latino or other under-
         represented communities

-3-

b.   Assure the active involvement of constituents in defining problems to be addressed, making policy, planning and evaluating the program;

c.   Address causes of social and economic inequities;

d.   Promote collective action and institutional change;

e.   Build the skills of emerging and experienced leaders and promote cultural pluralism.

3.   What were your fundraising goals? What did you actually raise? If there is a difference between your goals and actual funds raised, please indicate the reasons and explain how you managed. If the grant was not spent by the due date of this report, please explain your plans.

4.   Please attach an itemized financial statement for the current fiscal year, indicating all income and expenses. Please include project financial statement, if appropriate. Enclose your most recent audit.

We welcome your comments about this report.

I certify that this grant was used for the purpose designated.

_____

Name & Title   Date

- 4 -

Grantmakers that accept the
Common Grant Application & Common Report Form

Grantmaker	Telephone
1957 Charity Trust	610/828-8145
Advanta Corp.	215/784-5311
ARAMARK	215/238-3271
ARCO Chemical Company	610/359-3189
AT & T	215/963-1869
Isaac & Carol Auerbach Family Fdn.	610/667-8090
Black United Fund of Pennsylvania	215/732-9266
Byers' Foundation	215/822-6700
Claneil Foundation*	610/828-6331
Connelly Foundation	610/834-3222
Conrail, Inc.	215/209-4697
CoreStates Bank	215/973-5494
Douty Foundation	610/828-8145
Emergency Aid of Pennsylvania Fdn., Inc.*	610/527-1712
Samuel S. Fels Fund	215/731-9455
Elsie Lee Garthwaite Memorial Fdn.	610/527-1100
Grundy Foundation*	215/788-5460
The HBE Foundation	610/688-0143
Allen Hilles Fund	610/828-8145
Hunt Manufacturing Company Fdn.*	215/972-0123
Huston Foundation	610/832-4949
Stewart Huston Charitable Trust	610/384-2666
Independence Foundation	215/563-8105
Lukens Foundation	610/383-2159
McLean Contributionship*	610/527-6330
Penn Mutual Life Insurance Company	215/956-7785
The William Penn Foundation*	215/988-1830
The Philadelphia Foundation	215/563-6417
Philadelphia Newspapers, Inc.	215/854-4805
Phoebus Fund	215/557-7095
PNC Bank	215/585-6208
PNC Bank, Trustee	215/585-8174
The Prudential	215/784-2674
Rohm & Haas	215/592-2863
Rosenlund Family Foundation	not available
Seybert Institution	610/828-8145
W.W. Smith Charitable Trust	610/525-9667
Ethel Sergeant Clark Smith Memorial Fund	215/973-3704
Nathan Speare Foundation	610/566-8000
Sun Company	215/977-6524
United Way of Southeastern Pennsylvania	215/665-2500
Vanguard Group Foundation	610/669-1000
Waste Management of Pennsylvania	215/736-9400
Wawa, Inc.	610/358-8872
Wyeth-Ayerst Laboratories	610/971-5819

Other materials, such as a Proposal Cover Sheet may be required.
Please be sure to check with each grantmaker.
* accepts Common Grant Application but NOT Common Report Form

About Delaware Valley Grantmakers . . .

Delaware Valley Grantmakers is a membership association comprised of private and community foundations, corporate giving programs, charitable trusts and federated funds in the Philadelphia region. DVG's mission is to promote more effective philanthropy in the Delaware Valley. It is <u>not</u> the purpose of Delaware Valley Grantmakers to make or influence grants or to affect the fund raising efforts of individual organizations.

For further information . . .

To find out more about grantmakers in the Philadelphia region, contact The Foundation Center at the Free Library of Philadelphia at 215/686-5423. To purchase a copy of *The Directory of Pennsylvania Foundations*, contact Triadvocates Press at 610/544-6927.

Source: Reprinted with permission from Dale Mitchell, Executive Director, Delaware Valley Grantmakers, Philadelphia, PA, 1996.

Appendix 11–C

Sample Proposal

Container Recycling Institute

1400 16th Street, NW Suite 250
Washington, DC 20036-2217
tel. 202/797-6839 fax. 202/797-5411

August 26, 1996

Christopher Hormel, Executive Director
Global Environmental Project Institute
PO Box 1111
Ketchum, Idaho 83340

Dear Mr. Hormel:

The Container Recycle Institute (CRI) requests the opportunity to submit the enclosed proposal to the Global Environmental Project Institute for a Beverage Industry Watch Project.

CRI is a nonprofit, research and public education organization that compiles data on beverage container generation, recycling and disposal, studies alternative systems for recovering these containers from the waste stream, provides technical assistance to the government agencies and grassroots activists and serves as the National Clearinghouse for Deposit Legislation.

Again this year, Americans will throw away an estimated 50 billion beer and soda cans and bottles—300 per capita. These no-deposit, no-return cans and bottles are a corporate subsidy and a drain on government and taxpayers. We believe this is wrong, and that polluters should pay the price for one-way beverage containers.

The special interests fighting bottle bills and pushing for repeal of existing laws will outspend bottle bill proponents by 100 to 1. They have the muscle but we can win with the facts, if we have the resources to do the research and get the information out to activists, public officials and lawmakers.

Our own research, and numerous publicly and privately funded studies, show that deposit systems complement other materials recovery efforts such as curbside recycling and community drop-off programs. The city of Seattle, with the most comprehensive curbside program in the nation, has stated that a combined bottle bill/curbside program would divert more materials from the waste stream than a curbside program alone, and save the city money.

The beverage industry, which opposes internalization of the environmental costs of one-way beverage containers, has launched a major effort to repeal existing bottle bills by distributing slick booklets and "fact sheets" filled with half-truths and outright lies about recycling and bottle bills. There is an urgent need to "debunk" their myths and get the other side of the story to the public.

 Printed on recycled paper

Public officials and grassroots activists who have witnessed the tremendous success of the bottle bill in reducing litter and waste and creating jobs and new businesses, are actively working to expand the original bottle bill to include other beverage containers. They desperately need well-researched, well-documented, factual information to make their case to legislators and the general public.

CRI proposes to launch Beverage Industry Watch Project. Through the Beverage Industry Watch Project CRI will:

- provide grassroots activists with analyses of industry reports and claims,
- inform the public of the waste and pollution implications of no-deposit containers and the social, economic and environmental benefits of deposit systems,
- develop a network of contacts in government, media, industry and public interest organizations,
- link grassroots organizations through publication of our newsletter and published studies and fact sheets.

Next year, with the help of the Global Environmental Project Institute, we can get the message to millions of Americans in bottle bill states who take their deposit system for granted, and to millions more who are unaware of the substantial environmental and economic benefits of this system.

We have enclosed a proposal to the Global Environmental Project Institute for partial funding in the amount of $10,000 for the Beverage Industry Watch Project.

Sincerely,

Pat Franklin

Pat Franklin
Acting Director

BEVERAGE INDUSTRY WATCH PROJECT
"Debunking the Myths about Recycling"

SUMMARY

Disposal of glass, aluminum and plastic containers is increasing every year and recycling rates are decreasing, but the packaging industry has duped the public into believing that we are recycling more than ever before. Deposit systems are responsible for the lion's share of beverage container recycling, but the beverage industry claims that deposit systems are costly and conflict with curbside recycling programs. The recycling myths being perpetrated by the beverage and packing industries must be "debunked," so that the public knows the truth about beverage container reuse and recycling and deposit systems. The Container Recycling Institute is the only organization capable of "debunking" industry's myths about recycling.

DESCRIPTION AND EXPERTISE OF THE ORGANIZATION

The Container Recycling Institute (CRI) is recognized as the expert voice on beverage container reuse and recycling in the U.S. The small nonprofit, 501(c)(3) organization is playing a vital role in educating policymakers, government officials and the general public regarding the social and environmental impacts of beverage containers through our information clearinghouse service, quarterly newsletter, press releases, fact sheets and other publications.

CRI is the only repository for information on this issue, answering dozens of requests for information and technical assistance each month. Equally important as CRI's reputation for up-to-date information, and credible research, is CRI's ability to disseminate information and serve as a clearinghouse to citizen activists, linking state, national and international activities.

STATEMENT OF PROBLEM

The 50 billion beer and soda containers discarded each year in the U.S. are a national disgrace. The glass, aluminum and plastic manufacturing industries, eager to project a "green" image, spend hundreds of millions of dollars to advertise and publicize their recycling rates, in an effort to dupe the public into thinking we are succeeding in our war on waste and resource depletion. Trade associations, representing the beverage and packaging industry are extremely adept at getting their message to a broad audience of policymakers, lawmakers and the general public.

The message that "all's well with recycling" is a myth. The fact is, the recycling rate for glass bottles was only 37% again last year. The rate for aluminum cans dropped 5 percent in 1995 to a five-year low of 62% and the rate for PET soda bottles plummeted 16% to the 1993 level of 41%. Furthermore, Americans threw away 4 billion more aluminum cans and 23% more PET soda bottles in 1995 than they did in 1994.

There is no national group, other than CRI, willing or able to stand up to the beverage and packaging industries and refute their manipulated statistics. No other group can debunk their recycling myths and set the record straight on recycling rates for beverage cans and bottles, which make up 15% of all packaging waste. The public is not getting the truth about recycling.

NEED FOR THE PROGRAM

A growing number of citizen activists and government officials, aware of the energy consumption, resource depletion and pollution caused by the manufacturing and disposal of beverage containers, are advocating policies that will reverse this wasteful trend. They know that deposit-refund systems have proven to be an effective means of achieving beverage container recycling rates of 80 percent and higher, and that recycled content laws create a demand for recycled materials. But, they need well-researched information to deflect the propaganda of the well-funded, powerful, special-interest beverage industry lobby. They need help in educating lawmakers and the general public. They need help in "debunking the myths" about recycling.

Three examples of the myths being perpetrated by the beverage and packaging industries follow below:

- A 23-page booklet published by the National Soft Drink Association has been distributed to policymakers and lawmakers at every level of government. This document portrays bottle bills as a "threat to curbside recycling", a statement based on fiction, not fact. In fact, over one half of the U.S. population served by curbside recycling, lives in one of the ten bottle bill states and more than half of those living in bottle bill states are served by a curbside program. Curbside programs and bottle bills complement one another.
- A widely distributed Glass Packaging Institute "fact sheet" touts curbside recycling as the "best way to collect glass for recycling." But a US Environmental Protection Agency funded by GPI says that 20–40% of glass collected through curbside programs cannot be made into new containers.
- The American Plastics Council (APC) released its 1995 PET soda bottle recycling rate in June claiming that more PET soda bottles were recycled in 1995 than in 1994. They failed to mention that the rate dropped 16% last year, or that Americans threw away 140 million tons more PET soda bottles last year than in 1994.

LONG-TERM GOAL OF THE PROGRAM

To protect the global environment through conservation of energy and natural resources and pollution reduction by increasing beverage container reuse and recycling and eliminating one-way, no-deposit cans and bottles.

SHORT TERM OBJECTIVES OF THE PROGRAM

1. To increase public awareness of the wasted energy and resources resulting from the manufacturing and disposal of one-way beverage containers, and the benefits of deposit systems as a means of reducing waste and conserving energy and material resources.
2. To "debunk" the myths about recycling being propagated by the beverage and packaging industries.
3. To provide technical assistance to grassroots organizations and public officials working to implement, expand or prevent repeal of beverage container deposit programs.
4. To shift the social and environmental costs associated with manufacturing, recycling and disposal of beverage containers from government and taxpayers to producers and consumers.

STRATEGY AND PLAN OF ACTION

To begin to personalize the debate, we need to put Coke and Pepsi on the hot seat, and draw the major beverage and packaging companies out from behind their trade associations and public relations firms. In order to make them own up to their responsibility to reduce resource depletion and waste. Working with groups such as Essential Information, US Public Interest Research Group and Environmental Defense Fund, we will provide technical information to uncover and deflect the beverage industry's underhanded tactics, false claims and outright lies about recycling, reuse and deposit systems. We will produce materials that "debunk" their myths about recycling and provide educational information to the general public and local activist organizations. We will work to form a coalition to focus attention to the fact that public policies are needed to increase recycling and reuse.

Public Education: In order to get the message to the public that there is an alternative to the wastefulness and environmental degradation caused by one-way beverage containers, and uncover the truth behind recycling claims being touted by the container packaging industry, CRI will:

- develop a Beverage Industry Watch Project consisting of a bi-monthly press release, fact sheet and analysis of beverage industry reports and promotional propaganda,
- publish our quarterly newsletter, *Container and Packaging UPDATE* which highlights developments in beverage container recycling, reusable containers and packaging and reports on bottle bill activity in the U.S. and Canada,
- disseminate information to CRI's network of contacts in government, media, industry and public interest organizations linking these contacts with CRI and with each other. Without our critiques and reports these policymakers would rely almost exclusively on industry propaganda, and
- speak at state and national conferences.

Technical Assistance: In order to meet the objective of empowering grassroots activists seeking to reduce solid waste, reduce energy consumption and pollution, conserve natural resources, and reduce litter through beverage container recycling and reuse, CRI would engage in the following activities:

- develop critiques and analyses of industry funded studies as well as summaries of government studies. The beverage industry employs expensive, high-powered public relations firms to twist the data and package it in slick reports for public consumption. CRI will analyze and evaluate their data and point out flawed assumptions, skewed statistics and false conclusions,
- provide technical assistance to grassroots organizations through our central clearinghouse for information. (see enclosed letters from grassroots organizations),
- testify at public hearings,
- seek to get articles published in recycling magazines and periodicals, and
- provide activists with white papers, studies and other research products.

Research: CRI will collect and analyze beverage container generation, disposal and recycling figures. CRI will document the success of the bottle bill in the ten states that have enacted deposit legislation, particularly with regard to the compatibility of bottle bills and curbside recycling programs.

METHOD OF EVALUATION

One means of evaluating the project will be through media coverage, i.e., the number of articles printed, radio/tv interviews, etc. This would be done through a clipping service. The number of technical assistance calls/letters answered will also be a measure of the success of the program. Failure by industry to repeal one or more bottle bills and recycled content laws, and successful bottle bill expansion efforts will be a measure of the success of the project.

BUDGET

	Organization	Project
Salaries/taxes/benefits (Exec Dir & Assistant)	$65,000	$19,500
Consultants/professional fees/interns	9,000	3,000
Rent	10,800	2,700
Audit/legal/insurance	800	200
Telephone/fax/courier	3,800	2,000
Postage	10,000	5,000
Printing/copying	12,000	6,000
Supplies	500	150
World Wide Web Page	1,500	1,000
Travel (conferences/hearings)	2,500	1,000
Clipping service	1,000	500
Publication subscriptions	300	150
Contingency fund	600	200
Capital Equipment	1,500	500
Total	$119,300	$41,900

AMOUNT REQUESTED

CRI requests a grant in the amount of $10,000 for the "Beverage Industry Watch Project—Debunking the Recycling Myths", CRI's primary project for 1997.

Courtesy of Carol B. Waite, CFRE, member, Board of Directors, and Pat Franklin, Acting Director, Container Recycling Institute, 1996.

Chapter 12
Special Events—The Fun in Fund Raising

Chapter Outline

- The Fun in Fund Raising
- The Role of Special Events in Fund Raising
- Cost Versus Time of Special Events
- The Role of Volunteers
- The Role of Staff
- Donated Services and Goods
- How to Select the Best Location
- How to Budget for a Special Event and then Manage It
- Planning the Perfect Event
- What Must Be Done After the Event Is Over
- Contracting with Outside Vendors
- Using an Event Management Group
- IRS Regulations Regarding Special Events

Key Vocabulary

- Business Reply Envelope (BRE)
- Corkage Fee
- Gifts-In-Kind
- Graphic Artist
- Outsourcing
- Piggy Backing
- Public Service Announcement (PSA)
- Service Bureau/Mailing House
- Vendor
- Volunteer

The Fun in Fund Raising

Special events often are called the "fun" in fund raising. When people think of special events, they often think of the large charity balls or theme events such as "chili cook-offs," "walk-a-thons," "race-for-the-cures," golf outings, or the "roasts and toasts" that they have attended. Most individuals will attend many special events throughout their lives to honor individuals, create publicity, or raise money for a person or cause. This chapter focuses on the special events that are staged to raise funds to benefit an organization.

Normally, there are four reasons to hold a special event: (1) to highlight the public's awareness of the organization or person; (2) to raise money to support the interests of the organization or person; (3) to focus attention on the organization's programs or the causes supported by the individual; and (4) to garner attention from and for the organization's volunteers.

1. To create public awareness—An event can publicize a cause through coverage in the media by carefully placed public service announcements (PSAs), by direct mailing of invitations to people who ordinarily would not be aware of the organization, and by recruiting volunteers who had not been involved with the cause or person before to work on the event.
2. To raise money—The obvious way to raise money through a special event is by selling tickets. Yet, some events do not always break even, let alone make money. In addition to selling tickets, other items may be sold or raffled at the event to raise funds—t-shirts, mugs, cookbooks, posters, trips, etc. This is called "piggy-backing."
3. To create program awareness—Highlighting the mission and activities of the organization during a special event will create awareness. If someone decides to attend an event honoring a friend or acquaintance and then is exposed to the mission, programs, and activities of the organization, then the organization has expanded its audience. Contact can be made with the community's leadership, those financially able to support the organization, and those who may take an interest in working for the cause.
4. To recognize volunteers—Many events are held just to say thanks to the volunteers who sustain the organization throughout the year. These are not held to raise money, to raise the consciousness of the public, or to introduce new and innovative programs. They are instead held to say "thanks" to those who have given so unselfishly of their time to the cause. Other goals also can be obtained when

honoring volunteers. Well-placed feature articles on key volunteers can garner the recognition that the organization often needs and can attract more volunteers who want to be associated with a "winning cause" and the "right" people.

In capital campaigns, special events can provide an opportunity for continued contact with donors. Ground-breaking ceremonies, donor-recognition dinners, unveilings of donor recognition walls, tours of new facilities, and other special event opportunities associated with a capital campaign (see Chapter 14) are perfect forums for recognizing volunteers and attracting new volunteers and donors to the cause.

The most important questions to ask before considering planning or holding a special event are:

- Is it necessary to hold an event?
- What is this event expected to do for the organization—raise funds or public awareness?
- What type of event is best for the organization? Will it fit into the organization's mission and community?
- Is there adequate staff and volunteer assistance necessary to stage a successful event?
- Does the organization have the financial resources to undertake a special event and, if so, of what magnitude?
- Will an event bring cohesiveness to the staff and volunteers?
- What is the competition doing? Will this event compete with any events they hold or are planning?

Once these questions are answered and a decision is made to plan and hold an event, enough time must be allowed to organize it well. At least six months to a year should be allowed for planning and organizing a major event. Although it is possible to plan and execute an event in much less time, it is always wise to allow enough time for thorough planning. Exhibit 12–1 lists questions to help you determine if you are ready to have a special event.

In addition, the type of event should be carefully selected. Consider whether this event could be instituted as a yearly event for the organization. Just as the breast cancer organizations have the "race for the cure" 10 kilometer races each year and the National Kidney Foundation has "chili cook-offs," an organization may have a theme that could be made into an excellent special event. Another good example of this is the Texas State Society's "Black Tie and Boots" gala, which is held every four years in Washington, DC, to honor the newly elected President and Vice President of the United States. More than 3,500 people attend and enough money is raised to keep the organization operating for four years

Exhibit 12–1 Are You Ready to Have a Special Event?

Below are some key points to consider when deciding whether or not your institution should have a special event.

- Will your event be important enough to attract the attention of the groups you want to reach?
- Is the event significant in that it supports some aspect of the organization's overall program, policies, and purposes?
- Can you identify a cadre of volunteers who are willing to do the multitude of tasks necessary to be successful?
- Can your institution justify the time, effort, and cost involved?
- Do you have an idea that is interesting and different which can be presented in an entertaining or dramatic format in order to hold the attention of the audience?
- Will your event create a desire in people to respond in some way—to make a decision, to join or participate, to support through volunteer service, or to make a financial contribution?
- How much publicity will you be able to generate through newspapers, radio, and television?
- Have you attended and observed a variety of special events to assess what is appealing?
- Is there a special occasion which should be commemorated such as an anniversary, new administrator, etc?
- Are similar events already being done by organizations in your community and if so, is there room for another or can you do yours better?
- Is the proposed event appropriate for your institution?

Source: Reprinted with permission from LuAnn Davis, *Start Up: A Fund Raising Guide*, "Are you ready to have a special event?"

until the next inaugural gala. Another example is the annual "Black and White" ball, held in San Francisco.

After the type of event is decided, careful consideration should be given next to the theme and the location site. Aim for fun and excitement. Is there a building that recently has been opened or renovated that everyone is waiting to see? If so, determine if the event can be held there. Is there a site that is open to the public only during the day that

> People quickly tire of the same old black tie, sit-down dinner event and long for something creative and exciting.

would consider opening its doors in the evening for an event? Museums; zoos; parks; and public buildings such as post offices, banks, historic homes, or historic sites often will open their doors after hours for a fee. This helps to underwrite their operations as well as provides an exciting place for an event to be held. Look for something new and different. People quickly tire of the same old black tie, sit-down dinner event and long for something creative and exciting.

Establish your budget early. Determine all of the costs of the event, then price the tickets to not only cover the costs, but to make a profit. Then consider whether the community and the audience being invited can afford the price of the tickets. If they cannot, then rethink the event and what it offers to those attending. Can less be offered in the event and still interest people in purchasing tickets? Perhaps it is best to rethink the event entirely. On the other hand, the ticket price may be too low. After comparing what other organizations have charged for their events, rethink the ticket price. It is better to have conducted this analysis beforehand than to print and mail the invitations and find that no one attended because the tickets have been priced too high or be in the "red" because the ticket price did not cover all of the costs of the event.

Different levels of donor sponsorship also can be established for an event to increase the amount of money to be made. For example, a "Silver Circle" sponsor may receive a table for four and recognition in the brochure for a cost of $2,500. Those sponsoring at the "Gold Circle" level may receive a table for eight, recognition in the brochure, and have one of the honorees seated at their table for a cost of $5,000. "Platinum Circle" donors may receive a table for ten, recognition in the brochure, have an honoree seated at their table, plus be included in a private reception before the dinner with all of the honorees. The price for this level of sponsorship could be $10,000. Some donors will be willing to pay more for a higher level of recognition.

In addition to selling tickets, there are other ways of raising money at an event. For example, if programs are going to be printed for a special dinner, space in the program can be sold for advertisements. Also, if a cash bar is part of the event, a certain amount of the price of a drink can be set aside for the charity. Other merchandise can be sold in support of the cause or to celebrate the event. At some events, a photographer may be hired to take photos that are then sold to those attending. In addition, raffles or auctions can be held to bring in more revenue. The actual dinner may just break even after expenses, but an event can still make money through these other creative means.

One of the best ways to make money is to save money—by looking for donated goods and services. Seek the vineyard or liquor wholesaler who will donate the wine or alcohol for the event in return for recognition in the program, at the bar, and on the dinner table. Find the printer who works for the organization or others who will print invitations for free, or will at least provide upgraded paper from overstock or special ink colors at no charge. Locate the restaurants, merchants, and other vendors who would like to receive publicity by donating goods or "gifts-in-kind" to the event. If the item is part of the budget, look for creative ways to obtain it other than paying cash.

The Role of Special Events in Fund Raising

Special events are staged to call attention to the organization or person that they are honoring. Most special events don't raise a lot of money. It is fortunate if many just break even. Many are held with organizers aware that these events will cost the organization money. Why are they held? Because they bring something else to the organization—publicity. A special event provides the organization with the opportunity to promote its mission and goals to a constituency that may be unfamiliar with its basic tenets of operation. A new "public" may attend that is unfamiliar with the organization. This is the time to capitalize upon this opportunity by providing information about the organization. Have materials that guests can take home with them to learn more about the organization's programs. Don't let those attending leave without obtaining some record of their name, address, and phone number. If this isn't done when the tickets are sold, then it must be done at the event. These are the source of attendees at future events, potential donors, and possible volunteers. Keep track of who attends.

Just as publicity is important to an organization, so is a continual source of volunteer help. Special events also can help increase the public's awareness of the organization and can attract new volunteers. A special event can be a great opportunity to reach out to the community and recruit new volunteers for the event and for the organization. The excitement and spirit of working on the event can carry over into a desire of working for the organization's other programs and activities. A special event can make it possible for all types of people to volunteer, not just those that an organization would normally see involved with their cause. Special events can draw women and men, the young and the old, the rich and the poor, the working and the nonworking or retired, the highly educated and the not-so-well educated, and they can provide a cross section of the demographics of the area. The possibility of enriching the organization's volunteer pool through holding a special event may be as important as how much money the event will raise for the organization.

In addition to all of the previously stated advantages, special events allow the organization to enhance its image within the community through promotion and execution of the event. Securing the best possible volunteer leadership will attract others of comparable position and resources. The event must be first class in every way—this does not necessarily mean that it has to be expensive. The organization should be looking for an event that will not only attract people for the evening, but that will have a lasting effect upon those attending. If an event can be instituted—draw people year after year and be associated only with that organization—then it most likely will increase in popularity each year, draw more and more people, raise more and more money, and enhance the image of the organization within the community.

Organizations should not depend solely on special events for their funds, but should have a comprehensive, well-defined development plan and operation that includes special events.

Cost Versus Time of Special Events

Special events can be costly not only in dollars, but in time. The planning stages alone of a large event can take months. Staff time is taken away from other tasks that normally may bring money into the organization. Before deciding to undertake a special event, an organization must decide if this is the wisest method of raising money or creating publicity for the group. It may be the best event ever held in the city with the biggest names in attendance, yet the organization may lose a fortune in staff time and money.

Ask the following questions. Is there the time and staff to plan and execute this event? What will this event do for us? What could staff members be doing with their time if they are not working on this event? Which will bring the organization more income and/or publicity? Does the organization have the financial ability to hire an event management firm? Should the organization spend its money this way? There are no definitive answers. What may make sense to one organization may not be the answer for another. But, whatever the decision, make sure that these questions have been asked and the many options available are considered.

The Role of Volunteers

Most special events run on volunteer energy and expertise. Staff members usually plan and direct the event,

Most special events run on volunteer energy and expertise.

but the volunteer chair and help are the mainstays of many of the annually held events. Some events are so popular in the community that people vie to be the chair or co-chairs. Volunteers can be used to support events in many different ways. They may loan their homes for parties, house tours, etc.; chair events or committees; use their influence to get underwriting for an event; and cultivate other volunteers for the organization's activities.

Special events give volunteers an opportunity to learn something new and to have fun with people they know and people they would like to get to know. People will come to a special event one year and find that they have had such a good time that they will volunteer the next year to work on the event. They also will share their enthusiasm with their friends. The best way to find new volunteers is to ask the current volunteers to recommend people who they know who are interested in the organization's mission, would work hard on a project, and represent the organization well.

Volunteers can "make or break" a special event. A good volunteer board and a strong chair are no guarantee that an event will be successful, but they certainly can help. A weak volunteer chair and committee almost will surely bring disaster to an event, unless the staff is strong and large enough to rescue the foundering volunteer effort. Make sure that you select volunteers that will get the job done. It is the responsibility of the staff to make sure that volunteers have a clear understanding of all that is required of them and all of the tools with which to accomplish their job. Exhibit 12–2 lists special event committees.

Exhibit 12–2 Special Event Committees

- Event Management (Executive Committee)—sets direction, selects theme and date
- Arrangements—plans logistics, contracts for site, selects menus, delegates many details to subcommittees
- Ticket Sales—arranges for distribution and sale of tickets
- Promotion—promotes the organization and all event sponsors, as well as the event
- Publicity—publicizes through press, radio, television, and other media
- Decorations—plans and organizes all decorations around theme
- Finance—controls budget; collects funds; maintains records
- Clean-Up—cleans up after the event
- Gifts and Prizes—promotes door prizes and gifts (if there are to be any)
- Entertainment—selects and books entertainment
- Printing—arranges for printing posters, tickets, programs, etc.
- Advertising—arranges to sell advertising for program; places ads for benefit
- Program—is responsible for editorial content, printing, and distribution of program

Source: Reprinted with permission from Henry Rosso, "The Fund Raising Benefit," *The Fund Raising School Manual.*

The Role of Staff

In an ideal world, staff members are the planners and volunteers are the workers. In the real world, staff members and volunteers work side-by-side to produce special events. It is the responsibility of the staff to have the entire event planned in advance to the smallest detail. Then the staff must train and motivate the volunteers, and guide them through the many stages of the event. Also, the staff must later direct all of the accolades to the volunteers.

There are several points to keep in mind when working with staff and volunteers during the planning and execution of a special event. The following list is just a sample of what should be expected of both.

- Be selective when choosing which staff and volunteers will work the event. Not all people will be good representatives of the organization in a public event. Some people work well behind the scenes, but can not handle stressful situations, make quick judgment calls, or handle irate individuals.
- Train both the staff and volunteers well ahead of time. It is important for them to have a clear understanding of what will be expected of them during the event. Don't assume that they will have previous special event experience.
- Be cautious of the volunteer who wants to be part of the event because it will be fun. Staff and volunteers will be working at the event, not participating as guests.
- Arrange for a site visit before the event. All workers should be familiar with the general floor plans of the event location—the entrances, emergency exits, rest rooms, coat check rooms, security, and so forth.
- Provide volunteers and staff with guidelines on the appropriate dress for the occasion. If it is a black-tie affair, the males may have to rent tuxedos if they don't own them. This may be expensive so they should have ample time to prepare, budget, or choose not to volunteer for this particular event. Women should be encouraged to wear low-heeled shoes, and clothing that is comfortable.
- Have an adequate number of staff and volunteers assigned to work the event. It is better to have too many than too few. Plan on having several assigned to the chair or chairpersons in charge to act as "runners" and "special needs" persons. The last thing an event chair wants to worry about is "Where is the staff/volunteer?"
- No staff or volunteers should be seated before all of the guests are seated. Nor should they have drinks, unless it is appropriate. In fact, staff and volunteers should be instructed to ask the guests of honor if they would like to have their drinks held for them while photos are being taken.

- Staff should have adequate time to prepare for an event. Don't think that staff members can organize a major special event in addition to all of their other responsibilities. If the development director cannot be given the time to plan appropriately, then hire an events management firm and let the development director manage or coordinate the firm's activities.
- Don't depend on promises made by anyone. Plan ahead for all possible contingencies. Staff and volunteers should be empowered to make decisions on the spot. Only well-prepared and well-trained staff and volunteers can do this effectively.

Donated Services and Goods

A great way to save money on an event is to get as much of the goods and services donated as possible. This can be as small as the gifts to be given to the guests of honor and the favors to be given to the guests, or as large as having the printing, wine, or food donated. Use any contacts that the organization has—the contacts of the board members, the committee members, and the staff.

A printer may be willing to "run" an invitation package at the same time he or she is printing materials for another client and do the work for cost or provide the work for free for the visibility it will give to his or her company. The printer may be acknowledged in the program, on the back of the invitation, in the organization's newsletter, magazine, etc. See what similar "deals" can be struck with other vendors.

A speaker may be willing to donate his or her honorarium to the organization in return for a tax write-off. Also, don't be afraid to contact the celebrities who have an interest in the organization's cause and may be willing to donate their time to help the organization. But be careful with arrangements with celebrities. They may provide their time for free, but they may want to be reimbursed for their expenses, which can be greater than expected or reasonable for the organization's budget. Make sure that all agreements are in writing.

Think in terms of who can help and why they would want to be of service to your organization. For example, when planning an awards dinner honoring a top Russian official one year, the American Center for International Leadership (ACIL), based in Denver, Colorado, and associated with the University of Denver, contacted the Russian Consulate and asked to borrow a Russian flag to use at the podium along with a flag from the United States. They were pleased to comply and saved ACIL from having to purchase a flag costing approximately $100. For the same event, ACIL asked one of its board members who owned a vineyard to donate wine for the awards dinner. Even though the hotel charged a "corkage fee," it was substantially less than the cost of the wine, thus saving the organization considerable money on the event. Again, an alumna of ACIL who worked for a florist received an invitation to attend the dinner. She replied favorably and asked if ACIL had selected a florist to provide flowers for the evening. As they had not, they worked with her to not only give her the business, but to save ACIL considerable money on the purchase of centerpieces for the tables.

How to Select the Best Location

All cities have buildings that are available for special events, and, actually, some depend upon outside events for their operating budgets. Consider museums, historical homes, or places to which the invited guests normally would not have access.

> Consider museums, historical homes, or places to which the invited guests normally would not have access.

Many times people will want to attend an event to be able to enjoy the location or to be able to say that they have "been there."

Be concerned about the cost of the site. Many organizations just can't afford to spend $10,000 to $20,000 to rent a museum for an evening event. Be creative in your thinking. In Chicago, one of the most successful fundraising events held yearly to support the Boy Scouts is held in downtown Chicago in the "Loop" where the "financial block" of LaSalle Street is closed off for the evening and tables, bars, bands, etc. are set up right in the middle of this normally very busy thoroughfare. Businesses purchase tables, individual tickets are sold, and the merriment begins immediately after the close of the work day and goes well into the late evening or early morning. Obviously, the event is held in the summer!

You will have much more flexibility working with a site other than a hotel. There is room for bargaining at hotels, but not as much as when working with different vendors and caterers at private locations. Remember that caterers can serve food in locations where there are no kitchen facilities. Don't let the lack of a kitchen stop you from selecting a site.

If the location is to be in an urban setting, make sure that there is ample parking or that valet parking has been arranged. Being near a metro or bus stop also is helpful. Alerting taxi companies to the location and ending time of the event also is a courtesy to guests. Also, make sure that the site is safe and acceptable to all religious, ethnic, or special interest groups. If holding the event outside, be sure to plan for inclement weather, insects, and possible noise interference. Whatever site is chosen, be sure to make arrangements with someone with authority who works at the location to be available on the day of and during the event to coordinate or solve any unforeseen emergency that may arise.

How to Budget for a Special Event and then Manage It

Every special event should have a budget. To build a budget for an event, several things must be considered, including the following.

The Facility or Location

The first thing to consider is where the event will be held and how much it will cost to rent the facility. Will furniture be provided or will tables and chairs need to be rented? Is there a public address system and podium? What other audiovisual equipment is available, and is there a cost for its use? Is janitorial service provided both before and after the event and at what cost? Is parking available that is convenient and affordable for the guests? Will there be a need to contract for valet parking?

Food, Beverage, Catering, and Decorations

Does the location have food service capabilities and are they of the quality that will be needed for the event? What is the cost of these services compared to outside caterers? Can outside caterers be used? Are the linens of the quality or style that are desired for the event? Can other materials be used? What kind of food and drink should be provided? Will alcohol be served? Will it be an open or cash bar? What prices should be charged for drinks? Will the facility or caterer allow the organization to make money from the sale of drinks? Will they allow food or alcohol to be donated? Outside caterers may be more expensive than using the facility's food service.

Invitations, Programs, and Place Cards

How many people will need to be invited to "break even" or make money on the event? Will the facility being considered hold that many people? What are people in the community accustomed to paying for a special event of the type being planned? Can all of the costs be covered and a profit still be made when charging this amount? What type of invitation should be sent? Will a graphic artist design the invitation? What image should the invitation convey—flashy, conservative, frugal, wealth, sophistication, homey, excitement, glamour, etc.? Will there be a program for the event? Will place cards be used if the event is a sit-down breakfast, luncheon, or dinner? Exhibit 12–3 lists what to include in an invitation for a special event.

Mailing

Is the mailing to be personalized? Should first or third class postage be used? How long before the event should the invitations be mailed? Is money budgeted to have a mailing house do this work?

Exhibit 12–3 What to Include in an Invitation for a Special Event

- Name of the event
- Name of the organization holding the event
- Location of the event
- Date and time of the event—include p.m. or a.m.
- Compelling description of the purpose of the event or the cause it supports
- Price of admission—this may include several levels of pricing depending upon what is offered with the event
- RSVP date and phone number so people can inquire about any detail you may have forgotten, a way to contribute to the organization if they cannot attend the event,

to volunteer for the organization, or whatever may be of importance to a potential attendee
- Name of organization to which checks should be written
- Date by which checks must be received, tickets purchased, tables reserved, etc.
- Tax status of the organization and exactly how much of the cost is tax-deductible to the attendee
- Names of volunteer chairs and committee members
- Attire expected of attendees—black tie, white tie, country-western, tartan plaid of your clan, etc.

Source: Adapted with permission from Margaret Guellich and LuAnn Davis, *Fundamentals of Fundraising: A Capital View*, National Society of Fund Raising Executives, Greater Washington, DC Area Chapter.

All invitations to small, intimate events should be sent by first class mail with stamps affixed. Do not use a first class indicia, even though it will save time. Select a stamp that will coordinate with the invitation package. If it is springtime, select a stamp with flowers. If the event is being held around Christmas, select one of the Holiday stamps. If your event is political, then select the American flag or one of the many stamps with an eagle. Consider how it will look with the colors, shape, and size of the envelope. If money is available to spend and a mailing service has been budgeted for, a mailing house or paid staff can be hired to provide these services. However, a considerable amount of money can be saved by using volunteer help to produce this mailing—stuffing, sealing, and stamping the invitations.

If a large event is being produced, especially if mailing lists will be rented, it is not as necessary to use first class postage. For example, if the hottest ticket in town is to an inaugural ball or the annual Black and White Ball, then the recipient usually does not care if the invitation arrived with a first class stamp or was mailed bulk mail. If the event is that popular, then the organization can afford to skimp on postage. But, if the event is new to town and not everyone is vying for an invitation, then mail with a first class stamp. Also, if there is a short time frame, don't take chances with anything less than first class mail. An invitation that arrives after the event is held is not only an embarrassment for the organization, but definitely will not bring any people or money to the event.

Photographers and Video Operators

Is there a plan to have photos taken at the event? Will the photos be used for public relations or media efforts, or to make extra money by having photos available for sale after the event? Will the photos be used in future publications of the organization?

Is there a need to have the event videotaped? Can video footage be used in future videos developed for the organization?

Speaker(s) Honorarium

Will there be a speaker or speakers at the event? Will a fee be charged for their services? Will their expenses need to be paid—transportation, food, lodging, etc.? Will gifts be given to the speakers and their spouses? Be careful to select gifts that represent the organization and do not cost too much. Many quality stores have gift items such as crystal, silver, or pewter that can be personalized for the event or person.

Optional Items

What other items are needed to create a spectacular event that will raise money for the organization? Use all of the creative powers of the staff and volunteers to think of ways to make the event special.

> Use all of the creative powers of the staff and volunteers to think of ways to make the event special.

to think of ways to make the event special. Then include these expenses in the budget.

Planning the Perfect Event

It is not necessary to invent a new event each year. Many organizations use the same event year after year with great success. Often, though, an organization will want to try something new to create a sense of excitement and anticipation. Three examples of events of different sizes held in three distinct communities across the United States are included in Appendix 12–A. These or any of the other events in the book from which these were taken also may work for your organization. Exhibit 12–4 is a chart of various types of special events including the amount

Exhibit 12–4 Social Events at a Glance

MAJOR EVENTS	PLANNING TIME/PEOPLE NEEDED FOR PLANNING	OTHER ESSENTIALS NEEDED	PEOPLE NEEDED AT EVENT	OTHER BENEFITS BESIDES RAISING FUNDS
CONCERT	6 months 3–6 people	publicity, permits, talent, place, equipment, security, refreshments, tickets	Many	visibility, media, good time
AUCTION	3 months 3–4 people	publicity, items, place, microphone, permits, refreshments	1 auctioneer 4–5 others	visibility, media, expanded business contact gives tangible benefit
READING	3–4 months 1–2 people	publicity, place, refreshments, talent, microphone, tickets	poets/writers 2–3 others	visibility, low cost, good time, media possible
MARATHON/ WALK-A-THON	3–5 months 2–4 people	route permit, security, first-aid, refreshments, publicity	6–10	visibility, low cost, good time, exercise, media
PHONE-A-THON	1½–2 months 2–3 people	publicity, place with 6–10 phones, refreshments	20–30	visibility, low cost
MONTE CARLO NIGHT	2–3 months 2–3 people	gambling equipment, permit, publicity, refreshments	10 (some experienced dealers)	visibility, low cost, good time, media
TESTIMONIAL DINNER	6 months 3–5 people	tickets, publicity, place, microphones, notables, food, supplies	chef 3–5 others	expands constituency, media, opportunity to honor people
SMALL DINNER/ COCKTAIL PARTY	1½–2 months 1 person	place, hostess, food, supplies	1–2	low cost, easy
CONFERENCE	6 months 3–5 people	publicity, place, materials, equipment, experts, refreshments, tickets	6–10 (including trainers)	visibility, is educational, media
DANCE	3–4 months 3–4 people	permit, place, band, security, publicity, refreshments, tickets	6–8 (and a band)	visibility, media, good time
SALE	3–4 months 3–4 people	tickets, items, publicity	2–3	gives tangible benefit, visibility, low cost, expands business contacts
GARAGE SALE	3–4 months 2–3 people	publicity, items, place	4–6	low cost, quick, gives tangible benefit

Source: Reprinted by permission, United Way of America, *BoardWalk* Series, 1985.

of time needed to produce them, the number of volunteers needed, and the benefits these events could bring to an organization.

Information or Activities Required for a Successful Event

Timeline

Once a decision is made to hold an event, the most important step to take is that of developing a timeline. Start by working backward from the date of the event and include all the steps that will need to be taken to complete the event. For each task to be completed, ask questions such as the following: When do the invitations need to be received for individuals to RSVP by a particular date? When will the invitations need to be mailed? How much time is required for the printing, folding, inserting, and stamping process before they can be mailed? Will the invitation be the same as last year's or will new art work need to be designed? How much time will this require? By answering these questions, the amount of "lead time" can be determined and a timeline begun for each step of the event. No event should be undertaken without having developed a timeline. Exhibit 12–5 provides a timeline for producing a successful special event.

Budget

Once the timeline has been developed, the next step is to create a budget based on the needs identified within the timeline. Develop the budget by using the concept of "zero-based budgeting"—attach a cost to every item whether it is to be donated or the department already has it. From rental of the site, to the food served, to the printing of the invitation, to the salaries of the staff, to the reimbursed expenses of the volunteers, to the tape, paper, staples, etc. purchased—all should be included. The budget should reflect the real costs of the event. If items are donated, then this can be shown later as a savings. Also include in the budget other sources of revenue that are planned to be implemented such as the sale of t-shirts, mugs, hats, etc.; the raffling of items in an auction; or other opportunities that will bring in money from sources other than ticket sales. Ticket prices should be determined after the budget is completed. Exhibit 12–6 provides a checklist for budgeting for a special event.

Staffing

Determine the number of professional staff persons needed to successfully plan and execute the event. In addition, plan for the number of volunteer committees that will need to be chaired and staffed by volunteers. Don't forget to include these costs in the budget. It may be possible to determine these numbers based on how the event operated in the past. If the event is new, ask other organizations who have held similar events how they staffed their event. Make calls outside of the immediate area and ask similar agencies what they have done and how their events were staffed. This will be the time to decide whether an events firm will be hired. If it appears that it will cost the organization more in staff time, resources, and money to run the event internally than it would to hire an outside source to do the work, then the correct decision may be to hire an outside company with expertise.

Publicity

The success of a special event can depend upon the amount of publicity generated to promote it. To be successful, people need to know about the event and want to come to it. They need to perceive that it is something special and that they want to be a part of it. Publicizing an event is also another way to highlight the involvement of local volunteers. Photos can be taken during dress rehearsals or some other preliminary activity of the event and then sent to the local papers with an accompanying article featuring the event and the volunteer help. This can be a motivator for the volunteers, recruit additional interest in volunteering in the community, and further promote the event. The important point to remember is why the event needs media coverage and who will benefit from it. When this can be answered, there are several ways to publicize a special event.

> The success of a special event can depend upon the amount of publicity generated to promote it.

1. Radio stations—Public service announcements (PSAs) should be written and delivered to the local radio stations two to three weeks before the event. These should be fifteen, thirty, forty-five, and sixty seconds long. They need to cover the Who, What, Where, When, and Why of the event. Attach a fact sheet about the organization in case the station wishes to promote the event beyond what is written in the PSA. They also may wish to interview some of the celebrities who will be attending or the persons whom the event may be supporting or benefiting. It even may be possible to have the volunteer chair of the event interviewed. Plan to deliver the media package in person to the station manager, if possible.
2. Television stations—Contact the local television stations and provide them with the same media kit. Ask if they will be willing to tape a segment promoting the event. This may be possible if the event involves or benefits the entire community.
3. Newspapers—Develop a press release to distribute to all of the local newspapers, as well as those in surrounding communities. Don't forget the weekly community newspapers or the monthly "shoppers"

Exhibit 12–5 Timeline for Producing A Successful Special Event

EVENT PLANNING CALENDAR FOR MAJOR HOLIDAY BALL													
ACTIVITY	JAN	FEB	MAR	APR	MAY	JUN	JUL	AUG	SEP	OCT	NOV	DEC	JAN
Present fund-raising event idea to board for approval of event, goals, and budget.	X												
Develop, select, and recruit honorary committee and committee chairs.	X	X	X										
Establish dates for monthly committee meetings with tentative, more frequent meeting dates just prior to the event.	X												
Establish theme, type of food and beverage service, and ticket prices for the event.	X	X											
Identify honorees, speakers, or celebrities who are willing to lend their name to the event and solicit.		X	X										
Solicit sponsors for the event.			X	X	X								
Secure the site and date for the event.	X	X											
Meet with the caterer or hotel to arrange for food, beverage, flowers, AV, and other event details.			X			X	X				X	X	
Arrange for entertainment.			X	X									
Determine extent of decorations and make arrangements.			X	X					X				
Send "Hold the Date Cards" to constituency.							X	X	X				
Contract with artist to prepare event's printed materials.								X					
Approve artwork and order printing.									X	X			
Secure purchased or donated magazine space, and mail ads.								X	X				
Recruit and assign volunteers.											X		
Collect items donated by sponsors for raffle, silent auction, or door prizes.										X	X		
Mail invitations.											X		
Mail press releases to newspapers and PSAs for radio stations.											X		
Place announcements of the event in newspapers.											X	X	
Try to get a feature story about the event or the persons involved in the event in local newspapers and on television.											X	X	
Hold final committee meetings.												X	

continues

Exhibit 12–5 continued

ACTIVITY	JAN	FEB	MAR	APR	MAY	JUN	JUL	AUG	SEP	OCT	NOV	DEC	JAN
Script the event: devise a minute-by-minute event schedule.											■	■	
Get attendee list from sponsors.												■	
Call honorees, speakers, and celebrities to remind them of the event and provide them with event details.											■		
Call volunteers to inform them of their duties and confirm their attendance.											■		
Call the honorees, speakers, and celebrities to confirm their itinerary and the event schedule.											■		
Notify members of the media about the event and inquire about their attendance. Arrange escorts.											■	■	
Send out press releases after the event.												■	■
Hold a thank-you party or wrap-up meeting for staff and volunteers.													■
Send out thank-you letters to sponsors, speakers, celebrities, and volunteers.													■
Have chairpersons write a recap of the event, discussing what was both good and bad and suggesting ways to improve the event in the future.													■

Courtesy of Gerry Frank, CHA, *INN*dependent Management Group, 1992, Alexandria, VA.

papers. If there is a college or university in the area, be sure to include its papers (and radio or TV stations), also. Make sure that the press release is delivered to the correct editor (sports, food, entertainment, home, etc.) and that one is included for the editor of the community calendar.

4. Magazines—More lead time is required for information to be printed in a magazine than in a newspaper. Most magazines for large cities have a monthly calendar of events and this is probably the best location for an event to be publicized.

5. Local business—Ask the editors of corporate newsletters of local businesses to include an article on your event. This can be particularly successful if volunteers for the event work for one of these companies. The company probably will be pleased to highlight the volunteer activities of its staff. If the company provides services to the local and surrounding communities, it may be possible to have the company highlight the event in the newsletter that accompanies their monthly invoices. For example, the local electric or gas companies may include information on nonprofit events that will benefit their customers. In addition, local companies may be willing to post flyers or posters on their bulletin boards. Don't overlook banks, service stations, movie theaters, beauty salons, etc.

Exhibit 12–7 shows a sample planning calendar for event publicity.

Evaluation

Often it is easy to forget that all events conclude not with the close of the evening's activities, but with an

Exhibit 12–6 Checklist for Budgeting for a Special Event

A. The Facility/Location
  1. Cost of the facility — $_____
  2. Table and chair rental — $_____
  3. Public address system and podium — $_____
  4. Janitorial and grounds services — $_____
  5. Parking and valet services — $_____
  6. Tent, awnings, and canopies — $_____
  7. Flooring and carpeting — $_____

B. Food, Beverage, Catering, and Decorations
  1. Food — $_____
  2. Beverages — $_____
  3. Linens — $_____
  4. Flowers and plants — $_____
  5. Signs and posters — $_____
  6. Decorations and flags — $_____
  7. China and silver — $_____

C. Invitations, Programs, and Place Cards
  1. Invitation — $_____
  2. Reply card — $_____
  3. Carrier envelope — $_____
  4. Reply envelope — $_____
  5. Postage — $_____
  6. Inserts — $_____
  7. Program — $_____
  8. Place cards — $_____
  9. Table numbers and names — $_____

D. Mailing
  1. Postage — $_____
  2. Service bureau or mailing house — $_____

  3. Secretarial support — $_____
  4. Food for volunteers coordinating the mailing — $_____
  5. Cost of mailing lists — $_____

E. Photographer or Video Operators
  1. Photographer — $_____
  2. Film — $_____
  3. Video operator — $_____
  4. Videotape — $_____
  5. Lighting — $_____
  6. Staging and backdrops — $_____
  7. Staff assigned to work with photographer or video operator — $_____

F. Honorarium for Speaker(s)
  1. Fee — $_____
  2. Transportation — $_____
  3. Lodging — $_____
  4. Food — $_____
  5. Gifts — $_____

G. Other/Miscellaneous — $_____

SUBTOTAL OF COSTS — $_____

SUBTRACT COSTS OF ANY ITEMS DONATED — – $_____

GRAND TOTAL OF COSTS FOR THE EVENT — $_____

Courtesy of Gerry Frank, CHA, *INN*dependent Management Group, 1992, Alexandria, VA.

evaluation of the overall successes and failures of the event. An evaluation should not take place the morning after an event, but should be held within the following week—long enough to allow the staff an opportunity to rest from the stress of producing the event, but not so long that details are forgotten. This is also the time to plan for follow up on the event—how to capitalize on its success or to "mend fences" from its failures. All too often this step is forgotten. It may not take much to keep "the ball rolling" and continue the momentum of the moment. Have thank-you notes been sent to the volunteers and those who provided gifts-in-kind? Should telephone calls be made instead of writing notes? Have lists been made of those who attended the event who are new to the organization? How will they be included in future activities? Did this event make money? Could the event have made more money? What should be done to make the event better the next time? Use this opportunity to measure the success of the event and to set the course for the next year—whether it involves this event or some other in its place. Exhibit 12–8 depicts a special event evaluation form.

Special software programs are designed to help manage all aspects of special events—from invitations, registrations, and attendance to the "to do" lists, name badges, seating and group assignments, and "event-day" reports. These programs usually are flexible in design so they can handle all event types such as black tie dinners, class reunions, annual conferences, walk-a-thons, golf tournaments, etc. They also provide standard and custom reports to assist the development staff in reporting to its board or in analyzing the successes or failures of its events. These programs range in price and usually come packaged with other fund-raising software programs.

Exhibit 12–7 Planning Calendar for Event Publicity

ACTIVITY	6 MONTH	WEEK 12	WEEK 11	WEEK 10	WEEK 9	WEEK 8	WEEK 7	WEEK 6	WEEK 5	WEEK 4	WEEK 3	WEEK 2	WEEK 1 EVENT	POST EVENT WEEK
Send out "Hold Date" announcements.	■													
Write PSAs and identify media to which publicity will be sent. Develop a database.		■	■	■										
Send out press releases announcing the event to the calendar of events editor of area magazines.	■	■												
Develop database to whom invitations will be sent.	■	■	■											
Prepare labels or write addresses on invitations. Stuff envelopes.				■	■									
Send out invitations.					■	■								
Send out PSAs to local and regional radio and TV stations.										■	■			
Send out press releases announcing the event to all local and regional newspapers.										■	■			
Contact feature story editors of area newspapers and request that a feature story be written on the event.						■					■	■		
Arrange for the local media to cover the event. Assign personnel to escort each media group.													■	
Send out press releases recapping and publicizing the success of the event.														■

Courtesy of Gerry Frank, CHA, *INNdependent Management Group*, 1992, Alexandria, VA.

Exhibit 12–8 Special Event Evaluation Form

NAME OF EVENT _____

DATE _____

      SUCCESS OF DATE AND TIME _____

      SUGGESTED DATES AND TIMES _____

NUMBER OF GUESTS ATTENDING _____

NUMBER OF STAFF ATTENDING _____ WORKING_____

SITE LOCATION _____

      SITE APPROPRIATE OR NOT _____

      SUGGESTED SITES FOR FUTURE _____

VOLUNTEER LEADERSHIP _____

      GENERAL CHAIR _____

      COMMITTEE CHAIRS _____

                            _____

                            _____

                            _____

      TOTAL VOLUNTEERS INVOLVED _____

      ESTIMATED HOURS OF WORK _____

      SUGGESTED GENERAL CHAIR FOR NEXT YEAR _____

      SUGGESTED COMMITTEES FOR NEXT YEAR _____

                            _____

                            _____

                            _____

                            _____

SUGGESTED COMMITTEE CHAIRS FOR
NEXT YEAR   _____

                            _____

                            _____

                            _____

                            _____

NUMBER OF PROFESSIONAL STAFF WORKING EVENT _____

      EVENT DIRECTOR _____

      STAFF COMMITTEE ASSIGNMENTS _____

                            _____

                            _____

                            _____

                            _____

                            _____

                            _____

ESTIMATED HOURS OF STAFF WORK _____

MONEY RAISED

      TICKET SALES $_____

      OTHER SOURCES $_____

      GROSS $_____

      NET $_____

EXPENSES

      VOLUNTEER $_____

      STAFF $_____

      EVENT COSTS $_____

      TOTAL EXPENSES $_____

TOTAL—INCOME MINUS EXPENSES $ _____

continues

Exhibit 12–8 continued

1. Considering the time invested by staff and volunteers and the total net dollars raised, is the event worth repeating?
   YES _____   NO _____   COMMENTS _____
   _____
   _____

2. What are the benefits to those attending? _____
   _____
   _____

3. What are the drawbacks to holding this event? _____
   _____

4. What problems occurred while planning or executing this event that could be prevented in the future? _____
   _____
   _____

5. What changes should be made before holding the event again? _____
   _____
   _____

6. Why, in your opinion, was this event successful or unsuccessful? _____
   _____
   _____

7. Please comment on the overall performance of the professional staff in executing the event including both positive and negative observations. _____
   _____
   _____

8. Comment on the overall performance of the volunteer involvement with the event including both positive and negative observations. _____
   _____
   _____

9. Other remarks pertinent to this event. _____
   _____
   _____
   _____

10. _____ I would be willing to work on this event again.
    _____ I would NOT be willing to work on this event again.

NAME: _____

ADDRESS: _____

_____

PHONE: _____ FAX: _____

SIGNATURE: _____

DATE: _____

Courtesy of Gerry Frank, CHA, *INN*dependent Management Group, 1992, Alexandria, VA.

What Must Be Done After the Event Is Over

Many people think that when the event is over all of the work has been completed. Unfortunately, this is not so. In addition to the evaluation that must be conducted (see the section on evaluation mentioned previously in this chapter), everyone who has contributed to the success of the event must be thanked. This includes the chairs of the event to those who donated gifts-in-kind. All outstanding bills must be paid promptly. If the vendor provided special services, include a thank-you letter. It is important to ensure the vendor's participation the next time the event is held. Be in touch with all of those who attended the event. Put them on the list to receive the organization's newsletter. Try to cultivate these people to become annual donors or volunteers for the organization's next event.

Contracting with Outside Vendors

From caterers to printers, vendors are part of the special event scene. Providing the necessities for the event, vendors can make the event a success or a disaster! It is imperative that the development staff be familiar with the quality of work or goods that a vendor is going to provide. Check references. Attend an event that is featuring the vendors being considered. Listen to the music; sample the food; review printed materials. Call references before signing any contract with a company. It ultimately comes down to "doing your homework." Thoroughly investigate all vendors before agreeing to use them for an event.

Also, make sure that vendors are adequately insured or that the organization is insured in case someone is injured at the event. Usually, a rider can be purchased to attach to the organization's existing insurance policy. This will undoubtedly not be part of the organization's normal insurance unless conventions, meetings, and special events are a part of the organization's everyday operations. If the event is being planned for out of doors or during the winter months, event cancellation insurance should be considered. In all cases when alcohol is being served, liquor liability should be purchased.

Using an Event Management Group

Sometimes it is easier to hire a consultant and an events management group to plan and execute a special event than it is to use existing departmental staff. This is called outsourcing. First, consider the magnitude of the event and whether it has been held before; then consider the commitments, skills, and limitations of the current staff. If this is a "once in a lifetime" opportunity (and these are truly rare), then it may be wise to hold the event. If the staff has limited expertise in this area, then hire an outside firm to produce the event and use the staff to solely manage the firm's activities.

If this is the direction of choice, be very careful in negotiating the contract with the events firm so it is clear just what is expected from them, what will be managed by the development office, and what the true costs of the event will be. Also include performance standards, fee structures, and the schedule of payment. Don't overlook hidden costs! If you haven't negotiated a contract before, now is not the time to learn. Ask someone from the financial department to participate. It even may be wise to have a board member who can assist with the negotiations, or to even hire an attorney. Whatever is done, don't do it in a "vacuum." Show the contracts to the head of finance or the president of the organization before signing anything.

Most event firms are reputable and will do an excellent job. Ask for references and call them! Are the events these firms have organized in the past of the same type the organization wants to hold? Does the image of the event management firm fit with the organization's? If the organization is promoting gun control and the events firm does the majority of its work for the National Rifle Association, then the organization may not wish to hire this firm even if its credentials are impeccable. Discuss this with the board—do not have any surprises that the board may have to defend.

Events firms also may be able to negotiate better prices with vendors. They work with them every day and continuously steer business their way. Printers, musicians, caterers, florists, etc. are more likely to give a break in prices to those who use them frequently than to those who use them once a year. In addition, outside firms even may have better leverage with the organization's volunteers. If volunteers need to be firmly directed, it may be easier to have the events company's staff do the directing rather than those from the development office who will have to work with the volunteers in the future. Also, board members may perceive the events firm as being "more professional" than the development office when it comes to producing special events because this is what the event firm does day-in and day-out. They may be more willing to trust the expertise of this group and, as a result, not require as much direction or hand-holding from the development staff. Be sure to have only one person who is responsible for communicating with the firm managing the event. This is usually the most senior person on the staff of the development office. Don't just sign a contract and walk away. Keep open and frequent communications with the firm. Meet with staff persons from the firm often to make sure that they are on the right course for the organization.

One of the most overlooked advantages of using an outside firm to produce the organization's special events is that the work is not being done in the development office. The entire project will be organized outside—planning, design, mailings, envelope stuffing, telephone calls, and the management of any crisis will not interfere with the every-day workload of the staff. This alone can make it cost effective to hire an events firm. In addition, the events firm can bring people to the organization who may be interested in the organization's mission and activities—people who may have never heard of the organization before.

Finally, check references. Ask what other organizations similar in size have used the firm before. Determine if the events produced for other organizations are similar in scope and visibility to the one your organization wishes to produce. Call those persons who have worked with the firm and ask detailed questions about reliability, pricing structure, creativity, quality, etc. Request a capability package from each vendor—what they will be able to provide to the organization. Additional information regarding the use of consultants in fund raising may be found in Chapter 16.

"They want a receipt for their contribution to the dinner!"

Source: © Joseph A. Brown

IRS Regulations Regarding Special Events

Beginning January 1, 1994, the Internal Revenue Service (IRS) required that a charitable organization must provide a written disclosure statement to donors who make a payment described as a "quid pro quo contribution" in excess of $75. This new section 6115 of the Internal Revenue Code mandated that the charity notify in writing each participant in an event, indicating what portion of their contribution is tax-deductible. To determine what portion of the ticket price is tax deductible, consider the costs of the food and beverage, printing, postage, etc., and then deduct these from the price of the ticket. If the event includes a theatre ticket, then that also must be deducted at the full box office price charged by the theater, not at the discount price that the organization may have received. For example, if the event includes dinner, wine, and entertainment, and costs the organization $85 to hold, and the ticket price is $125, then the tax deductible donation to the guest is not $125, but is $45—the $125 cost of the ticket, minus the $85 in goods received.

If a person attends several events sponsored by the same charity during the year, but each event is under the $75 threshold, the payments cannot be aggregated to meet the $75 threshold. Also, a donor cannot submit several small checks to cover the costs of one event with a high ticket price to circumvent this ruling. Also, if a donor writes a check to a charity for $100 and receives in return $45 worth of goods or services, the $55 would be deductible; but, because the $100 payment, or quid pro quo contribution, exceeds the $75, the charity must provide the disclosure statement even though the amount the donor can deduct does not exceed the $75 limit. The safest way for the charity to protect itself after attempting to state the exact amount of the deduction on an invitation is to add "Tax deductible to the fullest extent as provided by law."

Any questions regarding these rules can be answered by reading the Internal Revenue Service publication 1771 (11–93), a copy of which is included in Appendix 12–B.

For more information about special events, see *Successful Special Events: Planning, Hosting, and Evaluating,* by Barbara R. Levy, ACFRE, and Barbara Marion, CFRE, another book in this series.

Appendix 12–A
Case Studies

"FESTIVAL OF TREES"
Women's Auxiliaries of Columbus Children's Hospital
Columbus, Ohio

Concept: Even Scrooge would be unable to resist getting into the Holiday Spirit while viewing a dazzling collection of more than a hundred magnificently decorated Christmas trees. He may even be tempted to buy one. Every year professional designers deck the halls of Columbus, Ohio's convention center by putting their unique "signatures" on artificial trees, and everyone who visits the display definitely knows it's Christmas.

Festival of Trees, which is sponsored by the women's auxiliaries of Columbus' Children's Hospital, is a five day event that takes place the week of Thanksgiving. After ten successful years it has become the unofficial opener to the Holiday Season in Columbus. At the Gala Opening Night Party on the Tuesday before Thanksgiving, the lavishly decorated trees go on sale at prices ranging from $400 to $2,000. The trees remain on display throughout the exhibition, and are then delivered to the purchasers on the Monday following the Festival. The highlight of the Opening Night Party is a live auction of four trees which have been decorated by the auxiliaries and include elaborate gifts that have been donated by local businesses or individuals.

Early Christmas shoppers can browse through *Giftland*, a display of handcrafted items that have been donated by auxiliaries; *Sweetland*, a collection of homemade cookies, candies, cakes, and breads; *Gingerbread Lane*, an exhibition of gingerbread houses created by local pastry chefs, and the *Avenue of Wreaths & Miniatures*, an array of beautiful Christmas decorations. Even the children can do some shopping at *Santa's Secret Shop*, where parents aren't allowed and most items are priced under $2. Santa is available for pictures and wish lists, of course.

Admission Price: 7 p.m. Opening Night Preview Party, $50 per person. 8 p.m. Opening Night Party, $20 per person. Exhibition pre-sale: Adults, $1.50, Children under 12, $.75. At door: Adults, $2, Children under 12, $1.

Attendance: Opening Night: 2,500; Exhibition: 75,000.

Net Profit: $290,000 total ($58,000 from auction)

Expenses: $75,000. Major expenses include the Opening Night Party ($24,000), rental of the Ohio Center ($20,000), and purchase of the trees ($7,000).

When: Wed., Fri., Sat. 10 a.m. to 10 p.m.
Thanksgiving, 4 p.m. to 10 p.m.
Sunday, 10 a.m. to 5 p.m.

Planning:	Planning for the event begins one year in advance. The committee is comprised of 115 to 120 members. Positions include Chairman, Chairman-Elect, Finance Chairman, Secretary, Vice Chairman of Sales, Vice Chairman of Physical Arrangements, Vice Chairman of Public Relations, and Vice Chairman of Volunteers. Some of the individual committees are titled: Decorators, Sponsors, Volunteer Scheduling, Area Design, Sweetland, Giftland, Funland, Tree Delivery, Opening Night Party, Calligraphy, Media, and Speakers' Bureau.
	The major planning tasks include: gathering sponsors, contacting sponsors and decorators through mail and phone campaign; organization of tree decorating process; compiling and producing the program; and arranging the Secret Santa area.
	The committee provides the artificial trees; some are donated by a local corporation, the rest are purchased. All the decorators donate their time and some donate materials. Reimbursement to those decorators not donating materials is done in accordance with the size of the tree that is being decorated, and the amount for reimbursement is established prior to the event. The decorators who request "early tree delivery" receive their trees one month before the Festival and then bring them fully or partially decorated to the convention center the day before the Opening Night Party. Other decorators elect to completely decorate their trees in place. These decorators arrive at 10 a.m. on the day before the Opening Night Party. 125–150 volunteers are needed to staff each day of the exhibition.
	The day after the event the trees are delivered to the purchasers by a local moving company, which donates vans and workers. Two members from the auxiliaries follow each van to assist the drivers with delivery, to make sure the trees are not damaged, and to help locate the correct addresses.
	The primary tasks required throughout the days of the event are: staffing Giftland, Sweetland, Santa's Secret Shop and Funland; selling raffle tickets; information hostessing; selling of trees.
Publicity:	Word of mouth, posters, fliers, mailers, ads in local newspapers and on buses.
Underwriting:	Each tree is assigned a sponsor. Sponsorships range from $350 to $1,000 or more, and the sponsor receives complimentary tickets to the Opening Night Party and scrip equal to the amount of their donation. The scrip may be used towards the purchase of one tree. (Scrip is not necessary to purchase a tree–anyone may be a purchaser.)
Awards:	Trees are judged by local media personalities and awards are given for Best of Show, Most Creative, Most Traditional, and A Child's Dream. Guests at the Opening Night Party vote for the winner of the People's Choice Award.
Raffles:	Raffles are conducted throughout the exhibition, with winners being announced on the last day. Items include quilts, trips, toys, hot air balloon rides, etc.
M.C.	A local television newscaster or radio D.J. emcees throughout the event, announcing the entertainment performances (school and church groups, singers and dancers) on an hourly basis each day. The M.C. donates his/her time and service.
Entertainment:	Continuous entertainment features magicians, choral and instrumental groups, and dancers, all of whom donate their time.
Printed Material:	A sixteen-page tabloid size program is available and includes paid advertising and benefactor lists, a map of the festival, lists of decorators, sponsors and an entertainment schedule. The program nets nearly $5,000.
Funding For:	The money is presented to the Columbus Children's Hospital board of directors to be used at their discretion, for such projects as research, unpaid patient care, construction costs or education. The four auxiliaries which support the hospital include TWIGS, Kinder Key, Women's Board and Pleasure Guild.

Comments: "The Festival of Trees is extremely well supported by businesses and individuals because it represents the unofficial opener of the Holiday Season in Columbus. Also, the community is very proud of Children's Hospital and goes to great lengths to support it because of its reputation for excellence in patient care, research, education, and its policy that it turns no child away because of the parents' inability to pay."

—Darlene DeRoberts, Event Chairman
Women's Auxiliaries of Columbus Children's Hospital

"DUCK DERBY"

American Diabetes Association
Montana Affiliate
Hamilton, Montana

Concept: Here's a quacky fundraiser that's easier than shooting ducks in a barrel. The event can be classified as a "race," if one calls putting hundreds of little toy duckies in a creek to see which one floats downstream the fastest a "race." Needless to say, this is not a high-speed, revved-up kind of a race.

The Duck Derby is held on a leisurely Saturday afternoon in a rural area of Montana. The participants who have sponsored the plastic toy ducks are just as welcome to come watch the spectacle as they are to stay home and drink a glass of lemonade. This is an event that has received some great community support, and the only requirements for participants are that they pay a "buck a duck" ($1 per sponsored duck) and have a good sense of humor.

There are ten qualifying heats in the Duck Derby with approximately 100 ducks per heat. Each heat has five winners. The fastest duck in each heat wins cash prizes, T-shirts and the chance to race in the final heat. All participants get to keep their ducks. The ducks can be purchased prior to the race at various downtown stores for a dollar or a five-dollar donation with the money going to the Montana Diabetes Association.

Next year, Duck Derby organizers plan to hold a special race for $10 per duck in which participants will be able to modify their ducks for improving speed as part of the competition.

During the four-hour event, a variety of unusual tasks are performed by the volunteer staff: Duck Dumpers are in charge of dumping sacks of the ducks into the water in groups of 100; Duck Herders are assigned to walk along the edge of the waterway and rescue any ducks that get tangled in the reeds; Duck Floaters act as general "gophers," floating from one task to another as needed; Duck Pluckers wait at the finish line to pluck the winning ducks out of the water.

According to the event's planners, the Duck Derby has proven to be a "ducky" way to raise money as well as awareness about the Diabetes Association within the community.

Attendance: Minimal. Owners do not need to be present to win prizes. 1,000 ducks are sponsored.

Price: $1 or $5 per duck

Net Profit: $1400

Expenses: $400. Major expenses include ducks, tickets, prizes, and T-shirts.

Location: The C&C Ditch in Hamilton, Montana.

When: Saturday, mid-July from 11 a.m. to 4 p.m.

Planning: Planning begins four to six months in advance. A committee of six people plans the entire event. The ducks are ordered from a carnival supply company and each one is numbered for identification. Prior to the race, collection cans are placed in local businesses throughout the town with posters describing the race and how to participate. Race organizers also find several sponsors to underwrite the cost of the ducks and the printing expenses.

The primary planning tasks include: handling publicity; selling tickets; recruiting and scheduling volunteers and arranging for event sponsors.

About 15 individuals work on the day of the event. Several of their responsibilities include: keeping track of the ducks; pulling ducks out at the end of the race; awarding prizes; and announcing the winners.

Underwriting: A variety of local businesses are approached to play a sponsorship role, donating the cost of most expenses.

Publicity: Because this is such a unique event, it garners excellent publicity. A local radio station broadcasts live from the race site and local newspapers cover the event that day, as well as featuring the race results after the race.

M.C. None

Entertainment: None

Food: None

Decorations: None

Prizes: Ducks that are sponsored for $1 are eligible to win a $25 prize. Ducks that are sponsored for $5 are eligible to win a $75 prize. (Next year they plan to award a $100 grand prize.) T-shirts with a Duck Derby logo are also awarded to the winners.

Printed Material: Posters, tickets and collection can labels.

Funding For: The money is used to improve public awareness of symptoms of diabetes for quicker detection; provide educational and instructional seminars for diabetics and their families, and professional persons associated with the care of diabetics; provide learning experiences through camps and retreats for young diabetics; and lend support nationally in the continued research for a cure for diabetes, and new means of living better with diabetes.

Comments: "The Duck Derby attracted a lot of support because it was something that had never been done before. The volunteers had a good time putting it on and the participants got a kick out of seeing if their ducks won. This was a simple, one-shot fund-raiser that took a minimum of coordination."

—Sandra Shull, Field Representative
American Diabetes Association

"NO-SHOW, NO-GO CELEBRITY BANQUET"

CARE
Atlanta, Georgia

Concept:	The tongue-in-cheek No-Show Banquet gets a lot of chuckles and a lot of money by throwing a bash to which no one is expected to come. Their humorous invitation reads: "Don't go to Atlanta's No-Show, No-Go Celebrity Banquet for CARE...No rubber chicken dinner. No pep talks from smiling celebrities...No renting a tux, hiring a sitter or tipping the parking attendants..." And then they ask for a donation. And it works!
	The South Eastern office for CARE, the world relief and development organization, throws their non-party on World Food Day each year in October, a time when many local residents are flooded with invitations to a variety of fund-raisers. The "non-event" pokes fun at the traditional black tie dinner dances that have a tendency to be yawningly long. This approach gives recipients the chance to participate with a contribution without leaving home. To entice people even more with the campaign, the group gets permission to use the names of renowned celebrities (i.e. Ted Turner) in writing their invitation... "Not one single, solitary word from Cap'n Ted." CARE asks contributors to send the amount they would usually spend on a formal fund-raising dinner—a fresh approach that may be just what many gala-goers ordered.
Invitations:	3,000 mailed
Admission Price:	The organization encloses return cards with suggested donation amounts, ranging from $25 to $500, or a fill-in amount.
Net Profit:	$24,000
Expenses:	Minimal, Postage only—everything else is donated.
When:	Mid-October
Planning:	Planning begins four months in advance. The major planning tasks include selecting a professional public relations firm to create and produce the invitation; soliciting sponsors to donate materials or services; soliciting volunteers to hand-address invitations; writing and distribution of press releases for support publicity. A total of 15 volunteers work during the planning stages.
	Since there is no actual event, the invitation is all the contributors will see—so it had better be good. With the aid of the P.R. firm, CARE comes up with invitations that are clever and attention-grabbing. The No-Show invitations have received several advertising industry awards for achievement in the non-profit category.
	Some examples of copy include: "Last year, no one came to the biggest social event in Atlanta. This year we hope to be even more successful..." Inside: "A party you'll be glad you missed...Chances are you'd give anything not to go. Give Anything." An example of an illustration is a harassed, tuxedo-clad gentleman being dragged by his wife to yet another charity ball. The creative ideas for the No-Show Banquet seem to flow every year, making much ado about "nothing" while bringing in substantial revenue.
Underwriting:	The P.R. firm donates all time and services. Other local companies donate paper, printing, photography, etc.

Funding For: In addition to feeding 22 million people worldwide on a regular basis, CARE is helping to establish or improve many basic services in the poorest countries of the world through a variety of health, nutrition and educational programs as well as community projects involving water, agricultural development and resource conservation.

Comments: "This is a light and clever way to get people to pay attention to the very serious issues addressed by CARE."

—Marilyn F. Grist, Southeastern Director
CARE

Source: Reprinted with permission from K. Kraatz and J. Haynes, *The Fundraising Formula: 50 Creative Events Proven Successful Nationwide*, 1987, KNI Incorporated.

Appendix 12–B
Charitable Contributions—Substantiation and Disclosure Requirements

UNDER THE NEW LAW, CHARITIES WILL NEED TO PROVIDE NEW KINDS OF INFORMATION TO DONORS. Failure to do so may result in denial of deductions to donors and the imposition of penalties on charities.

Legislation signed into law by the President on August 10, 1993, contains a number of significant provisions affecting tax-exempt charitable organizations described in section 501(c)(3) of the Internal Revenue Code. These provisions include: (1) new substantiation requirements for donors; and (2) new public disclosure requirements for charities (with potential penalties for failing to comply). Additionally, charities should note that donors could be penalized by loss of the deduction if they fail to substantiate. **THE SUBSTANTIATION AND DISCLOSURE PROVISIONS APPLY TO CONTRIBUTIONS MADE AFTER DECEMBER 31, 1993.**

Charities need to familiarize themselves with these tax law changes in order to bring themselves into compliance. This Publication alerts you to the new provisions affecting tax-exempt charitable organizations. Set forth below are brief descriptions of the new law's key provisions. The Internal Revenue Service plans to provide further guidance in the near future.

Donor's Substantiation Requirements

Documenting Certain Charitable Contributions.—Beginning January 1, 1994, no deduction will be allowed under section 170 of the Internal Revenue Code for any charitable contribution of $250 or more unless the donor has contemporaneous written substantiation from the charity. In cases where the charity has provided goods or services to the donor in exchange for making the contribution, this contemporaneous written acknowledgement must include a good faith estimate of the value of such goods or services. Thus, taxpayers may no longer rely solely on a cancelled check to substantiate a cash contribution of $250 or more.

The substantiation must be "contemporaneous." That is, it must be obtained by the donor no later than the date the donor actually files a return for the tax year in which the contribution was made. If the return is filed after the due date or extended due date, then the substantiation must have been obtained by the due date or extended due date.

The responsibility for obtaining this substantiation lies with the donor, who must request it from the charity. The charity is not required to record or report this information to the IRS on behalf of donors.

The legislation provides that substantiation will <u>not</u> be required, if, in accordance with regulations prescribed by the Secretary, the charity reports directly to the IRS the information required to be provided in the written substantiation. At present, there are no regulations establishing procedures for direct reporting by charities to the IRS of charitable contributions made in 1994. Consequently, charities and donors should be prepared to provide/obtain the described substantiation for 1994 contributions of $250 or more.

There is no prescribed format for the written acknowledgement. For example, letters, postcards or computer-generated forms may be acceptable. The acknowledgement does not have to include the donor's social security or tax identification number. It must, however, provide sufficient information to substantiate the amount of the deductible contribution. The acknowledgement should note the amount of any cash contribution. However, if the donation is in the form of property, then the acknowledgement must describe, but need not value, such property. Valuation of the donated property is the responsibility of the donor.

The written substantiation should also note whether the donee organization provided any goods or services in consideration, in whole or in part, for the contribution and, if so, must provide a description and good-faith estimate of the value of the goods or services. In the new law these are referred to as "quid pro quo contributions."

Please note that there is a new law requiring charities to furnish disclosure statements to donors for such quid pro quo donations in excess of $75. This is addressed in the next section regarding Disclosure By Charity.

If the goods or services consist entirely of intangible religious benefits, the statement should indicate this, but the statement need not describe or provide an estimate of the value of these benefits. "Intangible religious benefits" are also discussed in the following section on Disclosure By Charity. If, on the other hand, the donor received nothing in return for the contribution, the written substantiation must so state.

The present law remains in effect that, generally, if the value of an item or group of like items exceeds $5,000, the donor must obtain a qualified appraisal and submit an appraisal summary with the return claiming the deduction.

The organization may either provide separate statements for each contribution of $250 or more from a taxpayer, or furnish periodic statements substantiating contributions of $250 or more.

Separate payments are regarded as independent contributions and are not aggregated for purposes of measuring the $250 threshold. However, the Service is authorized to establish anti-abuse rules to prevent avoidance of the substantiation requirement by taxpayers writing separate smaller checks on the same date.

If donations are made through payroll deductions, the deduction from each paycheck is regarded as a separate payment.

A charity that knowingly provides false written substantiation to a donor may be subject to the penalties for aiding and abetting an understatement of tax liability under section 6701 of the Code.

Disclosure by Charity of Receipt of Quid Pro Quo Contribution

Beginning January 1, 1994, under new section 6115 of the Internal Revenue Code, a charitable organization must provide a written disclosure statement to donors who make a payment, described as a "quid pro quo contribution" in excess of $75. This requirement is separate from the written substantiation required for deductibility purposes as discussed above. While, in certain circumstances, an organization may be able to meet both requirements with the same written document, an organization must be careful to satisfy the section 6115 written disclosure statement requirement in a timely manner because of the penalties involved.

A quid pro quo contribution is a payment made partly as a contribution and partly for goods or services pro-

vided to the donor by the charity. An example of a quid pro quo contribution is where the donor gives a charity $100 in consideration for a concert ticket valued at $40. In this example, $60 would be deductible. Because the donor's payment (quid pro quo contribution) exceeds $75, the disclosure statement must be furnished, even though the deductible amount does not exceed $75.

Separate payments of $75 or less made at different times of the year for separate fundraising events will not be aggregated for purposes of the $75 threshold. However, the Service is authorized to develop anti-abuse rules to prevent avoidance of this disclosure requirement in situations such as the writing of multiple checks for the same transaction.

The required disclosure statement must:

(1) inform the donor that the amount of the contribution that is deductible for federal income tax purposes is limited to the excess of any money (and the value of any property other than money) contributed by the donor over the value of goods or services provided by the charity, and

(2) provide the donor with a good-faith estimate of the value of the goods or services that the donor received.

The charity must furnish the statement in connection with either the solicitation or the receipt of the quid pro quo contribution. If the disclosure statement is furnished in connection with a particular solicitation, it is not necessary for the organization to provide another statement when the associated contribution is actually received.

The disclosure must be in writing and must be made in a manner that is reasonably likely to come to the attention of the donor. For example, a disclosure in small print within a larger document might not meet this requirement.

In the following three circumstances, the disclosure statement is not required.

(1) Where the only goods or services given to a donor meet the standards for "insubstantial value" set out in section 3.01, paragraph 2 of Rev. Proc. 90–12, 1990–1 C.B. 471, as amplified by section 2.01 of Rev. Proc. 92–49, 1992–1 C.B. 987 (or any updates or revisions thereof);

(2) Where there is no donative element involved in a particular transaction with a charity, such as in a typical museum gift shop sale.

(3) Where there is only an intangible religious benefit provided to the donor. The intangible religious benefit must be provided to the donor by an organization organized exclusively for religious purposes, and must be of a type that generally is not sold in

a commercial transaction outside the donative context. An example of an intangible religious benefit would be admission to a religious ceremony. The exception also generally applies to de minimis tangible benefits, such as wine, provided in connection with a religious ceremony. The intangible religious benefit exception, however, does not apply to such items as payments for tuition for education leading to a recognized degree, or for travel services, or consumer goods.

A penalty is imposed on charities that do not meet the disclosure requirements. For failure to make the required disclosure in connection with a quid pro quo contribution of more than $75, there is a penalty of $10 per contribution, not to exceed $5,000 per fundraising event or mailing. The charity may avoid the penalty if it can show that the failure was due to reasonable cause.

Please note that the prevailing basic rule allowing donor deductions only to the extent that the payment exceeds the fair market value of the goods or services received in return still applies generally to all quid pro quo contributions. The $75 threshold pertains only to the obligation to disclose and the imposition of the $10 per contribution penalty, not the rule on deductibility of the payment.

Department of the Treasury
Internal Revenue Service
Publication 1771 (11–93)
Catalog Number 20054Q

Chapter 13
Fund-Raising Publications

Key Vocabulary

- Case Statement
- Desk-Top Publishing
- Thumbnails

The Need for Publications in Development

All fund raisers know that "people give to people." They also know that if you don't ask for the gift, it's highly unlikely that a gift will be given. But what most people don't understand is how important it is to have the right materials with you when soliciting a gift. By providing a potential donor with information before the visit or leaving materials behind after speaking with the individual or group, you leave a lasting impression not only with your words, but with the images in the brochures—the copy that describes the organization's mission or programs; the photos of the people working tirelessly on the organization's behalf; the numbers, graphs, or charts that relay the financial need of the organization; and the list of reasons why the prospect should make a gift to your organization. The person makes the "ask;" the materials provide the reminder of why the potential donors should support you and your cause.

For this reason, all materials used in development should reflect the style of the organization they represent. They need not be "slick," four color, bright, or fancy. They must be informative, accurate, fresh, error-free, and have a "feel" that makes the receiver

> All fund raisers know that "people give to people."

want to read and keep them. All development operations can produce materials that will fulfill this goal. What kinds and amounts an organization produces will depend upon the type of organization it is, the fund-raising effort it is undertaking, and the people that it will be soliciting.

Remember that there is almost no correlation between the ability of a fund-raising brochure to garner accolades and its ability to raise money for the organization. Publications are the "supporting players" in fund raising. The "stars" are the volunteers who solicit the funds face-to-face. Publications should never take the place of a direct person-to-person solicitation. The only exception to this rule is in direct-mail solicitation when the expected gifts are quite small.

There are, however, some basic materials that are used by all organizations both large and small in their fund-raising efforts. These materials include the case statement, an annual report, a general information brochure highlighting the organization and/or the fund-raising effort, a question-and-answer brochure, newsletters, press releases, pledge cards, and in some cases, posters. Following are descriptions of each of these pieces and how they are used in fund raising.

The Case Statement

A case statement is simply the organization's statement of need—an explanation of the needs and opportunities that confront the organization. The case statement does not need to be long. It should be concise, but comprehensive. All other documents that the organization will use for fund raising—personal letters, brochures, videos, etc.—will be based on the case statement. A case statement that is strong, well thought out, and well written will make it easier for the leadership and volunteers to promote the fund-raising effort.

A case statement will relate the history of the organization—why it was founded, what its mission is, how it has helped and served its constituents in the past, etc. It also will present the organization's current position—who does it serve, how its programs affect the public today, and what makes it different from other organizations with similar missions.

A case statement also will present the needs of the organization—why it needs funding, how much money it needs, a plan for how that money can be raised, and how the money will strengthen the organization's programs and change the world that the organization encompasses. It anticipates the questions and provides the answers. It concludes with a succinct wrap-up and leaves the reader with the feeling that the organization makes a difference and is worthy of support.

In Exhibit 13–1 Nike B. Whitcomb, CFRE, defines the uses for the case statement and gives suggestions on its design and printing.

Exhibit 13–1 Guidelines for Writing a Case Statement

The case statement is the vehicle used to recruit key volunteer leadership, to secure top gifts, and to open the door to other areas of fund raising. It is a printed document which uses copy, photography, and graphic art to present a first-class image. The case statement varies in size and number of pages based on several criteria, such as the following:

- The cause
- The urgency of the need
- The constituency being approached
- Previous style and type of printed materials

The copy in the case statement has a clearly delineated purpose—to convince the reader of the worth of the project and of the urgent need for a contribution. People give to what they know and understand. Therefore, the case must do the following:

- Identify the institution and establish its place in history
- Convey a sense of its value to society
- Give specific information regarding costs involved in solving the problems being addressed in the campaign
- Provide a means of response

Often the basic story can be enhanced through the use of personal "testimonials" from influential members of the community who already are committed to the cause. For example, if the cause is to raise funds for a new hospital wing, artists' concepts of the new building, floor plans, and pictures of people who will benefit from the improved services and facilities are helpful.

Generally, the case statement is printed in at least two ink colors to enhance graphic potential. Even agencies without large budgets for printing should consider modest use of four-color art work in a document like the case statement.

Before beginning the concept, design, and writing of the case statement and all other printed materials, several questions must be asked, such as the following:

- What is the overall budget for printing? What is the specific budget for this piece?
- Is this piece a part of a campaign (annual, capital, endowment, etc.)?

- What is the anticipated use of the piece? Recruitment? Solicitation? Short-term cultivation? Long-term awareness? All of the stated?
- How does/will the piece fit into the overall image of the institution?
- What is the timetable for creating the piece?
- What materials already exist that will add to the piece (graphs, charts, giving tables, photography, quotes)?
- Who will need to approve the copy? Design?

Costs to produce a case statement include those for writing, photography, design, and printing, and can range from as little as $2 to as much as $265 per copy. The press run usually will be short—1,000 copies is average for most small- to medium-size campaigns. Multiple pages, use of graphics and photos, multiple ink colors, and quality of paper will all add to or subtract from the cost.

To estimate the number of copies needed, look at the potential donor list. All top prospects should get a copy of the case statement. All board and staff members should have copies. All campaign workers should have copies. Extra copies also will be useful for distribution to media, to prospects in the middle tier of the potential donor list, and so on.

Once the rough estimate is made, add 10 percent for copies that may not be perfectly produced and for the inevitable "lost" copies that will need to be replaced. This is the number of copies to plan on.

Now is the time to consider the size of the piece. The following are a few things to keep in mind.

- Unless the piece is spiral or perfect bound, binding requirements for the document will be in increments of four. Small campaigns ($500,000 goal) may use only four pages—larger campaigns ($30 million plus) may use up to 100 pages.
- The vertical format of 8½" by 11" is the standard size but not mandatory.
- Ample room for white space, photos, and graphics will enhance the design and readability.
- The type font should be large enough (at least 10 point) and easy enough to read (most find serif type faces, such as Times Roman, easiest). Keep in mind that most prospects capable of large gifts are 40 years of age or older.

Source: Adapted with permission from Nike B. Whitcomb, CFRE, "Getting the Message Across," *Getting Started: A Guide to Fund Raising Fundamentals,* 1988, The National Society of Fund Raising Executives, Chicago Chapter.

An example of a well written, effective case statement developed as a brochure to be used in a capital campaign can be found in Appendix 13–A.

General Information Brochure

The fund-raising brochure is developed from the case statement and is the "professional" presentation of the

> The brochure should look professional, but not "slick" or expensive.

case statement. It is the polished package that accompanies all letters soliciting funds. It will restate the case, carry a message from the organization's leadership, describe the attributes of the organization, explain the funding needs, describe how to make gifts to the cause, list the gift recognition opportunities (if any), and leave the prospective donor with a sense of immediacy—the feeling that making a gift to the organization is the correct thing to do and it should be done now, not later.

The brochure should look professional, but not "slick" or expensive. It should include photos, quotes, graphs, charts, lists, and bulleted phrases. It should be concise and limit copy to keep from being overly wordy. Four color is preferred, but much can be done creatively with two colors of ink, which is much less expensive. Often the brochure is designed with a pocket either in the front or back into which a fact sheet, question-and-answer brochure, or other information can be inserted. The look of these other pieces is modeled after the design of the brochure.

Fact Sheet

Many times a donor will ask for specific facts and will not want to read an entire brochure. It is easy to provide a donor with a summary of the fund-raising need by developing a sheet of all important facts pertinent to the fund-raising effort. The design of this piece should be a complement to the brochure. The colors selected should be one or two of those used in the brochure. This piece need not be fancy, but should be laid out in a logical, easy-to-follow format.

Question-and-Answer Brochure

Questions that are commonly asked throughout the fund-raising effort can be anticipated, presented, and answered in a smaller brochure that accompanies the main fund-raising brochure. This can be called the question-and-answer brochure or the "Q and A" for short. In addition to being used along with the general informational fund-raising brochure, it also can be used separately. This is an inexpensive piece, often considered a "throw away" piece, and can be printed in two color, or "piggy-backed" with the printing of the major brochure and done in four color (if the brochure is being printed in four color).

Annual Report

As a complement to all fund-raising materials, the organization should develop and print an annual report. The brochure outlines the organization's programs and activities during the past year and reports on the financial stability of the organization. Produced annually, it can be used effectively as a supplemental brochure in multi-year fund-raising efforts.

Source: © Mark Litzler

Newsletters

Newsletters are used to communicate both within fund-raising campaigns and to the public being solicited for gifts. Written and distributed monthly, bimonthly, or quarterly, a newsletter can provide frequent updates on the fund-raising efforts by featuring stories on donors, campaign leadership, special events, and other activities of interest to the volunteers, members, potential donors, and others. Material for the newsletters should be planned in advance to set the stage for the fund-raising effort, introduce the volunteer leadership, announce key fund-raising events, and list the donors as they accumulate over the months.

In Exhibit 13–2, Whitcomb addresses the rules that apply to publications other than the case statement developed by the development office.

Press Releases

To inform the public of the organization's fund-raising efforts, the staff must write and distribute news releases to announce important happenings such as special events, the receipts of a major gift, the appointment of a campaign chairperson, etc. News releases can be distributed by mail or at a press conference, if the news is important

Exhibit 13–2 Developing Other Publications

The same rules that govern the creation of the case statement play an important role in other adjunct fund-raising literature. Newsletters, for example, can reinforce the message about a specific campaign and amplify basic information about the need. For example, institutions providing multiple services can profile each service and its associated personnel in successive issues of the newsletter over a one- or two-year time span.

The newsletter also can be used to update the constituencies regarding campaign progress. Story ideas include recruitment of volunteer leadership, announcement of early gifts, interviews with people who are and will benefit from the services, interviews with staff providing service, and interviews with key donors and lists of special needs.

Keep the format simple. For example, consider the following advice:

- Two colors are plenty.
- Stick to 10-point type.
- Stick to one or two type faces for the headline in no more than three sizes, using boldface and italics for variation.
- Use photos that are large enough to have visual impact but are not overpowering.
- Don't "continue" a story more than once within an issue.
- Four to six pages is enough space to tell the message and still invite the reader to keep reading.

Newsletters are not "newsy" if they are published less often than quarterly, although staff time and budget may dictate less frequency.

Source: Adapted with permission from Nike B. Whitcomb, CFRE, "Getting the Message Across," *Getting Started: A Guide to Fund Raising Fundamentals,* 1988, The National Society of Fund Raising Executives, Chicago Chapter.

enough to get the press to attend. If materials are distributed at a press conference, then a complete press kit should be developed including the press release, a brochure or fact sheet describing the organization, biographies of any persons involved, and any photographs (black and white) pertinent to the release.

The basic rules of producing a press release are the following: (1) Be sure to use letterhead or "press release" banner head stationery. (2) List a contact name and phone number before beginning the text of the release. (3) Keep the release short—one to two pages at the most. (4) Use quotes, short paragraphs, and a photo if possible. (5) Put the most important information in the first paragraph. (6) Type "more" on the bottom of the page if continuing to another page. (7) End the release with one of the following sets of marks—###, -30-, o0o.

Posters

Posters are effective fund-raising tools in many campaigns. Who can forget the March of Dimes poster child or the faces of the animals on the posters of the Society for the Prevention of Cruelty to Animals? A picture says a thousand words, and posters can raise thousands of dollars. They also can just be used to raise the public's awareness of the organization and its mission. They do not need to be in four color; but again, if it is in the budget, then use four color because it is usually more dramatic and appealing.

> A picture says a thousand words, and posters can raise thousands of dollars.

Pledge Cards

Pledge cards are integral to most campaigns. They allow the donors to convey their intentions—type of gift, size of gift, methods of payment, restrictions or designations, and whether a person or event is being commemorated.

Written materials are essential fund-raising tools. They present the image of the organization and the message of the institution's mission to potential donors. Quality materials are a must, and money should not be skimped when developing the materials to support the institution's fund-raising efforts. The goal of the development office is to produce quality pieces in a timely manner and within budget to assist in a successful fund-raising effort.

Publications Represent the Organization

All publications produced by the organization should be produced in a creative, professional, and cost-effective manner. Also, all printed materials used in fund raising should present a good image of the organization. For many who read the materials, this will be their first "image" of the organization. If the materials are sloppily conceived or poorly written or designed, they will leave the wrong impression with the potential donor. This may be a lasting impression of the organization and the potential donor may choose not to give at all.

Publications do not have to be expensive to represent the organization. Simple, neat, well-designed, two-color pieces can be more effective than crowded, complex, four-color pieces. Design the piece to fit the organization and the audience that you wish to reach. Having the image of being able to print expensive brochures may not be what you want to convey to your donors. Be careful of not only what you say, but of how it is reproduced and presented in printed materials.

How To Produce Low-Cost, High-Quality Pieces

Desk-top publishing is one method to use to design materials to be printed. If there is staff capable of producing design work with one of the many software products available, then consider using desk-top publishing, which enables you to produce camera-ready art directly from your own personal computer without using a designer. Some newsletters, brochures, and invitations are easily designed this way and save the organization thousands of dollars in design costs. The piece can go straight from the computer to the printer with the right software.

An organization that produces many brochures, a monthly newsletter, or other fund-raising pieces may wish to consider hiring a person whose sole responsibility is to produce these pieces in-house. Yet with the trend today for organizations to outsource projects, the production of these pieces probably will be one of the first duties to go in that direction.

Use of Consultants in Writing Publications

Working with a Designer
If an organization does not have in-house design capabilities, then it is imperative that it find a designer who can capture its spirit and mission and deliver these in smartly designed pieces. Finding the right "fit" between a designer and an organization can take some time and "shopping." Don't worry if you are not interested in the first few you interview. When you find the right person, it will be worth every minute of the search. Having confidence in a designer to produce the right look for a piece, or theme for a series of pieces, can ease the pressure from a fund-raising executive's already overburdened schedule. It will allow the fund raiser to pursue what needs to be done to bring the money in and to spend less time on the details regarding the fund-raising materials—art work, color, and design.

After selecting a designer to work with the organization, it is important to understand how to work with design firms. The tips listed in Exhibit 13–3 can make working with a design firm relatively easy. Do your homework before signing the contract!

When working with a designer, use the form shown in Exhibit 13–4 to help track your projects.

Working with a Printer
Finding the right printer is also key to producing successful fund-raising pieces. Begin by interviewing several printers. If the organization does not have a ready list of printers, ask similar organizations what printers they use. A different printer may be necessary for each type of piece being developed. A four-color brochure will require a printer with greater capabilities than one who prints stationery and business cards.

> Finding the right printer is also key to producing successful fund-raising pieces.

When selecting a printer, look for the following:

- Reliability—Does the printer complete the job on time and within budget?
- Responsiveness—If a rush job occurs, can the printer handle it?
- Costs—How do the printer's prices compare with others?
- Quality—Do the materials used as samples of the printer's work reflect the image your organization wants to project?
- Capabilities—Is it a large, small, or mid-sized operation? Does the printer have two- or four-color presses? Does it have a designer on staff? Does it require that you deliver all materials on a disk? Can the printer do the work you need to have done?
- Shipping and storage—Can the printer drop ship your pieces to your mail house? Or will you need to pick them up and deliver them? Does the printer have room to store your print job until you are ready to use it?

Before selecting a printer, make sure that you meet with representatives personally. In a small shop, you may speak with the owner directly. In larger shops, there may be one or more sales representatives. Ask for a tour of the plant and review samples of the printer's work. Don't just look at brochures or calendars it has printed; look at all sizes and types of materials. Consider the costs, location, and comfort level you have with the staff before making your final selection.

To keep the production of your materials within budget and on time, follow these guidelines:

- Get bids for each piece to be printed—at least two; usually three are preferable.
- Have several pieces printed at one time, if possible.
- Use standard paper sizes. Ask if the printer has any paper left over from another print job that could be used at a reduced price.
- Avoid unusual sizes, fancy cuts, die cuts, folds, flaps, pockets, etc.
- Proofread your materials to avoid making changes at the blue line stage.
- Avoid overtime charges by getting copy to the printer on time, with no mistakes or changes. Also, be wary of having proofs sent to you by messenger services.

Exhibit 13–3 Fifteen Tips For Working With Design Firms

1. Always provide the design firm with a budget.
   The design firm needs to know your budget to avoid presenting an unrealistic solution. Let them know if your budget includes design costs only or if it includes design, printing, and mailing costs.

2. Factor in alteration costs, and include them in your budget.
   Pad your budget by factoring in a 10-percent estimate for alteration charges. Here is an example using a budget of $5,000:
   $5,000 x .10 = $500; $5,000–$500=$4,500. Inform the design firm that your budget is $4,500.

3. Ask for overtime rates up front.

4. Get it in writing. Never start a design project without a written estimate.

5. Confirm the estimate with a memo or purchase order. Confirm the estimate by listing the specifications and cost.

6. Make arrangements for the printing yourself.
   Design firms typically mark up printing costs 15 to 20 percent. Handle the print management of a project (print estimates, review of blue lines and proofs, and press inspections) yourself. The hourly rate for print management should be included in the design firm's estimate. Be aware, however, that if a problem arises with the printed piece, you will have to negotiate with the printer, not the design firm.

7. Use internal courier service for deliveries.
   Design firms typically mark up delivery costs 15 to 20 percent. To avoid this mark-up, request that they use your internal courier service.

8. Request a production schedule.
   This will help you track your project's progress. The production schedule should include each step of the design process from layout to printing to delivery. It should include specific dates such as when copy needs to be submitted, first layout, two to three rounds of revisions, and return dates for proofs.

9. Think of thumbnails as an option.
   If you are not sure of the size or specification of a design project, have the design firm present thumbnail sketches (mini mock-ups, literally thumbnail size). You won't be able to read the text, but they will allow you to get a feel for the design. This is less costly than looking at two complete comprehensive layouts that require more time for the designer to produce.

10. Supply copy on disk.
    Most design firms use computers to produce your project. Providing copy on disk will save time and money. If the copy has to be keyed in manually, you will be charged for this at an hourly rate. Ask the designer what disks, formats, and software programs they can accept.

11. Get copy approved before it is submitted.
    Edit your copy thoroughly before submitting it to the design firm. This will help to cut down on alteration charges.

12. Get it in writing again.
    Before proceeding with any alterations, request an estimate of the alterations or a change order form. This will help you track the alteration cost while the project is being worked on and eliminate any surprises in your bill.

13. Keep alterations to a minimum.
    If your alterations result in more than 10 percent of the cost of the project, you're making too many changes.

14. Review and approve the colors.
    Always see a color proof of the project. A color photocopy sometimes can be made on the actual paper the project will be printed on. This will give you an accurate representation of the finished printed piece.

15. Make all alterations before sending the project to the printer.
    Avoid making changes at the blue line stage. This can be extremely costly. Not only are you paying the designer for alterations, but you are also paying the printer.

Source: Adapted with permission from Jill Jones Bank, "Fifteen Tips For Working With Design Firms," *Bank Marketing Magazine*, Bank Marketing Association, *ASAE Membership Developments Newsletter*, 1995, American Society of Association Executives.

The organization, not the printer, will pay for these services.

- Most printers will print 10 percent more than the guaranteed minimum number of items that you wanted printed. Be sure to ask if there will be a charge for this overrun, or if the printer provides it free of charge.

- Get all bids in writing. Don't rely upon verbal promises.

- Set deadlines for production of printed pieces well ahead of the deadlines for use or mailing of the pieces. Allow some delay times.

- Make photocopies of all corrections and directions given to the printer. These may be needed later to

Exhibit 13–4 Design Specifications Sheet

1. PROJECT TITLE _____

2. CONTACT _____

3. SIZE   FLAT _____   FOLDED _____

4. NUMBER OF PAGES _____ OR PANELS _____

   (Number of pages must be divisible by 4.)

5. COVER   Plus Cover _____   Self Cover _____

               Die Cut Pockets _____   Glued _____

6. COVER INK

   _____

   _____

7. TEXT INK

   _____

   _____

8. COPY PROVIDED:

   _____ On disk with hard copy.

   _____ Keystroke and proofread from original.

9. CHARTS AND GRAPHS

   Number _____   Note:_____

                          (Simple 2D or more complex 3D)

10. PHOTOS

    Provided (number) _____

    Stock (number) _____

    Photo shoot (number) _____

11. PAPER _____

12. BINDERY _____

13. DEADLINES _____

14. BUDGET _____

NOTE: The designer must "own" the design from the start through the printing.

           The designer will be required to provide the printer with a disk or camera-ready film, and must "pre-flight" the job with the printer after approval of the comps.

           The designer must approve blue line and match prints.

           The designer must accompany the project through a press check.

Courtesy of Susan Sarver, Special Projects, American Society of Civil Engineers, 1995, Washington, DC.

verify any claims against work not produced to your satisfaction.

Several steps are associated with the printing process. They include (1) writing the copy; (2) meeting with and selecting a designer and printer; (3) designing and laying out the piece to be printed; (4) selecting the ink colors (PMS) and ordering the paper; (5) reviewing the final layout before it is set in blue lines; (6) printing the piece; (7) attending a press check with the designer; (8) binding, folding, gluing, etc. to finish the piece; and (9) shipping and delivery of the piece to the client.

When producing publications, there are several lessons that usually are learned the hard way. Keep in mind the lessons highlighted in Exhibit 13–5 when working with a printer.

Coordinated Efforts Among Departments

If several departments within an organization are planning projects that need to be designed and printed, it may behoove them to bid their projects together—if not with the same designer, then at least with the same print shop to get a break in price for quantity work. This will work with a designer only if the pieces don't need to be produced within the exact same time frame. Remember that a large print shop may be able to handle several print jobs simultaneously, whereas a sole designer has only so many hours in the day.

It is equally as important for the departments to coordinate the styles of their materials as it is for them to work together to save money on printing. All printed materials should reflect the style and spirit of the or-

Exhibit 13–5 Lessons to Learn when Working with a Printer

1. If you are going to use a printer you have never used before, start with a relatively small project that's not on a tight deadline. If that project goes well, entrust the printer with more complex or time-sensitive projects.
2. In addition to any job order form you may use, prepare a letter outlining your expectations for the project. Have your contact sign the letter indicating the date the project is due.
3. Build good relationships with several printers. Favor those who can deliver a job before it is due, who call you with questions about issues that may seem trivial at the time, or who are candid enough to tell you immediately when they think they may have problems completing your job on time.
4. Realize that a printer who is donating services may give your project lower priority than other jobs from paying clients. Can your project afford to wait a day or two—or longer?

Source: Adapted with permission from Laurie Pumper, CAE, "Never Again," *Marketing Forum Newsletter*, 1996, American Society of Association Executives.

ganization. This does not mean that all brochures will look alike. Instead, there will be a theme or "look" to the pieces that immediately shows that they belong to that particular organization and not to another. Using one designer can assist in this effort.

Appendix 13–A
Sample Fund-Raising Brochure

"Many things we need can wait,

the child cannot.

Now is the time his bones are

being formed, his blood is being

made, his mind is being developed.

To him we cannot say tomorrow,

his name is today."

Gabriela Mistral, Chilean Poet

Courtesy of G. Gary Deverman, CFRE, Chief Development Officer, Arnold Palmer Hospital Center.

INTRODUCTION

ONE hundred twenty years ago a young child arrived on the doorstep of a hospital that had been created to nurse the large numbers of sick, poor children who had in many ways been casualties of the Civil War. The little boy could not breathe because of the cholera which had taken over his body, and he was not expected to live. The survival of that child was nothing less than a small miracle created by the intense and special care he received. His victory over death set the stage for the countless other victories Children's Hospital would claim over the next century.

We do not need to look back to the last century to see how the delivery of medicine has changed. In just the past 20 years, premature infants weighing as little as two pounds now have a good chance to survive and flourish. The five-year survival rate for children with acute lymphoblastic leukemia has soared to 70 percent, and improved diagnostic techniques have virtually eliminated exploratory surgery. Medical technology has introduced many new life-saving wonders like miniaturized heart-lung machines.

But these advances have been met by new conditions which resist obvious solutions and require unprecedented medical and social resources. Societal stresses of violence, drug abuse, and poverty are jeopardizing the potential of our youngest and most vulnerable citizens. Our hospital is witness to a growing number of children who are victims of premature delivery and low birthweight, HIV infection, substance abuse, poor nutrition, eating disorders, and critical injuries due to accidents, street violence, and child abuse.

In addition to these critical environmental forces, rapid changes in medical care constantly challenge our systems. Children's must continually respond to such far-reaching trends as accelerating outpatient versus inpatient services, increasingly complex inpatient care, and dramatic improvements in medical technology.

All of this can be achieved. We can continue to thrive as an institution and embrace the increasingly more complex, urgent needs of these children. But with this commitment comes a responsibility to remain the preeminent regional pediatric health care provider through our hospital, our research centers, and our community outreach programs. And we will continue to be a national leader with expanded efforts that have gained attention across the country and acted as a model for others.

WHAT SEPARATES US FROM OTHERS— OUR MISSION

THE qualities that separate us from others are not the bricks and mortar of the institution. They are the singular moments that may save a life or simply make a child's stay more comfortable. They are defined by multiple missions, symbolized by the acronym CARE: Care, Advocacy, Research, Education.

CARE

The mission of care is found in Children's staff and their determination to make each child's stay here more than a course of medical treatment.

This special quality of our care is especially seen in the code rooms of Children's **Emergency Medical Trauma Service**. What occurs there has become a national model that has saved thousands of lives of children who were crushed by cars, fell in water, were burned by fire and were victims of the most unconscionable forms of abuse. This department is so advanced in the field that Children's developed the first paramedic training program in the nation for pediatric emergency/trauma care.

Unequalled care also occurs in Children's **Critical Care** area where children are brought in the most fragile physical condition. Here specialized one-on-one nursing tends to every possible medical need these children might have. Monitors record all vital signs, and alert nurses and physicians to possible difficulties.

Our **ECMO** technology, which oxygenates a newborn's blood, and our highly specialized staff treat more patients than any other pediatric hospital nationwide and has the highest success rate. Children's offers one of only two training programs in the nation for this procedure.

Children's **Hematology/Oncology Department** synthesizes the best in pediatric cancer treatment. Collaboration with the **National Cancer Institute** puts the staff on the cutting edge of cancer care. Not only has the department performed successful bone marrow transplantations, it is the only one in the area to successfully achieve mismatched transplantation.

Most recently our **Cardiovascular Care Center** has entered a new world where certain conditions once needing open-heart surgery can now be treated with cardiac catheterization.

> "Committed individuals, organizations, and congregations can make life better for millions of children. The problems that too many of our nation's children see every day are very real – but they can be met if each one of us determines to make a difference in the lives of children."
>
> **Marian Wright Edelman**
> **Children's Defense Fund**

In the 1980s, Children's responded to the needs of families in the areas surrounding metropolitan Washington by establishing **satellite medical centers**. These convenient locations are staffed by Children's pediatric staff specialists who provide consultative evaluation and follow-up care for patients referred by community physicians.

ADVOCACY

Those who performed miracles in the code rooms of the Trauma Center realized that the greatest gift of all would be preventing these accidents. The urgency of this need became the motivation for the creation of the **National SAFE KIDS Campaign,** which has over 144 coalitions in 44 states, the District of Columbia and Canada actively committed to changing the way children and parents perceive safety.

Neglect can take a different form and requires another type of advocacy demanding a more intensive form of intervention. Children's was the first hospital to establish a hospital-based advocacy program in the nation. Our **Division of Child Protection**—the largest of its kind in the nation—is already a recognized national leader in helping children who are victims of child abuse and neglect. Each year more than 2,000 children at risk are seen by Children's staff of psychologists, social workers, physicians, and lawyers.

RESEARCH

Perhaps the most dramatic movement in medicine has occurred through research, which brings the laboratory to the bedside and reveals mysteries of the disease process and opportunities for treatment.

Children's has taken a bold step into the future with the creation of the **Children's Research Institute (CRI)** which will wrestle with the most stubborn and challenging medical conditions. CRI has created six centers of research:

I.   Center for Virology, Immunology, & Infectious Disease Research

II.   Center for Cancer & Transplantation Biology Research

III. Center for Molecular Mechanisms of Disease Research

IV.   Center for Applied Physiology Research

V.   Center for Behavioral, Mental Health, & Neurobiology Research

VI.   Center for Health Services & Clinical Research

The structure of the centers and the goals of the Institute have been reviewed and approved by a scientific advisory committee of physicians and scientists from across the country. Each center will be headed by strong and renowned investigative directors. The centers will be the homes of multiple laboratories working on programs related to specific goals.

CRI is well positioned to make a strong contribution to future research achievements. The hospital's staff represents an outstanding group of academically affiliated physicians in every specialty treating children's diseases. Children's National Medical Center is the clinical consultant to the **National Institutes of Health (NIH)** for pediatric patients, the only institution to provide this type of service to NIH.

EDUCATION

Training tomorrow's pediatricians is perhaps the greatest protection of our children's future health. Children's serves as the **Department of Pediatrics for The George Washington University Medical Center (GW)**. Today, this pediatric residency training program is recognized as one of the top in the nation. Children's is also one of the most distinguished educational facilities for subspecialty medical, surgical, and psychiatric training in the nation. And this impact can be felt by the fact that the majority of the area's physicians caring for children received some training at Children's National Medical Center.

Together, GW and Children's are already preparing for changes in medical education for the next century. We recognize that young physicians in the future will be more responsible than ever for high-tech yet cost-effective medical care. Training at Children's will give these residents the tools they will need to face the most challenging times ahead.

CREATING THE
MIRACLE

CHILDREN'S has the staff, the programs and the services of a national pediatric medical center. It has a carefully developed strategic plan, "Visions 2000," to guide it into the 21st century. It has a commitment to address the urgent health care needs of children today through plans to develop a National Child Protection, Trauma and Research Center.

But Children's does not have the physical environment consistent with the quality and level of its service or its goals. Without addressing its space and facility needs, Children's cannot continue to provide the health care this community and region expects, nor will it grow to its full national and international potential in the pediatric health field.

The management and medical staff of Children's has been integrally involved in assessing the most urgent needs at Children's. Together, with the support of board members and volunteers, they have embraced the objectives of a major initiative: **The Campaign for Children's.** The Campaign will address the following pressing needs:

- Expanded facilities to support the work of research centers established by Children's Research Institute. A new fifth floor added to the main hospital will accommodate this new laboratory space and facilitate scientific analysis and collaboration.
- Endowed chairs for two of the research centers.
- Expanded and reconfigured clinical care centers at the hospital, including a new one-story addition, and associated renovations in the existing structure.
- Medical equipment for these labs and clinics.

Our overriding concern is that the best science, the best medicine must have an environment in which to flourish. Children's cannot hold back the delivery of this expertise because of physical limitations. Nor can Children's deny access to care because of a physical inability to deliver it.

> "Will children's hospitals be the same in five years or perhaps even in ten? They will be the centers where expertise and compassion will be in easy balance. I cannot overstress the importance of an institution such as this."
>
> *C. Everett Koop, M.D.*
> *Speaking to the Boards of Children's National Medical Center*

FIFTH FLOOR RESEARCH ADDITION

Research in a medical center is critical to keeping the practical application of medicine connected to basic science. And, attracting top-flight physicians for clinical services today requires that we provide research facilities. The Campaign for Children's supports the vision of a fully potentialized research program with start-up funds that have provided 50,000 square feet of "shell" space on the fifth floor of the main hospital, plus 20 percent "fitup" of that space for basic science laboratories. The leadership and faculty of Children's Research Institute determined that this is a reasonable starting point, assuming that the research program will begin to fund itself and build on its own external grant funding.

CARE CENTERS

Emergency Medical Trauma Center   Children's Emergency Service handles more than 60,000 emergency visits a year, about double what the original emergency room was designed to accommodate. Many treatment rooms are now too small for today's complex trauma care which requires the presence of a number of physicians and nurses, as well as new technological equipment.

Not only is the space insufficient for current volume and projected caseload, it is also inadequate in terms of circulation patterns, and patient and staff traffic. In addition to addressing these space problems, the design of the new East Addition will also link the Emergency Medical Trauma Center with the new Helipad elevators. Thus, emergency or trauma patients who are flown to Children's will be moved directly into the code rooms.

Child Protection   The Division of Child Protection provides comprehensive services to emotionally and physically abused, neglected and sexually victimized children and their families. The program is the largest pediatric, hospital-based child protection service of its kind in the country. The Division's multi-disciplinary staff includes pediatricians, psychologists, social workers, nurses and legal support. An Emergency Response Service is available 24-hours-a-day for crisis assessment and intervention.

Construction of the East Addition will allow us to move Child Protection staff, currently housed off-site, to the hospital facility. The new space will also contain several private examination and consultation rooms which will enhance the quality of intervention by allowing children and families to receive services in a quiet, warm and supportive milieu, far from the hectic activities of the emergency room.

Ambulatory Care Clinics In the last ten years, ambulatory care at Children's has increased by more than 120 percent. In comparison to inpatient care, ambulatory clinics contribute substantially to reduced medical costs. But those departments continue to operate in the same space they were provided when the hospital opened in 1977.

The new East Addition will provide greatly expanded ambulatory space for primary care and other treatment capabilities in an integrated and efficient design. It will also be designed with patient and family convenience in mind. And it will be organized to deliver care in this new world of managed medical care. The Campaign for Children's will provide for a number of ambulatory clinics:

- Physicians Referral Center

  Currently, when a physician in the community wants to send a patient to Children's to get a complete diagnostic evaluation, the doctor may have to call six different departments to set up six separate appointments, trying to coordinate them so that a parent can finish the schedule in one day. Even so, that parent and child will be traversing the hallways looking for the various departments. The Campaign for Children's designates space for a clinic that can provide a complete diagnostic workup, facilitate the experience for the patient and the parent, and make it easier for the referring physician to access the system.

- Urgent Care Clinic

  Walk-in emergency patients with conditions that are not life-threatening also need quality medical care. Their recovery will be optimal if they can be treated and released as quickly as

"There will always be children in need of the most advanced medical care. When children are critically ill, they need a place where their illness can be treated. When children are seriously injured, they need a place where their bodies can be mended. For more than 100 years, Children's Hospital has been that place."

Donald L. Brown, President
Children's National Medical Center

possible and return home. The Campaign for Children's provides a new service for these patients with construction of the East Addition. Children seen in the Urgent Care Clinic will receive efficient, timely attention, while relieving crowded conditions in the Emergency/Trauma Center.

• Orthopaedics

Children's Department of Orthopaedics cares for more than 10,000 outpatients per year. Comprehensive services range from the treatment of simple bone fractures to surgical evaluation and treatment of advanced bone tumors, spinal deformities and genetic disorders such as spina bifida and cerebral palsy. Additional space is urgently needed to enhance the department's ability to meet the needs of patients and their families. Expanded facilities provided through the Campaign will increase the number of exam rooms, and provide two radiographic rooms and a casting room adjacent to and interfacing with Orthopaedics and Emergency.

In addition, the Campaign includes a brace shop to construct customized orthotic devices, and a gait lab, which will allow surgeons and specialists to evaluate a child's muscle and joint movements while walking. Currently there is no pediatric orthopaedics gait lab in the mid-Atlantic region.

• General Pediatric Ambulatory Clinic (GPAC)

The General Pediatric Ambulatory Clinic (GPAC) functions as a major primary care provider for economically disadvantaged children in the District of Columbia. Children are seen for routine health care, immunizations and minor injuries; as well as for more complex problems such as sexual abuse and HIV. GPAC also serves as the primary hands-on teaching and training area for pediatric residents rotating through the institution.

In addition to sharing its registration area with Emergency/Trauma, GPAC lacks appropriate isolation areas, and screening rooms where nursing and medical staff can evaluate patients.

At the same time, there are no areas for physician/parent conferences or teaching. New space is critically needed for GPAC's growing and increasingly important primary and preventive care services.

- Adolescent Ambulatory Care

Adolescent patients with a variety of health problems including acne, eating disorders, gynecological problems, sports injuries, substance abuse, and a range of psychological issues are treated in the Adolescent Ambulatory Clinic. In addition, the Burgess Clinic offers the only comprehensive health care service for patients ages 13-21 in the Washington area who are infected or at risk of infection from the Human Immunodeficiency Virus (HIV). Providing both acute and chronic care, the Clinic's health care team is experienced in dealing with the special issues of HIV infection in adolescents.

At the current time the Adolescent Ambulatory Clinic is located on the fourth floor of the hospital among inpatient units. Space is so crowded that the only waiting areas for patients are the hospital corridors. Examination and consultation facilities are inadequate, and patient education space is lacking. The Campaign for Children's will provide a new Adolescent Clinic on the first floor of the East Addition to correct these problems and improve Children's ability to address the needs of this special age group.

- Physical Medicine and Rehabilitation

Children's Department of Physical Medicine and Rehabilitation provides the most appropriate and complete rehabilitative care to children with disabilities in order to help them achieve the greatest degree of independence and function possible. Often these children face multiple obstacles early in their young lives which result from cerebral palsy, spina bifida, traumatic brain injury, burn trauma, limb deficiencies, amputations, neuromuscular disorders, connective tissue disorders and genetic diseases.

Children's Physical Medicine and Rehabilitation service suffers from especially inadequate and inefficiently designed space. It has only four exam rooms, which are shared with Rheumatology. Many patients are in wheelchairs, and clinical and administrative space are intermingled, making limited quarters especially congested. New facilities will offer improved opportunities to share equipment with the neighboring department of Orthopaedics, provide additional work and conference space for staff, and allow dedicated testing and observation rooms to be installed to provide comprehensive diagnostic and therapeutic services to patients and families.

• Blood Donor Center

Children's National Medical Center provides blood and blood products for any child requiring a transfusion. Currently blood donors must find their way to an inpatient area on the second floor of the hospital to contribute blood. Development of a new state-of-the-art Blood Donor Center on the first floor in the public area off the main hallway will help facilitate and attract volunteers who donate their blood. As more blood is donated, costs for acquiring blood from outside sources will decrease.

MRI Suite As diseases become more complex and more difficult to determine, the role of diagnostic technology grows. MRI (magnetic resonance imaging) now lets physicians see through bone to tissue that was once hidden. Computerized, colorized images illustrate tumors and abnormally functioning brains.

Diagnosis is critical to a child's timely, and often life-saving, treatment. Our ability to maintain responsive and accurate diagnostic technologies is critical to our patients' course of care. Children's National Medical Center has shared MRI equipment on a limited basis with neighboring Washington Hospital Center. However the demands on that equipment are tremendous, and jeopardize the ability of our patients to obtain these critical services. With the addition of an MRI suite at Children's, all patients will have access to this valuable technology on a timely basis. In addition, we will be able to provide MRI services to the Washington Hospital Center, thus relieving some of the demands on their equipment.

Surgery As Children's adds more surgical subspecialty staff and increases the technological abilities to perform various kinds of surgery, there is a predictable increase in surgical volume. Today it takes 50 percent longer, on average, to complete a surgical case in a major children's hospital than it did ten years ago. As operating time increases, so does the need for more operating rooms and more support areas. At no time do we want to have to postpone surgery or deny a child needing surgery because of space limitations.

Three of the operating rooms at Children's are undersized by today's standards. The Campaign will ensure that all operating rooms are of sufficient size, and provide critical support, utility, and equipment areas, as well as a Frozen Section Lab. Expansion of recovery room space will allow doctors to perform two more surgical procedures each day.

The Campaign for Children's will also dramatically increase the facilities for the A.M. Surgical Admission Center. Today parents and children of all ages must wait for registration and surgery in one cramped area. Parent consultation can take place only in hallways. Renovation plans provide for four private registration rooms, waiting and play/activity rooms for different age groups of children, private changing rooms, and additional induction rooms.

Clinical Laboratory Laboratory medicine is the backbone of all medical diagnosis and treatment at Children's. Every discipline in the hospital uses the laboratory every day, and Children's offers state-of-the-art diagnostic testing services to other hospitals and physicians throughout the region. More than one million laboratory tests are performed annually.

Accuracy and immediacy of lab results can mean the difference between life and death for a child—and they must not be compromised. The Campaign for Children's will allow a reconfiguration of this department's space, and will ensure that it remains on the cutting edge of medicine with new technology.

Critical Care: Intensive Care Unit, Burn Unit, Intermediate Unit Critical care medicine is a multidisciplinary specialty that cares for patients with life-threatening illnesses or injuries. It recognizes that

"Children's National Medical Center is committed to developing the resource base required to deliver vital health services and medical care. It has launched the Capital Campaign to help create the environment necessary to ensure that Children's will meet the challenges of pediatric care in the future."

C. Richard Beyda
Chairman of the Board
Children's Hospital Foundation

when one organ system begins to fail in a patient, all systems are affected. A crisis affecting the heart, for example, also affects the lungs, the kidneys, and the brain. Critical Care physicians and nurses care for the whole patient. Specialized one-on-one nursing tends to every possible medical need these children might have. Monitors record all vital signs and alert nurses and physicians to possible difficulties. With the advances in medicine, and the ability to treat patients who previously might not have survived, the children in intensive care today are sicker than in the past. And there are more of them.

The current configuration of the Intensive Care Unit does not allow for efficiency and flexibility in delivering care. Most beds are arranged in an open ward style with curtained cubicles. Extensive renovation is needed to convert this open ward arrangement to single and double rooms, and to provide proper isolation rooms, parent accommodations, consultation rooms, and space for nursing support. The units would be arranged to maximize their use by Intensive Care, the Burn Unit and the Intermediate or Step Down Unit.

Infectious Disease/Cystic Fibrosis As part of the use and alignment of inpatient space that will be made possible through The Campaign for Children's, the current Infectious Disease Unit will be expanded, and a newly designated Cystic Fibrosis Unit will be introduced. For the first time, this will bring all cystic fibrosis patients in the hospital together, and provide accommodations for the special needs of these patients and their families. Since the nursing support required for patients with infectious diseases and cystic fibrosis are similar, and patients require hospital stays at different times of the year, this move will greatly increase the efficiency of this inpatient service.

Cardiology Outpatient Clinic Eight of every 1,000 children are born with some type of structural heart problem, making heart disease the number one birth defect in the United States. The Cardiovascular Care Team at Children's treats approximately 6,000 outpatients yearly. The special talents of Children's team of physicians, surgeons and nurses makes the delivery of cardiovascular care unique among other cardiology teams in the Washington metropolitan area.

Like most medical specialities, more and more cardiology patients receive ambulatory treatment rather than require hospital admission. Along with this trend has come new types of equipment and testing facilities that to date have been "squeezed" into existing clinical areas. The Campaign for Children's will provide an expanded, reconfigured outpatient clinic for patients of the Cardiology Department.

Renal Cardiology The inpatient services for the Cardiology and Nephrology Departments will be combined for greater operational effectiveness and nursing support. The Department of Nephrology offers diagnostic procedures and treatment for the entire range of diseases of the kidney and urinary tract. Organ donor and recipient evaluation and long-term transplant management are provided for renal transplant patients. Care is provided for the acute and chronic renal-failure patient, including hemodialysis and peritoneal dialysis, and training for home dialysis.

Child and Adolescent Psychiatry Many children and families need mental health services at some point in their lives. Children's has served as the leading provider of mental health services for children and families in the Washington metropolitan area as well as a primary training ground for future child psychiatrists, psychologists and social workers.

Assessing the child's physical condition as well as his or her mental health and family makeup are key aspects of our psychiatry and psychology services. Children's offers both inpatient and outpatient services to patients ranging in age from infancy to 18. Our experienced staff works with children and families confronted with behavior disorders, depression, post-traumatic stress disorder, anxiety, phobias, psychoses and obsessive/compulsive disorders. Renovation plans provide for a ten-bed child psychiatry inpatient unit, and a ten-bed adolescent behavioral unit, with more private rooms in each unit.

Adolescent Inpatient Unit In 1955, Children's established the first inpatient unit devoted exclusively to the care of adolescents. It now operates as one of the largest units of its kind in the country. The atmosphere in the unit is conducive to both staff and patients; a place where teens have the opportunity to meet other patients their own age and experience a feeling of being "at home." Within Adolescent

Medicine, Children's manages an inpatient psychosomatic service in which a multidisciplinary group of health practitioners provide treatment to young people with eating disorders, depression or chronic illness such as diabetes, asthma or kidney disease. The treatment of many of these illnesses is coordinated between Adolescent Medicine and Psychiatry. A renovated ten-bed inpatient unit for Adolescent Medicine adjacent to the Adolescent Psychiatry unit will be provided through the Campaign.

Hematology/Oncology Outpatient Clinic Advances in the treatment of pediatric cancer have resulted in increased survival rates: more than two-thirds of children with cancer are now cured. The continued refinement of treatment, together with the increase in our patient population and increased rates of survival, have resulted in an increase of ambulatory clinical services. The outpatient hematology/oncology clinic has remained unchanged in size and configuration for the past twelve years. The Campaign provides support for updated and more comfortable facilities for our patients.

Short-Stay 23-Hour-Unit Many patients with medical problems who would previously have occupied beds for several days can now be treated as outpatients. In addition, a number of surgical patients do not require hospitalization following their operations, but may need to spend one night and require more follow-up and nursing than is available in the Short-Stay Recovery Unit. A new Short-Stay 23-Hour-Unit will provide space for for these patients, and for diagnostic tests, infusion therapy and other treatments. It will be open at night as well as during the day, and parents will be able to stay with their children.

Pediatric Rehabilitation Unit A comprehensive children's medical center needs an inpatient pediatric rehabilitation unit. Children's has the technology to return children to physical functionality. Yet there is no space for this program, and these patients are currently being transferred to other facilities. The East Addition provides space for a unit of 15 beds, allowing patients in rehabilitation to continue their follow-up care under the same medical staff.

Equipment and Technology One of the most remarkable miracles in medicine today is the advent of tools that have replaced the scalpel to see more clearly the cause and scope of many diseases. These noninvasive technological tools are also replacing surgical procedures for treatment in some cases. And computerized monitoring equipment ensures constant evaluation of each patient's condition.

The Cardiology Department illustrates the role equipment and technology play in providing the best possible care to our young patients. The role of heart catheterization in the management of children with congenital heart disease has changed dramatically in a very short time. Heart catheterization used to be the primary means of diagnosis for these children. Today, new noninvasive diagnostic tools, such as echocardiography which uses soundwaves, have diminished the role of heart catheterization for routine diagnostic purposes. At the same time, there has been a dramatic increase in techniques for treatment using heart catheterization.

Whether it is an exam table or a heart bypass pump, a microscope or a defibrillator, the Campaign provides for essential equipment vital to the diagnosis and treatment of children today. Equipment will be provided to all clinics and labs listed previously, and for Radiology, Neurology, Pulmonary, Neonatal Intensive Care, and Anesthesiology.

Fund for Emerging Programs and Technologies The rapid changes in medical care constantly challenge the medical staff at Children's National Medical Center to respond with the best treatment that is available for our children. In order to do so, The Campaign for Children's provides a special fund that will give our staff an "early start" in developing new programs and equipping our clinics with the latest in technology.

  **"The leadership of Children's Hospital have carefully planned for the tremendous challenges facing all health care providers today. The Campaign for Children's addresses our most critical facility and equipment needs. Our community can help ensure that children and families continue to receive the best medical care by supporting the campaign."**

Raymond S. Sczudlo
Chairman of the Board
Children's National Medical Center

THE CAMPAIGN FOR CHILDREN'S

The Board of Trustees of Children's National Medical Center has launched the Capital Campaign to help create the environment necessary to ensure that Children's will meet the challenges of pediatric health care in the future. Our goals are:

Research Facilities Fifth Floor Addition (50,000 square feet) to house:

Center I: Virology, Immunology, and Infectious Disease Research
Center II: Cancer and Transplantation Biology Research
Center III: Molecular Mechanisms of Disease Research

Endowed Research Chairs for Centers II and III

Patient Care Facilities

First Floor	**Second Floor**	**Third Floor**	**Fourth Floor**
New East Addition (45,000 sq. ft.)	New East Addition (6,000 sq. ft.)	Current Building Renovation	Current Building Renovation
Emergency Trauma Center	MRI Suite	Critical Care Units	Child Psychiatry
Child Protection Center		• Intensive Care Unit	Adolescent Psychiatry
Ambulatory Care		• Intermediate Unit	Adolescent Medicine
Clinics		• Burn Unit	Hematology/Oncology
• Physicians Referral	**Second Floor**	Infectious Disease/	Short-Stay 23-Hour
Center	Current Building	Cystic Fibrosis	Unit
• Urgent Care Clinic	Renovation	Cardiology Outpatient	Rehabilitation Unit
• Orthopaedics		Renal/Cardiology	
• Orthotics/Gait Lab	Surgery Suite		
• General Pediatric	A.M. Surgical		
Ambulatory Clinic	Admission Center		
• Adolescent Medicine	Recovery Rooms		
Clinic	Clinical Lab		
• Physical Medicine			
and Rehabilitation			
• Blood Donor Center			

New and Replacement Equipment

Fund for Emerging Programs and Technologies

"The need for new capital funds has never been greater. We've got to give these great doctors the facilities to take the hospital out on the cutting edge of research and the most modern treatment."

Benjamin C. Bradlee
Chairman, The Campaign for Children's

THE CAMPAIGN FOR CHILDREN'S: FUNDING GOALS

After a careful assessment of funding potential and the prevailing economy, a private sector Campaign goal of $40 million was established. Adding anticipated federal grants of $20 million provides a total of $60 million. In summary, the needs and the funding sources are:

Funds Required		Projected Funding Sources	
New Construction			
Research	$10.6 million	**Capital Campaign**	**$40.0 million**
Clinical Care	15.5 million	Capital Appropriations	20.0 million
Renovation	16.6 million		
Medical Equipment	10.4 million		
Research Equipment	0.5 million		
Emerging Programs and			
Technology Fund	3.4 million		
Two Endowed Research Chairs			
($1.5 million each)	3.0 million		
Total	$60.0 million	Total	$60.0 million

The Campaign for Children's is the foundation of our effort to respond to the growing crisis in child health today: the neglect, injury and illness that jeopardize the health and development of our children and, in turn, the well-being of our community and our nation. The Campaign will establish Children's as a national resource of clinical care, medical research and child health advocacy.

Perhaps most importantly, the Campaign will symbolize the realization that caring is more than medicine, that healing is more than mending the body, that physical health means little without mental and emotional well-being, and that a future of damaged children is really no future at all.

THE FUTURE: WHERE VISION BECOMES A REALITY

BY the year 2000, with the support of the Capital Campaign, Children's National Medical Center will have become a symbol of all that is possible in pediatric health care. It is no coincidence that Children's is in the nation's capital. This position carries with it special responsibilities. Our ability to thrive in the future will make us a model for those hospitals who struggle with many of the same issues that we do.

The Capital Campaign will provide critical momentum to this vision. Gifts to the Campaign for the needs outlined here will directly support a wider set of goals. These goals are nothing less than that:

Children's will provide comprehensive, quality care to any child no matter how injured or sick.

Through the development of our National Child Protection, Trauma, and Research Center, Children's will continue to meet the needs of victimized children and promote their successful treatment. We will assume an even stronger advocacy role on behalf of children with state and local legislatures and the federal government. We will expand our outreach programs. We will focus our education efforts on prevention of victimization and prevention of disease. We will aggressively pursue research efforts on the most difficult of diseases.

We will design a hospital that promotes the comfort and emotional well-being of our patients and their families—and that consolidates services for convenience. We will expand our outpatient facilities so that we can provide same-day surgery or treatment to thousands of new patients who might otherwise be hospitalized. We will continue to acquire the technologies needed to diagnose and intervene at the earliest possible moments of a child's illness or injury.

We will share our experience and findings with others so that they can help enhance quality of life and find cures for conditions which now defy medicine. We will serve as a model for the nation. We will stand for the health and well-being of children, our nation's most valuable resource.

Chapter 14
Capital Campaigns

Chapter Outline

- What Is a Capital Campaign?
- The Relationship Between Capital Campaigns and Annual Campaigns
- Campaign Readiness
- The Feasibility Study
- Developing a Case Statement
- Campaign Structure and Timetable
- Methods of Giving to a Campaign
- Campaign Materials
- Setting Up Internal Systems
- Maintaining Relationships with Leadership Donors
- What to Do When Campaign Momentum Wanes
- Campaign Evaluation

Key Vocabulary

- Active Phase
- Advance Gifts
- Campaign Brochure
- Campaign Chair
- Campaign Director
- Campaign Leadership
- Campaign Management
- Campaign Organization
- Campaign Staff
- Capital Campaign
- Capital Fund Campaign
- Case Statement
- Feasibility Study
- Fund-Raising Counsel
- General Gifts
- Gift Range Table
- Honorary Chair
- Initial Gifts
- Kickoff
- Leadership Gift
- Major Gift
- Pacesetting Gifts
- Pre-Campaign

- Private Phase
- Progress Report
- Rule of Thirds
- Pyramid of Gifts
- Sequential Giving
- Special Gifts
- Specific Situation Formula
- Table of Gifts
- Yardstick Gifts

What Is a Capital Campaign?

A capital campaign is an intensive fund-raising effort organized to meet a specific financial goal within a specified period for one or more major special projects such as the construction of a facility, the purchase of equipment, the expansion of programs, or the acquisition of endowment. At some time in its history, an organization will realize that it needs to conduct a capital campaign. New facilities (bricks and mortar) are needed, equipment must be upgraded, new programs or projects must be started and supported, or endowment must be raised—all reasons to start a capital campaign.

There is never a "perfect time" to start a campaign. Many campaigns just launched should have begun years earlier, but the organization's board was always waiting to find the "perfect" opportunity. Instead of waiting for that time, development staff can create the perfect time through careful planning.

> There is never a "perfect time" to start a capital campaign.

Capital campaigns are not necessarily inclusive. Most of the money raised in a capital campaign will come from a small number of donors. This is the direct opposite of an annual campaign in which a broad-based appeal is necessary to be successful.

Anyone thinking of undertaking a capital campaign will either read or be told about the many "rules" of a campaign. These rules include:

- The 80/20 rule—This rule applies to the fact that 80 percent of the money raised in capital campaigns comes from 20 percent of the donors. Some say that, today, this is even becoming the 90/10 rule.
- The rule of thirds—This second rule describes the formula that has been widely used in constructing gift range tables: The rule of thumb is that about ten donors account for the first third of funds raised during a capital campaign; about 100 donors provide the next third, and all remaining donors in the constituency furnish the final third. Any failure in achieving the objective of the first third of funds can be compensated for by exceeding the objective of the second third. The last third, however, cannot make up for failure in the first or second thirds.
- The sequential solicitation rule—This third rule is simple—gifts are solicited from the largest to the smallest gifts. This is a cardinal principle of capital campaign fund raising—that gifts should be sought "from the top down," that is, the largest gifts in a gift range table should be sought at the outset of a campaign, followed sequentially by the search for lesser gifts. Thus, the first gifts are called advance gifts, the second are leadership gifts, the third are major gifts, the fourth are special gifts, and the fifth and final gifts are general gifts.
- The 50 percent rule—This fourth rule relates to the concept that a campaign should never be announced to the public until 50 percent of the goal is achieved. Some will argue that a campaign can be publicly launched with only 30 to 40 percent of the gifts received. When in doubt, let the gift dollars accumulate before publicizing.

The success or failure of a capital campaign will rest with the decisions made and activities completed in the initial phases. A fully developed fund-raising plan, selection of the proper leadership, the full and complete support of the board and the staff of the organization, and having the proper systems and procedures in place are all necessary for a campaign to be successful. A lack of any of these will have such a negative impact that a campaign, once launched, may never recover.

Before undertaking a capital campaign, any organization should ask itself whether it is ready to embark upon such an endeavor. Are all the variables in place? Has all of the groundwork been laid? Are the board members, membership, other volunteers, and staff fully supportive and trained to begin? Eighteen questions to ask yourself before considering a capital campaign can be found in Exhibit 14–1.

If each of these questions has been addressed and can be answered realistically, then the organization can take the next steps toward beginning a capital campaign.

Exhibit 14–1 Capital Campaigns 101

Ask yourself these threshold questions whenever you are considering undertaking a capital campaign:

1. Do you need money?
2. Do you have a convincing case for support, appealing both to the heart and the head?
3. Do you have active and highly visible volunteer leaders?
4. Do you have enough staff to support a campaign?
5. Do you have a good access to funding sources?
6. Do you have (or can you get) a system in place for recording and acknowledging gifts and pledges?
7. What is "the competition" up to?
8. It costs money to raise money. Are you willing to make the necessary expenditures?
9. Is there a sense of urgency about your needs?
10. Does your organization have clear priorities?
11. How well have your fund-raising efforts worked up until now?
12. Do you have a positive image in the community?
13. Is your organization well known in the community?
14. How well does your organization work from a business perspective?
15. Can you identify five to ten top volunteer leaders?
16. Do you have an idea who your chairperson ought to be? Do you think that person will agree to lead?
17. Can you identify five to ten top prospective donors?
18. Can you identify two to three times the number of donors you will need for each gift category?

Source: Adapted with permission from Sinclair, Townes and Company, publishers of *The Digest of Southern Giving*, "Capital Ideas," 1996.

The Relationship Between Capital Campaigns and Annual Campaigns

Often, board members are fearful of embarking upon a capital campaign effort because they think it will negatively impact the organization's successful annual campaign. It is possible for a capital campaign to run concurrently with an organization's annual campaign. Although capital campaigns are a one-time fund-raising effort whereas annual campaigns occur year after year, capital campaigns should benefit annual giving by bringing in new donors and creating a higher profile for the organization. As annual campaigns usually support the operational needs of the organization, a capital campaign is held for a specific single purpose, usually to construct a building (bricks and mortar) or to raise money for endowment. See Exhibit 14–2 for a chart comparing an annual campaign to a capital campaign.

Exhibit 14-2 Comparison of a Capital Campaign and an Annual Campaign

CAPITAL CAMPAIGN	ANNUAL CAMPAIGN
Purpose is to raise large amounts of money for a specific goal.	Purpose is to raise smaller amounts of money for operating funds.
It is a one-time effort that is intensive and time-limited and it also has a high profile.	It is held yearly and has a lower profile.
Goals are based on findings of a feasibility study.	Goals are based on previous year's giving.
The organization's board members or trustees are directly involved.	The board members or trustees are indirectly involved; effort is mostly staff-driven.
Many volunteers at the highest levels are used for peer-to-peer solicitation to raise large sums of money.	Fewer volunteers are used to solicit smaller amounts of money, and this is usually not peer-to-peer.
The campaign chair is well known to the public, but is not necessarily active in the organization's activities.	The campaign chair is active in the organization but may not be well known to the public.
Prospects will come from a broad base, including more than just members.	Prospects most likely will come from the membership.

The organization's board of directors will have a greater commitment of time and energy in a capital campaign than in the annual campaign. Board members will need to lead by example. They will be the first to make their gifts to the campaign. In addition to the board, a special fund-raising committee will be developed to focus on the campaign during the period established for the capital campaign. The chairperson of the capital campaign must be a well-known, highly visible individual who has ties with major businesses and the leadership of the community, and is respected by almost everyone. Within a university or college setting, the chair may or may not have had a strong leadership role on the board of trustees; it is much more important that he or she have the global recognition, respect, and contacts, particularly with individuals or institutions controlling major financial resources. On the other hand, the chair of the annual campaign must be actively involved with the educational institution. In other organizations, the annual campaign chair may be less well known in the greater public but must have closer ties within the organization itself.

The leadership of a capital campaign—those selected to work with the chair in his or her cabinet—will often include individuals not frequently involved within the organization, those who are called upon only in special circumstances to come forward to "carry the torch" of the organization. These are usually very busy, influential people whose names are well known to everyone who is being targeted for solicitation of a gift. Prestige is the operative word.

Campaign Readiness

Before embarking on a campaign, the entire organization must be made aware of the importance of the effort and the impact it will have on the lives of those who work there. The president or executive director should meet with the entire staff to relay the big picture and explain why

> Before embarking on a campaign, the entire organization must be aware of the importance of the effort.

everyone must cooperate for the campaign to succeed. If this were a hospital, then the chief administrator and head of the hospital board would share in this responsibility. In a church, it would be the pastor and president of the council.

The success or failure of a fund-raising campaign will depend in great part upon the leadership selected and the decisions made early in the planning stages. No details should be overlooked or considered insignificant. Start with a plan and work the plan. Develop the plan from the information gathered during the feasibility study. Review the calendar of the organization and see what major events can be included in the plan. For example, can the campaign's kick-off be held in conjunction with the organization's annual meeting or the hospital's annual big fund-raising special event? Put everything down in writing and divide the plan into measurable segments. Financial goals should not be placed only at the conclusion of the campaign, but should be built into the plan on a quarterly, semi-annually, or yearly basis.

As the plan is being created, leadership gifts should be targeted and cultivated. This part of the campaign proceeds simultaneously as the campaign is being developed. In addition, an organization can begin writing the case statement and building the campaign's budget. One piece does not need to wait for the other to be completed.

Staff should divide the prospects into groupings to plan the solicitation targeted to them. These groups can be divided according to geographical distribution, giving capabilities, whether internal (board or staff) or external (community leaders or alumni) to the institution, and volunteer potential.

There are several issues that almost always arise during the planning and conducting of a capital campaign. They are:

- The readiness of an organization to carry out a capital campaign
- The question of whether to use a campaign counsel
- The ability of the current staff to carry out a capital campaign
- The use of nondevelopment office staff in the campaign
- The cost of the campaign
- The timing of the campaign's "kick-off"
- How to report the capital campaign vis-a-vis the annual campaign
- Whether premiums should be used to promote giving
- How to recognize donors

Before any organization undertakes a capital campaign, it must evaluate its resources. Does it have enough staff? Does it have the resources? Does it have the constituents? Is its base broad enough? Is its board strong enough? If an organization can answer positively to all of these, then it can consider a capital campaign. Planning and readiness have a direct effect on the results of a campaign.

Often, outside development professionals are hired to conduct both the feasibility study and the actual campaign. Sometimes, they are used only in the feasibility stage. An organization should not hire outside professionals who work for a percentage of the fee raised. Instead, look for those who work for "fee for service." Although there are many reasons to hire campaign counsel, the most common reasons are:

- They have broad capital campaign experience.
- They bring research and resources from other campaigns .
- They have the ability to keep the board and staff focused.
- They are objective.

Most organizations don't have development office staff with capital campaign operational experience. Staff members probably have operated in an annual campaign mode, soliciting gifts from within their membership while seeking grants from corporations and foundations. Few have had the opportunity to work on any capital campaign, either large or small. In addition, professional consultants from large consulting firms can bring many additional resources from other campaigns on which either they or other staff from their firm have worked. Plus, an outside consultant can view the organization objectively and is not placed in the position of having to please the board or senior staff to protect a job. Consultants also can keep the board and staff focused, and if necessary, be more blunt than staff in motivating board members to complete tasks assigned to them.

To be successful, a capital campaign needs the full support and cooperation of the organization's board members. Most board members probably will not have participated before in a capital campaign and will need to be fully briefed, if not trained. This is one of the best uses of a consulting firm—training the board to understand their roles and responsibilities.

The campaign will also look to the board members for a personal contribution as well as leadership and direction in the solicitation of prospective donors. These solicitations cannot be done by the staff or by any hired consultants. The board must be behind the campaign and accept full responsibility for as well as ownership of the goal.

The Digest of Southern Giving (1996) states, "If a capital campaign is in the offing, there are some key points to cover with the board.

1. The entire board must embrace the objectives of the capital campaign.
2. Each member of the board must be willing to make a financial commitment to the campaign.
3. The board will need to address the annual fund and the potential impact on the organization's cash flow.
4. The board should be involved in the selection of the consulting firm.
5. Board members must realize that this is their campaign.

Strong boards raise strong dollars. Remember the quotation attributed to John Paul Getty: 'The meek may inherit the earth, but not its mineral rights!'"

Setting a Goal

Before a goal can be established for a capital campaign, a feasibility study should be conducted to discover what amount of money is possible to raise and from whom. Usually conducted by an outside consulting firm, the feasibility study asks all of the difficult questions, such as the following: How is the organization perceived? Would people want to make a gift to the organization? Is the need to raise money real and necessary? Would this individual make a gift and of how much? Would this person recommend others who would make a gift? How is the leadership (the board) of the organization perceived?

After gathering as much information as possible from key individuals in the feasibility study, data are analyzed and categorized, and an attainable goal is set. The goal should be a "stretch" goal—one that will take a concerted effort to reach, yet one that the organization should be able to meet. A goal should never be set before a feasibility study has been conducted.

The Feasibility Study

All capital campaigns should begin with a feasibility study to determine if there is a need for a campaign. This is usually conducted by outside counsel, although, rarely, it can be conducted by staff. The study should address (1) the need for a campaign; (2) the strength of the case to be presented; (3) the resources available to use in a campaign—Is there an adequate number of staff and volunteers to conduct a campaign and are there enough donors available to successfully reach the goal and complete the campaign?; (4) the plan, budget, and calendar for the campaign; (5) the perception of the organization in the community; (6) potential leadership for the campaign; (7) potential sources for major leadership and major gifts; (8) the use of the information gleaned from the interviews to develop the campaign plan; and (9) the feasibility of the financial goal suggested for the campaign. This is also the time to develop an adequate base of public relations for the campaign.

Those approached in a capital campaign should include the leadership of the organization, those who benefit from the organization's services, those who are influential in the community or area served by the organization, and those who have the financial capability to made a contribution to the organization.

How many should be interviewed in a feasibility study? The more interviews conducted, the more potential donors are being cultivated for the organization. This of course assumes that the "right" people are being targeted in the first place. Some feasibility studies are conducted with as few as twenty persons interviewed. Others include more than 100 persons. When developing the list of interviewees, be sure to include leaders within the organization, those who benefit directly from the organization's services, and those capable of making a substantial contribution to the organization. Don't spend too much time and effort interviewing people who belong to constituencies that are not traditionally large givers.

After determining the list of people to be interviewed, a letter outlining the project and requesting a time for an interview is sent to each person on the list. Interviews can be conducted in person or by phone. This depends upon the budget of the organization. All local interviews should be done in person; those far away can be conducted by phone if the budget doesn't allow for travel expenses.

The letter should clearly explain the following: (1) the purpose for the visit, (2) the amount of time required, (3) what results are hoped to be achieved, (4) who will be conducting the interview and their relation to the organization, and (5) that the interview is completely confidential. A copy of the draft of the case statement should be included with the letter, so the interviewees have an opportunity to understand the reasons the potential campaign will be held.

The person conducting the interview will use a standardized form developed by all those who are conducting the interviews. It will cover the areas addressed by the following questions:

1. How does the person being interviewed view the organization, its mission, its goals, its staff, its volunteer leadership, and its finances?
2. Has this person ever supported the organization either financially or as a volunteer?
3. Does the organization tell its story accurately and effectively?
4. Does this person think that the organization can successfully raise large amounts of money within the community?
5. Does this person know of potential donors and the amounts they may be willing to give?
6. Would the person be willing to support the organization either financially or as a volunteer leader during the campaign?
7. Who else would this person recommend to become involved with the leadership of the campaign?
8. What are some suggestions regarding how high the goal should be set, who should head the campaign, and how long it should run?

It is important that the questions being asked allow the person to expand his or her comments beyond a simple yes or no answer; ask open-ended questions that draw out answers on each issue. Although it is easier to have a questionnaire that is quantifiable, valuable opinions and insight often can be missed if there isn't an opportunity for the interviewee to expand his or her answers.

Several points need to be followed when conducting an interview. First of all, be on time! If you are going to arrive later than the scheduled time, call ahead to alert the person being interviewed. This is only common courtesy. Calling the day before the interview to confirm the appointment is also a courtesy. At this time you can ask if the letter and draft case statement have been received and if the person has had time to read them.

Secondly, dress appropriately for the occasion. Professional appearance is a must! You are representing the organization or institution that is seeking advice and financial support from this person.

Third, when interviewing in the home, look for a place to be seated that will afford you good lighting and a writing surface. It is best that you have a portable writing surface such as a clip board on which you can write the notes during the interview. The goal is to get the questionnaire completed, so the person being interviewed must be comfortable and not anxious for the meeting to end before the task has been completed.

The results of a feasibility study should determine whether a campaign can be successful, identify potential leadership, determine what the gift goal (or range) will be, and identify potential gifts to the campaign.

Developing a Case Statement

When a business presents itself to its public through a brochure, it usually uses its annual report. If it is trying to generate business, it usually uses a brochure called a prospectus. When a nonprofit organization presents itself, it is usually through a general information brochure. When the nonprofit organization is trying to raise money and needs to present its fund-raising reasoning and strategies, it usually uses a document called a case statement. This document outlines the history of the organization, its mission, what the fund-raising needs and monetary goals are, who the leadership is, how to give to the organization, why one should make a gift to the organization, and how the money raised will be used by the organization. It is probably the most important document that an organization will ever write and use. It should be developed through a cooperative effort of both staff and board members. It requires the commitment and responsibility of both to be effective. Jerold Panas (19) lists nine essentials of a case statement. They are the following:

1. The history of the organization—It is important to include as much as possible about your organization's founding and history, but you also should be as succinct as possible. After all, it is the future that you wish to emphasize, not the past. The past is there to set the stage and should include your mission statement, why you were formed, the leaders of your organization, and any other pertinent information.
2. The problem and the opportunity—Explain the program for which you are raising money. Describe it in compelling terms—the urgency of the need, the people it will help, the lives it will change or help, etc. Don't focus on the institution; focus on the people who have a need and who will benefit from this new program.
3. Proposed solution—How is your institution going to solve the problem outlined previously? Explain why your institution is the best to do this and why it seeks the opportunity to do so.
4. The institution's unique role—Explain why your institution is the most or best qualified to respond to the challenge and meet the problem or need, and why it can do the job better than anyone else. Highlight the successes your organization has had in the past in the community. State how your organization has served its clients better than anyone else could have served them.
5. The goals—Describe the fund-raising project at this point including the reasoning behind the project.
6. The fund-raising equation—What will this fund-raising effort cost? Who is responsible for raising the money? Where will you find this money? Who will you be asking for this money and how much? Is there a combined effort to raise this money? If so, who will be involved and who will take the lead role? Is there to be a match of the initial gifts?
7. The fund-raising plan—Explain how you will raise the money and why the campaign will be successful. Include any leadership gifts that you have to date—by amount, not by name. Also describe the financial management and operations.
8. How to give—Describe the methods available for making gifts to the campaign. Also, include the level of giving for which you seek gifts. Also describe opportunities for giving other resources than money, such as time.
9. Leadership—Name those who already have agreed to help in the campaign. This will include your campaign chair, committee members, and other leaders who have agreed to assist with the fund-raising effort. This is the group responsible for raising the money and for determining how it will be spent. Explain who these leaders are, how they will function, and what their role is. Also invite your constituents to participate.

The structure of the case statement will vary. You may cover these nine essentials, but you also may include much more. Case statements will vary in length depending upon the history of the organization and the complexity of the need. Rarely are case statements printed pieces. Usually they are typed documents produced through word processing and some sort of desk-top publishing so a more polished (but not slick) appearance is created. They can be bound using any one of several formats—spiralled, three-hole punched, stapled with a plastic sleeve cover, etc. Whatever format is selected, the document should be easy to read, lay flat when pages are turned, and have plenty of white space for ease in reading and making notes on the pages.

Often, a cover letter signed by the chief volunteer will accompany the case statement. Usually, it is placed separately from the document (attached to the cover or left "loose"), but those following a growing trend bind it at the beginning of the case—after the cover page, but before the beginning of the document.

Some question the use of graphs, charts, and statistics in a case statement. If they will help illustrate a point by making it clearer, then use them. If they are being used as "filler," omit them from the document. Graphs can be effective in showing how much money needs to be raised in a specific amount of time. Other statistics can harm your case and deflate the emotional impact you may be trying to make. You can assist the reader by providing visual breaks using headings and sub-heads. Quotations from those well known and respected can add impact, also. In addition, use a thesaurus to vary your words and add impact.

Your case statement will serve as your basic marketing piece to explain to your public *who* your organization is, *what* your organization does, *where* it is located or *what* constituencies it serves, *why* it is raising money, *when* it will begin to raise these funds, and *how* and *when* it will spend them.

Sometimes it is difficult to write a case statement, particularly if you have never written one before. Begin by reviewing the materials previously written about your organization. Locate your organization's mission statement. If there is not one, then begin by writing a mission statement and obtain agreement on it from members of the board. Interview board members and senior members of the staff for their ideas on the who, what, where, when, and why of your organization. Visit the nearest fund-raising library and review samples of other organizations' case statements. Don't be afraid to copy ideas; just don't copy the written material! Then begin to write and rewrite. Share the document with staff and board members as you go along. Get input from others who will be making the final decision regarding the document. Have the key leaders of the campaign review the document. Finally, don't be afraid to revise the case statement again and again to gain consensus. Before using the case statement publicly, be sure all senior volunteers and staff members who will be using it "sign off" on the final document.

Don't forget to tailor the case statement to your audience. If members of your audience are used to seeing and

> **Don't forget to tailor the case statement to your audience.**

are comfortable with specific formats, type styles, and color combinations, then use these. Don't try to change now—keep a style that is appropriate for your audience. Use correct grammar and have your document free of errors.

Also, according to Panas (1995) there are six pitfalls to be avoided when preparing your case statement. They are the following:

1. Undefined purpose—If your organization's purpose is not clearly stated, then the persons from whom you are seeking money are not going to understand who you are and what you do. Your mission must be clear and concise.

2. Overstated emotionalism—It is important to appeal to your potential donors, to tug at their heart and purse strings, but it is equally important not to overstate your cause and make claims that may ultimately negatively impact your case.

3. The pleading of needs—Just because your organization has identified a need, doesn't mean that someone is going to give you money to satisfy that need. Every organization has needs. You shouldn't dwell on the financial problems, but on how your organization will solve those problems.

4. Misunderstanding what motivates a prospect—Keep the case statement succinct. Explain clearly what you need and why. Don't spend too much time on the history of your organization, particularly if your audience is its membership.

5. Vague plans—Know what it is that you want to do. Vague and unclear plans certainly don't inspire or motivate.

6. Unsubstantiated grand claims—It is easy to get carried away and make claims that far surpass what is possible to obtain. Don't be tempted to make the organization sound saintly when it isn't. People can easily ask for or seek substantiation for claims made. Be honest. It is the only right way to raise money.

A professional writer may be hired to develop the case statement, but staff and board members must become involved so that the document represents the organization. An outside writer can gather information and put it down on paper, but if he or she has no fund-raising experience, the document most likely will not have the necessary ingredients to effectively "make the case."

The "fail-proof" checklist in Exhibit 14–3 should be considered when developing a case statement.

Campaign Structure and Timetable

The long-standing formula for raising money in a capital or major gifts campaign is to divide the amount of the goal into thirds and allocate one third of the money to come from the top third (leadership gifts), the second third of the money to come from the middle third (major

Exhibit 14–3 The Fail-Proof Checklist

How is the institution positioned in the community and what is its heritage?

When was the institution founded?
What were the circumstances surrounding the beginnings?
What geographical area does the institution serve?
What are the natural resources in the area?
What is the industrial and business concentration?
What distinguishes the area from the rest of the county, state, or nation—a capital, a distribution center, a rural area?
Describe the population of the service area.
Describe population trends. Is the population increasing or decreasing? Is the population aging?
List level of affluence and occupational types of the population.
List educational level and cultural types of the population.
List ethnic origins.

How does the institution benefit the community and how and who does it serve?

What services does the institution offer?
How many people use these services? Have the services been increased or decreased? Why?
How much does each of these services cost? Are the services furnished free or subsidized?
What services do other organizations in the institution's service area offer?
Is there any duplication of services or is the organization's niche unique?
Does the institution cooperate with other organizations by joining programs or sharing use of facilities?
Is there a need for services not currently being met in the community that the institution could fill if the institution had increased funds?
How many potential new clients of the institution could you expect to attract if its programs were increased?

Why is a fund-raising program necessary?

Why does the institution need funds?

Is the purpose of the program to gain capital or endowment or both?
What are the specific components of the campaign and project?
How will the campaign improve the organization's ability to fulfill its missions?
How much money does the institution need?
How will the money be raised?
Have alternative sources of funding been investigated—government grants, bonds, etc.?

Is the institution fiscally sound?

What is the current operating budget?
Is the institution operating "in the black?"
Who makes the major contribution to the present operating budget?
Does the institution have a membership drive, annual support campaign, admission fee, or subscriptions?
Does it have an endowment?
What are the financial assets and liabilities of the institution?
Are the fees charged (if any) competitive?
Does the institution have a planned giving program?

Does the institution have strong leadership?

What is the composition of the board of directors or trustees?
How many are on the board?
Is the board representative of the varied community interests?
Are different ages and both sexes represented?
Are commercial interests and those of major businesses represented?
Are community minorities or the institution's constituencies represented?
Is the staff well qualified?
How many persons are on the staff?
What are the major strengths and accomplishments of the executive director and other key staff members?
Does the institution use volunteers and are they effective?
Do the administrative facilities meet the needs?

Source: Adapted with permission from Jerold Panas, "The No-Nonsense Guide To Help You Prepare a Statement of Your Case," © 1995, Young & Partners, Inc.

gifts), and the final third of the goal to come from the bottom third (small gifts). When placed on a triangle or pyramid, the top tier has a dollar amount equal to the middle and bottom tiers. This approach, called the "rule of thirds," is always discussed as the method to use, but actually is used less frequently today, because nothing is that simple or predictable.

Although the dollar amounts are divided equally, the numbers of prospective donors are not. The fewest individuals will make up the top third "leadership" level of

a donor pyramid, whereas the largest numbers of donors are in the lowest tier. In other words, very few people will make large, leadership gifts, whereas many people will give small amounts to campaigns. This holds true in most campaigns.

Pre-Campaign Planning and Preparation
For most campaigns, these phases will last approximately six months to a year. The organization should build consensus within its own ranks during the first three to six

months. The feasibility study has indicated that it is possible to conduct a successful campaign for a set amount of dollars; now, that information should be shared, confirmed, and forwarded within the various departments of the institution as well as with any volunteers who will be assisting with the campaign. This is the time for issues to be resolved that may affect the campaign and to bring on board all of those who questioned the feasibility of a campaign. It is also the time to identify the volunteer leaders and define their roles as well as those of the staff members. "Advance" and "leadership" gifts can be identified, and a structure for training the board and other volunteers can be initiated. The advance and leadership gifts also may be initially cultivated during this phase of the campaign.

During the next three to six months, the campaign leadership structure should be developed, the leaders identified and recruited, and the board members kept up to date on all activities and trained as much as possible regarding their roles in the campaign. Staff also should be involved in all of these stages and trained whenever necessary. Also, during this time, the case for support should be finalized and tested on various targeted constituencies. Decide what the benefits are for participating and giving to the campaign. Also use this time to solicit and confirm the advance gifts to the campaign. These are the gifts that have been identified in the feasibility study, will be received before the campaign is announced, and are usually the largest given to the campaign. Based on these advance gifts, final goals should be set, a calendar developed, and timetables established.

Recruitment of Volunteer Leadership and the Leadership Gift Phase

Recruiting volunteer leadership is one of the initial steps in organizing a capital campaign. If there is not a wealthy, powerful, or influential board of trustees in place at the organization to make or solicit gifts at the highest leadership level, a volunteer fund-raising committee, or campaign cabinet, must be developed immediately to solicit gifts at the highest levels (leadership gifts and major gifts). Everyone's energy must be used to develop this committee quickly. Individuals who know the organization, have an interest in its mission, and are willing to both give of their own personal, corporate, or foundation wealth and to work to raise money for the campaign must be identified. A commitment to serve on this committee is contingent upon the ability to either personally give or to raise large sums of money for the campaign.

Of course, the first step is to find someone to chair the overall fund-raising effort. Then, an organization of volunteer leaders will be recruited to form the Campaign Cabinet, a committee to implement the campaign. The structure may resemble that as follows in Exhibit 14–4.

The campaign cabinet is composed of national or local community leaders who will oversee and promote

Exhibit 14–4 Structure of a Campaign Cabinet

A campaign cabinet may include the following volunteer structure:

- Honorary chair
- General chair
- Vice chair (chair of campaign cabinet)
- Campaign cabinet
  - Individual major donor division chair
  - Capital gifts division chair
  - Special projects division chair
  - Corporate division chair
  - Foundation division chair
  - Every member campaign chair

the campaign. The cabinet may be expanded as the campaign grows to ensure representation of all necessary constituencies and to multiply leverage for recruitment and solicitations. Professional counsel may be hired to design the campaign and provide leadership, direction, training, and advice. The following roles are usually associated with the campaign cabinet:

- Honorary chair—An individual of prominence or influence who agrees to lend his or her name to a campaign organization with the understanding that he or she will not be expected to assume an active role. This is the person whose name recognition is so high among those to be solicited for gifts that the prospects would wonder why he or she was not involved.
- General campaign chair—The most visible leader in all phases of the campaign. This person must command the positive responses of peers in terms of agreement to assist the campaign in leadership and/or pacesetting gifts.
- Campaign vice-chair or cabinet chair—This volunteer works closely with the chair and is actually the "doer." Some campaigns operate without a volunteer at this level as the general chair assumes this role. If the general chair appoints a vice-chair or cabinet chair, this volunteer is key to the success of the campaign because he or she is the liaison between the trustees and the fund-raising committee or campaign cabinet. This person is the working head of the cabinet and works closely with the general campaign chair, the fund-raising counsel, the president, as well as the trustees.
- Division chairs/committee chairs—The divisional chairs/committee chairs will organize committees, recruit divisional leadership as required, and implement the campaign to their respective constituent prospects on a phase-by-phase basis.

The prospects for leadership gifts in each division will be solicited by campaign leaders including the divisional chairs. As the campaign progresses, donors may be asked to join the campaign cabinet to help solicit donations from their peers. Using the old adage that "people give to people," having a recent donor join in the solicitation of funds from another prospect is often a very successful campaign technique. Prospects for the smaller gifts in each division may be approached individually as deemed appropriate or may be contacted by mail with telephone follow up.

It is important for the campaign chair and other volunteer leaders to consider and understand the amount of time and effort that it takes to raise a gift—large or small—and then decide where that effort is best placed. If it takes the same amount of energy to raise a large gift as it does to raise a small gift, then it is probably wiser to direct this effort toward the highest level—the leadership and major donor levels. If there are no lower level potential donors on which to depend, or very few of them, the campaign will need to focus on leadership gifts and major gifts, allowing small gifts to "fall into" the bottom third, but gifts at that level are not actively sought.

> It is important for volunteer leaders to understand the amount of time and effort it takes to raise a gift.

When the campaign cabinet is in place and members are trained, approaches then will be made on a wider scale. But, as the committee is being developed, solicitations can occur simultaneously for leadership gifts—gifts at the highest level. Potential donors for leadership gifts can be identified by those currently working on the campaign; also, as the chair and committee members are identified and "brought on board," they will be asked to add to this list of potential donors. For each leadership gift needed, three to four prospective donors most likely will need to be identified. Thus, if a $1 million gift is needed, then three to four potential donors must be identified.

Solicitation of gifts in the middle tier—major donors—will begin once the leadership gifts have been received and the campaign cabinet is in place and actively soliciting donors. The cabinet members will help to expand the list of prospects in this category. Also, as some individuals, corporations, and foundations are asked for leadership gifts, they will decline to make gifts at that level and will instead make smaller, yet substantial gifts that will fall into this middle tier of major gifts. For each major gift received, approximately two prospects will need to be solicited.

The final two stages of the campaign—soliciting for special gifts and general gifts—will address the smallest gifts. Again, gifts will be made at this level throughout the campaign when donors wish to give; but the gifts will not be at the levels for which they were solicited. Again, approximately two prospects will need to be identified for each donor. The general gifts phase of the campaign may be unnecessary, if enough large gifts are obtained early in the campaign.

The greatest concern at this point is developing an accurate plan and a gift chart for the campaign. This is why a formal feasibility study was conducted. If a feasibility study is not done, the gift chart and accompanying prospect lists are developed without the benefit of this counsel and guidance. For the campaign to be successful, each step must be carefully evaluated to: (1) do the "right" cultivation of prospects; (2) have the "right" person(s) make the ask of each prospect, so as not to ask for too little; and (3) train volunteers to turn an initial "no" into a "yes" when soliciting a prospect.

Finally, the campaign gift chart, as well as the campaign plan, are evolving documents that need to be consulted frequently as the campaign progresses. If more money is raised than expected in the leadership phase, then less money will be needed to be raised in the later phases of the campaign. A gift chart is the statistical representation of patterns of giving. The gift chart is used as a planning instrument, as a tool for testing and measuring the availability of donor prospects in the various gift giving levels, and to raise the giving sites of potential donors. These are flexible documents that need to be revisited frequently during a campaign. A sample gift chart is included in Exhibit 14–5.

Private Phase of Campaign

The private phase includes all the phases of a campaign that take place before the campaign is announced to the public. It is also called by some the "silent phase," the "dark phase," and the "pre-public phase." During this time, all leaders of the campaign are recruited and trained, the case statement is defined, all publications are produced, advance or pacesetter gifts are obtained, leadership gifts are in place, and the focus is now on major and general gifts. Gift decisions have been made by the top 100 prospects, all of the board members have made their gifts, and more than half of the goal has been obtained. No short cuts should be taken to rush to the public phase of the campaign. It is imperative to complete all of the steps. Some fund raisers even propose that 100 percent of the campaign's donors should be identified before going public with a campaign.

Methods of Giving to a Campaign

Pacesetter, advance, leadership, or major gifts made to capital campaigns can take many forms. Gifts of cash can be given outright or pledged over several years (usually three to five) of the campaign. Most gifts are made with cash, yet some donors making substantial gifts to

Exhibit 14–5 Chart of Gifts

This table illustrates the number of qualified prospects and gifts needed in appropriate categories to conduct a campaign for $12 million for an organization. Gift range tables or charts of gifts are developed for each campaign undertaken and are based on the availability of prospects and their abilities to give.

GIFT LEVEL	# NEEDED	PROSPECTS	TOTAL	CUMULATIVE
$1,000,000	2	6–8	$2,000,000	$ 2,000,000
$500,000	8	24–32	$4,000,000	$ 6,000,000
$250,000	10	30–40	$2,500,000	$ 8,500,000
$100,000	15	30	$1,500,000	$10,000,000
$50,000	10	20	$500,000	$10,500,000
$25,000	25	50	$625,000	$11,125,000
$20,000	20	40	$400,000	$11,525,000
$15,000	15	30	$225,000	$11,750,000
$10,000	15	30	$150,000	$11,900,000
$5,000	15	30	$75,000	$11,975,000
<$1,000	25	50	$25,000	$12,000,000

the organization will use the types of gift vehicles outlined in Chapter 15—trusts, bequests, life insurance, etc. Some donors will make gifts of real property such as real estate, art work, jewelry, etc., whereas others will make gifts that can be matched by their corporations.

The giving of stock or securities may be of special interest to some elderly donors, for example, who are likely to have more in appreciated securities than younger persons. Stock can be used to establish a charitable trust that will generate tax-free income during their retirement years. When the donor dies, the charity will receive whatever money remains in the trust. See Chapter 15 of this book for further information on how to make planned gifts to a charity.

Another method of giving to an organization is through the transfer of appreciated stock. Many think that this is difficult to do, yet it is really quite simple. Most brokerage firms will make electronic transfers of stock for their clients at no charge. This precludes the hassles of obtaining stock certificates and paying to have them transferred to the organization. A gift of appreciated stock also affords the donor the opportunity to make a substantial gift to the institution and to not pay capital gains on the amount of appreciation; the donor also can "write off" the gift as a charitable deduction.

> **An organization should have systems established to handle different types of gifts.**

It is important for an organization to have a system established to appropriately handle these types of gifts. There is nothing more frustrating for a donor than to want to make a gift of stock to an organization, but the organization does not know how to handle such a gift. Simple instructions that provide accurate directions for a donor to transfer stock can be developed to be included with a standard letter responding to a donor's inquiry. This information should include the following: the organization federal identification number; the name, address, and telephone number of the brokerage firm handling the organization's account; the electronic transfer code for the brokerage firm; the organization's account number with the brokerage firm; and how to notify the organization when a decision to give a gift of stock has been made. A sample of such a letter and sheet of instructions are included in Exhibit 14–6.

Also, once a donor has given stock to an institution, he or she is more likely to do so again. Monitor the market to see if the prices of stock have increased or decreased since the last gifts were given. Don't hesitate to encourage these donors to make a second gift of stock. This time the gift may be to the institution's pooled income fund or used to establish a charitable trust. Of course, the organization should be in frequent touch with the donor over the years and ask again only at the appropriate time.

Exhibit 14–6 Sample Instruction Letter

December 5, 1996

Mr. John C. Smith
3700 Any Avenue
Anytown, USA 00000

Dear Mr. Smith:

Thank you for your inquiry regarding making a gift through the transfer of stock to the ABCD Foundation's *Building for the Future* campaign. The Foundation has opened an account with Charles Schwab & Company, Inc. to facilitate this giving opportunity. The following information describes how to make a gift to the campaign through the transfer of stock. Our hope is to make this transaction convenient for you by providing detailed directions.

As I mentioned in our conversation, Charles Schwab & Company notifies the Foundation on a monthly basis of any account activity, but the report does not include the name of the donor. It would be helpful for me to know when you actually transfer the stock to the Foundation, so I may assign the gift properly. Also, please complete and return the enclosed pledge form. In addition, I have included information on the various vehicles available to make a planned gift to the Foundation. If you have any questions regarding the enclosed information, please call me again at (222) 555-2277.

Again, let me reiterate how pleased I am that you are planning to make a gift to the Foundation's *Building for the Future* campaign. We hope you will join us at the ABCD Annual Convention in October in San Diego. The Foundation is planning a special event for donors, as well as a grand celebration of the successful completion of the campaign for all attendees.

Sincerely,

Jane S. Mitchell
Director of Development

Enclosures
cc: E. Smith

TRANSFERRING SECURITIES TO THE ABCD FOUNDATION

1. The Foundation has opened an account with Charles Schwab & Company, Inc. to facilitate this giving opportunity. The **Foundation's account number at Schwab is 1111-1111** and was opened at their **Washington, DC office.**

2. The Foundation's tax identification number is 54-262728.

3. **If you plan to give stock and it is in your name, please complete the attached Third Party Release form [INTER 476-2 (3/91] and have it notarized** before presenting it to a Schwab broker. Some Schwab offices have notary publics and others do not. If not, most banks and city clerks' offices have notary publics available for your use. When using a notary, you must have some form of photo identification with you.

4. Please call **1-800-435-4000, the toll-free number of Charles Schwab & Company, Inc.** to determine the Schwab office nearest to you and their hours of availability. At the same time, ask them if they have a notary public available.

5. At this time, you will be asked if the stock certificate is being physically held by you, by Schwab, or by another brokerage firm. **If you are physically holding the stock certificate,** you may either mail the certificate to Schwab with directions that it be transferred to the ABCD Foundation, Inc. whose Schwab account number is 1111-1111, or personally deliver the stock to a broker at the Schwab office nearest to you. In either case, **the back of the stock certificate must be signed by you and must be accompanied by the notarized Third Party Release form. Do not endorse anything on the back of the certificate other than your name** as it appears on the front. Your Schwab broker will complete the remainder of the information for you. All deliveries **MUST** include the Foundation's name and Schwab account number.

6. **If you do not physically hold the stock certificate and it is held by a brokerage firm,** either Schwab or some other firm, they may have the stock transferred electronically (using DTC Clearing 0164, Code 40) directly to Schwab by using the account number 1111-1111 and the complete name of the Foundation's account—The ABCD Foundation, Inc. Again, all delivery **MUST** include the Foundation's name and Schwab account number.

Using Commemorative Opportunities to Encourage Gifts and Recognize Donors

All capital campaigns should provide opportunities for donors to have their names identified with their gift. It may be as simple as placing their names on a plaque on a wall, or it may be the offering of specific rooms in a building at a set price for prospective donors to consider "naming." This is easy if the campaign is raising money for a new building. Most people like to see their names associated with their gifts. Gift clubs can be established and information included in all campaign publications. Some campaign organizers choose to put the gift clubs on the pledge card so donors can view the various club options when deciding upon the size of their gift. Development staff can promote gift clubs or other naming opportunities in newsletters and other publications.

Source: © Mark Litzler

Campaign Materials

To promote and conduct a capital campaign, most of the following marketing, communications, and training materials are required: (1) the case statement; (2) a brochure that focuses solely on the campaign; (3) a leadership or major gift prospectus; (4) a pamphlet that presents answers to the most frequently asked questions in the campaign—Q-and-A Brochure; (5) an annual report for the organization; (6) pledge cards; (7) a monthly or quarterly newsletter; (8) a theme or slogan for the campaign that is printed on or repeated in all materials; (9) banner paper for press releases; (10) a volunteer guidebook; (11) business cards; and (12) a poster, if appropriate to the campaign.

A case statement is more than just listing the needs of an organization. It also is the basis on which all other campaign materials will be developed. The case statement should put the campaign into perspective with all of the other activities of the organization as well as outline the plans for the use of the funds raised. Donors will

want to know how the money raised will impact the organization's future.

The Case Statement

The case statement is also sometimes called the statement of need. This piece presents the mission of the institution, the reason for the campaign, and the needs and opportunities—both long and short term—of the organization. The campaign brochure and all other promotional pieces are developed from the case statement.

The development of the case statement should include as many leaders of the institution as possible. If asked to develop the case, the volunteer is more likely to be able to articulate the case clearly and enthusiastically. This is the time to "bring along" potential leadership for the campaign. By involving individuals "up front," it more than likely ensures their positive involvement with the campaign.

The case statement should include a history of the institution, explain clearly where the organization stands today, what the organization's needs are, how the campaign will meet those needs, and a look into the future if the campaign is successful.

Campaign Brochure

The brochure will be the key sales piece for the fundraising initiative. The four-color brochure will convey the case in a concise and compelling way, and will be built around the central themes developed in the case statement.

Leadership and Major Gifts Prospectus

The leadership and major gifts prospectus is a special packet consisting of the following:

- Campaign brochure,
- Solicitation letter,
- Recognition opportunities sheet (if appropriate),
- Selected public relations materials,
- Annual report.

Question-and-Answer Brochure

Questions that are commonly asked throughout the fund-raising effort can be anticipated, presented, and answered in a smaller brochure that accompanies the main fund-raising brochure. This can be called the question-and-answer brochure or the Q and A for short. In addition to being used along with the general informational fund-raising brochure, it also can be used separately. This is an inexpensive piece, often considered a "throw away" piece, and can be printed in two color, or "piggy-backed" with the printing of the major brochure and printed in four color (if the brochure is being printed in four color).

Annual Report

As a complement to all fund-raising materials, the organization should develop and print an annual report. The brochure outlines the organization's programs and activities during the past year and reports on the financial stability of the organization. Produced annually, it can be used effectively as a supplemental brochure in multi-year fund-raising efforts.

Pledge Cards

A pledge card or pledge sheet is the official record of a donor's gift to a fund-raising campaign. The following information should be included on the card: the donor's name, address, and phone number; gift or pledge amount; payment schedule; method of paying the gift or pledge; information on what types of payments are available to the donor (check, credit cards, etc.); to whom to write the check and where to send it; the opportunity to indicate how the donor would like to have the gift recognized; a place for the donor's signature; and the date.

Newsletter

A newsletter from the organization's president, chair of the board, or chair of the campaign can be developed to promote the organization by reporting on new developments within the institution as well as the progress of the campaign. It provides an opportunity to give credit to donors and to recognize the campaign leadership. Any new donors should be highlighted in the next issue.

Theme or Slogan

Campaign themes or slogans will vary depending upon the reason for raising the funds. Many themes created today use the themes of "new millennium," "21st century," and "bridge to the future" in their titles. Use whatever is most fitting to the organization, its mission, and the campaign. Don't try to be cute.

Press Releases

To inform the public of the organization's fund-raising efforts, the staff must write and distribute news releases to announce important happenings such as special events, the receipts of a major gift, the appointment of a campaign chair, etc. Press releases can be distributed by mail or at a press conference if the news is important enough to get the press to attend. If the information is distributed at a press conference, then a complete press kit should be developed including the press release, a brochure or fact sheet describing the organization, biographies of any persons involved, and any photographs (black and white) pertinent to the release.

Volunteer Guidelines

A handbook of volunteer guidelines should be provided to all volunteers recruited to work on the campaign. It should provide a basic overview of the campaign including sample letters, scripts, etc.

Business Cards

All volunteers as well as staff members should have business cards that are designed specifically for the campaign. The cards should carry the slogan or theme of the campaign and should have all the necessary information on how to reach the campaign headquarters—address, phone number, fax, e-mail, etc.

Posters

A poster may be designed to augment the other campaign materials because posters can be effective fund-raising tools in many campaigns. Who can forget the March of Dimes poster child or the faces of the animals on the posters of the Society for the Prevention of Cruelty to Animals? A picture says a thousand words, and posters can raise thousands of dollars. They also can just be used to raise the public's awareness of the organization and its mission. They do not need to be in four color; but again, if it is in the budget, then use four color because it is usually more dramatic and appealing.

Setting Up Internal Systems

As important as trained volunteers are to the success of a campaign, so too are the systems established within the development office to manage a campaign. From research on a prospect to the collection of a gift to thanking the donor, a well-organized development office with systems in place is a must. Whether automated computer systems are used or paper files, the accuracy of data maintained is vital to the success of current and future campaigns. Some of the data that should be maintained for analysis for future campaigns include the following: number of gifts received, amount of cash received, dollar amount of pledges received, dollar amount of deferred or planned gifts received, number of donors, number of prospects contacted, percentage of those contacted who made gifts, average gift size, average advance or pacesetter gifts, average leadership gift, average major gift, average general gift, gifts by range, gifts by category, gifts by size, etc. In most campaigns, this information will be tracked on an ongoing basis and shared with the campaign leadership. The data can help staff manage the campaign and direct the volunteers in areas that need leadership.

All campaign gifts should be processed through the development office. If gifts are received by other offices, they should be sent immediately to the development office. One person in the development office should oversee the receipt of gifts. This person should make sure that all of the data requested on the pledge card is completely and accurately recorded, and that all cash gifts are accounted and deposited on the day they arrive. If this is not possible, then the cash gifts must be kept in a locked file cabinet or another secure place.

Acknowledging Gifts

All gifts should be acknowledged within forty-eight hours, if possible. If there is such a large number of gifts being made that this cannot be done, then additional staff should be hired temporarily to assist with this process. There is nothing more annoying to a donor than not to be thanked in a timely manner. Acknowledgment letters should be signed by the chair of the campaign or the president or executive director of the organization. If the gift is substantial, more than one thank-you letter can be sent from those representing the campaign and the organization.

Collection of Pledges

If the gifts are made in the form of a pledge, this information must be recorded accurately as a pledge payment schedule—monthly, quarterly, semi-annual, and annual remittances are common. Work with the organization's financial or accounting department to make sure that all requirements are being met for both the donor and the organization. It is important to track pledge payments, because delinquent accounts do not bring cash into the organization. If a donor misses two consecutive payments, a letter requesting payment should be sent. If this brings no results, then a phone call should be made by one of the campaign cabinet members.

Maintaining Relationships with Leadership Donors

Once a gift is made, the organization should never lose touch with the person who gave the gift. In particular, those who have made leadership gifts should be cultivated for future campaign volunteers, board leadership roles, and other future gifts to the organization. Major donors should be invited to all of the organization's major activities such as receptions, special events, private dinners, etc. Feature donors in the organization's newsletters whenever possible.

What to Do When Campaign Momentum Wanes

In almost every capital campaign there will come a time when the campaign appears to be "stalled" and no progress is being made. This is not a time to panic, but a time to assess what has been working well and what has not been successful. Taking the time to analyze the campaign's operations at this point can assist those responsible for its success in making decisions for the direction of the campaign in the remaining time.

Usually the momentum wanes just before the final phase of a campaign. In a three-year campaign, it is usually toward the end of the second year. In a five-year campaign, it is in year four. It is rare when a capital campaign doesn't halt at some point. People just tire of the routine. Also, natural problems occur around the summer months, the various religious holidays, and the long national holiday times such as Thanksgiving and the Fourth of July. Potential donors have other priorities on their minds and the campaign is usually not high on their list.

If the campaign plans for these "waning" periods, then the leaders can direct the volunteers through the valleys, and the overall campaign will not be affected. It is better to plan than to deny that a campaign can be stalled. Staff members can build certain "check points" into the campaign plan— a time when the leaders evaluate what has been accomplished, if the campaign is on target, and if the next stages planned for the campaign are still appropriate.

The Chronicle of Philanthropy (1996) stresses that organizations with inexperienced fund raisers can often jump into campaigns not realizing how difficult large goals are to achieve. The organizations then face potential public embarrassment as donations fail to appear as expected. An organization shouldn't publicly announce a campaign until it is certain it can reach its goal. If the best-planned capital campaign appears to be stalled, the following are some ideas to use to get out of those arid stretches:

1. Focus attention on the mission of the organization and not on the need to build a new building. Bring emotion back into the campaign.
2. Change the volunteer leadership. Bring new people in. Do not embarrass the current volunteers by removing them, but instead, add to their numbers. Others suggest removing the nonproducing volunteers totally as they most likely feel guilty that they haven't done a better job of soliciting funds and would be happy to be "let off the hook." Jerold Panas, a Chicago fund-raising consultant, says "You can't let a capital campaign or the welfare of an institution suffer because you're afraid to hurt someone's feelings. You need to take them off the hook and let them get rid of the guilt."
3. Solicit challenge grants that must be matched by other sources to lend a sense of urgency to the campaign.
4. Hire a new consultant. Sometimes the fund-raising consultant or consulting firm is the problem and should be replaced. The match with the volunteers may be wrong and this may lead to the inability to motivate.
5. End the campaign earlier than planned. Sometimes it is best to assess the situation, declare victory, and end the campaign.

Often if a campaign falters or stagnates in the middle of the drive, the leaders may be burned out, the economy may have changed, or the goal just may have been set too high. Whatever the reasons, it is important to evaluate the situation and make plans to either "jump-start" the campaign or to "declare victory" and end the campaign. Either decision is appropriate. What is not appropriate is to allow the campaign to continue to falter by taking no action.

> Evaluate the situation and make plans to either "jump-start" the campaign or to "declare victory."

First of all, evaluate why prospects have been slow to make their gifts. Were there enough prospects for each gift level? Does the development staff need to do more research on potential donors? Has the economy in your community changed and affected your prospect base? Is the case still relevant and timely? Were any shortcuts taken in starting the campaign? Were volunteers trained? Were all of the appropriate materials prepared? Were enough leadership gifts obtained before taking the campaign public? Have the donors been kept informed of the status of the campaign? They may be willing to increase their gifts to help you reach your goal. Plus, all donors must be nurtured for them to want to give again.

Options for a Troubled Campaign

To "jump-start" a faltering campaign, it may be necessary to reconstruct the campaign into smaller units or projects, based on the level of appeal to prospects. It may be that there were just too many programs involved with the campaign, and new priorities have to be set. Then, if these priorities become funded, those programs placed aside can be added again. Another, similar approach is to consider the campaign as a series of "mini" campaigns. Aim to complete the goal of the first mini campaign, then the second, the third, and so forth. It may be easier for donors to relate to a smaller scale campaign. Another option is to broaden the appeal. Review the case statement. Can it be expanded or changed to include new giving options? Consider ways to increase the number of prospects based on the expanded appeal. Also, watch how your money is being spent. Focus on the important tasks first. Organize your tasks by priority and size. Remember that it is possible to achieve victory one step at a time.

Campaign Evaluation

Changing Trends

Some people think that campaigns have to bypass the traditional rules to be successful. The face of capital campaigns today has changed in many instances. As the economic environment has shifted, so too has the structure of capital campaigns. It is becoming more and more difficult to find volunteers to work on campaigns. Individuals are becoming more concerned about their time commitments. With the downsizing of corporations, many persons are working second jobs to maintain their standards of living, and they think they no longer have time to volunteer. Others just don't want to have others ask them for favors, so they aren't interested in soliciting gifts in the first place. In addition to downsizing, yet another aspect of the changing world of the capital campaign is the merging of corporations, deleting the overall philanthropic dollars available to the nonprofit world. This lack of volunteers and shortage of available funds have forced some campaigns to take a nontraditional approach to undertaking a capital campaign.

The rules mentioned in the opening of this chapter are being, if not dismissed, at least changed. Although a strong chair is still essential to a successful campaign, development staff are taking on more and more of the work traditionally assigned to the volunteers. With fewer volunteers available to select and train, staff members often are forced to actually solicit gifts—this once being the sole domain of the volunteers.

Again, the rules have changed so that campaigns are being launched without large advance gifts and without reaching 50 percent of the goal. Instead of one or two lead gifts, a group of several smaller gifts may be used to launch the campaign. Sometimes the lead gift will come much later in the campaign, often as a closing gift or a gift to "top-off" the campaign total.

Donors are not contributing at the levels they once were, nor at the levels research suggests donors might contribute. Many are making challenge gifts or pooling their gifts with other members of their families to give less, but still a substantial gift. Yet others are making their gifts through planned giving vehicles instead of outright gifts of cash. The charity will not receive the cash for many years. All this underscores the great need today in the nonprofit world for professional development officers who are well trained to handle the realities of capital campaign fund raising.

Plus, with public funds dwindling, capital campaigns are becoming more common. They also are becoming larger than ever before. In 1994, Harvard University publicly launched a five-year, $2.1 billion capital campaign. This campaign was initiated just nine years after Harvard completed a $359 million campaign; of course, the private phase of the $2.1 billion campaign started much earlier than 1994. Some question whether the general public will continue to tolerate campaigns of this size, especially when an institution has $6 billion in its endowment. Certainly, it doesn't help when campaign goals seem to be determined by competition and not by the true needs of the institution or organization. But, the trend seems to be larger campaigns in both dollars and scope. One hopes that the donor is asking the questions that the organizations may not—What are the organization's priorities and is the money truly needed to help the organization fill its mission?

When To Start the Next Campaign

Some universities view capital campaigns as a source of "big money" with no ending. They ask donors for the next check as they thank them for the most recent. Donor burnout is happening more often and the nonprofit world should beware. With two major scandals (The United Way of America and the New Era Foundation) in fund raising still fresh in the public's mind, it is no wonder that many people are skeptical about giving and giving again to an organization that just has received a large sum of money from the donor. So, when is the right time to start the next campaign? Ask your membership and your constituents through a feasibility study. Listen carefully, because they will be honest and direct. It may be that the organization's prospects perceive the new programs or buildings to be unnecessary. If this is the case, it will be nearly impossible to raise the money being sought. The supporters need to think that there is a need and not just an organization caught up in a numbers game.

There have been attempts to regulate capital campaigns, especially among universities. Some have wanted capital campaigns to last no longer than seven years, oral pledges to not count in campaign totals, government dollars to not be counted in totals, and the full value of deferred gifts to not be counted, only the reduced value based on actuarial tables or other data to determine how much the gift is actually worth at the time it is made. Others have wanted a separation among outright gifts, pledges, and deferred gifts. This makes it easier to determine how much money would be available for immediate use. The fairness of these issues will continue to be debated. Whatever is done, it should not deter donors from making gifts to campaigns, and a firm belief should be instilled in donors that supporting organizations' and institutions' capital campaigns is the proper thing to do with their disposable cash or property.

For more information about capital campaigns, see *Capital Campaigns: Strategies That Work*, by Andrea Kihlstedt and Catherine P. Schwartz, another book in this series.

References

Capital Ideas: Highlighting Capital Campaigns, Planned Giving, and Ethics. 1996. *The Digest of Southern Giving*, 10 no. 6: 5–6.

Panas, J. 1995. *The no-nonsense guide to help you prepare a statement of your case.* Young & Partners, Inc.

Turning a Campaign Around—What Fund Raisers Can Do to Jump-Start a Stalled Campaign. 1996. *The Chronicle of Philanthropy*, 27 June.

Appendix 14–A
Capital Campaign Phases

The campaign will be conducted in five phases beginning in January 1996 through December 1999. Each phase will have a number of specific objectives.

PHASE I—Organizational
January 1996–August 1996

- Complete planning phase.
- Complete campaign brochure.
- Establish campaign calendar.
- Employ campaign counsel and support staff.
- Hold preliminary planning meetings.
- Recruit campaign volunteer leadership.
- Develop list of leadership gift prospects.
- Develop gift chart and rationale.
- Develop campaign materials—stationery, business cards, *Volunteer Handbook*.
- Request annual reports from corporations and foundations to be solicited.

PHASE II—Leadership Gift Solicitation
September 1996–May 1997

- Solicit prospects to obtain thirty-five leadership gifts totaling $8,500,000.
- Complete recruitment of campaign cabinet (volunteer committee).
- Identify additional leadership gift prospects.
- Complete campaign materials: brochures, pledge cards, prospect lists, letterhead, solicitation guides, *Volunteer Handbook*, etc.
- Identify major gift prospects.
- Recruit major gift volunteers (expand campaign cabinet) for various constituencies.
- Complete leadership gifts ($250,000 to $1 million).
- Develop pledge and gift tracking and collection procedures.
- Thank donors and enter into database.
- Send newsletter and annual report to donors.
- Develop donor recognition opportunities.

PHASE III— Major Gifts
June 1997–February 1998

- Announce publicly the campaign, goal, leadership, and leadership gifts totaling $8,500,000.
- Solicit major gifts from more than 100 prospects to raise $2,625,000.
- Expand volunteer organization for solicitation of special and general gifts.
- Identify special and general gift prospects.
- Train special and general gift volunteers.
- Initiate intensive publicity campaign.
- Monitor pledges.
- Thank new donors and enter into database.
- Send newsletter to donors.

PHASE IV—Special Gifts—Expansion of Campaign
March 1998–December 1998

- Complete major gifts.
- Conduct solicitation of special gifts from 100 prospects to raise $775,000.
- Finalize general gift prospect list.
- Monitor pledges.
- Thank new donors and enter into database.
- Send newsletter to donors.
- Train new volunteers.

PHASE V— General Gifts, Closure, and Victory Celebration
January 1999–December 1999

- Complete special gifts phase.
- Solicit general gifts from more than fifty-five remaining prospects to raise $100,000 for a general campaign totaling $12 million.
- Thank new donors and enter onto the database.
- Hold victory celebration—ribbon cutting or ground breaking with dinner for significant donors.

Appendix 14–B
Campaign Activities Timetable

1997 CAMPAIGN ACTIVITIES FLOW CHART
Month-to-Month Timetable

Activity	Jan.	Feb.	Mar.	Apr.	May	June	July	Aug.	Sept.	Oct.	Nov.	Dec.
ORGANIZATION/RECRUITMENT												
Campaign Cabinet/ Divisional Chairs	■	■	■	■	■	■						
Train Volunteers	■	■	■	■	■	■	■	■	■	■	■	■
SOLICITATION												
Leadership Gifts $250K to $1M	■	■	■	■	■							
Major Gifts $25,000 to $249,999							■	■	■	■	■	■
Identify Gift Prospects	■	■	■	■	■	■	■	■	■	■	■	■
Write Planned Giving Handbook	■	■	■									
PUBLIC RELATIONS/CAMPAIGN MATERIALS												
Announce Campaign					■	■						
Foundation/Newsletter	■			■			■			■		
Annual Report										■		
FOLLOW-UP												
Acknowledgments to Prospects/Donors	■	■	■	■	■	■	■	■	■	■	■	■
Collection of Gifts and Pledges	■	■	■	■	■	■	■	■	■	■	■	■

1998 CAMPAIGN ACTIVITIES FLOW CHART
Month-to-Month Timetable

Activity	Jan.	Feb.	Mar.	Apr.	May	June	July	Aug.	Sept.	Oct.	Nov.	Dec.
SOLICITATION												
Major Gifts $25,000 to $249,000	▓	▓	▓									
Special Gifts $10,000 to $24,999				▓	▓	▓	▓	▓	▓	▓	▓	▓
Identify Prospects for General Gifts	▓	▓	▓	▓	▓	▓	▓	▓	▓	▓	▓	▓
PUBLIC RELATIONS/CAMPAIGN MATERIALS												
Newsletter	▓			▓			▓			▓		
Annual Report										▓		
FOLLOW-UP												
Acknowledgments to Prospects/Donors	▓	▓	▓	▓	▓	▓	▓	▓	▓	▓	▓	▓
Collection of Gifts and Pledges	▓	▓	▓	▓	▓	▓	▓	▓	▓	▓	▓	▓

1999 CAMPAIGN ACTIVITIES FLOW CHART
Month-to-Month Timetable

Activity	Jan.	Feb.	Mar.	Apr.	May	June	July	Aug.	Sept.	Oct.	Nov.	Dec.
SOLICITATION												
General Gifts <$1,000 to $9,999	▓	▓	▓	▓	▓	▓	▓	▓	▓	▓	▓	▓
PUBLIC RELATIONS												
Newsletter	▓			▓			▓			▓		
Campaign Celebration										▓	▓	▓
Annual Report										▓		
FOLLOW-UP												
Acknowledgments to Prospects/Donors	▓	▓	▓	▓	▓	▓	▓	▓	▓	▓	▓	▓
Collection of Gifts and Pledges	▓	▓	▓	▓	▓	▓	▓	▓	▓	▓	▓	▓

Chapter 15
The Basics of Planned Giving

Chapter Outline

- Definition of Planned Giving
- The Steps to Establish a Successful Planned Giving Program
- Identifying the Best Prospects
- Marketing Your Planned Giving Program
- The Role of Volunteers
- The Bequest Society—The Simplest Way to Begin
- How Planned Giving Fits into a Major Gifts Program

Key Vocabulary

- Bequest
- Bequest Society
- Gift Policies
- Gift Vehicles
- Life Income Gifts
- Planned Giving
- Planned Giving Committee
- Wills

Definition of Planned Giving

For those new to the area of planned giving, there is a simple way to understand the difference between planned giving and major gift fund raising. Major gifts are defined as outright gifts from one's income (cash or securities) while planned giving primarily deals with gifts of assets such as real estate, works of art, life insurance policies, tangible property, and securities. The vast majority of these gifts are given after the donor has died and no longer has any need or use for his or her assets. You may discover that arrangements for a number of planned gifts have been made in a donor's will or estate planning. Planned giving opportunities also allow a donor to make a contribution and receive income back, after a certain age, from gift vehicles such as annuities or various charitable trusts. Exhibit 15–1 lists

reasons why planned giving is important to your organization.

This type of fund raising, with its own jargon, is by far the most technical in the development field. The best way for development officers to promote this type of giving is not to focus on the technical aspect but, instead, to focus on the donor perspective and what planned giving can do for the donor. What are the donor's philanthropic goals? Who are the people for whom the donor needs to provide, such as a spouse, children, and/or grandchildren? What type of assets (cash, stocks, bonds, insurance, real estate, art, antiques, family business) does the donor have? Are the donor's financial objectives to avoid capital gains tax or to increase income?

Exhibit 15–1 Why Planned Giving Is Important to Your Organization

- Planned gifts generally tend to be large gifts.
- Because many planned gifts are irrevocable, they allow organizations to do better planning for their future.
- Publicizing gifts can help generate interest of other prospective donors.
- Planned gift donors, when properly cultivated, are likely prospects for annual gifts and subsequent larger gifts including an additional planned gift.

The Steps to Establish a Successful Planned Giving Program

More and more organizations of all sizes and types are starting planned gift programs. The simplest way to begin is to provide information to donors about how to include the organization in their wills and estate plans. Exhibit 15–2 reveals highlights of a survey of more than 150,000 people as to whether they had a written will

Exhibit 15–2 Survey Highlights

According to a recent survey of 150,000 individuals by the National Committee on Planned Giving:

Over the next 20 years, approximately $8 to $10 trillion will be passed from a senior generation who is famous for making and saving their money to its children, the baby boomers.

Nationally:
- Forty percent of people have written wills.
- Approximately six percent of all people include a charity in their will.
- Age is not a determining factor.
- About 1 percent had participated in life income gifts.

Half of the wills were written within the past 1 to 5 years. Most wills are not changed. If they are changed, most changes increase the amount being left to the charity.

Source: Data from *About the Board*, Vol. 10, no. 1, October, 1995, p. 5, Semple Bixel Associates, Inc.

and if they included some type of charitable giving in their will. However, it is important to realize that some organizations are better suited for planned giving programs than others. The following factors are important to that success:

1. A track record of accomplishments
2. Stability and a plan for the organization's future
3. Strong constituency of older donors
4. A strong and mature annual fund program
5. A group of long-term consistent donors
6. The organization can afford up-front costs now with benefits not realized for several years
7. The organization has someone responsible for planned giving who is trustworthy, is able to deal with older people, believes in your organization, and is able to understand the financial and technical aspects of the program

If after reviewing these factors you believe your organization is suited to launch a planned giving program, one of the first things you may want to do is contact several organizations similar to yours that have planned giving programs underway. Important questions to ask include the following:

- When did they start their program?
- How many staff members did they start with?
- What were their first responsibilities?
- Who made the first gift? Board member? Staff member? Unsolicited gift?

- How long did it take to secure the first gift from outside the board and staff?
- How long before the organization can use the gift income?
- What is the current number and worth of the organization's planned gifts?

Having done your research, you will have a clearer picture of just what is needed to establish a successful program. The information you gather will help you develop the case for starting such a program, which you will need to present to your board and CEO. A basic requirement for all involved is patience. Your board and CEO must understand that when launching a planned giving program, an organization is investing in future stability. It is an ongoing, long-term effort. As in the other methods of fund raising, there is a series of steps involved, from identifying prospects, completing research, cultivating, making personal visits, soliciting, and finally working with the donor's tax and legal experts to secure the gift. Each step takes time. But, when you are talking about gifts of tens of thousands, hundreds of thousands, or millions of dollars, the investment of time will prove worthwhile.

Step One—Commitment from Organization's Staff and Board Leadership

First and foremost, to launch a successful program, you must have the support of the organization's CEO. With his or her help, you need to get a commitment from your board chair or development committee chair to pursue this effort. These three individuals, the CEO, board chair, and development committee chair, now have the task of securing the support of the entire board. The board should feel a sense of ownership of the program and be well informed about the operation of the program and the benefits the organization will reap in the long run. The board should pass a resolution to recognize the importance of planned giving and instruct the staff to start the program. Before you begin soliciting planned gifts, the board should approve a set of administrative policies including guidelines for which types of gift vehicles will be offered, procedures for accepting such gifts, and marketing strategies to promote these gift vehicles.

Step Two—Increase Knowledge of Planned Giving

It is extremely important for the staff involved in the program to have knowledge of planned giving. There are a number of resources available to you to increase your personal knowledge. They include seminars and conferences sponsored by the National Com-

> It is extremely important for the staff involved in the program to have knowledge of planned giving.

mittee on Planned Giving, the National Society of Fund Raising Executives (NSFRE), the Council for Advancement and Support of Education (CASE), the Association for Healthcare Philanthropy (AHP), and many planned giving consulting firms. Begin building a resource library with publications such as the *Practical Guide to Planned Giving,* published by Taft Publishers, and *Planned Giving Essentials: A Step by Step Guide to Success,* by Richard D. Barrett and Molly Ware, another book in this series.

Step Three—Set Realistic Goals and Priorities
Because this is only one of the many fund-raising programs going on each year, it is important to set clear and realistic goals and priorities. When you set your planned giving objectives, make sure they are achievable given the time and money allocated to the program in the organizational budget. Once you establish your goals and their importance, you can prepare performance objectives and detailed operational plans.

Step Four—Decide on Scope of Program
Closely related to goal-setting is determining the scope of your organization's planned giving program. You need to analyze the requirements for marketing and supporting the various types of gift vehicles and determine which gift vehicles you can include in your program. For example, although almost any organization can encourage donors to include planned giving in their wills, the organization may not have the staff or expertise to encourage charitable trusts. Most development professionals would recommend beginning by establishing a selective or partial planned giving program. As mentioned earlier, promoting bequests is by far the best way to begin. Depending on the type and size of the organization, there are varying opinions about which gift vehicles to include next. Exhibit 15–3 lists the different types of planned gift vehicles an organization can choose to include in its planned giving program.

Step Five—Prepare an Adequate Budget
No fund-raising program can be effective without adequate funding. In previous chapters, we listed many budget items necessary for running annual giving, direct mail, telemarketing, and major gift fund-raising programs. Planned giving programs are no different in that it takes money to raise money. Some additional items not found in the other program budgets but are necessary for planned giving include the following:

- legal fees
- bank administration fees
- consultant or vendor fees
- special subscriptions and publications
- additional professional memberships

Step Six—Develop a Well-Conceived Marketing Plan
Keep in mind the ways your organization communicates with its donors and prospective donors. When developing your marketing plan for planned giving include regular newsletters and publications, direct mail, personal mail, telephone cultivation, and personal visits.

Step Seven—Involve Volunteers
You can recruit volunteers to serve on a variety of committees—the board of directors; the board's development committee; the planned giving committee, which is covered later in the chapter; and special technical committees needed for planned giving.

LITZLER

"WHEN I GAVE HALF A MILLION DOLLARS TO THE CHURCH I DIDN'T COUNT ON BEING BLESSED WITH SUCH GOOD HEALTH THAT I WOULD OUT LIVE MY ASSETS."

Source: © Mark Litzler

Identifying the Best Prospects

After establishing your planned giving program, it is time now to identify those individuals and donors who are the best prospects for making a planned gift. To determine who your best prospects are, it is important to understand what is most important to them—financial security. The donor may need to feel secure now and in the future or may be more concerned about the financial security of a spouse and heirs. Remember, planned giv-

> To determine who your best prospects are, it is important to understand what is most important to them—financial security.

Exhibit 15–3 Ten Types of Planned Gifts

There are ten types of planned gifts with which development staff should be familiar. They are presented in priority order for implementation. The first three can help you to ease into planned giving with minimum complications. Numbers four, five, six can be incorporated once you begin to grow comfortable in your knowledge of planned giving. You can implement number seven in a few years when you feel confident in securing more than a few participants. Numbers eight and nine most likely will require special licensing through your state department of insurance. Number ten is designed for that extremely wealthy prospect down the road. Numbers four, five, seven, eight, nine, and ten now require an extensive disclosure statement presented to and signed by the donor(s) before the vehicle's legal documents are signed.

1. **Bequest**—One of the most common planned gifts. A nonprofit organization is bequeathed a gift in a donor's will. The gift may be designated as (1) percentage of the donor's estate, (2) specific dollar amount or description of property, (3) residual of the donor's estate or (4) contingent upon a certain event happening. Estate taxes are reduced by the value of the gift to the nonprofit organization.
2. **Outright gift**—Cash, securities, real estate, personal property, etc., the title of which is legally transferred to a qualified nonprofit organization. In most cases, an income tax deduction is allowed for the full market value and capital gains taxes are avoided, reducing the cost of the gift to the donor.
3. **Life insurance policies**—A relatively inexpensive way for a donor to leave a significant gift to a nonprofit organization. A new policy may be taken out on the life of a younger donor to "create" a major, deferred gift to a charity with the cost of the premium being a small fraction of the face value of the policy. Donors also may have existing policies that are no longer needed for their original purposes (to ensure a child's education). With a change of policy ownership and beneficiary to the nonprofit organization, the donor can contribute the premium amount to the charity and the policy's face value can be maintained, or, if the donor chooses not to continue payments, the face value or "paid up insurance" value can be significant. Donors' tax deductions are equal to their cash/replacement value or premiums paid, depending on the type of policy.
4. **Charitable remainder unitrust**—The donor receives a variable income from the gift for the rest of his or her life. The income to the donor is based on a specified percent of the trust principal, revalued each year, reflecting any increases in the value of the trust's assets. More than one person may receive income. The trust assets become the property of the nonprofit group upon the donor's death or in a pre-established time period. Additional contributions may be made to the trust. Income tax deductions for the donor are based on the current value of the remainder interest going to the nonprofit organization.
5. **Charitable remainder annuity trust**—Similar to the unitrust, except that (1) the donor receives a fixed income from the gift for the rest of his or her life, (2) the income amount is based on the original value of the trust's assets, and (3) additional contributions cannot be made.
6. **Life estate**—A donor deeds his or her personal residential property to a nonprofit organization. While the donor is still living, he or she has a legal interest in the life estate with full rights to live there, or to rent or sell those rights. The donor receives an immediate income deduction for the remainder interest value of the estate.
7. **Pooled life income fund**—Contributions from several donors are placed in a common trust fund for investment and management. Each donor has a pro rata share interest of the pooled fund and receives his or her share of the total net ordinary income earned. When the donor dies, his or her share becomes the nonprofit organization's property. Income tax deduction is based on the current value of the remainder interest going to the nonprofit organization.
8. **Charitable gift annuity**—A donor's gift is not placed in trust but immediately becomes the property of the nonprofit organization. In exchange, the nonprofit organization promises to pay a fixed income to the donor for the rest of his or her life. A portion of the income is not taxable, but considered a return of principal. An income tax deduction is allowed for the difference between the gift value and the amount required to fund the annuity (actuarial value). There is a maximum of two income beneficiaries.
9. **Deferred gift annuity**—A donor makes a gift now and receives an immediate income tax deduction. The donor begins receiving income at a later date—usually at retirement. Because the principal compounds between the date of the gift and the first date when the donor receives income, the amount of income can be significant and increase at a greater rate than that of the standard charitable gift annuity.
10. **Charitable lead trust**—A nonprofit organization receives income payments from the trust for a given number of years. At the end of the trust term, the assets of the trust are returned to the owner or his or her designee. This allows the transfer of assets to children while greatly reducing gift taxes.

Source: Reprinted with permission from D. Barnes, *National Fund Raiser Newsletter*, Vol. 22, no. 5, March 1996 Supplement, Barnes Associates.

ing is based on benefits to the donor such as tax advantages, income or net worth growth, or preservation of assets, while at the same time allowing for charitable giving.

To be successful in discussing planned giving with a prospect, you will need to learn the prospect's priorities relative to the benefits previously listed. Is there a spouse who needs special care? Are there grandchildren with future educational needs? Understanding the prospect's personal financial needs is your first responsibility. Then you can present those gift vehicles that best suit the donor's needs. Exhibit 15–4 lists possible criteria to use when analyzing your donor base for the best planned giving prospects, and Exhibit 15–5 is an evaluation form that can be used to gather more information on selected prospects.

Marketing Your Planned Giving Program

When marketing your program to donors, remember to stress the theme covered in this chapter—benefits to the donor! The best way to do this is to use real-life stories as well as fictional scenarios that illustrate how planned giving can help prospective donors address their needs and support your organization at the same time. To keep your program costs down, use publications and communications regularly sent to your donors and members.

Publications

Use organizational newsletters and publications such as magazines and annual reports to create awareness and promote the benefits of planned giving. Develop a series of advertisements that cover a variety of planned gifts. Exhibit 15–6 depicts an ad used in the Washington College of Law alumni magazine, *the Advocate.* Articles about donors who recently made a planned gift or published interviews with donors help to educate and in-

---

Exhibit 15–4 Criteria To Use When Selecting Planned Giving Prospects

Consider selecting someone as a planned giving prospect if he or she:

1. Is a current donor
2. Has given consistently over a period of years
3. Is 55 years old or older
4. Has no dependent heirs
5. Has highly appreciated assets not earning much income
6. Has an income and net worth range that indicate potential

---

form other prospective donors, as well as highlight the benefits shared by the donor and the organization.

Seminars

Depending on the size and type of the organization, seminars can be a useful tool in providing an overview of the estate planning process to donors and the general public. These seminars can increase your organization's visibility in the community but only if the presentations are of the highest quality. You must be sure that your seminars are accurate, educational, and polished enough to represent your organization. Presenting seminars may not be the best way to market your program because in many major cities there is much competition among organizations and companies offering free seminars on estate planning. These seminars are given by many nonprofit organizations, banks and securities houses, and financial planning professionals.

Direct Mail

Using regular or special publications does not prevent you from using direct mail as well. One easy way to use direct mail is to print a small box on all fundraising business reply envelopes (BREs) for donors to check if they would like information about wills and other planned gifts (see Exhibit 15–7). Focus each mailing on a specific area of planned giving and include a brochure. Remember to use real-life scenarios as often as you can to further educate your donors. Include a reply card that donors can return if they are interested in additional information. Those individuals inquiring about this type of giving should receive information as soon as possible with a follow-up call from you. To do timely follow-up, it is best to plan several smaller mailings rather than one large mailing so that time is available to follow-up on each inquiry.

> Using regular or special publications does not prevent you from using direct mail as well.

Telephone Follow-up

Personal outreach is very important in planned giving. You can determine a prospective donor's needs and priorities by speaking to them. Exhibit 15–8 describes a follow-up call to a prospective donor (fictionally named Mrs. Hansen) ten days after sending her a booklet on wills that she requested after receiving a planned giving mailing.

You will come across a number of objections when you make your follow-up calls. Remember, do not take these objections personally. The best offense is to have several responses prepared to deal with the most common objections. For example, if the objection is, "I re-

Exhibit 15–5 Planned Giving Prospect Evaluation Form

                                                   _____

                                                   last name

Title and full name of prospect: _____

Prefers to be known as: _____

Home address: _____

City, state, ZIP code: _____

Home telephone number: (   ) _____-_____

Salutation on correspondence: Dear: _____

Birth date:

                         _____ _____ _____
                         month   day   year

Spouse's title and full name: _____

Spouse prefers to be known as: _____

Salutation on correspondence: Dear: _____

Birth date:

                         _____ _____ _____
                         month   day   year

Names and ages of children: _____

Names of our board members or
administrators who are personally
acquainted with prospect and/or spouse: _____

Name of firm for which prospect works: _____

Position or title with this firm: _____

If no children, who are likely heirs: _____

Financial data: Estimated Net Worth: $_____ Estimated Annual Income: $ _____

Prospect's attorney and phone number: _____ _____

Prospect's CPA or CFP and phone number: _____ _____

Source: Reprinted with permission from D. Barnes, *National Fund Raiser*, Vol. 19, no. 5, March 1993, Barnes Associates.

---

ceived the booklet I requested but I haven't read it yet," your response could be, "It would be most helpful to me if when you read the booklet you note how it's written. Do you like the style? Are the examples clear? Do you have any suggestions on how we might improve it?"

Usually the donor will agree to do that, which allows you to set up a future time to call back. If the objection is, "I just asked for the booklet because I like to stay current on these matters," your response could be, "That's a good idea with all the changes taking place.

We will keep you on our mailing list and I will check in with you from time to time to see if some of the ideas might relate to you."

The most delicate type of objection to overcome is the one expressed by the donor who has spoken to his or her attorney about the gift, and the attorney advises against it. Offer to speak to the attorney to clarify any issues he or she may have, but be careful not to put the attorney in a negative light as you know the donor trusts his or her counsel.

Exhibit 15–6 Sample Advertisement

THE MOOERS SOCIETY

DEFERRED GIFT ANNUITY:

A contribution today that gives you an income tomorrow

A charitable gift annuity is an attractive gift vehicle for WCL alumni and an easy way to support the law school. A gift annuity—income from which is deferred for a period of years—can be a useful retirement planning device. Such a gift provides

- a guaranteed, fixed income for your lifetime
- an income tax deduction in the year the gift is made
- partially tax-free income
- avoidance of capital gains taxes
- a safe and secure investment opportunity

What really makes a deferred gift annuity appealing, however, is a rate of return higher than that of an immediate payment gift annuity. The longer you defer receiving income payments, the larger the income will be.

The income benefits and charitable deductions for a $10,000 deferred annuity would be as follows:

Current Age	#Years before Payment Begins	Rate of Return	Tax Deduction
50	15	13.5%	$6,200
55	10	10.5%	$5,705
60	5	8.1%	$5,096
65	5	8.5%	$5,632
70	5	9.5%	$6,050

If you are interested in an illustration of a deferred gift annuity for your personal situation, please send the birthdate(s) of the beneficiary(ies) and the amount of gift (minimum $10,000) to the WCL Development Office, American University, Washington College of Law, Suite 373, 4801 Massachusetts Avenue, N.W., Washington, D.C. 20016, (202) 274-4051. The law school will provide you with an illustration of your tax deduction and annuity income payments.

Source: Reprinted with permission from *the Advocate,* Fall 1994, American University, Washington College of Law.

Personal Visit

As was covered in Chapter 9 on major gift fund raising, you establish a relationship with a donor through a combination of telephone calls and personal visits over a period of time. Meeting with prospective donors will help you continue your information-gathering about their specific needs and priorities. Once a donor has expressed an interest in pursuing some type of planned gift, it is important to learn more about his or her personal circumstances. Always assure the donor that any personal information will remain confidential and is needed only to guide them in selecting the type of gift that best suits his or her needs.

One way to start this discussion would be to say, "I'm not trying to pry, Mr. X, but there is some information I'll need that will help me in suggesting some of the best ways to make your gift." Information you will need includes date of birth and, depending on the type and size of gift you are discussing, tax bracket, types of assets to be used in making the gift, income tax deduction needed, whether gift will be outright or life income, and name and age of beneficiary. More specific questions follow as a natural outgrowth of the conversation.

Keep in mind that you are working with those who have donated to your organization and they are interested in continuing to support it. Your role is to help them do it in a way that benefits them and the organization.

Exhibit 15–9 lists types of specific information that should be gathered for each planned giving prospect to assist in the individual's solicitation.

Exhibit 15–10 is a form for recording the results of a prospect contact.

Exhibit 15–7 Business Reply Envelope Sample Text

The Role of Volunteers

Considering another type of gift?

___I have included the Washington College of Law in my will or estate plans.

___Please send information about including a bequest in my will.

___Please send information about gifts to WCL that provide life or deferred income.

Courtesy of American University, Washington College of Law.

Just as in the other types of fund raising we have covered in this book, there is a role for volunteers in planned giving. The planned giving committee may be made up of members of the board or development committee or could be key volunteers and professionals from the community who would help strengthen the planned giving program. The committee chair probably should be a board member. However, consider the following list of individuals who could serve on this committee:

- Attorneys (estate planning practitioners)
- Trust officers
- Certified public accountants

Exhibit 15–8 Sample Follow-Up Call

Staff:	Good morning, Mrs. Hansen. This is Jane Smith with XYZ. How are you this morning?
Mrs. H:	Quite well, thank you.
Staff:	Mrs. Hansen, I'm calling you this morning for two reasons. First, I want to thank you for your generous support of XYZ. Because of you we are able to continue . . . . . (give an example of how gift will be used). We want you to know how much we appreciate it.
Mrs. H:	Well, I'm just glad I can do it.
Staff:	May I ask, Mrs. Hansen, how you became interested in XYZ? What prompted you to make your gift? (Commonly asked by nonprofit organizations which are not schools, or perhaps hospitals.)
Mrs. H:	I've always been interested in . . . . and heard about the work you're doing in that area.
Staff:	That leads me, Mrs. Hansen, to the second reason for my call. You said you are interested in the work we do, and your request for our recent publication on wills tells me you are interested in that as well. Would you mind telling me if there is anything in particular that prompted you to request that information?
Mrs. H:	Well, you hear so much these days about wills, trusts, and estate planning, I thought I'd better do a little reading on my own.
Staff:	That is a wise decision, Mrs. Hansen, and I'd like to help you, if I may. The information we sent was very general in nature. I would be happy to send you more specific information on the subject of estate planning or even stop by for a visit. Sometimes these matters are better discussed in person rather than over the phone.
Mrs. H:	Oh, a visit won't be necessary. Just send me something in the mail on trusts. You hear so much about them these days.
Staff:	I'll be happy to do that. I'll call you to answer any questions you may have or please feel free to call me if I don't get back to you soon enough. Thank you again, Mrs. Hansen. I look forward to speaking with you soon.

Other fact-finding questions that could be included are the following:

- Have you always lived in (city)?
- When was the last time you were in (location of XYZ)?
- If you plan to be in the area again, please give me a call or stop by for a visit. I'd enjoy meeting you and showing you some of the things your gifts have made possible.
- Does your family live in the area?

Exhibit 15–9 Prospect Information Checklist

The prospect:

- Has a will
- Does not have a will
- Owns primary residence
- Owns land or other residences
- Owns stock
- Owns closely held stock
- Owns life insurance

- Is retired or close to retirement
- Is living on fixed income
- Has independent income
- Inherited family wealth
- Has children who are provided for
- Has art or antiques
- Has obligation to grandchildren

Other:

Exhibit 15–10 Planned Giving Prospect Contact Record, Results

_____ last name

____ bequest

____ charitable remainder unitrust

____ life estate

____ charitable gift annuity

____ charitable lead trust

____ life insurance

____ charitable remainder annuity

____ pooled income

____ deferred gift annuity

____ outright gift of: _____

_____

_____

____ other: _____

	Month Date Year	Notes/Results
How was first contact made:	___ ___ ___	_____
What was follow-up to first contact?	___ ___ ___	_____
Follow-up:	___ ___ ___	_____
Follow-up:	___ ___ ___	_____
Follow-up:	___ ___ ___	_____
		_____
		_____
		_____
		_____
		_____

Source: Reprinted with permission from D. Barnes, _National Fund Raiser_, Vol. 19, no. 5, March 1993, Barnes Associates.

- Certified financial planners
- Certified life underwriters
- Real estate brokers
- Stock brokers
- Major donors
- Corporate executives

Each member of the committee needs to have a basic understanding of and commitment to planned giving.

Earlier in the chapter we outlined the steps involved in establishing a planned giving program. A planned giving committee will play an active role in helping the organization through these steps. One of the first tasks will be to develop a policy paper establishing the planned giving program guidelines. Subject to board approval, the paper will outline the scope of the program by prioritizing which gift vehicles will be implemented, define the processing procedure, and review the approval process for accepting such gifts. Input from this committee will help develop the multi-year marketing plan.

The planned giving committee should meet regularly to help accomplish the following:

- Provide names of individuals for the prospect list who should be cultivated
- Discuss and plan strategy for selected prospects
- Help provide personal and financial data on prospects without violating the prospects' confidence or any code of ethics
- Help prepare individualized proposals for selected prospects
- Review proposed gifts for acceptability
- Periodically review program's results in comparison to goals and objectives

The Bequest Society—The Simplest Way to Begin

You may be thinking now that planned giving is just too technical an area for you or your organization to pursue. Remember, a planned giving program can be implemented in stages beginning with simply asking your donors to include your organization in their wills and estates. Statistics show that 80 percent of the money raised through planned giving comes from bequests. The best way to solicit bequests is to invite donors to join a special recognition group or society. Many organizations often are surprised when they receive a bequest because they never knew it existed. By honoring those donors

> A planned giving program can be implemented in stages beginning with simply asking your donors to include your organization in their wills.

who have included the organization in their wills now, the organization can show its appreciation to the donors during their lifetime. Many benefits beyond the bequest can be realized by the organization through creating a bequest or legacy society today.

When creating a bequest society, do not spend too much time coming up with a creative name. Often there is an individual or family who has made a significant contribution to your organization whom you would like to honor in this way. At the Washington College of Law, American University, the Mooers Society is named after a much loved and respected alumnus and teacher, Dr. Edwin A. Mooers, class of 1914, whose involvement with the school spanned more than fifty years and continues to be carried on by his son, Edwin A. Mooers, Jr., class of 1941, also a former faculty member. If no individual or family comes to mind, commonly used names such as Heritage Society or Founder's Club can be just as successful in promoting planned giving.

The Gamma Phi Beta Sorority, whose international headquarters is in Englewood, Colorado, created a bequest society to honor all sorority members and friends who make gifts to Gamma Phi Beta's future through planned gifts. This special recognition society, the Tau Epsilon Pi Society, takes its name from the sorority's Greek open motto, *Tethemeliemenae Epi Petran*— Founded Upon A Rock. The sorority promotes its planned giving program by promoting this name. They declare that planned gifts are vital to the future of the sorority and to maintaining its tradition of excellence—the future of the Sorority can truly be "Founded Upon A Rock."

Once established, a bequest society gives you an excellent opportunity to communicate regularly with this special group of donors. These donors should receive regular publications and information about your organization. Sending them special mailings about planned giving and tax issues is also important. Remember to keep this group of donors updated on the mission of your organization and how their continued support makes a difference because this will be key to your organization remaining in their will.

Membership in this society should be as inclusive as possible. Include all donors who have informed you that your organization is in their will or estate plans, as well as individuals who have made one of the other types of planned gifts. Request copies of their wills or those portions that pertain to your organization for your files. Most of these gifts are revocable, which means the donor can change his or her mind in the future. List the members of this group as you would those of any of your other gift clubs.

Develop a special newsletter for the group if your budget allows. Use this as a marketing piece for other prospective members. Use regular publications such as the newsletter, annual report, or magazine to highlight society members and the activities of the group. Provide a sample of what language the donor should use when including your organization in his or her will, such as that listed in Exhibit 15–11, in appropriate publications.

Annual events such as luncheons, receptions, and other special events sponsored by the society are desirable benefits of bequest society membership, in addition to donor recognition. The type and number of events will depend on the size of your organization. An annual luncheon or tea is a wonderful way to show your appreciation to this group and keep them updated on the activities of the organization. Remember to invite bequest society members to other organization-wide events throughout the year so they can continue to see what the organization is doing and so others can meet the donors who are ensuring the organization's future. Your bequest society is the key to a regular planned giving awareness program. Bequests will be the most common type of gift to promote to donors, but other planned gift vehicles also can be incorporated over time.

How Planned Giving Fits into a Major Gifts Program

In the past, organizations of varying size and type have maintained separate efforts for major and planned gifts. This often creates an adversarial relationship between major gift officers and planned giving officers. The fundraising climate today is more competitive than ever. As a result, some organizations are rethinking the divisions between these two areas and are developing a "gift planning" philosophy, which brings major gift and planned giving staff together as a team.

In this new relationship, the major gift officer becomes familiar with the concepts of planned giving so that this information can be shared during meetings with donors who are unable to make outright gifts. He or she then involves the planned giving officer in developing a strategy that allows for the information-gathering necessary to determine which gift vehicle meets the donor's needs. The planned giving officer will assist in preparing gift proposals for use in solicitations or accompanies the major gift officer on the visit.

In turn, the planned giving officer must prioritize the tasks usually performed to allow for time to work with the major gift officer. One way is to develop better stewardship methods for the donors who give small, life income gifts, which will result in more free time for the planned giving officer. Another way is to streamline procedures used to follow-up general inquiries so that the planned giving officer is not spending as much time with people whose gift potential is in the $5,000 to $10,000 range. In general, the planned giving officer needs to spend more time with those individuals who are identified as major gift prospects.

This philosophy of including planned giving within major gifts programs is being espoused by many leaders in the planned giving field. In an article written for *Fund Raising Management* (1994), G. Roger Schoenhals urges readers to re-evaluate their development programs and place planned giving in a more prominent position. He explains that one future trend is defining the term "planned giving" to not only include deferred gifts but also any charitable gift that is considered in relation to someone's overall estate plan. Robert F. Sharpe, Sr., principal of a well-known planned giving consulting firm, is cited in that same article as saying that the wave of the future is to include estate planning in major gifts programs. He defines charitable estate planning as "estate planning which includes the planner's desire to make current and deferred gifts to charity(ies)."

For more information about planned giving, see *Planned Giving Essentials: A Step by Step Guide to Success*, by Richard D. Barrett and Molly E. Ware, another book in this series.

Exhibit 15–11 Sample of Language to Include XYZ in Your Will

Outright Bequests

I give, devise, and bequeath to XYZ (legal name should be provided), a tax-exempt organization, located at _____ , the sum of $ _____ or percentage of, (cash, real or personal property herein described) to be used for the general purpose of XYZ at the discretion of its board of directors.

Bequests for a Specific Purpose

I give, devise, and bequeath to XYZ (legal name should be provided), a tax-exempt organization, located at _____ , the sum of $ _____ or percentage of, (cash, real or personal property herein described) for the purpose of _____.

Reference

Schoenhals, G.R. 1994. Gearing up for the twenty-first century. *Fund Raising Management* (March).

Appendix 15–A
Case Study: Planned Giving

Several years ago, in a large Eastern seaboard city, there was a 501(c)(3) organization, about forty years old, that specialized in a rather esoteric form of language education. I was the director of development.

Some of the founding board members still sat in governance. One, a teacher in a midwestern state university, had created a charitable remainder unitrust for the organization some years earlier, on the condition that her identity always remain hidden. The other board members and I knew her identity but continued to reference her as "Ms. Anonymous."

During four decades, no one, except Ms. Anonymous, had given a thought to endowment-building. Yet, the esoteric language they fostered was growing in popularity and application. Not only was it used increasingly in the arts and in medicine, but even the CIA was exploring it as a surveillance tool. So, the organization needed to grow and stabilize.

Suddenly, there arose a *capital* need: the lease was about to expire; the options were to stay and renovate or to move with no place to go.

The board was distressed. They knew that they could not borrow the *whole* $150,000 for renovation from a bank. They could not raise it from normal sources on short notice, especially since we had just raised $500,000 from the major foundations for another major emergency project. It seemed that there were no solutions at hand.

At the board meeting, I explained that I was in an experimental course in deferred giving for mid-career professionals at the university, and it seemed that this problem might well be addressed as a class project. We have been exploring the efficacy of making loans to charities that were remaindermen of charitable remainder trusts anyway.

The board was delighted to contemplate a solution. How much could we obtain as a loan? How soon might we act? Must we pay it back, since we are the charitable remainderman? What's the interest rate? Are we personally liable? If we receive a loan of $100,000 on the charitable remainder trust, we think that we can raise the other $50,000.

Ms. Anonymous looked at me and *knew* that she was the solution I envisioned. Later, in private, she agreed. She knew that her charitable remainder unitrust trust had grown from $250,000 to $300,000 and that it would serve well as the basis of a $100,000 loan, the size of which the organization needed. She really did not *need* the 8% interest she was receiving annually; so she could afford to participate in an experiment to create the first such revolving loan for a charity. She cared about the organization and committed her help by agreeing to renounce her anonymity and work with the court to collapse her trust and reconstruct it with the loan language in place.

Ultimately, I worked with my teachers and lawyers, an enormous brokerage house, a major national accounting house, an actuarial firm, the SEC, the IRS, and many other agencies, and eleven months later, with thirty-one financial professionals on the telephone line with me, we called up on a computer monitor at the brokerage house a credit line of $100,000 for the organization. It was a checking account against which the organization could write the capital improvement checks it needed.

Several conflicts ensued. I defended the fiduciary responsibility of the organization's board by curbing the investment house's inclination to loan out 90 percent of the corpus of the trust. I insisted that both sides observe a 30 percent maximum. The investment company said, "You don't have to pay it back. After all, we can collect the trust corpus as collateral upon the death of Ms. Anonymous." I said, "You *will* pay the loan back in ten years, to restore the corpus for the organization."

Both sides won. The charity got the loan of needed capital renovation funds and paid them back on a schedule that it could afford without destroying the integrity of the charitable remainder trust. The credit remained as a revolving line for the future. The investment house got a new product to sell to its nonprofit organization section. The donor had the pleasure of helping her favorite organization twice instead of once. I facilitated a major change for the fund-raising field and got an "A" for the course.

Courtesy of Beverly Hoffmann, President and CEO, Center for Social and Economic Leadership.

Chapter 16
Working with Consultants: Hiring and Using Consultants in Your Fund-Raising Programs

Chapter Outline

- Determining the Need for a Consultant
- What Consultants Can Offer to a Development Operation
- How to Convince Your Board and Staff to Use a Consultant
- What to Expect from a Consultant
- How to Find a Consultant Who Can Work with You
- How to Hire a Consultant
- How to Develop Trust with a Consultant
- Determining the Amount to Pay Consultants
- The Contract
- Evaluating the Work of a Consultant
- Employee or Consultant According to the IRS

Key Vocabulary

- American Association of Fund-Raising Counsel (AAFRC)
- Fund-Raising Consultant
- Paid Solicitor

Determining the Need for a Consultant

Inevitably, at some point in a development officer's career, he or she will need to or want to employ a consult-

> At some point in a development officer's career, he or she will need to employ a consultant.

ant to do the following: provide advice or consultation on an issue; actively steer a campaign; motivate a board; or provide needed expertise in some areas. Some of the best and most experienced development officers employ consultants on a regular basis. This does not mean that these officers are having fund-raising difficulties or do not know their business. Instead, it may be more cost effective to use a short-term consultant rather than adding permanent staff to the payroll. Or, it may be that board members or other volunteers need

specific specialized training, something the development officer cannot do or does not know as well as a consultant.

Individual consultants and consulting firms are hired to provide a variety of specialized services. In fact, an organization may use several firms at one time. One firm may produce an organization's special events, another firm may conduct the capital campaign, another may provide computer expertise, and another may provide strategic planning or board training. The use of consultants is increasing, and fund-raising consultants have matured just as their field has.

There are many reasons to consider when hiring a professional fund-raising consultant. It is important for the organization to know the difference between a fund-raising consultant and a paid solicitor. A fund-raising consultant will not solicit or retain custody of the organization's contributions. A paid solicitor or solicitation firm that is employed to solicit contributions for a charity may have possession of the contributions before turning the money over to the organization. Many telemarketing firms work in this manner. Most states require paid solicitors to post bond before rendering their services. If a consultant is needed, most nonprofit organizations will want to hire the fund-raising consultant and not the paid solicitor.

But first, question if there is a need for a consultant at all. Ask yourself the following questions: What can a consultant do for me—generally and specifically? Do I need general advice about or specific assistance on a project? Should I use a large or small consulting firm or an individual contractor? How much will I have to pay a consultant? Should I pay by the project or by the hour? How do I set priorities, goals, and objectives for the person or persons, and will I know how to evaluate the work produced by the consultant?

What Consultants Can Offer to a Development Operation

Let's answer the basic questions first. What does a consultant do? Consultants bring a level of wisdom, expertise, and creativity to a fund-raising effort. They may provide staff and board training, or strategic guidance to a capital campaign. They can furnish a sense of objectivity and candor, and they *assist* you in raising money—*they do not raise it for you.*

According to Rutter (1994), "Fundraising consultants do not solicit funds for organizations in large part because of donor perception. Donors want a relationship with the cause they are considering helping rather than communication with a paid representative of the organization. Therefore, consultants manage the behind-the-scenes aspects of fund-raising campaigns, developing plans, surveying prospects, organizing committees, designing marketing strategies, and training volunteer leaders."

Michael Y. Walters (1996) states there are some considerable things a consultant or consulting firm can bring to the table for a nonprofit organization (Exhibit 16–1).

How to Convince Your Board and Staff to Use a Consultant

Often it is a member of the board who suggests bringing in a consultant to assist with a particular project or campaign. Staff should not feel threatened by this suggestion, because consultants can provide a fresh perspective to a department that may be mired in its day-to-day operations. The familiar phrase of "not being able to see the forest through the trees" often can apply to any staff. A consultant can relate issues to the senior management or board that staff cannot. Instead of fighting the prospect or opportunity of hiring a consultant, embrace it. Be glad that the board is open to using a consultant and begin the search for the right consultant for the organization.

If board members need to be convinced that a consultant would be beneficial to their fund-raising efforts,

---

Exhibit 16–1 Contributions of Fund-Raising Consultants

- **Experience**
  This can be especially helpful for an organization with a new or young development program. Even in instances when a nonprofit organization has a chief development officer with considerable experience, the development officer and his or her staff may lack experience in a specific program or area of development.
- **Objectivity**
  Frequently, development programs, even comparatively sophisticated programs, need an experienced outside observer whose viewpoint is not influenced by internal institutional politics or other considerations. Often, simply a fresh point of view is required.
  Objectivity is good in the creation and management of a capital campaign, but is particularly important when the organization is having a "development program audit."
- **Focus**
  This is especially important in a capital campaign. There is a clear distinction between the mind set that is "development" in approach and that which is "campaign" in approach. A development officer must keep the long-term future of the organization and its development programs in mind, whereas the campaign consultant focuses everyone's attention to the matter at hand.
  A campaign has an established time frame and a goal that must be met within the time allotted. Therefore, the consultant will keep the group's attention focused on the campaign process—as distinct from other details of a development operation.
  Regular development operations focus on the cultivation of the gift for the long-term enrichment of the insti-

tution. A campaign requires a clear sense of urgency to meet a specific goal. Therefore, the consultant's job is to "hold everyone's feet to the fire," including the board and campaign committee, a task frequently outside the staff's capability.
  It is almost always necessary to create a group that is separate from the organization's board to oversee the operations of a campaign. The board may be concerned about facility maintenance, bonding, staff salaries, endowment management, etc. The campaign steering committee focuses on the operation and structuring of the effort at hand. A consultant can be decisive in selecting and organizing the best available committee from among a group's many constituencies.
- **Prospect Research**
  Few consulting firms will match large university development programs with staff and resources devoted to an established long-term research program. But, a good consulting firm will make a commitment to research resources to which most organizations, except for the larger ones, will not have access. Also, a consulting firm's research resources will cover a wider variety of data and sources than the in-house programs of even the largest universities.
- **Breadth of Staff Resources**
  Staff of most consulting firms include several individuals with particular expertise. Although a particular skill may not be required for the entire course of a campaign, an individual with a critical skill can be brought aboard on an *ad hoc* basis, without requiring the institution to make a long-term commitment to new staff.

Source: Data from Michael Y. Walters, Senior Fundraising Consultant, Community Counselling Services, Inc., New York, NY, 1996.

---

remind them that a consultant also would provide valuable training for the current staff in areas that it may lack expertise, as well as for the board. Even though the consultant eventually will leave, the knowledge will stay behind. This is one of the major benefits of hiring a fundraising consultant.

But keep in mind that there can be some negatives when working with consultants. If an organization hires only consultants or a consulting firm to do its fund raising without permanent staff, it will lose any sense of history when the contract is completed. Organizations need to be cautious about staffing a campaign entirely with consultants. Although many tasks such as proposal writing, data entry, event coordination, or public relations all can be handled by consultants, will it be in the best interest of the organization over the long run? After the consulting firm leaves, who will be trained to carry on with the work? Relationships developed with the volunteers and members may disappear when the consulting team departs. If permanent staff is used alongside the consulting team, then some permanent bonding may occur, with new relationships developing or old ones strengthening.

> Organizations need to be cautious about staffing a campaign entirely with consultants.

What to Expect from a Consultant

Before any work begins, a written proposal should be submitted. Be sure that it includes the scope of work for which the consultant will be paid, what tasks will be performed for that fee, and on what dates they are to be completed. Spell out clearly who is responsible for incidentals such as postage, printing, mileage, etc. In addition, references including telephone numbers should be listed. Call all references listed and ask for more if necessary. Agree upon a fee, and sign a contract before any work begins.

When hiring a consultant, look for qualities that complement the organization. The person or firm should meet the standards set by the organization. Seek a professional who can represent the organization well. Find someone who is able to mix well with the staff, who is experienced and knowledgeable, who is a specialist in the area in which the organization seeks help, who has a good ability to present materials at all staff and volunteer levels, who is a good writer and communicator, and who is able to devote the full amount of time needed for the tasks at hand. Remember to seek a fund-raising consultant, not someone who just solicits money for your cause—there is a difference between the two.

How to Find a Consultant Who Can Work with You

Your first inclination when hiring a consultant may be to hire the person or firm that a board member recommends. Another potential mistake is hiring someone that looks and sounds like you, with whom you feel comfortable. Don't forget that what you are seeking is expertise, not necessarily a friend, buddy, or clone! The consultant may need to play the role of the "tough-guy," the person who has to say "no" to board members, the person who has to "insist" that schedules be met during a campaign. If he or she is too close to you, or a friend of a member of the board, an important dynamic can be lost—that of separation. The consultant needs to be free to tell you what you "need to know," not "what you would like to hear!"

Again, the best way to find a consultant that fits your and your organization's comfort level is to ask development staff members in other organizations similar to yours what consultants they have used and if they would recommend them.

"YOUR CAMPAIGN IS IN SERIOUS TROUBLE WHEN THE CHAIRMAN'S PRIMARY CONCERN IS RENAMING THE GIFT CLUBS AFTER HIS GRANDCHILDREN."

Source: © Mark Litzler

How to Hire a Consultant

There are at least sixty major consulting firms in the United States, with each major city having at least that many independent consultants who operate solely, apart from a firm. How do you know where to find a consultant or consulting firm? You first may want to contact the American Association of Fund-Raising Counsel (AAFRC), the professional association of fund-raising consultants. Independent consultants likely will be members of the National Society of Fund Raising Executives (NSFRE). Both of these organizations require that their members adhere to a code of ethics.

Before hiring any consultant, at least three competitive bids should be received and reviewed. Previous and current references should be included in bids. Call these references before meeting with the consultant and ask them detailed questions concerning the work that the consultant did for them. Did the consultant complete the work on time, within budget, and successfully? Would you rehire the consultant? Would you recommend the consultant to others?

When working with larger consulting firms, there may be a clause in the contract that prevents the organization from permanently hiring any person who at the time of the contract was employed by the consulting group or any of its affiliates. This prevents organizations from hiring account executives from the consulting group without giving some sort of remuneration to the group.

It is recommended that an organization not use an open-ended contract to hire a consultant. There always should be a cancellation clause—the ability to terminate the contract. Any contract should be reviewed by legal counsel. Fees and reimbursable expenses should be spelled out in detail in the contract.

Before you sign a contract with a consultant or firm, there are six areas you should consider. They are listed in Exhibit 16–2.

How to Develop Trust with a Consultant

By clearly stating up front what is expected from the consultant or the consulting firm, much of the anxiety of both sides can be alleviated. Regular meetings with the consultant allows monitoring of the consultant's progress without presenting the "feeling" of too much supervision. Expect expertise, assistance, advice, and knowledge from the consultant in addition to quality workmanship. Treat the consultant with respect and fairness. Don't try to add on work that was not in the original contract. If more work is needed and expected, then add a rider to the contract spelling out the additional work and the additional fee. Treat the consultant as you would want to be treated. They will then trust you and you will trust them.

Exhibit 16–2 Areas to Consider When Hiring a Consultant

1. Talk with a variety of other organizations. They will be glad to share their experiences and make recommendations.
2. Talk with several firms. Initial consultations are free. Ask every question you can think of, and make sure you understand how the firm interacts with clients in providing the kinds of services you want.
3. Ask the firms that interest you for a list of five to seven other clients they have served in the last few years, and call them. Ask the clients the following questions: "Was the firm responsive when you had questions or needed help? Were the budgets reasonable? Were they close to initial estimates and, if not, were there good reasons for the divergence? Were there any problems and if so, exactly what were they?
4. Get proposals from several firms, spelling out what they will do, their fees, and the estimated budget for additional costs. Although none can guarantee their results, find what they think you can raise and the basis for their projection.
5. Before you sign, have a frank and thorough discussion with the firm about your goals and expectations. Are they realistic? Because this is the yardstick by which you will measure the firm and the campaign's success, a mutual understanding is important. Also, make sure you know what is expected of your organization to help make the effort a success.
6. Finally, have your lawyer review the proposed contract—but not just for legal problems. Make sure he or she understands exactly how you perceive the relationship, your commitments, and what the firm will do, and that the contract reflects your understanding.

Source: Reprinted with permission. Copyright, 1979, *Insight*, a solicitations review newsletter, published by Council of Better Business Bureaus, Inc., 4200 Wilson Blvd., Suite 800, Arlington, VA, 22203-1804.

Determining the Amount to Pay Consultants

Consulting fees vary depending on the size of the project or campaign and what the consultant thinks that the organization can pay. Fees usually cover the cost of the people involved, travel and living expenses, telephone, fax reproductions, copies, etc. Never allow the fees to be based upon the goal of the campaign or a percentage of the development office's budget. Fees should be based upon the services

> Never allow the fee to be based upon the goal of the campaign or a percentage of the development office's budget.

provided to the organization. Also, never allow the fund-raising firm to hold any of the funds being raised for the organization. Most established firms will have a schedule for billing professional fees. Compare the fees of the persons or firms that the organization has asked to submit bids. Are they in line with one another? If so, then look at the other areas of importance when deciding a contract and know that it will not be the money that decides the selection.

It is suggested that three bids be obtained for each project being undertaken. Any more than this can be counter-productive—more of your time is taken up in interviews than in getting the project completed. It is not necessarily the wisest choice to choose the lowest bid. Consider all aspects of the proposal and select the bid best suited to the organization and the work to be accomplished.

It is best to hire a consultant for a specific fee to cover specific duties. NSFRE discourages organizations from hiring consultants who work on a percentage basis. This does not meet their code of ethics for professional fund raisers. In their Code of Ethical Principles and Standards of Professional Practice (Exhibit 16–3), it states: "Members shall work for a salary or fee, not percentage-based compensation or a commission," and "Members may accept performance-based compensation such as bonuses provided that such bonuses are in accord with prevailing practices within the members' own organizations and are not based on a percentage of philanthropic funds raised."

Beware of the consultant who suggests an open-ended fee. It may be the invitation to paying open-ended bills. Ask for a proposal with a set fee for a specific scope of work. Also beware of the consultant who asks for a large advance. One month's fee or a quarter of the cost of the project up-front is acceptable. Establish a payment schedule up-front that is acceptable to both parties.

The Contract

All major agreements between a client and a firm should be put in writing to avoid any problems based on misunderstanding. It is important for the client to understand what the firm is capable of doing for the organization and at what price and, it is equally important for the consulting firm to understand what the client (1) expects, (2) wishes to keep in its own control, (3) wants to have reported and at what intervals, (4) expects to be charged, etc. All contracts should include some basics that protect both the client and the consulting firm. These basics are covered in the following.

> All major agreements between a client and a firm should be in writing.

Fees and Expenses

The consulting firm must list all of its fees and expenses that it expects to charge. This may mean developing a detailed budget for the assignment for the client's review. Other projects may be detailed by task with one sum covering all of the work to be performed. Then, if additional expenses occur during the course of the contract, the expenses must be agreed upon before being incurred. A provision should be included that will address this issue. For example, before an expense can be incurred that is not already included in the agreed upon budget, the client and firm must both "sign off" on it. Flexibility must be built into a contract because it is impossible to know exactly every charge that will occur. The important point to keep in mind is that there must be open communication between the client and the firm. A consultant should never spend money that has not been agreed upon in advance!

As important as agreeing upon the price to pay is agreeing upon the method of payment. After obtaining competitive bids, selecting a firm, and agreeing upon a price, next negotiate the type of payment structure. Will the money for the work to be done be paid in advance? Will it be paid monthly, quarterly, or at the end of the contract? How will bills from other vendors be paid? Should these bills be given directly to the organization or go through the consulting firm first? All of these items should be discussed and placed in the contract. Make sure that whether the consulting firm can receive any mark-up on these outside contracts is discussed and agreed upon in advance. For example, if consulting firms have accounts with supplies stores, caterers, or printers, should their discounted prices be passed along to the client? Ask these questions before the contract is signed, not after.

Services

Spell out clearly what services will be provided by the consultant or firm, when they will be provided, and what happens if they are not provided on time. Also, clearly state what the obligations are of the organization hiring the consulting services. For example, if the firm is providing design work for a piece to be printed, will the client or the firm own the art work after the project is completed? This is particularly important if additional work is to be done at a future time with the same art work. Resolve up-front who "owns" the art.

Determine ahead how many staff members will be assigned to the contract and where they will work. If the consulting staff is responsible for written materials, determine who on the organization's staff will be responsible for sign-off tasks. Never allow any materials to be distributed or printed without the approval of the client. The client must have control of what is being said, how it is being said, and the frequency of the message being disseminated.

NSFRE Code of Ethical Principles and Standards of Professional Practice

Statements of Ethical Principles
Adopted November 1991

The National Society of Fund Raising Executives exists to foster the development and growth of fund-raising professionals and the profession, to preserve and enhance philanthropy and volunteerism, and to promote high ethical standards in the fund-raising profession.

To these ends, this code declares the ethical values and standards of professional practice which NSFRE members embrace and which they strive to uphold in their responsibilities for generating philanthropic support.

Members of the National Society of Fund Raising Executives are motivated by an inner drive to improve the quality of life through the causes they serve. They seek to inspire others through their own sense of dedication and high purpose. They are committed to the improvement of their professional knowledge and skills in order that their performance will better serve others. They recognize their stewardship responsibility to ensure that needed resources are vigorously and ethically sought and that the intent of the donor is honestly fulfilled. Such individuals practice their profession with integrity, honesty, truthfulness and adherence to the absolute obligation to safeguard the public trust.

Furthermore, NSFRE members

- serve the ideal of philanthropy, are committed to the preservation and enhancement of volunteerism, and hold stewardship of these concepts as the overriding principle of professional life;
- put charitable mission above personal gain, accepting compensation by salary or set fee only;
- foster cultural diversity and pluralistic values and treat all people with dignity and respect;
- affirm, through personal giving, a commitment to philanthropy and its role in society;
- adhere to the spirit as well as the letter of all applicable laws and regulations;
- bring credit to the fund-raising profession by their public demeanor;
- recognize their individual boundaries of competence and are forthcoming about their professional qualifications and credentials;
- value the privacy, freedom of choice, and interests of all those affected by their actions;
- disclose all relationships which might constitute, or appear to constitute, conflicts of interest;
- actively encourage all their colleagues to embrace and practice these ethical principles;
- adhere to the following standards of professional practice in their responsibilities for generating philanthropic support.

Standards of Professional Practice
Adopted and incorporated into the NSFRE Code of Ethical Principles November 1992

1. Members shall act according to the highest standards and visions of their institution, profession, and conscience.
2. Members shall avoid even the appearance of any criminal offense or professional misconduct.
3. Members shall be responsible for advocating, within their own organizations, adherence to all applicable laws and regulations.
4. Members shall work for a salary or fee, not percentage-based compensation or a commission.
5. Members may accept performance-based compensation such as bonuses provided that such bonuses are in accord with prevailing practices within the members' own organizations and are not based on a percentage of philanthropic funds raised.
6. Members shall neither seek nor accept finder's fees and shall, to the best of their ability, discourage their organizations from paying such fees.
7. Members shall effectively disclose all conflicts of interest; such disclosure does not preclude or imply ethical impropriety.
8. Members shall accurately state their professional experience, qualifications, and expertise.
9. Members shall adhere to the principle that all donor and prospect information created by, or on behalf of, an institution is the property of that institution and shall not be transferred or utilized except on behalf of that institution.
10. Members shall, on a scheduled basis, give donors the opportunity to have their names removed from lists which are sold to, rented to, or exchanged with other organizations.
11. Members shall not disclose privileged information to unauthorized parties.
12. Members shall keep constituent information confidential.
13. Members shall take care to ensure that all solicitation materials are accurate and correctly reflect the organization's mission and use of solicited funds.
14. Members shall, to the best of their ability, ensure that contributions are used in accordance with donors' intentions.
15. Members shall ensure, to the best of their ability, proper stewardship of charitable contributions, including timely reporting on the use and management of funds and explicit consent by the donor before altering the conditions of a gift.
16. Members shall ensure, to the best of their ability, that donors receive informed and ethical advice about the value and tax implications of potential gifts.
17. Member's actions shall reflect concern for the interests and well-being of individuals affected by those actions. Members shall not exploit any relationship with a donor, prospect, volunteer, or employee to the benefit of the member or the member's organization.
18. In stating fund-raising results, members shall use accurate and consistent accounting methods that conform to the appropriate guidelines adopted by the American Institute of Certified Public Accountants (AICPA)* for the type of institution involved. (* In countries outside of the United States, comparable authority should be utilized.)
19. All of the above notwithstanding, members shall comply with all applicable local, state, provincial, and federal civil and criminal law.

Amended: March, 1993; October, 1994

Courtesy of the National Society of Fund Raising Executives, Alexandria, Virginia.

Termination Clause

Always build a cancellation clause into the contract for use by either party. Most would agree that a thirty-day escape clause is reasonable, whereas sixty- to ninety-day clauses may be more reasonable when a contract involves direct mail, a capital campaign, or a major special event. Also, the longer time may be insisted upon when a consulting firm has made a large investment such as paying for the expenses of moving a consultant and his or her family to the client's location.

Be wary of the consulting firm that wants to "manage" the organization's funds as it helps to raise them. This is dangerous, can be a direct conflict of interest, and most likely will not benefit the organization. Consulting firms may not negotiate the best sub-contracts for the client or exercise the best control over expenditures. An organization should not pre-finance a project and should retain control over expenditures.

Also, consulting firms should be wary of the organization that expects them to be paid only after they have raised money for the client. Some clients will want a firm to be paid a percentage of the money that the firm raises. This type of payment is not permitted for members of NSFRE, nor is it recommended for consulting firms or clients. Payment should be based on services provided and should not be a percentage of funds raised. A con-sultant or firm may wish to delay payment for a few months as a campaign "gets off the ground" and then, when money starts to flow into the organization, begin to receive payments. The client still would be responsible for the fees, even if the money raised wasn't as much as expected. Is a doctor not paid for services even if the patient dies? Fund raising also is a profession and its professionals should be paid based on services rendered.

Evaluating the Work of a Consultant

Evaluating a consultant's work should not wait until the end of the project. Regular progress reports from the consultant and a review of the work completed should be undertaken on an ongoing basis. Reports may be either written or verbal, but the important factor is that there is communication between the consultant and the organization. Weekly meetings between the staff and the consultant are a must. Taking the time to make sure that the consultant understands what is expected by the organization can prevent many mistakes from happening. Some organizations expect the consultant to be a visible part of their staff, whereas others would prefer that a low profile be maintained. Whatever the case, one person should act as the liaison or contact with the consultant and provide the direction and guidance. Although

Exhibit 16–4 IRS Guidelines to Determine Consultant Status

1. Do you require the worker to comply with another person's instructions about when, where, and how he or she is to work?
2. Do you provide training for the worker that indicates you want services performed in a particular method or manner?
3. Are the worker's services integrated into the business operation? That is, does the success or continuation of the business depend to an appreciable degree upon the services performed by the worker?
4. Do you require the worker to personally render his or her services? If so, you are demonstrating interest in the methods used to accomplish the work as well as in the results.
5. Does the person to whom the worker reports hire, supervise, and pay assistants?
6. Do you have a continuing relationship with the worker?
7. Do you establish set hours of work?
8. Does the worker devote substantial time to your business?
9. Is the worker required to perform his or her services on your premises?
10. Do you require the worker to perform services in a set order or sequence?
11. Do you require the worker to submit regular or written reports?
12. Do you pay the worker by the hour, week, or month?
13. Do you pay the worker's business or traveling expenses?
14. Do you furnish the worker with significant tools, materials, and other equipment?
15. Does the worker invest in facilities he or she uses to perform services that are not typically maintained by an employee, such as renting an office or setting up a home office?
16. Can the worker realize a profit or suffer a loss as a result of his or her services?
17. Does the worker perform work for several unrelated persons or firms at the same time?
18. Does the worker make his or her services available to the general public on a regular and consistent basis?
19. Do you have the authority to discharge the worker?
20. Does the worker have the right to terminate his or her relationship with you at any time without incurring liability?

Source: Reprinted with permission from *Association Management*, copyright 1994, American Society of Association Executives, Washington, DC. From "Guiding Your Consultant," by Arleigh Greenblat.

the consultant may work with many people on the staff, the direction and monitoring must be done by one person. How the consultant is directed and guided through the maze of internal politics will make the difference in the success or failure of the consultant's work and how satisfied the client will be with the work produced.

Make sure that everything expected from a consultant is written in the initial contract. Also, indicate if a final written report is expected.

Employee or Consultant According to the IRS

An organization may have a consultant on its payroll for a long time. What makes this person different from an employee? According to the IRS, if this person is consulting solely with this organization, works in the organization's office every day, and is supervised to the point of being able to exercise limited independent judgment, then the consultant well may be considered an employee by the IRS. Be careful of this when hiring a consultant. Make sure that written contracts clearly indicate that these are independent contractors with federal tax identification numbers, that they pay quarterly income tax and FICA payments, and that they have other clientele.

Exhibit 16–4 lists twenty questions based on IRS guidelines that can be asked to gauge whether a contractor should be considered an employee or a consultant. If the answer is "yes" to questions 1 through 14, 19, and 20, then the employer controls or has the right to control the manner in which services are performed. This generally indicates an employer-employee relationship and not an organization-consultant relationship.

References

Rutter, E.J. 1994. Hiring a fundraising consultant—Sending shivers up the organization's spine. *The Funding Connection*, Winter.

Michael Walters, 1996, Fundraising Consultant, Community Counselling Services, Inc., New York, NY.

Chapter 17
Fund Raising As a Career

Chapter Outline

- The Characteristics of a Successful Fund Raiser
- Career Mapping
- Career Questions for All Disciplines
- Ethics in Fund Raising
- The Fund Raiser As a Donor Steward
- Growing Career Opportunities
- Conducting a Job Search
- The Importance of Networking
- Certification

Key Vocabulary

- Advanced Certified Fund Raising Executive (ACFRE)
- Council for Advancement and Support of Education (CASE)
- Certified Fund Raising Executive (CFRE)
- Downsizing
- Ethics
- Fund Raising
- Independent Sector
- Association for Healthcare Philanthropy (AHP)
- National Society of Fund Raising Executives (NSFRE)
- Private Sector
- Public Sector
- Stewardship
- Third Sector

The Characteristics of a Successful Fund Raiser

> Few of the professional fund raisers today even knew of the profession when they were in college.

For the past five years, *Working Woman* magazine has listed fund raising as one of the hottest professions for women in the 1990s. Female or male, what is it that makes a good fund raiser? Why would someone want to become a fund raiser or development officer? Certainly, few of the professional fund raisers today even knew of the profession when they were in college, let alone considered it as a career option. Yet most of them probably had done some fund raising by that stage in life. What are the personality traits and skills that an individual should have to be a successful fund raiser?

In a survey of 1,800 fund raisers recently completed by the University of Pittsburgh, the most frequently mentioned traits or abilities associated with successful fund raising were (1) good writing, (2) the ability to work well with volunteers, and (3) strong managerial skills. In addition to these three are (1) a flexible, adaptable personality; (2) strong self esteem (without having an inflated ego); (3) the ability to listen to others; (4) integrity and honesty; (5) strong leadership skills; (6) attention to details; and (7) a good sense of humor. If asked to put these in order of importance, it would be nearly impossible, but all of the traits listed in Exhibit 17–1 are absolute requirements of the successful development officer.

Having a good sense of humor may be the most important trait of all. One had better have a sense of humor in a profession where the working hours in the day can average ten to twelve and the tenure of the job itself can be as short as 18 months. Working with people

---

Exhibit 17–1 Characteristics of a Development Professional

- Strong leadership skills
- Good writing skills
- Ability to work well with and motivate volunteers
- A flexible and adaptable personality
- Ability to listen to others
- Attention to details
- Strong managerial skills
- Strong self esteem, but with the ability to give credit to others, especially when you've done all the work
- Integrity and honesty
- Sense of humor

with various personalities in itself can require an active sense of humor. A quick smile or hearty laugh at oneself can help to ease tensions, generate cooperation, and inspire confidence in your role as a leader in the organization.

"THE IDEAL FUND RAISING EXECUTIVE WILL KNOW A LITTLE BIT ABOUT ESTATE PLANNING, TAX LAW, MARKETING, AND HYPNOTISM."

Source: © Mark Litzler.

Career Mapping

If considering a career in fund raising, one can investigate the profession by doing the following: (1) reading and research, (2) interviewing those currently in the profession, (3) volunteering, (4) joining the professional organizations, and (5) networking. Some individuals will do all of the aforementioned; some will choose one approach only. Whatever method selected, make sure to thoroughly gather information. Remember, selecting a career or making a career change involves investments of time, energy, and money. Take time to thoroughly investigate this possible next career path.

"Ultimately, the decision to take a new job must be based not only on what you feel you are looking for in a career shift; it must also be based on what you need and

want for personal and professional satisfaction," says Kay Sprinkel Grace, CFRE (1991), organizational consultant. She describes five "basic questions that transcend all disciplines within the not-for-profit sector." They form the critical negotiating platform for any job search and offer an effective filter for analyzing opportunities. Ask the following questions when considering a career change: What am I looking for? What do I need to be successful in a job? What do I want to learn? What do I know already, and how do I apply it elsewhere? What will be different?

"The most successful career laddering occurs when you find a 'fit' within the culture of an organization and between the organization's mission and your own personal values," says Grace. "Without this match, the transition will still leave you hungry and searching."

Many fund raisers state that one of the reasons for entering the field was the ability to do good works. Many choose to work for a particular organization because they believe in the cause of the organization. Although we would like to think that an orientation to public service is what brings people into the field, it usually isn't the reason. For the most part, the reason is the ability of the person to become genuinely enthusiastic about the mission of an organization or a cause that strikes his or her heart. If it is an emotional level that draws a person to the profession, the individual should not lose sight of the practical side of the profession. Fund raisers have goals to meet, deadlines to keep, and a responsibility to the board, just as those in other professions. For persons to find a "fit" with an organization, they must find a connection between the organization's mission and their own personal values. If this match doesn't occur, there is not much to keep an individual working there. A development professional must be able to promote the organization enthusiastically and honestly. If they cannot, then the organization is wrong for them.

There is a trend today for people to be offered "early retirement" by their employer. With the downsizing of the U.S. military and many government agencies, as well as many regional banks and U.S. firms such as IBM and AT&T, many middle-aged people are faced with finding new jobs. In many cases, they are seeking new career paths as well. Many of these individuals are considering the field of fund raising. They are well educated and committed people who have thoroughly investigated the field and find that becoming a fund raiser offers a role that meets their need to do something with their life that will benefit society and also offer personal growth. They are not as concerned with upward mobility as they are with finding self-satisfaction. As more people consider the field, the development profession is becoming more recognized. It is important that those who enter the field bring to it the high standards that the profession requires.

As broad as the backgrounds are of those considering the field, there are just as many career opportunities for a person to investigate within the development profession. It is not likely that someone will enter the field at the senior level (vice president for advancement, chief development officer, director of development) unless he or she has had extensive nonprofit experience in another area that required fund raising, yet was not a development position. Rather, most will enter the field by working in a specific area of fund raising such as direct mail, special events, corporate fund raising, major gift fund raising, the annual campaign, or planned giving.

How do you decide on a particular field within the development profession? Begin by selecting an area in which you have an interest, some experience as a volunteer, or, at the minimum, some knowledge. Most individuals know little about planned giving, but if your background is in banking, the law, or estate planning, this may be the perfect area in which you should begin your development career. Likewise, if you have worked extensively with senior corporate leaders and understand the corporate world, then perhaps corporate fund raising is where you should begin. Also, if you have spent years coordinating dinners and other special events, then perhaps the special events area is what you should seek.

While deciding on a career direction, a person may wish to volunteer at a nonprofit organization. This will give him or her an opportunity to experience the profession of fund raising first-hand and help to determine the area in which there is the best fit. Whatever career path is selected within the development profession, a person will be challenged. To the novice, this can be a strange, but fascinating field. People frequently can feel exhilarated or exhausted. It can be the best job ever and it always will demand the highest quality work. To adapt a slogan of the Peace Corps, fund raising can be the toughest job you'll ever love!

Career Questions for All Disciplines

What is the future of the fund raising profession? What types of people are entering the field? Who can be expected to enter the field tomorrow? Will the same skills be necessary? The following quote is attributed to McDiarmid (1993):

> Tomorrow's fund-raising leaders will have a financial management rather than a public relations background. They will be initiators rather than accommodators, and will use research-based strategies to deal with big issues in a bold fashion. Few of tomorrow's fund raisers will succeed because of their knowledge about producing news releases or ad copy. Rather, they will succeed because they are effective at complex analytical thinking and can manage the movement of large gifts to the treasuries of well-managed organizations. This is not to say that these managers will be unskilled speakers, writers, or listeners. In fact because they will be dealing with original, complex concepts, they will have to be particularly effective and aggressive communicators.

> Tomorrow's leaders must also be adept at creating alliances among donors, program managers, governing board members, and financial and legal advisors. . . . Tomorrow's fund raisers should not expect to organize large numbers of volunteers and oversee phonathons. Rather, their primary task will be to understand and communicate organizational opportunities to major prospects.

Also, more and more of the professional development officers are women. This trend started in the 1980s and continues today. The reasons of some as to why are interesting. For those interested in additional information on this topic, read Judy Rosener's (1990) article, "Why Women Lead," in *Harvard Business Review*. According to McDiarmid,

> Those of us who have watched the relative feminization of the fund-raising field during recent decades have speculated on why this process has occurred. In part, the answer may be that women have been socialized from early age to be effective managers in ambiguous situations. These female managers operate productively in fast-changing, international organizations in which they do not have the benefit of "formal sources of power." Further, they are skilled at helping others transform "their self interest into the goals of the organization."

Similar characteristics will be required of the next generation of fund raisers. Because ambiguity will become a dominant fact of life, they must create innovative alliances in order to manage successfully.

Ethics in Fund Raising

"Fund-raising executives are not merely raising money for the institutions that pay their salaries; they are a vital component of a sector that defines the very distinctiveness, indeed the uniqueness, of our society," says Dr. Joel Fleishman. In a recent lecture on philanthropy, Fleishman urged all fund-raising executives to exert themselves to do the following:

- Shape the kinds of persons chosen to serve on the boards of your organization.

- Raise standards of accounting, planning, and stewardship in your organization.
- Have your organization report more fully to public authorities and to the public itself.
- Seek education and certification.
- Take pride in fund raising and volunteerism.

"You have every reason to demand accountability and propriety," says Fleishman. "Your capacity to produce funds for your employer or client depends directly on your organization's public reputation, a reputation that is likely to suffer damage as a consequence of any publicly noted failure of accountability."

Two scandals have rocked the world of fund raising in the 1990s. The first was the downfall of the head of the United Way of America for improperly using the organization's funds. The second involved the fleecing of both donors and their nonprofit recipients by the head of the New Era Foundation. Unfortunately, both of these have drawn negative publicity and attention to the field of fund raising. The general public can tend to forget all of the honest, hardworking professionals who make up the field. This is why it is imperative that the profession "police" itself and hold all who enter its doors to the highest of ethical standards.

> It is imperative that the profession "police" itself and hold all who enter to the highest of ethical standards.

Increasingly, as more organizations downsize and more and more people consider fund raising as a career opportunity, the issues of how many employees are needed to raise funds and how much to pay them come to the forefront. Staff numbers will vary per the overall size of the organization and its fund-raising plans. So, too, will the level of salaries being paid to professional staff. Most development professionals work for small or mid-size organizations and do not receive large salaries. Some larger trade associations, universities, and hospitals may offer higher salaries. Yet, more and more frequently, nonprofit employers are asking fund raisers to take smaller salaries and work on a commission of what they raise for the organization. This creates ethical questions that need to be addressed.

Members of the National Society of Fundraising Executives (NSFRE) adhere to a code of ethics that prohibit them from working on commission (See Exhibit 16–3). They may accept performance-based compensation such as bonuses, but not percentages of monies raised for an organization. Why is this important for a person entering the field to understand? If a person comes from the profit sector with a sales background, he or she may have been compensated based on the percentage of whatever it was that he or she sold that month or quarter. It may be difficult for this person to understand that this is not the practice in the development profession. For example, if a development officer was working with a major donor whose gift to the organization was to be in the six-figure range, would that donor still want to give as much if he or she knew that the development officer was going to receive 10 percent of the gift? Probably not. Another example is, what would prevent a fund raiser from accepting money from a source not appropriate to the institution so he or she could receive a percentage of the gift? Would the American Cancer Society want a gift from one of the tobacco firms? Probably not. Yet, if a person knew that a large gift could be made, the temptation to accept it would be great. Many other scenarios can be discussed, but NSFRE guidelines do not permit its members to work for a salary based on commission. If a person's sole interest is earning a great deal of money, then another profession should be considered. Although a respectable salary can be earned, the development professional puts the donor's interest above all other interests. It is imperative in our profession to "do the right thing!"

The Fund Raiser As a Donor Steward

Fund raisers are continually being asked to build relationships with members of their board, donors, clients, staff, and the public in general. Probably the most important relationship to develop is that with the donor. Not only must donors be comfortable with the organization's mission, but they must trust the judgment of the institution's board and staff who will be managing their contribution. After donors have chosen to make gifts to an organization, the board and staff must maintain contact with them to keep them informed of the activities of the organization and how their gift was used in support of the organization's mission. Donors should be sent reports on the use of their gifts at least annually. These may be letters re-thanking them for their gifts and may include a copy of the organization's annual report, calling their attention to whatever program they were supporting.

If there have been any changes in the mission, programs, or activities of the organization that affect the intentions of the donor in making this gift, then the donor immediately must be informed of the change. It is probably best to arrange a face-to-face meeting to discuss the changes and not to talk over the phone, especially if this is a large gift. This becomes more difficult when an organization may be phasing out a program that was established years before by an endowment fund and the original donor is deceased. It is still the responsibility of the organization to contact the remaining family or official representative of the donor to inform them of the changes and then ask their permission to alter the use of the gift. This may even require a court order. It is unethical to use a donor's money for any other purpose than that which was initially specified, unless permission is received to do so.

It is also important to understand that upon accepting a gift, the organization is responsible for the proper investment of the funds. There should be no high-risk investment of donor's money placed in endowments. The last thing an organization should want is to erode the corpus. The financial committee of the board of the organization must establish written policies that will govern all gifts made to the organization. These should be published and made available to donors upon request. In fact, it may be useful to print them and use them when discussing possible major gifts with prospective donors.

> Upon accepting a gift, the organization is responsible for the proper investment of funds.

NSFRE along with the American Association of Fund Raising Counsel (AAFRC), the Association for Health Care Philanthropy (AHP), and the Council for Advancement and Support of Education (CASE) developed *A Donor Bill of Rights* to support donors in their desire to make gifts to nonprofit organizations and to help them feel that they have made the right decision in giving their money to another in support of a cause. *A Donor Bill of Rights* is included in its entirety in Appendix 1–A. It begins by stating, "Philanthropy is based on voluntary action for the common good. It is a tradition of giving and sharing that is primary to the quality of life. To assure that philanthropy merits the respect and trust of the general public, and that donors and prospective donors can have full confidence in the not-for-profit organizations and causes they are asked to support, we declare that all donors have these rights:"

In addition to *A Donor Bill of Rights*, NSFRE has included in its Code of Ethics basic principles under which its members work when acting as stewards of a donor's money. Members are directed "to the best of their ability, ensure that contributions are used in accordance with donors' intentions" (Standard No. 14) and "ensure to the best of their ability, proper stewardship of charitable contributions, including timely reporting on the use and management of funds and explicit consent by the donor before altering the conditions of a gift."

Growing Career Opportunities

Finding a job takes time; building a profession can take a lifetime. In the 1980s and 1990s, the development profession expanded rapidly. Membership in NSFRE increased from 3,559 in 1982 to more than 16,100 today—an increase of 452 percent! There are more than 136 NSFRE chapters represented throughout North America. Expansion of the field was not only successful, but necessary. More nonprofit organizations were formed to support new causes that required more people to raise money.

With these large increases in position openings, new names and titles were created for the fund-raising executive. The most preferred term today seems to be development officer, but one can find advertisements for the following: advancement officer, fund-raising executive, director of development, account executive, special events coordinator, major gifts officer, planned giving specialist, vice president for institutional development, annual gifts coordinator, director of resources development, manager of organizational fund raising, etc. Whatever the titles listed for this vocation, those entering the field can expect to be challenged and required to work for the right to use the title—it is one that has to be earned.

Conducting a Job Search

If you have decided to pursue a career in fund raising, the next decision to make is to determine for what type of institution you would prefer to work. Universities, colleges, hospitals, and almost all nonprofit organizations need fund raising and, thus, hire development professionals. The right place for you need not be found by chance. You can seek a new career or position in an organized way. Ask questions! Remember, it is your future.

First, look for an organization whose mission is of interest to you, something you can believe in, something you can support. Consider those groups to which you already have given your time and/or money. Then look for those organizations whose work is similar, but with which you are not as familiar. For example, if you have been a supporter of The Sierra Club, you could then look into other environmental groups such as The National Wildlife Federation, Conservation International, The Nature Conservancy, Defenders of Wildlife, The Wilderness Society, American Rivers, etc. If you attended and/or strongly believe in small liberal arts colleges, then you may not want to work for a development operation in a large university. Similarly, if you are attracted to liberal causes, you may not want to work for an organization that supports conservative, right-wing programs.

Sooner or later, most development professionals will work in several of the many philanthropic areas—health, the arts, social science, education, etc.—and will be required to know about all facets of the profession. Often, the development professional is asked to relocate to secure the kind of job he or she is best suited for and really wants. This is no different from most other ca-

> Sooner or later, most development professionals will work in several of the many philanthropic areas.

reers. To be successful in a career, one may have to go to where the job is.

Second, determine whether the organization is legitimate. How many years has it existed? Who sits on its board? Is it legally incorporated? Does it have a worthy cause? What is its track record in its business and what is its record in fund raising? Ask for an annual report and other materials. Review its mission statement. Is it clear and understandable? Does it put forth the group's purpose and reason for existence? After all, if it doesn't communicate its mission clearly, is it a place where you will be comfortable working?

Third, review the volunteer leadership and executive management. Who heads the board? What is their commitment? Are they working members of the board or have they been asked to serve for use of their name only? Are these the types of individuals whose values and ethics coincide with yours? Could you work for a cause in which you did not believe even if you had the opportunity to "mingle with" Hollywood or Wall Street personalities? Also, considering that the responsibility of the board is to raise money, look at the board members critically. Do they have contacts? Do they have job descriptions that state the amount of money they are to bring yearly to the organization? Have they actively assumed financial oversight of the organization to provide it with stability? Is there a long-range plan for the organization?

Fourth, review the professional staff and operations. How long have the staff members been employed by the organization? How is the organization structured? Where does the development operation fit in the overall structure? Does the head of development have direct access to the board? If not, beware! It is almost impossible to raise money for an organization if you are not directly working with or have access to its leadership.

Fifth, use your professional organizations and their resources to help you in your search. For example, NSFRE and CASE have created a database of individuals from culturally and ethnically diverse backgrounds to assist in networking and job placement. In addition, NSFRE offers a course in fund raising tailored to those entering the profession. More than 500 persons have participated in this course, which is offered at twelve different sites. NSFRE continues to attract thousands of people each year at their international conference, which is usually held in March. In addition, more than 80,000 people per year attend meetings of their NSFRE local chapter or monthly luncheons, round tables, and seminars.

Sixth, ask who will be your supervisor and how that person manages daily activities. Is training provided for staff? Will the organization pay for your membership in your professional organization? Does the organization encourage attendance at professional meetings and monthly luncheons? How long has the current staff been employed by the institution? What is the institution's method for evaluating performance?

Upon completion of these tasks, the next important step is to make sure that others know that you are seeking a position in the development world, that your qualifications are superb, and that you wish to be referred to those who have positions open.

The Importance of Networking

Remember the old adage that "it's not what you know, it's who you know"? Well, networking has its place in the field of fund raising just as it does in all other fields. Learning about the profession of fund raising can be as easy as becoming involved with fund raisers, their activities, and their professional organizations. Whether you select to volunteer for a specific organization's development office or attend conferences, monthly seminars, or weekly luncheons and round tables, opportunities are available for you to talk and work with those who are experienced in the field. Most development officers are members of and active in their professional organizations. Some of the organizations to which fund raisers belong are the following:

- National Society of Fund Raising Executives (NSFRE)
- Council for Advancement and Support of Education (CASE)
- Association for Healthcare Philanthropy (AHP)
- Institute of Charity Fundraising Managers (ICFM)
- American Association of Fund-Raising Counsel (AAFRC)
- National Catholic Development Conference (NCDC)
- International Society for Third-Sector Research (ISTR)
- Canadian Society of Fund Raising Executives (CSFRE)
- Southern Africa Institute of Fundraising (SAIF)
- EUCONSULT
- Club des Fundraisers
- National Committee on Planned Giving (NCPG)
- National Council for Resource Development (NCRD)
- United Way of America
- Independent Sector

To learn more about the previously listed organizations or other philanthropic-related organizations, refer to Appendix B, or visit a fund-raising library. Then call or write to obtain more information regarding their membership requirements, costs, and benefits.

Another form of networking is selecting a mentor, someone who cares about you and your success. Meet with this person on a weekly or monthly basis and share your professional desires. Ask for direction and guidance. Your mentor should be someone you trust and respect.

In October of 1996, NSFRE released the results of a survey that it conducted in 1995 to gather data about those who work in the development field. Those surveyed were members of NSFRE. The results revealed that the active membership of NSFRE was more than 57 percent female and that minorities represented approximately 4.9 percent. While the average age of the respondents in 1988 was just above 35 when entering the field, the average age of those responding in 1995 was 32 when they entered the profession. Of the minorities reporting in 1995, 43 percent of the Asians were 25 or younger when entering the field, while 20 percent of the African Americans were older than 40.

There continues to be a significant gap between salaries earned by male fund-raising executives and those earned by females. Although the median salary in 1995 was $46,100, women earned an average of $41,207 while men averaged $52,917. Again, the highest salaries were earned by those who fund raise for hospitals and medical centers ($62,294 median) and educational institutions ($50,535 median). Those who work for conservation and wildlife organizations earned the lowest median salaries.

More executives are staying in the field longer than had been previously reported, although the concern about the perceived frequency of job changes continues to be discussed. NSFRE determined in 1992 and reconfirmed in 1995 that statistics do not support the opinion that fund raisers switch jobs more frequently than the national average in other fields. "More than half of the respondents report they have been with their organization for more than ten years in almost every category of employer type, with the exception of youth organizations (37.5%), retirement communities (46.2%), religious organizations (42.9%), and local service organizations (28.3%). In the aggregate, 79.1 percent of respondents have been with three employers or fewer in their fund-raising careers. A third have worked for only one employer."

There has been little change in the number of hours that the average fund raiser works. In the 1995 survey, 12.9 percent of those responding worked 40 hours or fewer, compared to 12.2 percent in 1992. Also, those working more than 63 hours per week in 1995 was only 4.1 percent compared to 5.3 percent in 1992. Approximately one third (31.9%) work an average of an extra hour or two each day.

Finally, according to NSFRE's Profile (1996), "the typical respondent to the 1995 career survey is a 45-year old who entered the fund-raising field at age 32, has 17+ years of education, has held two jobs in fund raising, has an annual salary of $46,100, and overall, expressed a strong level of satisfaction with their careers."

Certification

Once a development professional has five or more years of experience in the fund-raising field, it may be time to consider certification. NSFRE offers a certification program called the Certified Fund Raising Executive (CFRE), which is considered "the ultimate mark of distinction for the profession." Exhibit 17–2 outlines how CFRE certification can benefit a fund-raising professional's career, how to obtain the certification, and the criteria on which it is based.

> Once a development professional has five or more years of experience, it may be time to consider certification.

A development professional can take the certification examination for the Advanced Certified Fund Raising Executive (ACFRE) after (1) being in the field a minimum of ten years, (2) earning an undergraduate degree, (3) holding active CFRE certification status with at least one renewal, (4) attending at least two national fund-raising conferences within the past five years, and (5) participating in at least twenty-four hours of senior-level development seminars and/or courses. Details describing this opportunity for the advanced professional can also be found in Exhibit 17–2.

References

Fleishman, J. Maurice G. Gurin, CFRE, Annual Lecture on Philanthropy.

Grace, K. S. 1991. Shifting gears: The excitement and challenge of changing disciplines in your fund-raising career, *NSFRE Journal*, Winter.

McDiarmid, J. 1993. The next generation of fund raisers. *AHP Fall Journal*, Fall.

National Society of Fund Raising Executives. 1996. *Profile—1995 Membership Survey*. Alexandria, VA: NSFRE.

Rosener, J. 1990. Why women lead. *Harvard Business Review*, November–December.

Exhibit 17-2 NSFRE Certification

NSFRE Certification

The NSFRE Certification Program affords fund-raising professionals with five or more years of experience the opportunity to be certified by an objective body and recognized by their employers and their colleagues for exceptional expertise and professionalism. The designations "Certified Fund Raising Executive" (CFRE) and "Advanced Certified Fund Raising Executive" (ACFRE) are marks of distinction that provide heightened professional recognition for fund development professionals in North America and elsewhere.

Benefits of Certification

- Enhance knowledge of fund-raising practices through preparation for certification;
- Gain credibility as a fund-raising executive;
- Build personal esteem in the fund-raising profession;
- Enhance job opportunities in the development field.

Becoming a CFRE

The Certified Fund Raising Executive (CFRE) Program is open to any eligible fund-raising executive, whether or not they belong to NSFRE. All potential candidates must meet the following qualifications:

1. Currently employed as a fund-raising executive;
2. Minimum of five years of full-time experience as a professional member of a fund-raising staff or as a fund-raising consultant to not-for-profit organizations within the previous eight years; and
3. Written pledge to uphold the NSFRE Code of Ethical Principles and Standards of Professional Practice.

The program consists of an evaluation of a candidate's experience, fund-raising accomplishments, post-high school education, continuing professional education and service to the profession and society. In addition, the candidate's knowledge of fund-raising principles and techniques is measured by a written exam. Areas covered include: case statements, prospect identification, public relations, marketing, use of volunteer leadership, annual campaigns, direct mail, capital campaigns, planned giving, foundation proposals, campaign evaluation, corporate solicitation, fund-raising managerial planning, staff relations, ethics and professional practices, and use of fund-raising counsel.

Certification involves four steps: submission of an application; evaluation and verification of the personal and professional history record submitted by the applicant; examination of the candidate's knowledge of fund-raising principles and techniques; and certification approval by the Certification Board.

Because fund raising is a dynamic and rapidly changing field, continuing education and other professional development activities are required to maintain certified status. Recertification is required every three years in order to maintain CFRE status. The NSFRE Service Office staff will send a courtesy notice approximately three months prior to the expiration of certification. However, full responsibility rests with the individual CFRE to assure that the application for recertification is submitted by the stipulated deadlines.

Fund-raising executives who are retired or retiring and would like to keep the CFRE designation should notify the Certification Board in writing of retired status and circumstances, including a description of the level of future activities. The Certification Board may extend "retired" status to the CFRE who has recertified three times. A one-time processing fee is required. CFRE (ret.) is for life.

Becoming an ACFRE

The Advanced Certified Fund Raising Executive (ACFRE) Program is the most rigorous step in the certification process. The successful completion represents a significant level of mastery within the profession. It offers professionals a means to distinguish themselves, employers a way to identify exceptionally accomplished fund raisers and philanthropy an opportunity for enriched interactions with donors. Those seeking the ACFRE credential must meet the following qualifications:

1. Current CFRE credential and at least one three-year recertification;
2. Minimum of 10 years of full-time paid professional experience in the fund-raising field;
3. B.S./B.A. or equivalent experience;
4. Adherence to NSFRE's Code of Ethical Principles and Standards of Professional Practice;
5. Active participant in NSFRE and/or other fund-raising organizations with demonstrated service to other not-for-profit organization;
6. Completion within the previous five years of at least two national fund-raising conferences, one of which must be sponsored by NSFRE; and
7. Attendance or instruction within the previous five years of at least 24 educational contact hours in other senior-level development seminars and/or courses.

The ACFRE certification process is challenging, and involves an application, written examination, portfolio review and oral evaluation. The application assesses performance including amounts and kinds of funds raised. The second phase, written examination, measures a candidate's knowledge of general development, management, leadership and fund-raising skills. Next, the candidate presents a portfolio of development materials, prepared within the last five years, to a peer committee. The portfolio must emphasize at least two special skill areas and written synopsis of use and results. A planning document relevant to the portfolio must be included with the portfolio. Finally, the candidate must complete an oral evaluation by demonstrating a mastery of advanced-level knowledge and understanding in fund-raising management, leadership and two of the candidate's specialty areas. Upon successful completion of all four steps, the ACFRE designation is conferred for life.

Courtesy of National Society of Fund Raising Executives, Alexandria, Virginia.

Appendix A
Fund Raising and the Law

A nonprofit organization is defined as an organization that pertains to or provides services of benefit to the public without financial incentive. It is qualified by the Internal Revenue Service (IRS) as a tax-exempt organization with the designation of 501(c)(3) from the federal tax code. Because of this special designation, nonprofit organizations are subject to certain federal, state, and local government laws and regulations. Of particular importance to development professionals are those regulations pertaining to charitable solicitations and fund-raising administration.

According to Bruce R. Hopkins, an attorney and author who specializes in corporate law and taxation for nonprofit organizations, the nonprofit sector will see increasing legislation and regulation of fund raising in the future. In the Fall 1995 issue of *Advancing Philanthropy*, he makes this prediction based on actions by the federal government and state governments during the past twenty-five years. They include the following*:

- the enactment of the Tax Reform Act of 1969, which brought about most of today's statutory charitable giving rules as well as the public charity and private foundation rules;
- growing sophistication in the application of the unrelated business income rules;
- increased emphasis on reporting and disclosure including expansion of public access to organization's annual information returns;
- more involvement of tax law in the administration of the fund-raising process;
- a decision by Congress to make litigation of charitable organizations' tax issues in federal court easier;
- a decision by Congress to become more involved in planned giving and the emergence of agencies other than the IRS (such as the U.S. Postal Service for postal regulation and the Federal Trade Commis-

sion for telemarketing) as regulators of fund raising; and
- expansion of the role of state attorneys general, often augmented by secretaries of state and directors of consumer protection departments.

There are many reasons for these trends. The IRS believes revenue is lost because many organizations are advising their donors that contributions are tax deductible when these contributions are not or when only a partial deduction is allowed because the donor received a service or product. Thus, new substantiation and disclosure rules went into effect in 1994 resulting in increased administrative responsibilities for nonprofit organizations. This negative attitude of the IRS toward charitable giving promises unfavorable consequences for the future. The need for increased revenue to aid federal and state deficits is leading legislators to narrow the range of tax exemptions available to nonprofit organizations. Many in government and the general public believe the distinction between for-profit and nonprofit organizations is not as clear as it was because many nonprofit organizations are adapting business practices that had been viewed as those of for-profit organizations. These practices include product endorsements, corporate sponsorships, affinity cards, tours, and cruises. Public confidence and trust in nonprofit organizations wane as headlines report on the conviction and imprisonment of the former president of the United Way, based on fraud charges, and the donors and charities who are short millions of dollars as the New Era for Philanthropy Foundation files for bankruptcy.

Hopkins believes that federal and state regulation of fund raising will continue to intensify in the short term. Regarding the long term, the future effects of any changes in federal tax policy may present the possibility that there no longer would be any tax advantage for giving.

Recent IRS Rule Changes

As discussed earlier, the IRS is the main agency of the federal government involved in regulating fund-raising

---

*Source: From B.R. Hopkins, A Struggle for Balance. Copyright 1995, *Advancing Philanthropy*, NSFRE, Alexandria, VA. Reprinted with permission.

administration. The Omnibus Budget Reconciliation Act of 1993 tightened substantiation requirements for taxpayers claiming charitable deductions. It also enacted a change in the tax code to include the earlier IRS position that charities should provide donors with information regarding the amount of their contribution that is deductible.

Substantiation

In a case of a donation of $250 or more, no charitable deduction is allowed unless the donor obtains written acknowledgment from the charity in a timely manner and keeps this document. The acknowledgment must describe and declare the value of any goods or services provided by the charity to the donor.

With this new rule, it is no longer permissible to use a canceled check as documentation of a charitable gift of $250 or more.

Disclosure of Quid Pro Quo Contributions

When a payment exceeding $75 to a charity includes a donative element but also entitles the donor to goods or services, the organization must provide a written statement that (1) informs the donor that the deductible amount of the contribution is limited to the excess of the cash or property contributed over the value of the goods and service provided by the organization and (2) provides the donor with a good faith estimate of the value of such goods and services.

Nonprofit organizations revised their acknowledgment procedures to comply with these two new rules. Receipts and acknowledgment letters now use such language as the following:

"No goods or services were received in exchange."

"We very much appreciate your gift of $XXX (or description of property). In consideration of your gift, we provided you with _____ (insert description) which we estimate has a value of $ _____. The amount of your contribution that is deductible for federal income tax purposes is limited to the excess of your contribution over the value of goods and services we provided to you."

The States' Role in Regulation

Most of the laws regulating fund raising come from the states. How many laws an organization encounters depends on the number of states in which it solicits gifts. All but three states—Delaware, Montana, and Wyoming—have some form of statutory law governing the solicitation of gifts. For organizations soliciting gifts nationally, state regulation creates significant registration, reporting, disclosure, and other requirements demanded by the various state charitable solicitation acts.

Giving USA Update provides an annual survey of state solicitation laws provided as a service of the American Association of Fund-Raising Counsel, Inc. The following provides a sampling of state regulations reported in their January 1, 1996 issue.

GEORGIA

STATE REGULATORY AGENCY: Secretary of State, Business Services and Regulation
CHARITABLE ORGANIZATIONS:
    REGISTRATION/LICENSING: Registration, $25 fee.
    REPORTING DATES/REQUIREMENTS: Annual report due on organization's renewal date. $10 fee.
    Certified financial statement required if proceeds are $500,000 or more; independent CPA review required for proceeds of $100,000 to $500,000; file form 990 if proceeds are less than $100,000.

PAID SOLICITORS:
    REGISTRATION/LICENSING/BONDING: Registration, $250 fee and $10,000 bond. File solicitation notice before campaign.

FUND-RAISING COUNSEL:
    REGISTRATION/LICENSING/BONDING: None. If counsel has custody of funds, register as paid solicitor.

SOLICITATION DISCLOSURE REQUIREMENTS (ALL PREVIOUSLY STATED): Organization must disclose to donor names of solicitor and organization. If telephone solicitation, solicitor must disclose his or her location and that full description of the charitable program and the financial statement are available upon request.

NEW JERSEY

STATE REGULATORY AGENCY: Charities Registration Section
CHARITABLE ORGANIZATIONS:
    REGISTRATION/LICENSING: Annual registration. Fee scale: $30 to $250, depending on receipts.
    REPORTING DATES/REQUIREMENTS: Annual financial report due within 6 months of fiscal year end.

PAID SOLICITORS:
    REGISTRATION/LICENSING/BONDING: Registration, $250 fee and $20,000 bond. Registration for individuals working for paid solicitor, $15 fee.

FUND-RAISING COUNSEL:
    REGISTRATION/LICENSING/BONDING: Registration, $250 fee. No bond.

SOLICITATION DISCLOSURE REQUIREMENTS (ALL PREVIOUSLY STATED): Printed solicitations, written confirmation, receipts, or written reminders issued by a charitable organization, independent paid fund raiser, or solicitor must contain the following statement, which must be conspicuously printed. Solicitation disclosure statement: "Information filed with the attorney general concerning this charitable solicitation may be obtained from the attorney general of the state of New Jersey by calling 201-504-6215. Registration with the attorney general does not imply endorsement."

ILLINOIS

STATE REGULATORY AGENCY: Attorney General, Charitable Trust Division

CHARITABLE ORGANIZATIONS:
  REGISTRATION/LICENSING: Initial registration.
  REPORTING DATES/REQUIREMENTS: Annual financial report due within 6 months of fiscal year end. CPA opinion must accompany report if revenues exceed $100,000 or if professional solicitor is engaged.

PAID SOLICITORS:
  REGISTRATION/LICENSING/BONDING: Registration and $10,000 bond. No fee.

FUND-RAISING COUNSEL:
  REGISTRATION/LICENSING/BONDING: Registration every two years. No fee.

SOLICITATION DISCLOSURE REQUIREMENTS (ALL PREVIOUSLY STATED): None.

CALIFORNIA

STATE REGULATORY AGENCY: Registry of Charitable Trusts

CHARITABLE ORGANIZATIONS:
  REGISTRATION/LICENSING: Initial registration for organizations located or doing business in state. More than 200 cities and counties have solicitation ordinances that may require registration. Contact Registry of Charitable Trusts for more information.
  REPORTING DATES/REQUIREMENTS: Financial report due four and one-half months after fiscal year end.

PAID SOLICITORS:
  REGISTRATION/LICENSING/BONDING: Annual registration, $200 fee for commercial fund raisers who receive and control funds. $25,000 bond.

FUND-RAISING COUNSEL:
  REGISTRATION/LICENSING/BONDING: None.

SOLICITATION DISCLOSURE REQUIREMENTS (ALL PREVIOUSLY STATED): Paid solicitors must disclose name, address, and telephone number of solicitation firm; if contribution is not tax-deductible; and that solicitor is paid. Telephone solicitor must disclose address and telephone number from which solicitation is being made. See statute for details.

Source: Giving USA Update, Issue 1, 1996, American Association of Fund Raising Counsel Trust for Philanthropy, New York. Reprinted by permission.

What a Development Professional Should Know About a Nonprofit Organization

The Mission Statement
The mission statement explains an organization's purposes, goals, and objectives. It describes why the organization was founded and what it is committed to accomplish. The basic purposes must be of "public benefit" for the organization to qualify as a tax-exempt charitable organization, 501(c)(3).

The Legal Structure
A voluntary board of directors assumes responsibility that all services provided will be faithful to the mission and that all funds received will be used in fulfillment of that mission and not for the personal benefit of any board member, employee, client, or other person involved.

The Articles of Incorporation
The articles list the specific charitable purposes intended to be fulfilled by the mission statement. These purposes, which represent the uses for public gifts that qualify the organization for tax exemption, can differ depending on the type of organization.

Reporting Requirements Mandated by Law
Reporting requirements exist for federal, state, and local jurisdictions. Nearly all tax-exempt organizations are required to file an annual information form with the IRS known as the Form 990. This return reflects an organization's support and revenue, disbursements, and expenses.

Federal law requires that all charities make available its three most recent annual Internal Revenue Service (IRS) returns, form 990s, and supplemental schedules for inspection by the public. A public information file available for inspection also should include a copy of the original tax-exempt application sent to the IRS including a copy of the group's charter and bylaws and a description of its purposes and programs. A nonprofit organization's IRS annual return reports expenses for programs, fund raising, and for administration, along with names of board members and officers and their compensation and benefits. It also includes the names of and compensation levels for the five highest-paid staff persons and five highest-paid professional advisors.

Other types of federal and state filings include unrelated business income tax returns, reports of gift property sold by the charity, state annual reports, and reports required by various state charitable solicitation acts.

Fund raising for charitable purposes is regulated by the states. These laws impose registration, reporting, record-keeping, and other requirements on charitable organizations that solicit within the jurisdictions.

How a Development Professional Helps an Organization Comply with Regulations

There are specific duties and responsibilities that are assigned to the development staff that help an organization comply with laws and regulations pertaining to fund raising.

Gift Processing and Recording
The development professional is responsible for complying with IRS and American Institute of Certified Public Accountants (AICPA) guidelines. A single processing procedure should be used regardless of the number of different solicitation programs in operation. Each gift

goes through a process of deposit, data entry, fund account assignment, and acknowledgment.

Regular reports should group data by source, purpose, and method of solicitation. Both the number of gifts and total revenue should be tallied in reports for public use. Formal financial statements, audits, and summary reports required by federal, state, and local authorities must be prepared and submitted by deadlines.

Management of Funds Raised
The development officer is responsible for proper deposit of all funds received as well as their correct use in accordance with donors' wishes, especially when they are restricted gifts or are designated for special purposes. Proper accounting ensures that each donor is thanked (in a timely fashion), that the funds are used correctly, and that reports on all solicitation activities are accurate.

Donor Relations
A very important duty for a development professional is donor relations, which involves donor recognition and communications. No one else in an organization has the primary responsibility for this area except the chief development staff person.

Keep in mind that donors expect the following:

- an organization to keep accurate records
- to receive an acknowledgment of their gift and the appropriate recognition
- to receive a report on how funds are used
- invitations to organization's public events
- access to information about programs, services, and financial affairs

Appendix B
Philanthropic-Related Organizations

American Association of Fund-Raising Counsel (AAFRC) & AAFRC Trust for Philanthropy
25 West 43rd Street
Suite 820
New York, NY 10036
212-354-5799

American Association of Museums
1225 Eye Street, NW
Washington, DC 20005
202-289-1818

American Council for the Arts
One East 53rd Street
New York, NY 10022
212-223-2787

American Council on Education
One Dupont Circle, Suite 209
Washington, DC 20036-1193
202-655-0177

Association of Charitable Foundations
34 North End Road
London W14 OSH
England
01-603-1525

Association of Professional Researchers for Advancement (APRA)
414 Plaza Drive, Suite 209
Westmont, IL 60559
708-655-0177

American Symphony Orchestra League
1156 15th Street, NW, Suite 800
Washington, DC 20005-1704
202-628-0099

Applied Research & Development Institute
2121 S. Oneida Street, Suite 633
Denver, CO 80222
303-691-6076

Association of Art Museum Directors
41 East 65th Street
New York, NY 10021
212-249-4423

Association for Healthcare Philanthropy (AHP)
313 Park Avenue, Suite 400
Falls Church, VA 22046
703-532-6243

Association for Research on Nonprofit Organizations and Voluntary Action (ARNOVA)
Indiana University Center on Philanthropy
500 West North Street, Suite 301
Indianapolis, IN 46202
317-684-2120

Australian Association of Foundations
8th Floor, 20 Queen Street
Melbourne 3000
Australia
03-614-1491

Canadian Centre for Philanthropy
74 Victoria Street, Suite 920
Toronto, Ontario M5C 920
Canada
416-368-1138

Center for Nonprofit Management of Central Florida
1900 N. Mills Avenue, Suite 3
Orlando, FL 32803
407-894-2151

Center for Philanthropy
550 West North Street, Room 301
Indianapolis, IN 46202
317-274-4200

Charities Aid Foundation
48 Pembury Road
Tonbridge, Kent
TN9 2JD England
011-44-771333

CIVICUS: World Alliance for Citizen Participation
919 18th Street, NW, 3rd Floor
Washington, DC 20006
202-331-8518

The Conference Board
845 Third Avenue
New York, NY 10022-6601
212-759-0900

Corporation for Public Broadcasting
901 E Street, NW
Washington, DC 20004
202-879-9600

Council for Advancement and Support of Education
(CASE)
11 Dupont Circle
Washington, DC 20036-1261
202-328-5887

Council for Aid to Education
342 Madison Avenue, Suite 1532
New York, NY 10173
212-661-5800

Council of Jewish Federations
730 Broadway, 2nd Floor
New York, NY 10003
212-598-3500

Council on Foundations
1828 L Street, NW, Suite 300
Washington, DC 20036
202-466-6512

Dance USA
1156 15th Street, NW, Suite 820
Washington, DC 20005
202-833-1717

The Foundation Center
79 Fifth Avenue
New York, NY 10003-3076
212-620-4230

Foundation for Independent Higher Education
5 Landmark Square, 330
Stamford, CT 06901-2502
203-353-1544

The Fund-Raising School
Indiana University Center on Philanthropy
550 West North Street, Suite 301
Indianapolis, IN 46202-3162
317-274-7063

The Grantsmanship Center
PO Box 17220
Los Angeles, CA 90014
213-482-9860

Independent Sector
1828 L Street, NW
Washington, DC 20036
202-223-8100

International Society for Third Sector Research (ISTR)
The Johns Hopkins University Institute for Policy
    Studies
Shriver Hall
Baltimore, MD 21218

National Association of Independent Schools
75 Federal Street
Boston, MA 02110
617-451-2444

National Catholic Development Conference
86 Front Street
Hempstead, NY 11550
516-481-6000

National Center for Nonprofit Boards
2000 L Street, NW, Suite 510
Washington, DC 20036-4907
202-452-6262

National Charities Information Bureau (NCIB)
19 Union Square West
New York, NY 10003-3395
212-929-6300

National Committee for Responsive Philanthropy
2001 S Street, NW, Suite 620
Washington, DC 20009
202-387-9177

National Committee on Planned Giving
310 North Alabama, Suite 210
Indianapolis, IN 46202-2103
317-269-6274

National Federation of Nonprofits
815 Fifteenth Street, NW, Suite 822
Washington, DC 20005-2201
202-628-4380

National Network of Women's Funds
1821 University Avenue, Suite 409 North
St. Paul, MN 55104
612-641-0742

National Society of Fund Raising Executives
  (NSFRE)
1101 King Street, Suite 700
Alexandria, VA 22314
703-684-0410

NEW Center (Nonprofit Enterprise at Work, Inc.)
1100 North Main Street, Suite 101
Ann Arbor, MI 48104
313-998-0160

Nonprofit Resource Center
50 Hurt Plaza, Suite 220
Atlanta, GA 30303
404-688-4845

Nonprofit Sector Research Fund
1333 New Hampshire Avenue, NW, Suite 2070
Washington, DC 20036
202-736-5800

Nonprofit Support Center of Santa Barbara County
5266 Hollister Avenue, Suite 102
Santa Barbara, CA 93111
805-683-9770

Philanthropic Advisory Service
Council of Better Business Bureaus
4200 Wilson Boulevard, Suite 800
Arlington, VA 22203
703-276-0100

The Society for Nonprofit Organizations
6314 Odana Road, Suite 1
Madison, WI 53719
608-274-9777

Support Center
166 West Washington, Suite 530
Chicago, IL 60602
312-606-1530

Support Center/Executive Service Corps
8361 Vickers Street, Suite 304
San Diego, CA 92111
619-292-5702

Support Center for Nonprofit Management
706 Mission Street, 5th Floor
San Francisco, CA 94103-3113
415-541-9000

Support Center of New York
305 Seventh Avenue, 11th Floor
New York, NY 10001-6008
212-924-6744

Support Center of Oklahoma—Oklahoma City
525 NW 13th Street
Oklahoma City, OK 73101-2238
405-236-8133

Support Center of Oklahoma—Tulsa
1120 South Utica Avenue
Tulsa, OK 74104-4090
918-579-1900

Support Center of Rhode Island
Simmons Building
10 Davol Square, 3rd Floor
Providence, RI 02903
401-861-1920

The Support Center—Washington, DC
2001 O Street, NW
Washington, DC 20036
202-833-0300

Support Centers—International

Europe
Support Center
Calea Mosilor 278, 20 Bis
Apt. 16, Sector 2
Bucharest, Romania
40-1-619-0670
FAX 40-1-210-3382
e-mail: thomas@sci.buc.soros.ro
(+7 hours from US East Coast)

Middle East
Support Center
17 El Saraya Street, Apt. 1
P.O. Box 293
Dokki, Giza, Egypt
20-2-348-8134
FAX 20-2-349-3958
Telex: 21736 UN DIBOK
e-mail: rgking@rusys.eg.net
(+7 hours from US East Coast)

United Way of America
701 North Fairfax Street
Alexandria, VA 22314
703-836-7100

World Fundraising Council
The World Fundraising Council Secretariat
1101 King Street, Suite 700
Alexandria, VA 22314
703-684-0410

Glossary

AAFRC *n.* American Association of Fund-Raising Counsel—a professional organization for fund-raising consultants.

ACFRE *n.* Advanced Certified Fund Raising Executive

acknowledge *v.t.* to express gratitude for (a gift or service) in written or oral form, communicated privately or publicly. **acknowledgment,** *n.*

acknowledgment form *n.* standardized form used to acknowledge a contribution.

acknowledgment letter *n.* type of correspondence used to thank and acknowledge a contribution.

acquisition *n.* the process or act of acquiring new donors.

active phase *n.* the period of public solicitation during a campaign that usually follows the successful completion of a campaign's nucleus fund and the establishment of a pattern of giving. This phase consists of solicitation activity in contrast to campaign planning. Also **intensive phase.**

ad hoc *adj.* concerned with a particular purpose, such as an ad hoc committee.

advance gift *n.* a donation, often from a trustee or director of an organization, that demonstrates a commitment to a campaign and provides momentum at the outset before external solicitations are undertaken. Also **initial gift; nucleus gift; strategic gift.**

advisory board *n.* a group of usually influential and knowledgeable people that offers counsel and prestige to the organization or cause with which it is associated, but that usually does not have any fiscal or policy authority.

advisory committee *see* **advisory board.**

AHP *n.* Association for Healthcare Philanthropy—a professional association of health-care development professionals, formerly known as National Association for Hospital Development.

analyze *v.* to make an analysis of, such as fund-raising data.

annual giving *n.* **1.** an amount given annually; **2.** a fund-raising program that generates gift support on an annual basis. Also *(Austr.)* **budget fund raising.**

annual report *n.* a yearly report of the financial and program status of an organization or institution.

anonymous gift *n.* a gift that is not publicly attributed to the donor.

appreciated security *n.* a security with a market value greater than its original tax basis.

back up *v.t.* to copy (information) from the hard drive of a computer to either a floppy disk or a tape drive.

backup *n.* **1.** the procedure for making security copies of computer data; for example, from a hard drive to either a floppy disk or a tape drive; **2.** the disk, tape, or information copied.

bellwether *n.* **1a.** a gift, action, or other leading indicator in a movement or campaign; **1b.** anything that sets a standard for a campaign.

benefactor *n.* a generous donor, usually at the highest gift level.

benefit *n.* **1.** something of value; **2.** a social event from which net proceeds are designated as a donation to one or more causes.

Source: Portions of this glossary reprinted from *The NSFRE Fund-Raising Dictionary,* by John Wiley & Sons, Inc., New York. Copyright 1996 John Wiley & Sons, Inc. Reprinted by permission.

bequest *n.* **1.** the act of bequeathing; **2.** something bequeathed. Also **legacy.**

bequest society *n.* a membership group made up of donors who informed an organization of their intention to provide for the organization financially in their will.

bleed *v., n. v.i.* of text or an illustration or embellishment, to be extended into the margin of a trimmed printed page. *v.t.* **1a.** to extend (such material) into the margin; **1b.** to print so that this occurs. *n.* any printed material that bleeds.

blue line *n.* in printing, the final corrected pages of a print job, used as a review before printing.

board *n.* **1.** governing board; **2.** an advisory board; **3.** in printing, material that is camera-ready (also **mechanical**).

board member *n.* one who serves on a governing or advisory board.

board of trustees *n.* another name for a governing board.

BRE *n. see* **business-reply envelope.**

bricks and mortar campaign *n. (informal)* a capital campaign to meet the financial needs for constructing a physical plant, including facilities and furnishings.

briefing *n.* a formal or informal report prior to or subsequent to an event or situation that prepares a participant or that reports or relates the outcome.

brochure *n.* a printed pamphlet or booklet used to promote an organization and/or its programs.

bulk rate mail *n.* second, third, or fourth class mail that qualifies for special postage rates that are lower than first-class rates. This mail is presorted by an organization or a service before going to the post office.

business-reply envelope (BRE) *n.* a self-addressed, return envelope with postage paid by the receiving organization or institution. Also **postage-paid envelope; return remit.**

campaign analysis *n.* a report on the results and effectiveness of a campaign. The report may include a quantitative and qualitative review of income and expense, number and size of gifts, and other considerations. *See* **evaluation.**

campaign brochure *n.* a summary statement most often accompanied by a pictorial depiction of an organiza-

tion's case—the relevance of its mission, the urgency and legitimacy of its needs, and the compelling reasons for campaign goals.

campaign chair *n.* the overall volunteer leader of a campaign organization who is in charge of all volunteer forces.

campaign director *n.* a fund-raising executive, from either a consulting firm or an organization's staff, who is assigned to direct a campaign.

campaign leader *n.* a volunteer who helps recruit and motivate other volunteer members of a campaign organization and who sets the pace for the giving of gifts and active participation in a campaign.

campaign management *n.* the administration and implementation by appointed staff of the overall operations of a campaign.

campaign organization *n.* a chart or table delineating the responsibilities and relationships among fund-raising committees.

campaign staff *n.* paid personnel who perform clerical, research, record keeping, and other coordination and support functions essential to campaign operations under the supervision of the campaign director.

capital campaign *n.* an intensive fund-raising effort to meet a specific financial goal within a specified period of time.

carrier envelope *n.* an envelope, containing an appeal letter and other material, that is attached to a direct-mail package.

CASE *n.* Council for Advancement and Support of Education, a professional organization for individuals working in higher education.

case statement *n.* a presentation that sets forth a case. **case-stating,** *adj.*

cash gift *n.* a contribution made by writing a check.

cause-related marketing *n.* marketing in which a for-profit organization, by using the name of a not-for-profit organization, promotes its product and in return provides financial support to the organization according to a predetermined formula based on sales and purchases.

CD-ROM (compact disk read-only memory) *n.* an information storage device capable of storing large amounts of material read by a specially equipped computer.

CFRE, Certified Fund Raising Executive *n.* **1a.** a designation, developed and administered by the National Society of Fund Raising Executives, that is awarded to a professional fund raiser who has met specified standards of service, experience, and knowledge. **1b.** a person who has earned this designation.

challenge gift *n.* a gift donated by a person made on condition that other gifts or grants will be obtained using some prescribed formula, usually within a specified period of time, with the objective of encouraging others to give.

challenge grant *n.* a challenge gift donated by an organization, corporation, or foundation.

charitable *adj.* **1a.** giving to those in need. **1b.** giving for benevolent purposes.

charitable deduction *n.* the portion of a gift to a qualified charity that is deductible from a person's or corporation's federal income tax, a person's gift tax, or a person's estate tax.

charity *n.* **1.** that which is given in willingness to aid those in need; **2.** a not-for-profit organization or institution that is active in humanitarian work and supported entirely or in part by gifts.

closed-face envelope *n.* a type of envelope that does not have a window.

cold list *n.* a list of prospects that has not been previously tested.

cold prospect *n.* a potential donor that has never contributed to a particular organization.

community foundation *n.* a not-for-profit organization that receives funds and distributes them, or any income from them, for charitable purposes in a specific geographic area.

computer hardware *n.* any piece of physical equipment that is used in the computer. (*See* **software.**)

computer software *n.* the computer language that gives the computer instructions for the execution of tasks.

computer virus *n.* in computer security, a self-propagating program that infects and may damage a software program.

constituency *n.* people who have a reason to relate to or care about an organization. These people typically fall into customary groupings, such as faculty, alumni, medical staff, users, parents, donors, etc.

consultant *n.* a person with expertise in a specific field of knowledge who is engaged by a client to provide advice and services. A consultant usually does *not* directly solicit funds on behalf of the client.

consulting firm *n.* a company of fund-raising consultants.

contribution *n.* a gift or donation.

control package *n.* a mailing package used as a model against which a different mailing package is tested.

corkage fee *n.* the fee charged by vendors, hotels, or other establishments to open wine, hard alcohol, or other beverages and provide the glasses and other necessities for service when the beverages have been donated and not purchased from the vendor or hotel.

corporate foundation *n.* a private foundation, funded by a profit-making corporation, whose primary purpose is the distribution of grants according to established guidelines.

corporate-giving program *n.* **1.** a grant-awarding program established and controlled by a profit-making corporation. **2.** an organization's activities to solicit donations from a corporation.

corporate philanthropy *n.* support from corporations and corporate foundations through gifts of cash, equipment, supplies, and other contributions.

cost per dollar raised *n.* a measure of the productivity of a fund-raising program calculated by dividing the expenses incurred in raising the funds by the total dollars raised.

cost-benefit guidelines *n.* a formula or set of parameters used to evaluate the cost effectiveness of a fund-raising program.

CPU *n.* central processing unit, the heart and brains of the computer. It is where the actual data processing is performed.

cultivate *v.t.* to engage and maintain the interest and involvement of a donor, prospective donor, or volunteer with an organization's people, programs, and plans. **cultivation,** *n.*

cultivation event *n.* a special event (such as a dinner, meeting, or similar affair) to enhance interest in and enthusiasm for the work of an organization.

database *n.* indexed information held in computer storage, from which a computer user can summon selected materials. In a database, data are organized so that various programs can access and update information.

decoy *n.* a name and address placed in a database file to monitor use of the file.

deferred gift *n.* a gift (such as a bequest, life insurance policy, charitable remainder trust, gift annuity, or pooled-income fund) that is committed to a charitable organization but is not available for use until some future time, usually the death of the donor.

demographics *n.* the study of the characteristics of human populations, such as size, growth, density, distribution, and vital statistics.

designated gift *n.* a gift, the use of which is designated by the donor. This gift is either a temporarily restricted gift or a permanently restricted gift.

desk-top publishing *n.* producing camera-ready artwork on a personal computer using software developed to give the non-professional the ability to design and lay out brochures and other materials.

development *n.* the total process by which an organization increases public understanding of its mission and acquires financial support for its programs.

development audit *n.* an objective evaluation, sometimes conducted by professional fund-raising counsel, of an organization's internal development procedures and results.

direct mail *n.* **1.** mass mail sent by a not-for-profit organization directly to prospects. **2.** the soliciting by this method of donations, product sales, or subscription sales.

diversity *n.* **1.** the quality or state of being different. **2.** the quality or state of encompassing people of a different race, gender, religion, physical disability, age, sexual orientation, and income.

donor *n.* a person, organization, corporation, or foundation that makes a gift. Also **contributor**.

donor acquisition *n.* the process of identifying and acquiring new donors.

donor list *n.* a listing of donors who give to an organization.

donor pyramid *n.* a diagrammatic description of the hierarchy of donors by size of gifts. The diagram reflects that: as the size of donations increases, the number of donations decreases; as the number of years a donor is asked to renew increases, the number of donors decreases; as campaign sophistication progresses from annual giving to planned giving, the number of donors decreases; as donor involvement increases, the size of the donor's contribution increases and the response to campaign sophistication increases. Also **pyramid of giving**.

donor recognition *n.* the policy and practice of providing recognition to a donor, by a personal letter, a public expression of appreciation, a published list of donors, or in another appropriate way.

DOS *n.* Disk Operating System, software that directs the flow of data between disk drives and a computer. Without an operating system, a computer can do nothing.

downsizing *n.* the decision by businesses and the government to reduce the number of persons being employed.

electronic funds transfer (EFT) *n.* **1a.** a process or act by which a person may authorize automatic and periodic deductions from his or her bank account to be credited to another account, as to a not-for-profit organization. **1b.** money transferred in this way.

electronic mail (e-mail) *n.* **1a.** a system for sending a message or data file in machine-readable form by means of a computer network. **1b.** the transfer of a message or data sent by electronic mail. **1c.** a message or data sent or received by this method.

electronic screening *n.* the process or act of comparing an organization's database to national databases to gain address, telephone, and household information to be added to an organization's records. The process also usually involves ranking prospects by both capacity and likelihood to make gifts.

endowment *n.* a permanently restricted net asset, the principal of which is protected and the income from which may be spent and is controlled by either the donor's restrictions or the organization's governing board.

evaluation *n.* examination, judgment, appraisal, or estimate.

face-to-face solicitation *n.* the soliciting in person of a prospective donor. Also **personal solicitation**.

fact sheet *n.* a brief statement of an organization's purposes, programs, services, needs, plans, and other pertinent information prepared in summary form for use by volunteers involved in a campaign.

family foundation *n.* a type of private foundation.

fax *n., v.t., adj., n.* facsimile. *v.t.* to send a fax of. *adj.* of or producing a fax.

feasibility study *n.* an objective survey, usually conducted by fund-raising counsel, of an organization's fund-raising potential. The study assesses the strength of the organization's case and the availability of its leaders, workers, and prospective donors. The written report includes the study findings, conclusions, and recommendations.

federated campaign *n.* a unified fund-raising program administered by a not-for-profit organization that distributes funds to similar agencies. The United Negro College Fund and United Way are examples of federated campaigns.

font *n.* in printing, a complete set of type of one size and style (or face).

foundation *n.* an organization created from designated funds from which the income is distributed as grants to not-for-profit organizations or, in some cases, to people.

fund raiser *n.* **1.** a person, paid or volunteer, who plans, manages, or participates in raising assets and resources for an organization or cause. **2.** an event conducted for the purpose of generating funds.

fund raising *n.* the raising of assets and resources from various sources for the support of an organization or a specific project. **fund-raising,** *adj.*

fund-raising counsel *n.* a person or firm contracted to provide service to not-for-profit organizations seeking advice, evaluation, or planning, for the purpose of fund raising. Also **consulting firm; development counsel; professional counsel.**

fund-raising goals *n.* number of gifts, donors, and total dollars to be raised.

fund-raising tripod *n.* the three components of a fund-raising program: the case, leadership, and sources of support.

general gift *n.* **1.** a gift derived from a general appeal. **2.** a gift within the lower range of giving in a campaign.

general-purpose foundation *n.* an independent, private foundation that awards grants in many different fields of interest.

gift *n., v.t. n.* donation. *v.t.* to endow or present with a gift.

gift-acceptance policy *n.* the rules and regulations developed by a donee organization to determine which types of gifts should or should not be accepted.

gift-in-kind *n.* a gift of a service or a product rather than a cash or stock gift.

gift opportunities *n.* a list of campaign needs, usually within a range of donation levels, that are used in an appeal to the various special interests of prospective donors.

gift receipt *n.* an official acknowledgment, required by the Internal Revenue Service, issued to a donor by a recipient organization in response to a donation of (currently) $250 or more, requiring information naming the charity, the asset donated, and any benefits received by the donor in exchange for the gift.

gift table *n.* a projection of the number of gifts by size (in descending order: leadership gift, major gift, general gift) so as to achieve a particular fund-raising goal. Also **gift range table.**

giving club *n.* one of various donor categories that are grouped and recognized by a recipient organization on the basis of the level of donations. Also **gift club.**

grant *n., v.t., n* **1.** a financial donation given to support a person, organization, project, or program. Most grants are awarded to not-for-profit organizations. **2.** *informal (incorrectly for)* a grant proposal. *v.t.* to give or confer (such as the ownership or a right) by a formal act.

graphic artist *n.* a designer who provides art work either hand done or by computer for brochures or other publications.

hardware *n.* any piece of physical equipment that is used in the computer. See **software.**

honorary chair *n.* a person of prominence or influence who agrees to lend his or her name to a campaign organization.

identification *n.* the first phase in the fund-raising process.

Independent Sector (IS) *n.* an alliance (headquartered in Washington, DC) of donors and donees that promotes the interests of the independent sector. The organization is composed of memberships from corporations and foundations with national giving programs, as well as from national, not-for-profit organizations concerned with philanthropy.

indicia *n.* (singular, *indicium*) markings printed on bulk mail in place of stamps, metered postage, or other postmark.

initial gift *n.* advance gift.

ink-jet printer *n.* a printer that uses an ink spray to print the characters on a sheet of paper.

Internet *n.* a global computer network consisting of a loose confederation of interconnected networks. The Internet provides many services, such as file transfer, electronic mail, electronic journals and other publications, discussions, and community information service.

kick off *v.t.* to begin an official, public launching of (a campaign), usually at a special event to which major prospects have been invited and where major funds, committed or already in hand, are announced.

lapsed donor *n.* a donor who has contributed at any time prior to the current year.

laser printer *n.* a printer that uses a laser beam to print the characters on a sheet of paper.

leadership gift *n.* a gift, donated at the beginning of a campaign, that is expected to set a standard for future giving.

letter shop *n.* a commercial enterprise that addresses, inserts, sorts, bags, ties, and delivers a mailing to a post office. Printing services are also frequently available.

life-income gift *n.* a gift arrangement by which a donor makes an irrevocable transfer of property to a charity while retaining an income interest to benefit the donor and any other beneficiary for life or a specified period or years, after which the remainder is distributed to the charity.

list broker *n.* a commercial firm that buys, sells, and rents mailing lists. **list-brokering,** *adj.* **list-broking,** *n.*

list exchange *n.* the exchange of constituent lists between two or more organizations, often on a name-for-name basis, that enables each organization to mail to the other's constituency.

logo *n.* two or more letters, a figure, symbol, or other identifying representation associated with an organization or other enterprise.

mail house *n.* a commercial business that addresses, inserts, sorts, bags, and delivers a mailing to a post office. See **letter shop.**

mailing list *n.* a list of donors or prospective donors to receive a mailing.

mailing package *n.* a package that usually contains an appeal letter, a brochure, and a response device.

major gift *n.* a significant donation to a not-for-profit organization, the amount required to qualify as a major gift being determined by the organization.

matching gift *n.* **1.** a gift contributed on the condition that it be matched, often within a certain period of time, in accordance with a specified formula. **2.** a gift by a corporation matching a gift contributed by one or more of its employees.

megs *n.* a measure of computer storage space.

memory *n.* computer's temporary data storage area.

merge-purge *v.t., n., v.t.* to both combine (two or more computer files) into one file and delete duplicate records. *n.* the process, act, or an instance of doing this.

mission statement *n.* a statement about a societal need or value that an organization proposes to address.

modem *n.* a device that transmits data normally over a telephone line. A modem is necessary for telecommunications—e-mail, fax, web pages, etc.

monitor *n.* the screen on which you view the output of the computer.

multi-tasking *n.* the capability of some applications to run several other applications or several documents at one time. The user can switch between applications or documents instead of exiting and reloading.

needs assessment *n.* the study of an organization's program or situation to determine what activity or activities should be initiated or expanded to satisfy a need.

nine ninety (990) *n.* an Internal Revenue Service financial information return submitted annually by most tax-exempt organizations and institutions, except religious.

nixie, nixy *n.(plural,* nixies). *Informal.* an undeliverable piece of mail returned to the sender because of incorrect address, illegibility, or other reason.

nonprofit sector *n.* any not-for-profit or tax-exempt organizations collectively that are specifically not associated with any government, government agency, or commercial enterprise. Also **independent sector; not-for-profit sector; third sector.**

not-for-profit *adj.* that pertains to or provides services of benefit to the public without financial incentive. A not-for-profit organization is qualified by the Internal Revenue Service as a tax-exempt organization. Also **nonprofit.**

NPO *n.* nonprofit organization.

NSFRE *n.* National Society of Fund Raising Executives, a professional organization whose members are fund raisers for nonprofit organizations.

on-line databases *n.* databases of information retrieved by a computer.

operating foundation *n.* a private foundation that, rather than making grants, conducts research, promotes social welfare, and engages in programs determined by its governing body or establishment charter.

operating support *n.* contributions that are used so that the organization can operate. It funds salaries, utilities, supplies, travel expenses, etc.

outsourcing *n.* contracting work to be done outside of the office by another firm and not by staff of the organization. Most often used to save the organization money by not hiring full time staff and not paying their salaries and benefits. Outsourcing can also produce a high quality product, decrease costs, and reduce stress on the staff.

pace-setting *adj.* **1a.** (said of gifts), that set a standard for all subsequent gifts. **1b.** related to the gift range table of anticipated giving. Also **pattern-setting.**

package *n.* **1.** a proposal for support incorporating a combination of gift opportunities. **2.** all components of a mailing package.

paid solicitor *n.* a person who will ask for donations on behalf of an organization for which they are working.

personal solicitation *n.* face-to-face solicitation.

philanthropy *n.* **1.** love of humankind, usually expressed by an effort to enhance the well-being of humanity through personal acts of practical kindness or by financial support of a cause or causes, such as a charity (for example, the Red Cross), mutual aid or assistance (service clubs, youth groups), quality of life (arts, education, environment), and religion. **2.** any effort to relieve human misery or suffering, improve the quality of life, encourage aid or assistance, or foster the preservation of values through gifts, service, or other voluntary activity, any and all of which are external to government involvement or marketplace exchange. **philanthropic,** *adj.* **philanthropical,** *adj.* **philanthropically,** *adv.* **philanthropist,** *n.*

Phone/Mail *n.* **1a.** *(trademark) n.* a simulation of face to face solicitation technique used in a mass solicitation procedure utilizing a carefully orchestrated sequence of telephone and mail contacts. **1b.** the process or act of using Phone/Mail.

piggyback mailing *n. informal.* a letter or other communication that accompanies a mailing but covers a different topic.

piggy-backing *v.* the act of raising additional money by including the request or opportunity along with a request for another purpose. For example, mailing a dues renewal to a member and including a request for funding of a new project, or selling t-shirts, mugs, caps, etc. at a charity dinner in addition to charging money for the ticket in order to raise additional funds.

planned giving *n.* a systematic effort to identify and cultivate a person for the purpose of generating a major gift that is structured and that integrates sound personal, financial, and estate-planning concepts with the prospect's plans for lifetime or testamentary giving. A planned gift has tax implications and is often transmitted through a legal instrument, such as a will or a trust. Also **gift planning** or **deferred giving.**

planned giving committee *n.* a group of volunteers who assist an organization in planning, promoting, and implementing a planned giving program. Members usually include attorneys, accountants, insurance agents, certified financial planners, etc.

planning *v.t.,* formulating a scheme or program for the accomplishment or attainment of a goal.

pledge *n., v.t, n.* **1a.** a promise that is written, signed, and dated, to fulfill a commitment at some future time;

specifically, a financial promise payable according to terms set by the donor. Such pledges may be legally enforceable, subject to state law. **1b.** the total amount of such a pledge. **2.** a verbal pledge. *v.t.* to commit (a specified amount of money) as a pledge. Also **promise to give.**

pledge card *n.* a printed form used by a donor as a response to an appeal.

pooled-income fund *n.* a trust to which a donor transfers property and contributes irrevocably the remainder interest to a qualified charity, retaining a life-income interest for one or more beneficiaries. The transferred property is commingled (pooled) with gifts made by other donors, and each income beneficiary, the fund's trustee severs from the fund an amount equal to the value upon which the beneficiary's income interest was based and distributes that amount to the charity.

postage-paid envelope *n. see* **business-reply envelope.**

precampaign *adj.* of or pertaining to the period preceding the launching of a campaign.

premium *n.* **1.** goods or services, or both, offered as an inducement to a prospective donor to make a donation. **2.** a payment made on an insurance policy.

press kit *n.* a packet of informational materials, usually used for supporting a news release, an organization's program or a particular situation within an organization.

private foundation *n.* as designated by federal law, a foundation whose support is from a single source (usually a person, family, or company) and that makes grants to other not-for-profit organizations rather than operating its own programs. Its annual revenues are derived from earnings on investment assets rather than from donations. Private foundations are subject to more restrictive rules than public charities. Also **family foundation.**

private phase *n.* the phase of a campaign that precedes the public announcement of the campaign. The private phase is also called the "quiet phase," the "dark phase," and the "pre-public" phase.

private sector *n.* the area of a nation's economy and civic enterprise that is under private, rather than any governmental, control.

professional ethics *n.* standards of conduct to which members of a profession are expected to adhere.

program officer *n.* a staff member of a foundation who reviews grant proposals and makes recommendations for action.

progress report *n.* a report prepared periodically during a campaign for distribution to leaders and workers of the campaign organization as well as for the record.

proposal *n.* a written request or application for a gift, grant, or service.

prospect *n., v.t. n.* any potential donor whose linkages, giving ability, and interests have been confirmed. *v.t.* to identify (a prospect).

prospect list *n.* a listing of those individuals who are evaluated to be candidates for making contributions to an organization.

prospect profile *n.* a research report detailing the pertinent facts about a prospective donor, including basic demographic information, financial resources, past giving, linkages, interests, potential future giving, and such.

prospect research *n.* **1.** the continuing search for pertinent information on prospects and donors; **2.** identification of new individual, foundation, and corporate prospects. **prospect researcher,** *n.*

prospecting *n.* the act of performing prospect research.

PSA *n.* public-service announcement.

public charity *n.* as designated by federal law, a foundation that, during its most recent four fiscal periods, has received one-third of its support from donations from individuals, trusts, corporations, government agencies, or other not-for-profit organizations, provided no single donor gives two percent or more of the total support for the period. Normally the charity investment income. A public charity escapes the stringent rules that apply to a private foundation.

public sector *n.* the area of a nation's economy that is under governmental, rather than any private, control.

pyramid of gifts *n.* a reference to the distribution of gifts by size to a capital campaign within the context of the principle that larger gifts, although limited in number in relation to the total gifts received will account for a larger and disproportionate share of the total objective—the classic gift pattern for a campaign that, graphically represented, resembles a pyramid.

RAM *n.* Random Access Memory. The working space or temporary storage area for the program being used and the document on the screen. RAM is erased when the computer is turned off.

reinstated donor *n.* a donor who reinstates his or her support after a period of not contributing.

rejection letter *n.* the term used to describe the letter sent by a funder when a gift request is turned down. This denial letter is sent by many funders to applicants explaining why the gifts the applicants requested were not made.

research *n.* the second phase in the fund-raising process.

restricted gift *n.* a former accounting term for a temporarily restricted gift or a permanently restricted gift.

return on investment (ROI) *n.* **1a.** a measure of the efficiency of an organization or program, calculated as the ratio of net income received to the expended funds. **1b.** the monetary amount derived by this calculation.

roll-out *n.* the extension of an earlier test program, such as a direct-mail appeal, to a larger number of people on a given list or within a given population.

rule of thirds *n.* a formula for constructing a gift range table for a capital campaign, based on the premise that ten donors account for the first third of funds raised, the next hundred donors for the next third, and all remaining donors for the final third.

screening and rating sessions *n.* volunteers and staff members gathering together to identify individuals they know from prepared lists of names and evaluate or rate each individual's ability to give at certain levels.

seed money *n.* an early gift by a donor used for launching a program, thereby establishing credibility and momentum for that program.

segment *v.t., n. v.t.* to subdivide (such as donors or prospects) into smaller groups with similar characteristics. *n.* a segmented portion or group.

self-mailer *n.* a package for mailing that requires no separate carrier envelope or reply envelope.

sequential giving *n.* a cardinal principle of capital campaign fund raising that gifts should be sought "from the top down,"—that is, the largest gifts in a gift range table should be sought at the outset of a campaign, followed sequentially by the search for lesser gifts.

service bureau *n.* a professional firm that handles all facets of an organization's database management. Also may offer mailing services.

site visit *n.* a visit by a potential donor to inspect a project or review a program for which donations are being sought.

slug *n.* a device used with a postage machine that will imprint a message to the left of the printed postage each time an envelope is put through the postage machine. This message can be changed to promote an organization's many causes.

software *n.* the computer language which gives the computer instructions for the execution of tasks.

solicit *v., v.t.* **1.** to ask (a person or group) for a contribution of money, resources, a service, or opinion. **1b.** to request or appeal as for such a contribution. **solicitation,** *n.*

solicitor's kit *n.* a packet of materials to be used by volunteers when doing personal solicitations. The kit contains general information about the organization, the case for support, brochures about the organization, materials for making a gift such as pledge cards, and envelopes.

special event *n.* a function designed to attract and involve people in an organization or cause.

special gift *n.* a gift among the higher ranges of the gift range table.

special-purpose foundation *n.* a public foundation that focuses its grantmaking activities on one or a few special areas of interest.

specific situation formula *n.* a variation of the "rule of thirds" that focuses on the actual giving potential of the individual organization's prospects, mainly its prospects for the largest gifts. This approach assumes special importance for organizations with inadequate giving potential at or below the middle gift levels. For example, if an organization has ten prospects capable of gifts at a sufficiently high level, the top ten donors could provide two-thirds or more of the total goal.

sponsor *v.t., n. v.t.* **1.** to endorse (an organization or cause). **2.** to agree to assume the financial responsibility of (all or part of the cost of a special event or a special event or a special program or activity). *n.* a person or corporation that sponsors.

steering committee *n.* a committee of top volunteer leaders who oversee and manage a campaign or other fundraising effort. This committee is often composed of the chairmen of other working committees.

stewardship *n.* **1.** a process whereby an organization seeks to be worthy of continued philanthropic support, including the acknowledgment of gifts, donor recognition, the honoring of donor intent, prudent investment of gifts, and the effective and efficient use of funds to further the mission of the organization. **2.** the position or work of a steward.

strategic plan *n.* a program incorporating a strategy for achieving organizational goals and objectives within a specific time frame and with substantive support in the form of methods, priorities, and resources.

stretch gift *n.* **1.** a donation that fulfills a donor's optimum capacity to give. **2.** a gift that is larger than a donor originally intended to make.

surge protector *n.* a device that protects both hardware and software from being damaged by a surge in power through the electrical or telephone wires. Some will even maintain a power supply for up to thirty minutes.

suspect *n.* a possible source of support whose philanthropic interests appear to match those of a particular organization but whose linkages, giving ability, and interests have not yet been confirmed.

target *n., v.t. n.* **1.** a specific objective in a fund-raising program or campaign; **2.** a campaign goal; **3.** a prospective donor. *v.t.* to identify, single out, or make as a target.

teaser copy *n.* the wording or phrase found printed on the carrier envelope of a direct mail fund-raising solicitation letter.

technology consultant *n.* a consultant who specializes in database management and computer technology.

telemarketing *n.* the raising of funds or the marketing of goods or services by volunteers or paid solicitors, using the telephone.

telethon *n.* a television program in which entertainment features are integrated with a fund-raising message that is broadcast over a television station. During the program viewers are asked to call and make pledges.

third sector *n.* independent sector.

three "G's" *n.* give, get, or get-off—the phrase attributed to a board member's ability to raise money for an organization.

three "W's" *n.* work, wisdom, and wealth—the phrase that describes what board members can bring to an organization.

thumbnail *n.* mini mock-ups of a design project that are literally thumbnail size.

token gift *n.* a gift considerably below the capacity of the donor.

trust *n.***1.** an arrangement establishing a fiduciary relationship in which a trustor conveys property to a trustee to hold and manage for the benefit of one or more beneficiaries. Trusts can be revocable or irrevocable. **2.** something (such as property or financial securities) managed by a trustee for someone else's benefit. In the phrase **in trust**, in the care or possession of a trustee.

typeface *n.* in printing, **1a.** the printing surface of a piece of type. **1b.** a single design of type. **1c.** all the characters of a single design of type.

typeset *v.t.* to set (copy) into printing type.

unrestricted funds *n.* those gifts that donors have not directed for a specific purpose.

unrestricted gift *n.* a gift made without any condition or designation.

upgrade *v.t. n.* **1.** to increase or attempt to increase (the level of donor giving). **2.** to reconfigure (a computer) to increase its computing power. *n.* **1.** donor upgrade. **2.** a new release of a brand of computer software, containing usually major changes.

vendor *n.* a manufacturer, wholesaler, or retailer who sells a product or service.

volunteer *v.i., n. v.i.* to work without compensation in behalf of an organization, cause, benefit, etc. *n.* a person who volunteers. Also **worker. volunteerism,** *n.*

wallet envelope *n.* a contribution envelope with a large flap that can be used for giving information about a requested contribution.

will *n., v.t. n.* a legally executed statement of a person's wishes about what is to be done with the person's property after his or her death. Also **last will and testament.** *v.t.* to give or dispose of by a will.

window envelope *n.* an envelope with a window through which you can read the name and address of the recipient; commonly used for pledge reminders and receipts.

world wide web (WWW) *n.* an electronic system, connected with the Internet, that allows viewing of images and text and allows sound to be received.

yardstick gifts *n.* large gifts obtained early in a campaign that can be held up as models to other potential major contributors—gifts against which other gifts can be measured.

year-end gift *n.* a gift made in the last two months of a calendar year.

Bibliography
Fund-Raising Books, Periodicals, and Directories

General Interest

AAFRC Trust for Philanthropy. *Giving USA*. New York: AAFRC Trust for Philanthropy. Updated annually.

Advancing Philanthropy. National Society of Fund Raising Executives (NSFRE). Quarterly journal.

AHP Journal. Association for Healthcare Philanthropy.

AHP Primer Manual. Association for Healthcare Philanthropy. Annual.

Berendt, Robert J. and Richard J. Taft. *How To Rate Your Development Office*. Rockville, MD: The Taft Group, 1983.

Broce, Thomas E. *Fund Raising: The Guide to Raising Money from Private Sources*. Norman, OK: University of Oklahoma Press, 1986.

Case Currents. Council for Advancement and Support of Education (CASE).

The Chronicle of Philanthropy. Trade publication published twice a month.

Contributions Magazine. Contributions. Bimonthly trade publication.

Development Director's Letter. CD Publications. Newsletter.

The Digest of Southern Giving. Sinclair, Townes, & Company. Monthly newsletter.

Duronio, Margaret A. and Bruce A. Loessin. *Effective Fund Raising for Higher Education: Ten Success Stories*. San Francisco: Jossey-Bass Publishers, 1991.

Flanagan, Joan. *The Grass Roots Fundraising Book*. Chicago: Contemporary Books, 1992.

Flanagan, Joan. *Successful Fundraising: A Complete Handbook for Volunteers and Professionals*. Chicago: Contemporary Books, 1993.

FRI Monthly Portfolio. The Taft Group. Newsletter.

FRM Weekly. Hoke Communications. Newsletter.

Fund Raising Management Magazine. Hoke Communications. Monthly.

Giving and Volunteering in the United States. Washington, DC: Independent Sector, 1994.

Grassroots Fundraising Journal. Chardon Press.

Greenfield, James M. *Fund-Raising: Evaluating and Managing the Fund Development Process*. New York: John Wiley & Sons, 1991.

Greenfield, James M. *Fund-Raising Cost Effectiveness: A Self-Assessment Workbook*. New York: John Wiley & Sons, 1996.

The Heart of the Donor. Study conducted by Direct Marketing Association Non-Profit Council, New York, 1995.

Josephson, Michael. *Ethics of Grant-Making and Grant-Seeking: Making Philanthropy Better*. Josephson Institute of Ethics, 1992.

Klein, Kim. *Fundraising for Social Change*. Berkeley, CA: Chardon Press, 1994.

Mixer, Joseph R. *Principles of Professional Fundraising: Useful Foundations for Successful Practice*. San Francisco: Jossey-Bass Publishers, 1993.

The NSFRE Fund Raising Dictionary. New York: John Wiley & Sons, 1996.

National Fund Raiser. Barnes Associates. Newsletter.

New Directions for Philanthropic Fund Raising. San Francisco: Jossey-Bass Publishers. Quarterly series of sourcebooks.

Nichols, Judith E. *Growing From Good to Great: Positioning Your Fund-Raising Efforts for Big Gains*. Chicago: Bonus Books, 1995.

The NonProfit Times. Monthly trade publication

Panas, Jerold. *Official Fundraising Almanac*. Chicago: Precept Press, 1990.

Philanthropy Trends That Count. Judith E. Nichols, editor. Capitol Publications. Newsletter.

Reiss, Alvin H. *Arts Management*. Rockville, MD: The Taft Group, 1992.

Robinson, Andy. *Grassroots Grants*. Berkeley, CA: Chardon Press, 1996.

Rosso, Henry A. *Rosso on Fund Raising*. San Francisco: Jossey-Bass Publishers, 1996.

Rosso, Henry A. and Associates. *Achieving Excellence in Fund Raising: A Comprehensive Guide to Principles, Strategies, and Methods*. San Francisco: Jossey-Bass Publishers, 1991.

Seymour, Harold J. *Designs for Fund-Raising*. Rockville, MD: The Taft Group, 1988.

Shaw, Sondra C. and Martha A. Taylor. *Reinventing Fundraising: Realizing the Potential of Women's Philanthropy*. San Francisco: Jossey-Bass Publishers, 1995.

Stotz, C. *Handbook for Designing and Opening a New Development Office*. Southeast Missouri Hospital Foundation, 1992.

Successful Fund Raising. Stevenson Consultants. Monthly newsletter.

Warner, Irving R. *The Art of Fund Raising*. Rockville, MD: The Taft Group, 1992.

Worth, Michael J. *Educational Fund Raising: Principles and Practice*. Phoenix, AZ: Oryx Press and Council for Advancement and Support of Education, 1993.

Nonprofit Boards and Volunteers

Board Fund Raising Strategies. Aspen Publishers. Newsletter.

Carver, John. *Boards That Make A Difference*. San Francisco: Jossey-Bass Publishers, 1993.

CarverGuide Series on Effective Board Governance. San Francisco: Jossey-Bass Publishers, 1996.

Conrad, William R., Jr. and William E. Glenn. *The Effective Voluntary Board of Directors*. Athens, OH: Swallow Press, Ohio University, 1983.

Duca, Diane J. *Non-Profit Boards: A Practical Guide to Role, Responsibilities, and Performance*. Phoenix, AZ: Oryx Press, 1986.

Ellis, Susan. *The Volunteer Recruitment Book*. Washington, DC: Points of Light Foundation, 1994.

Gale, Robert. *Building A More Effective Board*. Washington, DC: Association of Governing Boards, 1984.

Gurin, Maurice. *What Volunteers Should Know for Successful Fund Raising*. Lanham, MD: University Press of America, 1982.

Howe, Fisher. *The Board Member's Guide to Fund Raising*. San Francisco: Jossey-Bass Publishers, 1991.

Howe, Fisher. *Welcome to the Board*. San Francisco: Jossey-Bass Publishers, 1995.

Joyaux, Simone. *Strategic Fund Development: Building Profitable Relationships That Last*. Gaithersburg, MD: Aspen Publishers, 1997.

Lord, James Gregory. *The Raising of Money: 35 Essentials Every Trustee Should Know*. Cleveland, OH: Third Sector Press, 1987.

National Center for Nonprofit Boards. Publications for board members and chief executives.

O'Connell, Brian. *Board Overboard*. San Francisco: Jossey-Bass Publishers, 1995.

O'Connell, Brian. *The Board Member's Book*. New York: The Foundation Center, 1985.

Panas, Jerold. *Boardroom Verities*. Chicago: Precept Press, 1991.

Struck, Darla. Fund Raising for Nonprofit Board Members. Gaithersburg, MD: Aspen Publishers, 1995.

Struck, Darla and Sheri Campbell, eds. *The Board Fund Raising Manual*. Gaithersburg, MD: Aspen Publishers, 1995.

Vineyard, Sue and Steve McCurley. *101 Tips for Volunteer Recruitment*. Washington, DC: Points of Light Foundation, 1988.

Volunteer—We Belong Together: The 1996 Volunteer Center Directory. Washington, DC: Points of Light Foundation, 1996.

Wood, Miriam, ed. *Nonprofit Boards and Leadership*. San Francisco: Jossey-Bass Publishers, 1995.

Technology

Bergan, Helen. *Where the Information Is: A Guide to Electronic Research for Nonprofit Organizations*. Alexandria, VA: BioGuide Press, 1996.

Warwick, Mal. *Technology and the Future of Fundraising*. Berkeley, CA: Strathmoor Press, 1994.

Annual Giving

Gee, Ann D. *Annual Giving Strategies: A Comprehensive Guide to Better Results*. Washington, DC: Council for Advancement and Support of Education, 1990.

Gratsy, William and Kenneth Sheinkopf. *The Annual Fund*. Los Angeles: The Grantsmanship Center.

Greenfield, James M. *Fund-Raising Fundamentals: A Guide to Annual Giving for Professionals and Volunteers*. New York: John Wiley & Sons, 1994.

Peirce, Susan P. ed. *Gift Club Programs: A Survey of How 44 Institutions Raise Money*. Washington, DC: Council for Advancement and Support of Education, 1992.

Williams, Karla A. *Donor Focused Strategies for Annual Giving*. Gaithersburg, MD: Aspen Publishers, 1997.

Direct Mail/Telemarketing

FRI Phonathon Orientation Kit. Rockville, MD: The Taft Group, 1987.

Kachorek, Joseph. *Direct Mail Testing for Fund Raisers*. Chicago: Precept Press, 1991.

Kuniholm, Roland. *The Complete Book of Model Fund-Raising Letters*. Englewood Cliffs, NJ: Prentice Hall, 1995.

Kuniholm, Roland. *Maximum Gifts by Return Mail: An Expert Tells How to Write Highly Profitable Fund Raising Letters*. Rockville, MD: The Taft Group, 1989.

Lautman, Kay and Henry Goldstein. *Dear Friend, Mastering the Art of Direct Mail Fund Raising*. Rockville, MD: The Taft Group, 1991.

Lewis, Herschell Gordon. *How to Write Powerful Fund Raising Letters*. Chicago: Precept Press, 1991.

Squires, Con. *Teach Yourself to Write Irresistible Fund-Raising Letters*. Chicago: Precept Press, 1993.

Warwick, Mal. *The Hands-On Guide to Fundraising Strategy and Evaluation*, Gaithersburg, MD: Aspen Publishers, 1995.

Warwick, Mal. *How to Write Successful Fundraising Letters*. Berkeley, CA: Strathmoor Press, 1994.

Warwick, Mal. *999 Tips, Trends and Guidelines for Successful Direct Mail and Telephone Fundraising*. Berkeley, CA: Strathmoor Press, 1993.

Warwick, Mal. *Raising Money by Mail*. Berkeley, CA: Strathmoor Press, 1995.

Warwick, Mal. *Revolution in the Mailbox: How Direct Mail Fundraising Is Changing the Face of American Society—and How Your Organization Can Benefit*. Berkeley, CA: Strathmoor Press, 1990.

Warwick, Mal, ed. *Successful Direct Mail & Telephone Fundraising*. Strathmoor Press. Newsletter.

Warwick, Mal. *You Don't Always Get What You Ask For: Using Direct Mail Tests to Raise More Money for Your Organization*. Berkeley, CA: Strathmoor Press, 1992.

Prospect Research

Bergan, Helen. *Where the Money Is: A Fund Raiser's Guide to the Rich, Second Edition*. Alexandria, VA: BioGuide Press, 1992.

Bergan, Helen. *Where the Information Is: A Guide to Electronic Research for Nonprofit Organizations*. Alexandria, VA: BioGuide Press, 1996.

FRI Prospect Research Resource Directory, Second Edition. Rockville, MD: The Taft Group, 1991.

Leadership Directories—Corporate Yellow Book, Federal Yellow Book, Law Firm Yellow Book. New York: Leadership Directories, Inc., Published annually.

Nichols, Judith E.. *Changing Demographics*. Chicago: Precept Press, 1991.

Nichols, Judith E. *Targeted Fund Raising*. Chicago: Precept Press, 1992.

Nichols, Judith E. *Global Demographics: Fund Raising for a New World*. Chicago: Precept Press, 1995.

Philanthropic Digest. Association of Professional Researchers for Advancement.

Strand, Bobbi and Susan Hunt. *Prospect Research: A How-to Guide*. Washington, DC: Council for Advancement and Support of Education, 1986.

Major Gifts

Donovan, James A. *Take the Fear Out of Asking for Major Gifts*. Donovan Management, 1993.

Gough, Samuel N. *Major Gift Programs: Practical Implementation*. Gaithersburg, MD: Aspen Publishers, 1997.

Mai, Charles F. *Secrets of Major Gift Fund Raising*. Rockville, MD: The Taft Group, 1987.

Matheny, Richard E. *Major Gifts: Solicitation Strategies*. Washington, DC: Council for Advancement and Support of Education, 1994.

Muir, Roy and Jerry May, eds. *Developing an Effective Major Gift Program: From Managing Staff to Soliciting Gifts*. Washington, DC: Council for Advancement and Support of Education, 1993.

Nichols, Judith E. *Pinpointing Affluence: Increasing Your Share of Major Donor Dollars*. Chicago: Precept Press, 1993.

Panas, Jerold. *Mega Gifts: Who Gives Them, Who Gets Them*. Chicago: Precept Press, 1988.

Prince, Russ A. and Karen M. Rile. *Seven Faces of Philanthropy: A New Approach to Cultivating Major Donors*. San Francisco: Jossey-Bass Publishers, 1994.

Williams, M. Jane. *Big Gifts: How to Maximize Gifts From Individuals, With or Without a Capital Campaign*. Rockville, MD: The Taft Group, 1991.

Corporate, Foundation, and Government Support

America's New Foundations 1996. Chicago: The Taft Group, 1996.

Carlson, M. *Winning Grants Step by Step*. San Francisco: Jossey-Bass Publishers, 1995.

Corporate Foundation Profiles. New York: The Foundation Center.

Corporate Giving Directory. Rockville, MD: The Taft Group. Updated annually.

Corporate Giving Watch. Rockville, MD: The Taft Group. Newsletter.

Corporate Giving Yellow Pages. Rockville, MD: The Taft Group. Updated annually.

Corporate Philanthropy Report. Capitol Publications. Newsletter.

The Directory of Corporate and Foundation Givers Rockville, MD: The Taft Group. Updated annually.

Directory of International Corporate Giving in America and Abroad. Updated annually.

Federal Assistance Monitor. CD Publications.

Federal Grants and Contracts Weekly. Capitol Publications.

Federal Support for Nonprofits. Rockville, MD: The Taft Group. Updated annually.

Foundation and Corporate Grants Alert. Capitol Publications. Newsletter.

The Foundation Directory. New York: The Foundation Center. Updated annually.

The Foundation Directory, Part 2. New York: The Foundation Center. Updated annually.

The Foundation Directory Supplement. New York: The Foundation Center. Updated annually.

Foundation Fundamentals. New York: The Foundation Center.

Foundation Giving Watch. The Taft Group. Newsletter.

The Foundation Grants Index. New York: The Foundation Center. Updated annually.

The Foundation Grants Index Quarterly. New York: The Foundation Center.

Foundation News and Commentary. Council on Foundations.

The Foundation 1000. New York: The Foundation Center. Updated annually.

The Foundation Reporter. Rockville, MD: The Taft Group. Updated annually.

Frost, Gordon Jay, ed. *Winning Grant Proposals*. Rockville, MD: The Taft Group, 1993.

Geever, Jane C. and Patricia McNeill. *The Foundation Center's Guide to Proposal Writing*. New York: The Foundation Center, 1993.

Gooch, Judith Mirick. *Writing Winning Proposals*. Washington, DC: Council for Advancement and Support of Education, 1987.

Grant Guides on various topics. New York: The Foundation Center. Updated annually.

The Grantsmanship Center Magazine. Los Angeles: The Grantsmanship Center.

Guide to U.S. Foundations, Their Trustees, Officers, and Donors. The Foundation Center.

Krauth, Diana. *How to Use the Catalog of Federal Domestic Assistance*. Los Angeles: The Grantsmanship Center. Year.

Margolin, Judith B., ed. *Foundation Fundamentals: A Guide for Grantseekers*. New York: The Foundation Center, 1994.

Murray, Vic. *Improving Corporate Donations: New Strategies for Grantmakers and Grantseekers*. San Francisco: Jossey-Bass Publishers, 1991.

National Directory of Corporate Giving. New York: The Foundation Center.

National Directory of Grant Making Public Charities. New York: The Foundation Center.

National Grant Guides on select topics. New York: The Foundation Center.

Nelson, Donald T. and Paul H. Schneiter. *Gifts-In-Kind: The Fund Raiser's Guide to Acquiring, Managing, and Selling Charitable Contributions Other Than Cash and Securities*. Rockville, MD: The Taft Group, 1991.

Plinio, Alex and Joanne Scanlan. *Resource Raising: The Role of Non-Cash Assistance in Corporate Philanthropy*. Washington, DC: Independent Sector, Year.

Scanlan, Eugene A. *Corporate and Foundation Fund Raising: A Complete Guide from the Inside*. Gaithersburg, MD: Aspen Publishers, 1997.

Seltzer, M. *Securing Your Organization's Future: A Complete Guide to Fundraising Strategies*. New York: The Foundation Center, 1987.

Spomer, Cynthia Russell. *Federal Support for Nonprofits 1995*. Rockville, MD: The Taft Group, 1994.

Winning Federal Grants: A Guide to the Government's Grant-Making Process. Capitol Publications, 1994.

Special Events

Brown, S. *Capital Events '88*. Washington, DC: The Brown Group, 1988.

Catherwood, D. and R. Van Kirk. *The Complete Guide to Special Event Management*, New York: John Wiley & Sons, 1992.

Elliot, Chuck, ed. *Aspen's Guide to 60 Successful Special Events*. Gaithersburg, MD: Aspen Publishers, 1995.

Farb, C. *How to Raise Millions Helping Others Have a Ball*. Austin, TX: Eakin Press, 1993.

Freedman, H. *The Role of the Event Manager*. Rockville, MD: The Taft Group, 1993.

Freedman, Harry A. and Karen F. Smith. *Black Tie Optional: The Ultimate Guide to Planning and Producing Successful Special Events*. Rockville, MD: The Taft Group, 1991.

Harris, April L. *Special Events: Planning for Success*. Washington, DC: Council for Advancement and Support of Education, 1988.

————— *Raising Money and Cultivating Donors Through Special Events*. Washington, DC: Council for Advancement and Support of Education, 1991.

Jackson, Robert and Steven Schmader. *Special Events: Inside & Out*. Washington, DC: Points of Light Foundation, 1990.

Levy, Barbara R., and Barbara Marion. *Successful Special Events: Planning, Hosting, and Evaluating*. Gaithersburg, MD: Aspen Publishers, 1997.

Plessner, G. *Golf Tournament Management Manual*. Arcadia: Fund Raisers, Inc., 1980.

————— *Charity Auction Management Manual*, Arcadia: Fund Raisers, Inc., 1986.

Study of Cause-Related Marketing. Sheridan Associates and Zimmerman Associates. Washington, DC: The Independent Sector, 1988.

Ukman, L. *The Special Events Report*. International Events Group, Chicago. Bi-weekly.

Wilkinson, D. *The Event Management and Marketing Institute*. Ontario, Canada: The Event Management and Marketing Institute, 1988.

Publications

Gayley, Henry T. *How to Write For Development, Revised Edition*. Washington, DC: Council for Advancement and Support of Education, 1991.

Capital Campaigns

Dove, Kent E. *Conducting a Successful Capital Campaign*. San Francisco: Jossey-Bass Publishers, 1988.

Hauman, David J. *The Capital Campaign Handbook*. Rockville, MD: The Taft Group, 1987.

Kihlstedt, Andrea and Catherine P. Schwartz. *Capital Campaigns: Strategies That Work*. Gaithersburg, MD: Aspen Publishers, 1997.

Quigg, H. Gerald, ed. *The Successful Capital Campaign: From Planning to Victory Celebration*. Washington, DC: Council for Advancement and Support of Education, 1986.

Planned Giving

Barrett, Richard D. and Molly E. Ware. *Planned Giving Essentials: A Step by Step Guide to Success*. Gaithersburg, MD: Aspen Publishers, 1997.

Jordan, Ronald R. and Katelyn L. Quynn. *Planned Giving: Management, Marketing, and Law*. New York: John Wiley & Sons, 1995.

Practical Guide to Planned Giving. Rockville, MD: The Taft Group. Updated Annually.

Planned Giving Today, G. Roger Schoenhals, ed. Newsletter.

Schmeling, David. *Planned Giving for the One-Person Development Office: Taking the First Steps*. Deferred Giving Services, 1990.

Schoenhals, G. Roger. *19 Articles You Can Use (To Acquire Planned Gifts)*. Seattle, WA: Planned Giving Today, 1995.

Schoenhals, G. Roger. *On My Way in Planned Giving: Inspiring Anecdotes and Advice for Gift-Planning Professionals*. Seattle, WA: Planned Giving Today, 1995.

White, Douglas E. *The Art of Planned Giving: Understanding Donors and the Culture of Giving*. New York: John Wiley & Sons, 1995.

Working with Consultants

Kibbe, Barbara and Fred Setterberg. *Succeeding with Consultants*. New York: The Foundation Center, 1992.

Fund Raising As a Career

Cohen, Lilly and Dennis Young. *Careers for Dreamers and Doers: A Guide to Management Careers in the Nonprofit Sector*. New York: The Foundation Center, 1989.

Duronio, Margaret and Eugene Tempel. *Fund Raisers: Their Careers, Stories, Concerns, and Accomplishments*. San Francisco: Jossey-Bass Publishers, 1996.

Gurin, Maurice. *Confessions of a Fund Raiser*. Rockville, MD: The Taft Group, 1985.

Knott, Tonald Alan. *The Makings of a Philanthropic Fundraiser*. San Francisco: Jossey-Bass Publishers, 1992.

Panas, Jerold. *Born to Raise: What Makes a Great Fundraiser*. Chicago: Precept Press, 1989.

Index

A

Acquisition programs, direct mail, 87

Action plan calendar, 73, 75

Address verification, firms for, 156

Advanced Certified Fund Raising Executive, 283

Advisory committees, to board of directors, 17–18

American Association of Fund-Raising Counsel (AAFRC), 2, 276, 296

American Prospect Research Association, 156

America Online, 49, 111

Anniversary giving, 83

Annual giving
  annual campaign calendars, 83
  capital campaign, compared to, 238–239
  case for support, 78–80
  elements for success, 79
  evaluation of campaign, 83–84
  gift clubs, 82
  increasing gifts, methods, 83
  management of volunteers, 81–82
  phases of, 83
  purpose of, 78, 79
  pyramid of giving, 79
  recruitment of volunteers for, 80
  solicitation methods, 80
  steering committee, 81
  training volunteers, 81

Annual report
  capital campaigns, 250
  corporate donor information, 155
  fund-raising material, 212

Appeal letter, direct mail, 86

Arts, amount in contributions, 4

Association for Healthcare Philanthropy (AHP), 33, 60, 263, 286

Association of Professional Researchers for Advancement (APRA), 117
  mission statement, 121–122

B

Bentz Whaley Flessner, 112

Bequests, 260

Bequest society, planned giving, 266–267

Bill of Rights
  for donors, 6
  for volunteers, 8–9

Biographical resources, prospect research, 110

Board of directors
  advisory committees to, 17–18
  age of members, 9
  chief development officer, role of, 18–19
  communications with staff, 19–20
  development committee, 17
  diversity of, 10
  evaluation of member effectiveness, 18
  existing board, working with, 15–16
  expectations of staff, 20
  gender of members, 9
  geographic representation of members, 10
  give and get commitment form, 19
  job description, 10, 12–13
  member questionnaire, 11–12
  motivating board, 16
  qualities of good trustees, 14–15
  race/ethnicity of members, 9–10
  recruiting members, 10
  retiring member, 18
  role of chairperson, 15

  staff expectations of, 20
  training/development for, 16–17

BoardLink, 111

Brochures
  annual reports, 250
  capital campaigns, 249
  example of, 218–236
  general information brochure, 212
  question-and-answer brochure, 212

Budget
  for development office, 30, 31–33
  plan for fund-raising, 68–69
  planned giving, 259
  special events, 186, 189–190, 192, 195
  telemarketing, 95

Business cards, capital campaigns, 250

Business journals, corporate donor resources, 145

C

Calculator, 28

Capital campaigns
  annual report, 250
  brochure, 249
  business cards, 250
  campaign cabinet, 245–246
  case statement, 242–243, 249
  commemorative opportunities, 249
  evaluation of, 252–253
  fail-proof checklist, 244
  feasibility study, 241–242
  gift range table, 247
  giving methods, 247
  goal setting for, 240–241
  instruction letter, example of, 248
  internal system, 250–251

About the Authors

BARBARA KUSHNER CICONTE, CFRE, is Associate Dean for Institutional Advancement at the Washington College of Law at American University. As Director of Development at the law school, she successfully completed its $20 million capital campaign. Prior to joining the law school staff in 1991, Ms. Kushner Ciconte served as Director of Major Gifts and Director of the Annual Fund at American University, and Manager, Fund Raising Projects, for NARAL, a national advocacy organization.

She was elected to the national Board of the National Society of Fund Raising Executives (NSFRE) in 1996. Ms. Kushner Ciconte has served as co-chair of the national NSFRE–Georgetown University Law Center conference, "Fund Raising and the Law," and on several national task forces and committees. In 1992, Ms. Kushner Ciconte served as president of the NSFRE/Greater Washington, DC Area Chapter.

She has presented trainings and workshops for NSFRE, The Support Center, Howard University, the American Heart Association/Montgomery County Chapter, the American Diabetes Association, the National Capital Area YWCA, and the American Horse Trails Foundation. In addition, she has taught fund raising at The George Washington University's Center for Continuing Education.

Prior to her career in development, Ms. Kushner Ciconte was an elementary and junior high school teacher for 11 years in upstate New York. She received her Bachelor of Arts degree in Education from the State University of New York (SUNY) at Oneonta and her Master of Arts degree in Education from SUNY Cortland.

JEANNE GERDA JACOB, CFRE, is Director of Development for the American Society of Civil Engineers Foundation (ASCEF) in Washington, DC, where she successfully completed a capital campaign for ASCE's new international headquarters building raising $4.4 million on a goal of $3.5 million. Prior to joining ASCEF she worked with INNdependent Management Group (IMG) as Vice President for Public Affairs and Development serving IMG clients that included: American Association of University Women, Water Environment Federation, Women in Development Office of U.S.A.I.D., American College of Nurse Mid-Wives, American Center for International Leadership, Greater Washington Society of Association Executives, and National Technological University.

Before joining IMG, she was Director of Development for seven years at the National Academy of Engineering (NAE), where she spearheaded a major, five-year capital campaign for NAE that raised $46 million with a goal of $30 million. Prior to NAE, she worked eight years for YFU International Student Exchange, where she began her career in development. In addition, she has taught the Fundamentals of Fund Raising course for seven years at The George Washington University's Center for Continuing Education.

In her volunteer life, she served: as Chair of four Presidential Inaugural Balls (Reagan in 1985, Bush in 1989, and Clinton in 1993 and 1997); as President of the Illinois State Society, and a member of its Board for 15 years; and on the boards of the Big Sisters of the Washington Metropolitan Area, the American Center for International Leadership, and the Alexandria Symphony Orchestra League.

Ms. Jacob was elected to serve two terms on the board of the NSFRE/Greater Washington, DC Area Chapter, holding the office of Secretary of the board during one term. In addition, she assists her husband in his fund raising for The Hill School in Pottstown, PA, as well as supports the development efforts of her sorority, Gamma Phi Beta, on both the national and local levels.

Prior to her development career, Ms. Jacob worked for five years in the field of college admissions for Mount Holyoke College and the University of Chicago, and was a teacher of English for two years at Glenbard West High School in Glen Ellyn, Illinois. She received her Bachelor of Arts degree in English from the University of Iowa in Iowa City, Iowa.